The Debate
on
Soviet Power

The Debate on Soviet Power

Minutes of the All-Russian
Central Executive
Committee of Soviets

Second Convocation,
October 1917–January 1918

Translated and Edited by
JOHN L. H. KEEP

Clarendon Press   Oxford
1979

Oxford University Press, Walton Street, Oxford OX2 6DP

OXFORD LONDON GLASGOW
NEW YORK TORONTO MELBOURNE WELLINGTON
IBADAN NAIROBI DAR ES SALAAM CAPE TOWN
KUALA LUMPUR SINGAPORE JAKARTA HONG KONG TOKYO
DELHI BOMBAY CALCUTTA MADRAS KARACHI

© *John L. H. Keep 1979*

British Library Cataloguing in Publication Data

The debate on Soviet power.
  1. Russia – Politics and government – 1917–1936 –
Sources
  I. Keep, John
  354'.47'0009   JN6526   78–40489
  ISBN 0–19–822554–7

*Printed in Great Britain by
Richard Clay (The Chaucer Press) Ltd,
Bungay, Suffolk*

Preface

THIS volume presents a composite text, reconstructed according to published primary sources, of the proceedings of Soviet Russia's first quasi-legislative assembly, the All-Russian Central Executive Committee of Soviets of Workers', Soldiers', and Peasants' Deputies (here abbreviated to CEC; the Russian acronym was VTsIK). In this makeshift revolutionary forum were discussed some of the most important questions to arise in the aftermath of the Bolshevik seizure of power in October 1917. The vital issue, on which all else depended, was the nature of the new government. How was the world's first socialist state to be ruled? The Bolsheviks had carried out their insurrection in the name of 'soviet power', but just what this term implied was initially far from clear. The soviets were councils elected directly by the most radical groups of the population. A congress of these bodies, in which the military element predominated, gave endorsement to an all-Bolshevik cabinet, the Council of People's Commissars (CPC; Sovnarkom), immediately after the *coup*. But very few of these representatives, or of the men for whom they spoke, were in favour of unlimited dictatorship by a single revolutionary party, the form which 'soviet power' quickly assumed.

The debate which took place in Petrograd's Smolny Institute during the first weeks of Soviet rule, between October 1917 and January 1918, is by no means of mere historical interest. It anticipated one that is still in progress wherever parties of a Marxist–Leninist type exercise or contend for power. The fundamental problems which it poses have not yet been solved satisfactorily even in the USSR, where the Soviet system is entering its seventh decade, to say nothing of eastern European countries which have inherited a different political tradition. How are the incontrovertible principles of 'scientific socialism' to be reconciled with the natural variety of opinion found among citizens of any modern state? Where should the line be drawn between dissent and opposition? How can the ideal of popular self-government be realized when the ruling party regards itself as the guardian of supreme ideological verities and claims to express the immanent interests of the working masses? The answers given to these basic questions will determine the nature of the regime's policies in the economic and social domain, as well as its relations with other states, above all those that have a more pluralistic political system.

It is as a contribution to this ongoing discussion, as well as to our knowledge of the Russian revolution, that this neglected historical document is here made available in English translation. The commentary is designed to clarify allusions in the text whose meaning might not be readily obvious even to specialists. Such a critical edition could not be published as matters stand at present in the USSR.

Historians of the Russian revolution, both western and Soviet, have neglected the CEC. This is partly due to the state of the sources. So far as the first convocation (June–October) is concerned, the more public aspects of its affairs were widely reported in the contemporary press; but in order to write a definitive account of the important role it played in the country's political life during these months one would need to consult the original records. These have been preserved in Soviet archives, but are apparently in a defective state. One Soviet historian who consulted them was Vera Vladimirova, who in 1923–4 helped to compile a valuable chronicle of events during the revolutionary year. During the 1920s the proceedings of a number of deliberative bodies active in 1917 were published in scholarly editions. Among them were the First and Second Congresses of Soviets, held in June and October respectively, and the Constituent Assembly, which met for a single session on 5–6 January 1918. However, no equivalent treatment was accorded to the CEC, even for the period after October 1917, when it had come under Bolshevik control.

The reasons for this seem to have been partly practical and partly political. There already existed an edition of the second convocation's minutes, which had appeared in Moscow in 1918; although deficient in many respects, it was adequate for the needs of Soviet scholars at this time. On the political side, the modest role played by the soviets in the governmental system during the post-revolutionary era would have made it embarrassing to publicize their far more significant functions in 1917.

Nor would it have been expedient to encourage close examination of the attitude then taken by non-Bolshevik maximalists
who had since been excluded from political life. Some scruples
may also have been felt about portraying in detail the divisions
among Bolshevik leaders of the day—although these were not
concealed when the Bolshevik Central Committee's minutes for
the revolutionary period were first published in 1929.

Whatever the reasons may have been, the onset of Stalinism
halted scholarly work on the Russian revolution for more than
two decades and permanently disfigured the official Soviet
interpretation of 'Great October'. In the post-Stalin era, especially in works published between 1956 and the mid-1960s, the
1918 edition of the CEC's minutes is occasionally cited, but
always in selective fashion. Hundreds of documentary collections devoted to the events of 1917 have appeared in recent
years; but among them one would look in vain for the proceedings of Soviet Russia's first legislature. Even to mention the
names of certain participants, except in a pejorative context, is
to break a taboo.

The 1918 Moscow edition of the minutes is something of a historical curiosity. It was published by the CEC itself, as part of a
series of propagandist tracts. No editor or compiler is identified.
It was evidently a reprint of reports which had appeared at the
time in the CEC's official organ, *Izvestiya*. These reports provided only an incomplete record—the last two sessions were not
covered at all—but nothing was done to supplement them; on
the contrary, some excisions or amendments were made, without any indication of the fact, apparently for political reasons.
Speeches by dissenters were an obvious target for the censor's
blue pencil. The text was poorly presented and at several points
defective. Such technical shortcomings were to be expected in a
publication which simply sought to inform the general public
about the regime's first legislative moves. It was printed under
difficult physical conditions, when paper and other materials
were in short supply. The volume soon became a bibliographical rarity, and few western libraries possess a copy.

The present English translation is based upon a comparison
of the 1918 text (referred to here as *Prot.*) with contemporary
newspaper sources. The proceedings were reported in the maximalist press of Petrograd, notably in the Left SR daily *Znamya*

truda ('Banner of Labour') and in the USDI's *Novaya zhizn'*. The CEC's affairs were all but ignored by the moderate socialists and liberals, who took no part in it and whose newspapers were at this time battling for survival; occasionally, however, these organs do add significant details. The *Pravda* accounts are usually identical with, but sometimes briefer than, those in *Izvestiya*. In newspapers of any political tendency dispatches were liable to be cut short on technical grounds as well as for reasons of editorial policy.

Where the present text is taken from press reports, this is noted by alphabetical references; where there are none, the source is *Prot*. The choice of text has been governed solely by concern for historical accuracy and completeness. Where significant divergences of meaning occur, these are indicated, but minor differences of wording have been ignored, since we are dealing with summaries of debates, not with a full stenographic record. Wherever possible, direct speech has been used. The elliptical style of the original has necessitated a number of editorial insertions (in square brackets) to clarify the meaning or to conform to normal grammatical usage. Occasionally, where the text is very repetitive, some phrases have been omitted, indicated in the usual way, but care has been taken to reproduce the speakers' meaning and style accurately, even at the risk of some prolixity.

For some sessions the sources include an agenda. This has not been reproduced since it was so seldom adhered to; instead the items are numbered as they were taken and have been given headings. Sessions that lasted overnight are dated according to the day when they were convoked. Texts of laws and public documents have been included only where they relate directly to the CEC's debate. Also omitted are the (incomplete) lists of those present that were occasionally published, and the form of address 'comrade'.

Since the press reports generally follow a standardized form, it is conceivable that some official or semi-official stenographic record was compiled. However, Soviet historians in a position to examine the relevant archive materials (in TsGAOR, *fond* 1235) do not mention one. Access to these unpublished documents (which in accordance with Soviet custom are not identified in citations) probably would not add very much to our knowledge of what happened in the CEC's debating-chamber, although they may contain information about the private discussions in the Presidium. It would be pleasant to think that this volume might lead to a relaxation of the stringent controls enforced on research into matters such as this, so that Soviet as well as western historians might at last be able to consult freely the records not only of the CEC but also of that inner sanctum of 'soviet power', the Council of People's Commissars.

The transliteration system is that used by the *Slavonic and East European Review*, with certain minor adaptations, including the omission of the soft sign from Russian personal and place-names. The form Zinoviev has been preferred to Zinovyev, as being more familiar to English readers. The word 'soviet' has been capitalized only where it refers to the state order of the USSR: thus 'Soviet government', but 'soviet power'. Dates are given in the Old Style until 1/14 February 1918, when Russia adopted the Gregorian calendar. In measurements of weight, one pud is equivalent to 36·11 pounds (16·38 kg).

The editor gratefully acknowledges receipt of a grant from the Canada Council towards preparation of this volume and warmly thanks the staff of the Bibliothèque de documentation internationale contemporaine, Paris (BDIC), for kindly permitting use of their facilities. The views expressed in the introduction and notes are the editor's sole responsibility.

Contents

CONTENTS

List of Abbreviations

PPS	Polish Socialist Party (*Polska partia socjalistyczna*)
PSR(SRs)	Party of Socialist-Revolutionaries
RC	Revolutionary Committee (*revkom*)
RCP(b)	Russian Communist Party (Bolsheviks); formerly RSDRP(b); subsequently AUCP(b), All-Union Communist Party (Bolsheviks), and CPSU, Communist Party of the Soviet Union
RSDRP	Russian Social-Democratic Labour Party (*Rossiyskaya Sotsial-demokraticheskaya rabochaya partiya*)
RSFSR	Russian Soviet Federation of Socialist Republics
Rumcherod	Executive Committee of Soviets of Workers' and Soldiers' Deputies of the Romanian Front, Black Sea Fleet, and Odessa Military District
SDKPiL	Social-Democratic Party of the Kingdom of Poland and Lithuania
SDP	(German) Social-Democratic Party
SDs	Social Democrats
SEC	Supreme Economic Council (*Verkhovny sovet narodnogo khozyaystva*; *Vesenkha*)
SRs	see PSR
Stavka	(Army) General Headquarters
Tsentrobalt	Central Committee of the Baltic Fleet
Tsentroflot	Central Committee of the All-Russian Navy
USDI	United Social-Democratic Internationalists
USDP	Independent Social-Democratic Party of Germany
Vikzhel	Executive Committee of the All-Russian Union of Railwaymen

NEWSPAPERS AND JOURNALS

Iz.	*Izvestiya*
NZ	*Novaya zhizn'*
Pr.	*Pravda*
RG	*Rabochaya gazeta*
ZT	*Znamya truda*

Introduction

THE second convocation of the CEC (October 1917–January 1918) was held at an extremely difficult moment in the history of the Russian people. The state administration and the national economy had virtually collapsed under the strain of war. The remarks that follow are designed to explain why the new order assumed the shape it did. We may examine in turn the revolutionary regime's relations with the outside world, its efforts to reconstruct the Russian economy on socialist lines, and finally its institutional structure, in which a key place was occupied by the CEC. It was in this deliberative assembly that the 'debate on soviet power' was articulated most clearly.

THE RUSSIAN REVOLUTION AND THE WAR

From the 1890s onward most Russian socialist intellectuals regarded themselves as internationalists. In the tsarist empire patriotic sentiment had so often been abused by conservatives and reactionaries that their radical opponents tended to go to the other extreme. In doing so they were prone to overlook Russia's legitimate state interests and to underestimate the strength of national feeling among the population at large; but there is no doubt that these views were sincerely held. Many revolutionaries were forced into exile in western Europe, where their experiences helped to foster a cosmopolitan outlook. In this respect they were generally to the left of their comrades in the Second International. They looked forward enthusiastically to a socialist Europe in which the peoples of Russia, liberated from tsarism and perhaps from capitalism as well, would play a vigorous and influential part.

Within this common world outlook there were of course several gradations of view, implicit and explicit. They were part of the pattern of factional conflict that had characterized the Russian socialist movement from its beginnings. The rift be-

tween Populists and Marxists, which loomed large at the turn
of the century, was superseded during and after the 1905 revolution by one between moderates and radicals which affected
both the main left-wing parties, the agrarian socialist Party of
Socialist-Revolutionaries (PSR, SRs) and the Marxist Social
Democrats. Among the latter the principal groups were the
Mensheviks and Bolsheviks, whose feud went back to the historic second congress of the Russian Social-Democratic Labour
Party (RSDRP) in 1903. Personal as well as doctrinal differences were involved in this dispute. The Mensheviks by and
large favoured a strategy and organizational pattern modelled
on that of the German Social Democrats, whereas their rivals
held to the ideas developed by V. I. Lenin, acknowledged
leader and virtual embodiment of Bolshevism, who in 1912
formed his followers into what was virtually an independent
party. Its most obvious feature was its élitism—the belief that
the party should act as a 'conscious vanguard' in directing the
revolutionary struggle, which led its adherents to adopt an intransigent attitude towards those elements within the RSDRP,
and in other left-wing parties, who did not accept Lenin's interpretation of the tasks facing Russian socialists. Within the PSR
divisions were less acute, since it took a rather less dogmatic
stance; however, its influence was slighter than that of the
RSDRP. The rank and file of both parties professed a vulgar-
ized form of Marxism which stressed the allegedly beneficent
role of inexorable class conflict in furthering the cause of social
progress.

Throughout Europe the outbreak of the First World War
provoked a deep schism among socialists. The Second International collapsed. In each belligerent country a majority faction supported the national government in maintaining the war
effort in the interests of defence—hence the term 'defensist'.
They sought to attenuate social antagonisms, to the extent that
this was possible, so long as hostilities continued. Their radical
critics proudly called themselves 'internationalists'. They regarded the war as the product of rivalries inherent in contemporary capitalism; the task of the proletariat was to end the
conflict from below, by mass action, and so to weaken the
position of the propertied classes and the governments that
allegedly served their interests, and theirs alone. This theory

was taken to an extreme by Lenin, who from his refuge in neutral Switzerland called for the 'imperialist war' to be converted into an international civil war. This, he hoped, would bring about the revolutionary overthrow of the entire political and social order: the bourgeoisie, which had in his view deliberately launched the mass slaughter to advance its own selfish interests, was to be dispossessed; the new socialist Europe would be ruled by an international organization (the future Third International, or Comintern); this body was to be run on centralized lines, like the Bolshevik party, and so would be proof against the 'revisionist' tendencies that had caused the disintegration of its predecessor. Lenin's ideas were too far-fetched for most anti-war socialists outside Russia, but he was able to form an active pressure group within the so-called 'Zimmerwald movement' (named after the Swiss village where internationalists from several countries held their first conference in 1915).

By the third winter of the war the centre of gravity within European socialism was shifting rapidly to the left. The high rate of casualties, the military stalemate, and the unprecedented hardships inflicted upon civilians brought about a change in the popular mood. This was more evident in Germany and Austria–Hungary than it was in any of the Entente countries—with the conspicuous exception of Russia. Here the sudden collapse of the Imperial regime in February 1917 created a totally new situation. The liberal Provisional Government, which sought to continue the war in fulfilment of Russia's obligations to her allies, rapidly lost credit with the population. Russia's armies on the Eastern front had been severely mauled and morale was at a low ebb among troops as well as civilians. In the spring of 1917 soldiers' committees were formed in many units and discipline was soon seriously undermined. At first the prevailing attitude among the troops could be described as 'revolutionary defensism', which meant that they were willing in principle to carry on such defensive operations as were necessary to consolidate the gains of the revolution, on condition that action was taken at once to conclude a general democratic peace 'without annexations or contributions'. This formula, which had originated with partisans of the Zimmerwald movement, was publicly endorsed, as early as 14 March, by leaders of the Petrograd soviet of workers' and soldiers' deputies, and this gave it a broad popular appeal.

From the start of the Russian revolution the authority of this body rivalled, and indeed exceeded, that of the Provisional Government, in which the tone was initially set by liberal Constitutional-Democrats (Kadets) and other non-socialists. The soviet was controlled by parties of the moderate left, principally Mensheviks and Socialist-Revolutionaries, who were anxious to end the hostilities as soon as possible by negotiation among the powers. These leaders believed that the moral example of the Russian revolution would encourage the war-weary peoples in other belligerent countries to exert massive pressure upon their governments, which would be forced to revise their war aims and to accept a restoration of the *status quo ante*. This view was not realistic. In Britain and France, where hopes of victory had been reinforced by the entry of the United States into the war, official and unofficial opinion was, with few exceptions, unsympathetic to the aspirations of the Russian socialists. They were widely seen as irresponsible demagogues bent on subverting the Allied cause, and the influence which the Petrograd soviet exerted over the Provisional Government aroused considerable misgivings.

Within Russia criticism of the soviet's peace policy was voiced not only by politicians of the right and centre, who advocated national solidarity against the external enemy, but also by the extreme left. Those most eager to end the war at once maintained that the moderate socialists were failing to act with sufficient energy and were showing too much concern for the Kadets, whose presence in the Provisional Government they (the moderates) thought essential. These ultra-radicals were commonly referred to at the time as 'defeatists' or 'maximalists'. The former expression was used pejoratively, to mean that they were not merely willing to accept Russia's military defeat as a *fait accompli* but were actually seeking to bring it about, in the interests either of international revolution or of the Central Powers—whose agents they were therefore alleged to be. The other term, 'maximalism', is a useful one, in that it expresses the spirit of utter irreconcilability which inspired these angry men, whose main strength was drawn from the war-weary soldiers. The maximalists comprised a loose alliance of malcontents, ranging from dissident SRs and Mensheviks to Anarcho-syndicalists; but it derived its sense of purpose and its organizational cohesion from the Bolsheviks. The latter were able to become a major political force precisely because they belonged to this broad front of radicalized elements.

Lenin had from the start bitterly attacked the Provisional Government and the moderate leadership of the Petrograd soviet. Soon after his return to Russia on 3 April he persuaded the waverers in his party to adopt an attitude of outright hostility towards all those whom he termed 'conciliators', i.e. socialists who sought to compromise with the so-called 'bourgeois' groups. In his eyes such persons were no better than traitors to the people's cause. He insisted that the Provisional Government must be overthrown and replaced by a new revolutionary regime based on the soviets; only such a government, he maintained, would enjoy genuine popular support and be able to bring the war to an end. It would do so not just by pressing for negotiations but by undertaking direct action, in particular by promoting fraternization among troops on either side of the front.

By June maximalist propaganda had made considerable headway. It was assisted by the failure of an ill-prepared offensive launched on the Galician sector. Some troops turned on their officers or deserted to the rear; others, notably in the turbulent Petrograd garrison, tried to force the Petrograd soviet leaders to take power (3–4 July). The attempt was clearly premature and the Bolsheviks belatedly disowned responsibility for it. The affair caused some embarrassment to Lenin's party, but it soon recovered from the setback. The Provisional Government was more seriously harmed; reconstituted under the premiership of A. F. Kerensky, it had a socialist majority and was more dependent than ever upon the goodwill of the soviet leaders. It was in no position to take decisive action against its maximalist critics. To be sure, information was made public to the effect that the Bolsheviks had been in contact with the Imperial German authorities, and had received from them through clandestine channels a far from negligible subsidy with which to finance their 'defeatist' agitation. However, the charge was not driven home. Lenin strongly denied the accusation that he was in any sense a German agent, but he preferred to go underground rather than face trial. It is now generally thought that he did not in fact enter into any explicit obligations towards his party's financial backers, but remained faithful to his principles as an internationalist socialist; he intended to use this aid to bring down all 'imperialist' governments, that of the Kaiser included. Nevertheless the Bolsheviks' short-term interests clearly coincided with those of the German high command, and their opponents were perfectly entitled to suppose that, should a maximalist regime come to power, it would be forced to make extensive concessions to the Germans.

The prospect of a Bolshevik government still seemed remote in July and August 1917. However, opinion was turning against the ruling coalition for a variety of reasons, not least because the Allies were less disposed than ever to listen to its pleas (now somewhat muted) for a revision of war aims. The erosion of the government's authority caused its opinions to be treated with scant respect in other capitals. Nor were the leaders of the soviet movement any more successful in their peace policy. Those who still adhered to the idea of bringing public pressure to bear upon the belligerent governments put their hopes in an international socialist conference, to be held in neutral Stockholm, which was to rally anti-war sentiment throughout the continent; but nothing came of this scheme, and its failure enhanced the credibility of the course of action advocated by the Bolsheviks and their partners.

The turning-point came at the end of August, when Kerensky alleged—without adequate grounds, as it later transpired—that General L. G. Kornilov, the Supreme Commander-in-Chief, was conspiring to bring down the government and to establish a right-wing military dictatorship. In order to avert this threat the prime minister turned to the soviet leaders, who mobilized their supporters; the supposed plotters were promptly disarmed and arrested. The 'Kornilov affair' gravely discredited military and civilian authorities throughout the land, especially in the metropolitan areas of Petrograd and Moscow and at the front. It strengthened the maximalists, who claimed that their warnings of treachery had been proved correct by events. Passions ran high, and officers were widely suspected of harbouring 'counter-revolutionary' designs. Criticism was also directed against Allied representatives, who had been urging the Russian authorities to tighten military discipline in the interests of the common war effort. Even so few people in Russia were as yet prepared to endorse the idea of a separate peace with the Central Powers, since it was generally recognized that such a bilateral agreement could not fail to be extremely onerous.

The Bolsheviks were aware of this sentiment, and for that reason took care not to spell out too clearly what their peace programme entailed. It was their good fortune that ordinary folk, in and out of uniform, were in no mood to examine their slogans coolly. Transfer of power to the soviets came to be regarded as something of a panacea. It was expected to give such a tremendous impulse to the international peace movement that the belligerent governments would be powerless to resist it. This optimistic view was shared by many leading Bolsheviks as well as by ordinary workers and soldiers. Yet it was as much a chimera as the peace strategy of the moderate socialists had been. Statesmen in the Allied countries would pay even less heed to the demands of a maximalist government than they did to one comprising left-wing democrats. They would automatically write it off as 'pro-German'. The hostility of the Entente powers could be taken for granted, and there was no likelihood of this attitude being seriously modified by public pressure, at least within the foreseeable future. So far as the Central Powers were concerned, the situation was slightly more favourable, in that the Russians could hope to spread revolutionary propaganda among their troops, with whom they were in face-to-face contact. On the other hand Germany's policy in the east was dictated by the high command; she enjoyed overwhelming military superiority; and she could impose her will upon her allies. It followed that, until the revolutionary threat in their homelands became actual, the German leaders could deal an annihilating blow against the infant Soviet regime whenever they chose. The chances of it surviving seemed slight indeed.

Nevertheless the risk was taken. On 25 October the Bolsheviks rose in insurrection in Petrograd; the Provisional Government was overthrown. Within a few weeks they had consolidated their hold over much of the country. They owed their survival in large part to sheer good luck. Neither the Allies nor the Central Powers were willing or able to take decisive action

against them. To put matters baldly, they were saved by the
continuation of the war in the west, which held first priority in
the thinking of all the protagonists. This factor was certainly
more important than the desperate military and diplomatic
measures which the Soviet authorities took to bolster their
regime, significant though these were in long-term perspective.

The Allies ignored Lenin's and Trotsky's appeals for a
general democratic peace. The Central Powers, however,
responded favourably to their initiative. An armistice was concluded at Brest-Litovsk on 2 December, and this was followed
by negotiations for a separate peace. The Bolshevik leaders
rapidly reconciled themselves to such a prospect, if indeed they
had not reckoned with it in their hearts all along. The treaty
was eventually signed, under duress, on 3 March 1918 (N.S.).
The Soviets thus had nearly four months in which to do what
they could to improve their security and to wear down their
adversaries' resolve by a propaganda campaign unequalled in
the annals of diplomacy to date. The prolonged parleying was
an endeavour to gain time, a substitute for the military force
which Russia no longer possessed. The armistice dealt the final
blow to army discipline, so that the front lay wide open to German attack. There was no realistic possibility of waging successfully the 'revolutionary war' which the maximalist leaders
(Lenin included) had expected to launch in the event of
'imperialist' aggression. This became evident when the Central
Powers called the Soviet bluff and ordered their troops to
advance; they met virtually no opposition, and the government
in Petrograd had no choice but to accept the stiffer terms
subsequently presented and embodied in the Brest-Litovsk
treaty.

Not only was the Soviet regime militarily defenceless, and in
constant jeopardy, throughout this period; the impact of revolutionary propaganda on the morale of their antagonists was also
much slighter than had been anticipated. This was true both of
the direct exchanges across the front line which were permitted
under the armistice agreement and of the messages addressed to
public opinion in general, and socialist opinion in particular, in
Germany and Austria–Hungary. Central European radicals
and pacifists were well disposed towards the October revolution
(whose deeper implications they, like most people, did not fully

comprehend); but a mass movement comparable in scope to that which had developed in Russia did not materialize until the autumn of 1918, by which time the international situation had been transformed by the ending of the First World War. Anti-war and anti-élitist sentiment did not merge to the same extent as it had in Russia. Basic differences in the social and political structure ensured that, once revolution did break out in central Europe, it would take a less cataclysmic form.

This meant that at the peace negotiations Soviet Russia could not rely upon the vast groundswell of international popular support to which her leaders had confidently looked forward. The basic issues were made clear already during the first round of the talks, held in December 1917; what followed was a public relations exercise, a test of nerves on either side. The principal question at issue was the fate of the vast belt of territory situated between Soviet Russia and the Central Powers, most of which was under German occupation. Both sides acknowledged that in this region the new order should be based upon the principle of national self-determination; but each construed this principle in a partisan manner. The German high command was concerned to preserve what it considered to be Germany's vital military security interests, which it interpreted so broadly as to render fictitious such national rights as it was prepared to grant. The German Foreign ministry, and the Austro-Hungarian government, took a less intransigent approach, but the difference was tactical rather than substantial. On the Soviet side the principle of national self-determination was likewise applied in a flexible manner. Marxists judged such questions dialectically: the overriding priority was the interest of the international socialist revolution as they themselves defined it. To the extent that achievement of national independence facilitated this objective, by strengthening the Soviet regime and weakening its enemies, it merited support; where this was not the case, it was 'objectively counter-revolutionary' and must be opposed. This self-serving doctrine was enunciated with exemplary frankness by early Soviet official spokesmen, who saw nothing illogical or immoral in professing a dual standard. In their view this was an inescapable concomitant of the class struggle, which the October revolution had internationalized.

This mode of reasoning was still novel to diplomats and others who had had no previous contact with the revolutionary milieu, and they found it hard to contend with. At Brest-Litovsk the public relations battle was won by the Bolsheviks, in the sense that by applying physical force the Germans antagonized domestic and international opinion: this was the price they paid for short-term material gains. (Nor did the Allies fare much better: their representatives in Russia were ill equipped to offer a sophisticated rebuttal of the Bolsheviks' ideological claims.) It was perhaps to be expected that professional revolutionaries should excel in adapting the art of propaganda, with which they were so familiar, to the world of international relations. But the corollary of this was that they risked falling victim to their own distorted perception of reality. The belief that the situation in other countries was as explosive as it had been in Russia, and that their own survival depended upon speedy extension of their power abroad, led to a mood of 'revolutionary messianism'. Some of the most fanatical maximalist's, carried away by their Utopian fantasies, were willing to immolate themselves, and the regime they served, in order to bring about the long-promised general conflagration.

The Bolsheviks were by no means immune to this way of thinking, but in their case romantic euphoria was seasoned by an element of rational calculation, indeed even of cynicism. Lenin shared the conviction that the international proletariat would rise in revolt at Soviet Russia's signal, but he had a far more realistic notion of the time that this would take to materialize. A master of political tactics, he was ever alert to the changing balance of forces and ready to adjust his position to take account of unexpected setbacks or fresh opportunities, while adhering rigidly to basic principles. In his eyes the 'correct' course was invariably the one that served to bolster his party's power, since on that the fate of the revolution ultimately depended.

This hard-headed pragmatism led him to accept, much more easily than most of his comrades, a *Diktatfrieden* which would deprive Soviet Russia of much of its most valuable resources and seriously weaken its ability to promote international revolution. He was prepared to make whatever concessions might be necessary in order to bring such a peace about—partly to appease the

war-weary troops, upon whose support his government so con-
spicuously rested, and partly because a continuation of external
conflict would hinder prosecution of the domestic struggle
against real or suspected 'counter-revolutionaries'. The Brest-
Litovsk treaty, he argued, was but a temporary reverse, which
would give Soviet Russia a badly needed breathing space; the
losses incurred could be made good later.

Within nine months Germany and her allies lay prostrate.
Central Europe was in turmoil, apparently ripe for an expansion of Soviet influence. The 'robber treaty' could be denounced
with impunity and the revolutionary forces primed for a new
offensive. Lenin's flexible strategy appeared to have been vindi-
cated. Yet this seemed so only when viewed in short-term perspective. What followed was not the world-wide revolution of
Marxist prophecy but two more years of bitter civil and international conflict, which ended in an uneasy truce between
Soviet Russia and her western neighbours. By 1920 the Communists (as the Bolsheviks now called themselves) were masters
of Russia, but they could not feel secure so long as 'imperialism'
continued to exist. The ruling party's combative ideology led it
to assume a posture of confrontation *vis-à-vis* the external world.
This imposed a heavy burden upon the population, which had
to be conditioned politically and psychologically to accept it;
and this in turn demanded the creation of a centralized administrative machine. The goal of international revolution was not
abandoned, but it was to be brought about not so much by
fomenting mass upheavals as by extending the might of the
'apparatus-state'. The long-term result of the maximalist victory in 1917 was thus paradoxical: peace with the Central
Powers, a major aim of the Russian people at the time, was
achieved—but only at the cost of plunging the country into an
interminable struggle against a host of new adversaries.

TOWARDS A NEW SOCIAL AND ECONOMIC ORDER

The victors in the October revolution inherited a catastrophic
economic situation and a society on the verge of falling apart.
Unhappily, neither by intellectual background nor by practical
experience were they well equipped to undertake the super-
human task of reconstruction: that is to say, of repairing the
damage, establishing reasonably harmonious relations between

producers and consumers, and fulfilling the expectations harboured by most ordinary working people that the revolution would bring an immediate improvement in their material conditions.

In the last decades of the nineteenth century Russia had embarked upon a painful process of modernization which brought few rewards to industrial labour and fewer still to agricultural producers. Forty years of administrative neglect lay between the peasants' emancipation from serfdom in 1861 and their emancipation from the traditional rural commune in 1906. The reformist agrarian legislation of prime minister Stolypin (1906–11) had scarcely begun to achieve its principal object, the creation of a stable property-owning yeomanry, when the war intervened. Although per capita GNP was rising, and industrial growth was mopping up more and more surplus village labour, in 1914 living standards were still extremely low by international standards. Social distress was widespread both in the towns and in the countryside. Those who were discontented with their lot tended to blame it on the selfishness of the social élite. They were fortified in this simplistic view of their plight by the teachings of radical intellectuals. As the latter saw it, Russia had entered upon a path of 'capitalist' development which had led to exploitation of the labouring classes by the 'bourgeoisie' (a term of alien origin which carried overtones of moral condemnation); from this she could be liberated only by social revolution, in the course of which the country's wealth would be redistributed according to egalitarian principles. What would be the effect of such measures upon productivity, and hence upon income levels, in a land still so close to a subsistence economy? Such questions were of little concern to these theorists, who were preoccupied rather with the attainment of social justice, by which they understood *inter alia* the expropriation of those who owned capital in any form. The entrepreneurial and managerial elements in Russian society were generally deemed to have forfeited any claim to considerate treatment. In the new order their functions would be exercised, in some still unspecified way, by publicly controlled authorities. On such basic propositions all Russian socialists, with very few exceptions, were agreed. Differences arose between Marxists and Populists, or between Mensheviks and Bolsheviks, as to certain details of the expropriation process, but these were of little immediate relevance.

In Russia as elsewhere the First World War led to increased state intervention in economic life. Controls were introduced over the output and marketing of a wide range of commodities, including some basic foodstuffs. An effort was also made to regulate prices, but the diversion of resources to war production led to serious inflation, and most wage-earners' real incomes declined. The tsarist authorities received very little credit from the public for their hesitant moves towards *dirigisme*. Liberals as well as socialists tended to blame all the scarcities and short-comings upon the autocratic regime—even where they were clearly due rather to structural weaknesses in the economy, to wartime dislocation of commercial relationships, or to other factors for which the government could not fairly be held responsible. It came to be widely assumed that Russia's economic problems were basically organizational in nature, and that therefore a democratization of the political and administrative system would suffice to make it perform more efficiently.

After February 1917 the opportunity arose to put these notions to the test. Almost overnight a host of new regulatory bodies appeared. Most of them were popular in character, in the sense that they emerged spontaneously in response to pressure from below, although some were sanctioned by the Provisional Government. As a rule they were staffed by unpaid volunteers who were prone to place loyalty to their electors ahead of loyalty to their superiors in the disintegrating and proliferating bureaucratic hierarchy. A network of supply committees came into existence to procure foodstuffs and distribute them to the hungry townspeople. Their powers were duplicated by the economic departments of local soviets and similar *ad hoc* agencies. These bodies would also intervene to settle labour disputes by endorsing bargains that gave the inflationary spiral a further twist. More serious still was the widespread erosion of managerial authority by factory (enterprise) committees, which were usually under maximalist influence. A wave of violence spread across the country which the various official and unofficial organs tried in vain to check. In rural areas peasants began to confiscate the land and livestock of individual owners (including fellow-peasants) as a step towards the long-awaited general redistribution of property. This could not but adversely affect the output and marketing of agricultural produce, so adding to the hardship in the towns. The northern and central provinces, which normally imported supplies from the more fertile south, and the army suffered most from this dislocation. The chief reason for the food shortages, however, was not peasant unrest but the breakdown of the transport system. The railways could not handle the greatly increased demand for goods. Their reserves of skilled labour, rolling-stock, and fuel were all but exhausted.

By the autumn of 1917 Russia had fallen into a state of economic chaos from which no government, however sagacious, could have extricated her with ease. Business life was almost at a standstill; the printing-presses were flooding the market with paper currency; and the country's foreign credit rating had sunk close to the zero mark. In such circumstances the advent to power of a maximalist regime committed to a far-reaching socialist programme was not so much a misfortune as an irrelevancy. In the short term, at least, its economic measures could only accelerate the process of dissolution already under way. Recovery could not begin until the fighting had ended and a stable political authority had been established. That stage was not to be reached until 1921 or 1922.

The Bolsheviks and their allies had laid no detailed plans for management of the economy after the seizure of power, and at first tackled problems as they arose by trial-and-error methods. They were not agreed among themselves. Most activists believed that the country's ills could be remedied by a further dose of administrative decentralization: that is to say, by transferring real decision-making power to agencies of the local soviets, to the trade unions, or to enterprise committees. The slogan of the hour was 'workers' control', often interpreted very literally to mean direct self-government by the men at the factory bench. Managerial and technical personnel were frequently ejected or placed under strict restraints which, added to their other difficulties, prevented them from operating effectively. The general assumption seemed to be that problems of industrial production, finance, and transport could be handled in much the same way as the land question was being settled by the peasants. This crude approach could be rationalized by reference to Anarcho-syndicalist or Marxist theory, or to some caricature of it, but the main impetus to action came from the desperate situation in which many workpeople found themselves. Local labour leaders, faced with idle plant and masses of unemployed, could not but resort to rough and ready measures of self-help, whatever the economic cost.

This elemental mass sentiment came into conflict with the more sophisticated Marxist precepts professed by Social-Democratic intellectuals and cadre elements, with which most other Russian radical socialist leaders tacitly concurred. Mensheviks and Bolsheviks differed as to whether the present revolution ought properly to be termed socialist, but they shared a common commitment to economic planning and administrative centralization. Basic industries, banks, and the transport system were to be managed by state officials, the bulk of whom, they hoped, would be recruited from the ranks of organized labour. Only the most complex technical matters—and they were thought to be relatively few—would be reserved to 'bourgeois' experts operating under the supervision of these functionaries. Such a system could also be designated 'workers' control', if this term were stretched to mean control by officials of the 'workers' and peasants' state'. Partisans of this view held that public ownership, by liberating wage-earners from capitalist oppression, would give them a strong moral incentive to increase labour productivity; and that the consequent improvement in industrial discipline, coupled with the application of scientific methods of organization, would lead to a rapid rise in living standards.

Thus there were two opposing philosophies within the maximalist camp. Tension between them developed immediately after the October revolution. It was most evident in disagreements over the nature and extent of 'workers' control'. Many trade-unionists could not see why rights which they had won in struggle against the employers should now be surrendered to organs of the new state. They were out of sympathy with the argument that there was no place for labour militancy under socialism since the interests of the community as a whole took precedence over those of any sectional group. The trade unions in particular became a reservoir of 'autonomist' sentiment that would take years to eradicate.

The tendency towards a centrally-controlled economy may be thought inevitable, or at any rate preferable to continuation of the anarchy that prevailed in the autumn of 1917. The misfortune was that for some time to come such benefits as it conferred were reaped by the state rather than by the mass of citizens, whether as consumers or as producers. Industrial output fell sharply (except perhaps in the armaments branch), and matters were not noticeably improved in this respect by introduction of public ownership. This was decreed somewhat haphazardly, on a sectoral or even enterprise basis, largely in response to pressure by organized labour. Banks and credit institutions were among the first institutions to be subjected to what latter-day Soviet historians, using a term of Lenin's, call 'the Red-guard onslaught on capital'. In the maximalist view they were the nerve-centres of the capitalist economy, and so had to be brought under state control forthwith. This action certainly dealt a serious blow to the free-market economy; alas, it almost destroyed the market as such, for the new functionaries, inexperienced in financial and commercial affairs, could not cope with their enormous task. Of the limited amount of trade carried on under 'war communism' (as the economic policy of the civil-war years came to be known) a great deal escaped official control. It took the form of speculative black-marketeering, conducted in a manner more reminiscent of the sixteenth century than the twentieth. Money lost all value, being replaced by barter. By 1920 Russia had sunk back into a state of nature.

As an agrarian country still in the initial stages of development she could withstand this trial better than most; nevertheless the sufferings that befell ordinary folk during this period beggar description. Massive unemployment emptied the cities; personal savings were wiped out; family life was disrupted; famine and epidemics took a heavy toll. This profound social crisis was not just the product of Bolshevik rule, as conservative critics alleged, for Bolshevism was as much symptom as cause. Nevertheless the actions (or inactions) of the revolutionary regime helped to make the average citizen's lot harder than it need have been. Its efforts to ease distress by legislation were little more than well-meaning or propagandist gestures. Measures of a more realistic kind were ruled out by the official ideology, which encouraged the party cadres to approach all problems in terms of 'class struggle'. At its best this doctrine perplexed ordinary people or diverted their energies from more constructive activities; at its worst it stimulated deeds of brutal savagery. It was not just the Russian economy that took a great leap backwards as a result of war and revolution: Russian society, too, lapsed into a condition of semi-barbarism in which the life of mere individuals seemed of little account. This was soil in which the seeds of tyranny were sure to sprout.

THE INFRASTRUCTURE OF DICTATORSHIP

The maximalist leaders were as ill prepared to assume responsibilities in the political sphere as they were in the economic domain. In the late nineteenth century Marxism had been received by Russian radical intellectuals as a ready-made doctrine imported from the west, as a secular faith or *Heilslehre* which gave promise of untold future benefits as a reward for present sufferings. Revolution came to be seen as a supreme end, to achieve which virtually any means were justified. The individual was considered duty-bound to subordinate himself to the collective. Those who thought otherwise, and who pursued personal or material ends, were referred to contemptuously as *obyvateli* ('philistines'). Russian revolutionaries believed that they had a mission to bring 'enlightenment', by which they meant political knowledge as well as cultural improvement, to the 'dark' masses. They took it for granted that the common people (*narod*)—the toilers in field or factory—were engaged in a righteous struggle against injustice and oppression bound to culminate in a cataclysmic act of self-liberation in which the radical intellectuals' function would be to provide leadership.

This quasi-religious, messianic vision of politics generated many acts of courage and self-sacrifice that won admiring respect from contemporaries in Russia and abroad. In the final analysis, however, it left a pernicious legacy. It encouraged Russian revolutionaries to become exclusive, intolerant, and authoritarian; to substitute slogans for reasoned analysis; and to attach a supreme value to conflict rather than consensus. Lenin's party came to embody these traits to a fault, but they ought more properly to be seen as generic to an entire subculture in Imperial Russian society.

When political repression was relaxed, as it was after 1905, the radicals had an opportunity to emerge from their state of psychological alienation. They had to adjust to the unfamiliar world of competitive open politics, in which much of their traditional way of thinking was exposed as shallow or irrelevant. They were led to reconsider their ideas in the light of fresh experience. In the last pre-war years Russian socialist thought was becoming more mature. A demythologizing process was under way which was accompanied by the rediscovery of spiritual values. However, this movement was obstructed by the reactionary policies adopted in ruling circles and after 1914–15, when tsarism entered upon its death agony, it may be said to have gone into reverse. Wartime sufferings naturally revived apocalyptic hopes for deliverance from present evils by the *deus ex machina* of revolution. By 1917 a situation had developed in which maximalist ideas were bound to evoke a sympathetic response among broad segments of Russian society.

There is no doubting the enthusiasm with which, in the spring of that year, hundreds of thousands of ordinary folk rallied to the cause of what was loosely called 'revolutionary democracy'. To most of them this modish phrase denoted social levelling, the elimination of privilege in every form. To a minority who thought in political as well as social categories, it meant a far-reaching devolution of authority. In general the populace had an ambiguous attitude towards the central state power (*vlast*): on one hand they held it in discredit as 'reactionary' and oppressive (at least potentially so); on the other hand they expected it to accomplish miracles if it were sufficiently 'democratized'. Fantasies of uninhibited self-rule were combined with unexpressed longings for a firm directing hand. Such a naïve and contradictory outlook was to be expected in Russia, given the lack of a pluralistic political tradition. The danger was that this inchoate state of public opinion gave great leverage to any party which could combine an ultra-democratic image with an authoritarian core. Here the Bolsheviks, or to be more precise the Leninist Bolsheviks, entered the lists with an inestimable advantage.

Russian political development between the February and October revolutions is mainly characterized by a contest which ranged the moderates against the maximalists: on one hand stood the parties of the democratic or centre-left (the Kadets and most SRs and Mensheviks), and on the other the Bolsheviks and their allies, about whom more will be said below. This struggle is sometimes presented as a propaganda war in which victory went to those whose slogans were best attuned to the popular mood. This is, however, only part of the story. It also involved a fight for control of the mass organizations which proliferated throughout Russia during 1917: of trade unions, militia groups, enterprise, land and supply committees, and— last but not least—soviets. Some one thousand such councils of deputies, elected by workers, soldiers, and (less frequently) peasants, had come into being by the time of the October insurrection. They varied greatly in significance and composition, some uniting representatives of two or even three of the social groups eligible to join. They were most densely concentrated in the north-west and on certain sectors of the front. Those in the provinces modelled themselves to some extent upon the soviet in Petrograd, which had been formed as early as 27 February, before the tsarist regime expired.

Common to all soviets was a form of organization that permitted them to be influenced—indeed, manipulated—by the radical activists who assumed leading positions in their executive committees or other standing bodies. These men were as a rule intellectuals or semi-intellectuals with more political experience than the rank-and-file deputies (or delegates, as they should properly be called). Such 'core organizations' soon came to overshadow the plenary assembly, and in fact to substitute themselves for it. The plenum's function was not to take decisions but rather to mobilize support for the leadership and to confer upon its actions the sanction of an affirmative popular vote. Ordinary deputies had little opportunity to debate the merits of the policies they endorsed. Their attitudes were shaped by discussions in one or other of the party-political caucuses ('fractions'), in which contentious issues would as a rule be thrashed out before they were presented at meetings of the executive committee and then laid before the generality of members.

Powerful centralizing tendencies made themselves felt within the soviet movement from the spring of 1917 onwards. They were facilitated by the arbitrary nature of the electoral process.

Soviets were free to determine for themselves the criteria whereby representatives were chosen. Their electorate was unstable, especially where soldiers were concerned. Voting as a rule took place by show of hands. Only sporadic efforts were made to ensure that elections were held regularly or that minority views were fairly reflected. These practices at first benefited the moderate socialists, but as mass opinion shifted to the left it was they who had cause to complain of discrimination. Both moderates and maximalists employed manipulative techniques, but the latter did so more consistently and with greater sense of purpose. Such practices enabled the soviet leaders to institutionalize the popular support they had won and to prevent transitory changes in mass sentiment from endangering their control.

Lenin had always impressed upon his followers the importance of organizational work. This was an essential precept of Bolshevism, which had asserted its identity as a separate faction in the RSDRP by carrying on a long drawn-out struggle against rival groups and tendencies. That party's cohesion and the sense of comradeship among its members had been strained and all but destroyed by incessant squabbling for which the Leninists bore much of the responsibility. They launched one campaign after another to secure control of various party organizations and to expel from them those suspected of deviant views. They thought it quite acceptable to apply administrative measures against opponents in order to maintain discipline and ideological purity. To a lesser extent their adversaries became infected with the same way of thinking.

After February 1917 a new arena of political activity was suddenly opened up to the leaders of the revolutionary parties who emerged from clandestinity or returned from emigration or exile; yet the traditions of the underground milieu lived on. In seeking to outmanœuvre their rivals for influence over the masses these cadre elements could draw upon a whole armoury of stratagems and *ruses de guerre*. To be sure, countervailing tendencies also were present, particularly among new recruits to the cause, in the direction of party unity and common action by socialists generally. To many rank-and-file members of the RSDRP it seemed unnecessary, and even improper, to engage in intensive party-political warfare at a time when the maximalist cause was winning broad popular support. However, this pressure from below could be contained without great difficulty by the senior activists, and no one was more outspoken than Lenin in condemning what he described as 'conciliationist' tendencies.

The political battle within the soviets centred upon the role they were to play in the revolutionizing process. Most Mensheviks and other moderates thought that these organizations' value lay in their ability to articulate the masses' demands during a period of crisis. They assumed that, once Russia had settled down to a more normal pattern of existence, these bodies would come to play a subordinate role in the new institutional structure. In a democratic order soviets would assist the government in carrying out certain tasks and help to keep it responsive to popular opinion; but they should not seek to supplant duly constituted state authorities, for they were but class organs representing a limited segment of the community; sovereignty rested with the people as a whole, whose will should be expressed through the national legislature. The moderate socialists thus professed allegiance to the principles of representative government as commonly understood, even though in practice they might accord the soviets a political weight scarcely consonant with western European constitutional theory.

These ideas were challenged root and branch by the maximalists. In their view it was precisely the soviets' class character that made them more democratic than a 'bourgeois' parliament, however progressive. In his pamphlet *State and Revolution* Lenin roundly declared that under capitalism democracy could not but be fraudulent, since exploiters and exploited had no interests in common. He hailed the soviets as authentic popular artefacts and potential organs of state power. Their merits were deemed to lie in their informal, spontaneous character: not only was membership in them confined to the labouring classes, but deputies were chosen at their workplace, instead of their area of residence; they were given imperative mandates which their electors could revoke at any time; and they exercised integral power, combining the legislative, executive, and judicial functions which 'bourgeois' advocates of constitutional rule sought artificially to distinguish. This meant that under 'soviet power' the mass of working people would be continually involved in running their own affairs, so realizing one of the basic goals of Marxist socialism.

This theory, derived from Jacobinism by way of the Russian radical tradition, left many questions obscure. Lenin paid remarkably little attention to the operative practices of the soviets as they developed in Russia during 1917. While praising them for their revolutionary accomplishments, he showed virtually no interest in the actual workings of the institutions upon which the socialist order was supposedly going to rest: how decisions were taken, or how the various soviet organs interacted at different levels. Nor was he disposed to forecast the attitude of a Bolshevik government to the soviet movement's anarchistic features, which so crassly contradicted the centralist principles to which his own party was committed. This silence was in large part tactical: Lenin realized that by entering into too much detail he would spoil the bright image of the future that he was delineating. If taxed on concrete points, he could plead that experience alone would provide the answer: let the soviets first take power, and then the masses would be able to develop freely their creative talents.

This appealing doctrine, coupled with superior organizing ability (to say nothing of good fortune), enabled the Bolsheviks and their allies to seize the initiative in the soviet movement. In September, in the wake of the 'Kornilov affair', they won control of two of the most important councils, in Petrograd and Moscow. From this base they challenged the authority of the moderate-controlled central soviet executive (the CEC) and of the Provisional Government. The October insurrection met with little resistance, at least in Petrograd, and was almost an anti-climax: Kerensky's fall had been expected for some time. What did come as a surprise to many was the formation of an all-Bolshevik government, the Council of People's Commissars, with Lenin at its head. Was this the long-heralded 'soviet power'?

The new regime based itself in large degree *upon* the soviets, but it was not *of* the soviets. It derived an appearance of legitimacy from its endorsement, on the night of 26–7 October, by delegates to the Second Congress of Soviets: this was a gathering of the most radical elements in the movement, whose title to speak for all soviets in the country did not go unchallenged.

Most of these men seem to have desired a regime in which major decision-making power would rest with the soviets which had elected them. In so far as they recognized the need for a central Soviet government at all, they expected it to consist of representatives from all the parties and groups active in these bodies, in proportion to their strength. It would be a new coalition ministry, but unlike its forerunners one which excluded those moderate leaders who stood for collaboration with non-socialists, for continuation of the war pending conclusion of a general peace, or for delaying major domestic reforms until the Constituent Assembly met. It was expected to embark at once upon a radical restructuring of Russian society, but to do so with as much support as it could muster within 'revolutionary democracy'.

This was not Lenin's view. Looking at the problems of government with an eye to the realities of power politics, he reckoned that the soviets performed a relative, not absolute service to the socialist cause: they could certainly strengthen Bolshevik influence over the masses, but equally they might weaken it by articulating popular dissatisfaction. To avert this they had to be kept under firm control. Lenin conceived of the soviets as instruments of rule rather than sovereign bodies. He never modified his conviction that his party had a 'vanguard role' to play, not only in winning state power but also in constructing the new society. His opinions on this fundamental point were at least consistent, if not always fully explicit.

It was therefore inevitable that the soviets' real decision-making power should be rapidly eroded in the post-October period, at the centre as well as in the various localities. They increased in number and complexity of organization, but their deliberative function atrophied; they lost such spontaneous vitality as they had once possessed and became still more 'other-directed' than before. The plenary assembly, where it continued to be called, acted as a mere sounding-board for the executive, or more often than not for a small directing nucleus (usually a group of three, or *troyka*). The local leaders were soon obliged to take their cue from agents of the central power, the ubiquitous commissars. The soviets became administrative bodies whose operations were subjected to close regulation by functionaries from within the mushrooming bureaucracy. The electoral process, from which they derived their representative character, became more of a formality than ever. Already in 1918 voters could no longer choose between different parties; soon afterwards the same was true of alternative tendencies within the single ruling party. Deputies came to be pre-selected on the electors' behalf. Dissenters were expelled or cajoled into acquiescence, since unanimity of views was regarded as a talisman of ideological good health. If a soviet resisted this pressure, it would be unceremoniously dissolved.

The same treatment was meted out to all other public bodies, official or semi-official, that were permitted to survive. The process of organizational *Gleichschaltung* was carried through with impressive thoroughness. The system of centralized control included a special police agency to safeguard the regime's security, the 'Cheka'. Established in December 1917 on Lenin's personal initiative, it took over from an organ of the Petrograd soviet which had operated in and around the capital since the overturn in October. The arbitrary acts of these organs, censorship of the press, and the loss of civil liberties caused much dissatisfaction and alarm, which was not confined to educated people. Critics, aware of the French revolutionary precedent, were soon speaking of government-sponsored violence as 'terror'. At the time such a term seemed uncalled for: few lives were actually lost as a result of this repression, which seems to have been designed to harass the opposition rather than to eliminate it *tout court*. Nevertheless the potential significance of all these measures was immense. It was not just that the new regime adopted a harsh style: it had set up machinery which could turn the 'dictatorship of the proletariat' into a state run by cadres of professional revolutionaries on the people's behalf. Taken together with the Bolsheviks' commitment to ideological conformity and their disregard for conventional legal or moral limitations upon the exercise of power, this portended the birth of nothing less than a new type of government. Within a few years, at the hands of Lenin's successor, it would assume dimensions beyond the imagination of most witnesses to the events of 1917.

OPPOSITION AND DISSENT

From the start the dictatorship met with overt and covert resistance from several quarters. However, this opposition lacked a unifying centre or a common programme. It was divided into two camps whose mutual suspicions made concerted action virtually impossible.

Russian conservatives (and some liberals, too) saw Bolshevism as plebeian, anarchic, and anti-national. Most of them believed that it would collapse of its own accord, and therefore adopted a passive attitude. A minority took the view that it should be countered by physical force, but found the military leaders, to whom they turned for support, less than enthusiastic: the latter, preoccupied with the defence of Russia against her external foes, did not want to encourage fighting among their men. They were also somewhat contemptuous of civilian politicians, especially if they bore a socialist label. Even if the generals had wished to intervene actively in the affairs of Petrograd during the crucial early weeks, this would have been rendered difficult by the soldiers' angry mood. The political organizations in the armed forces often exerted an influence greater than that of the commanders.

The Bolshevik insurrection was greeted with satisfaction by many soldiers, particularly on the key Northern and Western fronts, and the news that an armistice was imminent turned this sentiment into one of approval. It was not so much a matter of the troops being converted to any party credo as of their deciding to abandon their positions and to make their way home as best they could. In the winter of 1917–18 few could be found who were willing to bear arms against the Soviet regime, even among the officer corps. Some active resistance was offered by the cossack 'hosts' in south-eastern Russia, but within a matter of weeks it had been largely overcome, and the first 'White' units formed in that region were forced on the defensive. In this small-scale war, a political as much as a military conflict, the advantage lay overwhelmingly with the 'Reds'. The course and outcome of these initial campaigns gave an accurate foretaste of what was to occur in the next three years of civil war. The anti-Bolsheviks lacked their adversaries' ideological drive and propagandist skills; they were disunited and poorly organized; and they did not receive the timely aid from foreign powers that might have turned the scales in their favour.

The other element in the opposition looked for leadership to politicians of the democratic centre and moderate left. These liberals and socialists regarded Bolshevism as a recrudescence of tsarist autocracy in new guise. They too believed, although for different reasons, that its chances of survival were slight, and so were none too inclined to undertake active measures against it. Where they did, their response took the form of a defence of the legal order, and above all of the Constituent Assembly, which for so long had symbolized the aspirations of Russian democracy.

In considering the rhetorical appeals and declamatory statements issued by these leaders one should bear in mind that their purpose was to remind the public of its basic rights and responsibilities. A didactic approach was only to be expected in view of the general lack of civic education. Nevertheless these affirmations lacked credibility. There were several reasons for this. First, most of the politicians involved had been associated in one way or another with the Provisional Government, and were naturally blamed for its errors and shortcomings. Second, they were still racked by partisan discord and failed to rally behind any leader of stature. Third, they had no physical force at their disposal which they could set against that which the maximalists, or for that matter the conservatives, could bring to bear. This last factor was undoubtedly the most important. Moral protests by the unarmed seldom inspire respect.

Yet before one dismisses out of hand (as is the fashion) these pacific-minded politicians—who commanded majority support among the electorate, as the poll for the Constituent Assembly showed—their achievements should at least be placed on record. For some weeks they maintained a shadow administration, with the aim of providing legal continuity between the defunct Provisional Government and the future national executive to be established, as they hoped, by the Constituent Assembly. They set up an umbrella organization uniting representatives of various public bodies that had not yet fallen under maximalist control; and when this agency was suppressed they replaced it by another. In many provincial cities and towns there appeared 'committees of public safety' based on the same principle, which served to co-ordinate the activities of local groups, some of which performed functions essential to the life of the community. In this way they provided a minimum of security at a time when anarchy was rife. Finally, the moderates gave a good account of themselves at the single session of the Constituent Assembly which the Bolsheviks permitted them to hold. The forcible dissolution of this national legislature on 6 January 1918, after some people who demonstrated peaceably on its behalf had been shot and killed, was a confession of weakness on the part of the maximalists, who feared that from this tribune the democratic politicians might appeal effectively to a populace that was beginning to resent dictatorial rule.

It should also be noted that in those regions where the centre and moderate left parties had the rising tide of nationalism behind them, as was the case in Finland, the Baltic lands, the Ukraine, and Georgia, they were able to offer more resolute opposition to dictatorship than they could in Great Russia. The Ukrainian leaders, in the main Socialist-Revolutionaries or Social Democrats, aspired to national independence within a genuinely federal system. This was incompatible with the Bolshevik drive for hegemony and led to war between the Ukraine and Soviet Russia. This conflict, which in one form or another dragged on for years, obliged the Bolsheviks to modify their initial intransigence towards minority claims, at least on paper, by giving the Soviet state a federal constitution and conceding a measure of economic and cultural autonomy. In Finland, which won its independence from Russia in 1917, and later in the Baltic lands, they had to accept a compromise. In Georgia a moderate socialist government survived until 1921, when it was overthrown by Soviet armed intervention. Among the Muslims and other eastern peoples of the former Russian empire national consciousness was to prove more difficult to accommodate to Communist purposes than Lenin had expected.

Apart from these adversaries the Bolsheviks had to deal with the problem of dissent. Within the maximalist camp there were many who accepted the basic principles of 'soviet power' but questioned the way in which they were being implemented. The dividing-line between opposition and dissent was not always clear at the time, and critics on both flanks were inclined to blur it; nevertheless the distinction is fundamental.

In the PSR factional strife led to a formal schism a few days
after the October revolution, when the party's Central Committee expelled those left-wing elements that had participated in
the insurrection. They soon established themselves as a separate
entity under the label of the Party of Left Socialist-Revolutionaries (PLSR; Left SRs). Foremost among their objectives was
the immediate seizure of privately-owned land and its redistribution among the 'toiling peasants', whose spokesmen they
considered themselves to be. Both the Left SRs and the SR
Maximalists, another breakaway group whose ideas were
strongly coloured by Anarchism, were profoundly egalitarian
in spirit. They hated privilege with an emotional intensity that
appealed to many soldiers and peasants who came fresh to
politics. After some involved bargaining the Left SRs accepted
portfolios in Lenin's government, but resigned from it in March
1918. Critics have dubbed them 'history's first fellow-travellers',
while sympathetic observers have seen them as embodying the
conscience of the revolution.

Among the (non-Bolshevik) Social Democrats, too, the
centre of gravity shifted leftwards during 1917, and by September the so-called Menshevik Internationalists, led by Yu. O.
Martov, were calling the tune in the Central Committee of the
RSDRP. (The Mensheviks had inherited the title of the once
united party.) Martov had fewer illusions than the PLSR chiefs
about the Bolsheviks' intentions, but the pressure which his
group brought to bear upon the Provisional Government indirectly played into their hands. After the October insurrection
the Mensheviks rallied in opposition to the new regime, but
there was a moment when they nearly crossed the line from
opposition to dissent. This occurred on 31 October, when their
Central Committee decided, by a one-vote margin, to seek a
socialist coalition government that would include Bolsheviks.
However, nothing came of this scheme and after a few days the
party reverted to a stand that excluded political collaboration
with the 'usurpers'. One Menshevik faction refused to abide by
this ruling and challenged the Central Committee's authority.
The members of this group called themselves United Social-
Democratic Internationalists (USDI). (The word 'united' in
the title signified their ambition to bridge the gulf between
Mensheviks and Bolsheviks.) Led by V. Bazarov and V.

Stroyev, this minuscule coterie had a political weight out of proportion to its size since it published an influential newspaper, *Novaya zhizn'* ('New Life'), of which Maxim Gorky was one of the editors. Unlike the PLSR, the USDI did not join the Soviet government, but it was represented in the central executive committee of soviets (CEC).

In addition to these elements the dissenters included Anarchists and Anarcho-syndicalists of various shadings and, last but not least, certain independent-minded Bolsheviks who jibed at the constraints of party discipline. They were thus as diverse ideologically as they were fragmented organizationally. If there was any single idea that united them, it was a desire for the new regime to exercise its power in a more responsible manner and to show greater regard for mass opinion (or to be precise, for that sector of radical mass opinion which they claimed to represent). They considered that the maximalist bloc as a whole had a common interest which the Leninists, with their self-assured headstrong ways, overlooked. Unnecessarily forceful actions threatened to isolate the government from its popular base, and so to increase the risk that the civil war might end in a victory for 'reaction'.

More was involved here than mere cowardice. Half-intuitively the dissenters realized that the revolutionary regime might manage to survive at an unacceptable cost. The danger, as they saw it, was that the 'dictatorship of the proletariat' might degenerate into the rule of a repressive self-contained oligarchy which would justify its actions by reference to its own ideological premises rather than to the actual opinions of its supporters. This would allow privilege, which the social revolution had supposedly eliminated for good, to re-emerge in new guise; and the dissenters were egalitarians and collectivists *à l'outrance*. They believed in the natural wisdom and virtue of the common man, provided that his conduct conformed to their own stereotype. Although they called themselves democrats, the term was inappropriate. Their attitude to the Constituent Assembly and other representative institutions was governed by considerations of political expediency; in this they did not differ from the Bolsheviks. Likewise the dissenting maximalists were inconsistent in their defence of civil liberties and other basic human rights. If they advocated what would today be called pluralism, this was chiefly because this would enable their own voices to be heard, and not because they objected on principle to Lenin's monist *Weltanschauung*. Indeed, a number of them were inwardly attracted by the self-confidence which such doctrinal certainty conferred, and therefore did not find it too difficult later to shed their doubts and to convert to the victors' creed. Other dissenters, however, continued to adhere to their convictions.

This ambivalence towards Bolshevism was particularly marked in the case of the Left SR leaders, for whom the revolution was above all a moral triumph for the Russian people, which had liberated itself from injustice by a feat of daring heroism. No one idolized the *narod* more fervently than these Populist ideologues, who stood in an ancient intellectual tradition. In entering upon an active partnership with the Bolsheviks, they realized that they were setting their ideals at risk; yet they hoped that by acquiring positions of authority within the Soviet government they could exert an influence in favour of less exclusive policies. They reckoned that, as 'soviet power' was consolidated and the regime's security improved, the Bolsheviks would relax their doctrinaire intransigence: for how could they stand against the whole Russian people? Since the industrial working class was but a small segment of the 'toiling masses', its spokesmen would be obliged to yield before the will of the vast majority.

What these idealists left out of account was the Leninists' superior skill in organization and political manœuvre. To them the Left SRs were errant, vacillating comrades whose 'petty-bourgeois' class affiliations hindered them from adopting a consistent proletarian viewpoint. Lenin contended that the dictatorship required a strong central power free from restraint of any kind. Having broken with 'bourgeois' notions of legality and morality, one had to go *jusqu'au bout*. 'The safety of the revolution is the supreme law': this maxim should inspire the judicial and ethical norms of the new socialist order. He agreed that mass support was essential, but what counted most was its quality rather than its quantity. Where mass support was lacking, it was the task of those in power to manufacture it by providing resolute leadership.

Against such arguments the dissenters tentatively advanced

the notion of a *constitutional* socialist order based on the soviets. The rights of these representative bodies should be preserved and expanded, so that they might act as a check upon the authority of those charged with dictatorial power. This was indeed a quixotic and contradictory idea. How, one might ask, could a revolutionary regime be both dictatorial and constitutional? Yet a brief glance at later Soviet history suggests that it might have been worth trying. The Communists proceeded to construct a state order in which the constitutional norms safeguarding individual and group rights became mere fictions, not intended to be taken seriously, wherever their implementation might have harmed the interests of the party apparatus. As a result political life acquired an artificial character and eventually atrophied. Yet society was never wholly bureaucratized, for the population was expected to participate actively in 'the construction of socialism', and this allowed an awareness of individual and group rights to survive. Once controls were relaxed, citizens were bound to press for recognition of these rights in real life, and for their institutions to become more responsive to their needs; but these popular aspirations could not be satisfied without demolishing the whole totalitarian edifice.

Such ossification of the governmental system might well have been avoided if the dissenters' suggestions had been followed. Not all twentieth-century dictatorships, after all, have found it necessary to go so far along the road of fraudulent constitutionalism. A more authentic soviet order might well have proved more stable, more resilient in times of crisis, and more successful in harnessing popular energies to its purposes. There is no need to assume *a priori* that it would have fallen victim either to internal dissension or to external attack. It is another question, to be sure, how the dissenters could have made their views prevail, given the Leninist Bolsheviks' dictatorial cast of mind—and the Russian political tradition. Nevertheless in 1917 the options were not yet closed, and they were justified in presenting an alternative design for the socialist state order. The issues they raised would remain topical long after they themselves had passed from the scene.

THE CENTRAL EXECUTIVE COMMITTEE

If the soviets were to remain vigorous institutions of popular self-government, their rights had to be defended in their central deliberative organ, the CEC. This had been set up by the First Congress of Soviets in June 1917, ostensibly to co-ordinate the activities of workers' and soldiers' soviets throughout the land. (A separate committee existed for peasant soviets.) It served mainly as a channel of communication between the socialist party leaders—at first the moderates, then the maximalists—and their most active supporters. A revolutionary parliament of sorts, it debated all the issues of the day that were of interest to the left. Its notoriously chaotic proceedings reflected the immediate concerns of rank-and-file cadre elements, but its decisions were the work of the politicians who staffed its core bodies. This was the pattern throughout the soviet movement, and it was particularly evident in the Petrograd organization whence the central soviet executive sprang.

Although the CEC was supposedly an all-Russian body, its view of events was strongly coloured by developments in the capital. There was no clear demarcation line between its organs and those of the Petrograd soviet, which continued to exist alongside it. Nor was its competence differentiated from that of the socialist parties or of the Provisional Government. Such ambiguity was natural in the fluid situation in which Russia found herself during 1917, when the old institutions had all but collapsed and new ones were still being born.

The CEC of first convocation (June–October) had well over 300 members, the bulk of whom were activists from the capital. Only a proportion of these men actually attended plenary sessions of the committee. Many were absent on various assignments in the provinces, since in accordance with the generally accepted theory they combined an executive function with their deliberative one: each member was supposed to be actively engaged in revolutionary work. The core organizations consisted of a 50-man Bureau and a Presidium of nine. The chairman was the Menshevik N. S. Chkheidze; his party and the PSR each had four representatives on the Presidium. L. B. Kamenev, who spoke for the Bolsheviks, was for some weeks incapacitated by arrest on a political charge, but this did not seriously inhibit the maximalists in the CEC, whose influence was clearly on the increase from mid-July onward. To counteract their pressure, the moderate leaders shifted the centre of decision-making to the Bureau. In the three months July to September this body met 48 times and the plenum 30 times; both types of session were held with declining frequency. Meanwhile the Presidium members were in constant touch behind the scenes with Kerensky's cabinet and were able to influence many of its major decisions. The CEC's authority suffered in consequence, and it lost further prestige once the Bolsheviks had won control of the Petrograd and Moscow soviets. The moderate socialist leaders were unable (or unwilling) to convert the two central soviet executives into an effective source of support for the Provisional Government, but on the contrary allowed them to undermine its authority.

When the Bolsheviks rose in insurrection the CEC of first convocation was voted out by the delegates to the Second Congress of Soviets, who chose a new Bolshevik-controlled executive in its stead. By this time the CEC had acquired a considerable bureaucratic apparatus, as befitted an organ whose members treated it as an alternate government. It had some eighteen administrative departments, whose functions to some extent paralleled those of state ministries. Thus there were rudimentary agencies for international, military, and agrarian affairs, local government, economic planning, public health and so on, in addition to those concerned with propaganda and agitation, which were the most active.

It was generally assumed on the left that, once 'soviet power' had been won, these agencies would take over from the ministries of the old regime. Precisely the reverse happened. By the end of the year those of the CEC's departments that exercised quasi-governmental functions had been absorbed, along with whatever remained of the ministerial staffs, into the apparatus of the relevant people's commissariat (PC)—the name which the Bolsheviks gave to the central administrative bodies they set up. Similarly the new government was not constituted out of the CEC. Instead the Council of People's Commissars 'formed itself', so to speak, secured endorsement from the Second Congress of Soviets, and then coexisted with the CEC. Thus in a sense there were now two parallel governments. This ambiguous situation reflected the fundamental paradox of the October revolution.

Had Bolshevik theory made allowance for the separation of legislative and executive power, the problem would have been manageable: each agency would have had its distinct role to fulfil. But to Lenin such an arrangement smacked of 'bourgeois parliamentarianism'. For ideological as well as practical reasons he was determined to concentrate as much authority as possible in the CPC, which ruled the country under close supervision by the Bolshevik party's Central Committee. The CPC issued edicts as it thought fit, often in an impromptu manner after hasty discussion, and passed some of them on to the CEC for confirmation when such a procedure seemed expedient. It was reluctant to allow these laws to be considered in detail even by maximalist cadres in good standing, whose experience might have been of value; instead it preferred wherever possible to operate in secret. In theory sovereignty lay with the CEC when the congress of soviets was not in session; but in practice this sovereignty was nullified by the rights which the people's commissars arrogated to themselves. The Bolshevik leaders paid no more than lip service to the principles of government they had proclaimed, and resorted to familiar manipulative devices in order to keep the deputies in line.

Control over the CEC was exercised mainly through its Presidium. This was headed from 8 November by Ya. M. Sverdlov, a member of Lenin's inner circle who managed the potentially troublesome assembly with considerable skill. He understood very well how to evade inconvenient provisions in the statutes which ostensibly governed its procedure. Sessions were held irregularly, at short notice, and without prior publication of the agenda. They were usually preceded by meetings of the Presidium, held in private, at which the party leaders would seek to agree upon a common approach. This inevitably gave the debate that followed a somewhat stage-managed character, although spontaneous interventions from the floor were still possible and the official agenda was seldom adhered to. Much time was devoted to matters of secondary importance, whereas such major issues as the establishment of the Cheka were not discussed. The tendency for sessions to be held with diminishing frequency, which had begun before October, continued. The CEC of second convocation met four times in each of the first two weeks of its existence, but by December only one or two weekly sessions were held. These were often restricted, rather than plenary, meetings; of the latter three had a purely ceremonial character, which limited freedom of debate, and were in fact little more than mass meetings.

The CEC's composition did not remain stable throughout the brief life of the second convocation (27 October 1917–6 January 1918). On 14 November it was agreed that it should be expanded to include deputies from peasant soviets, thus ostensibly making it representative of the entire labouring population. But simultaneously it received an infusion of men from armed forces' organizations and trade unions, which safeguarded it from any possible deviation towards Populism. This compromise produced an assembly with a theoretical complement of 366 members. The Bureau (which was of no practical account) and the Presidium were subsequently reformed to take account of this new situation. They continued to be constituted according to the principle of proportionality between the parties and groups represented, each factional caucus making its own nominations. On the Presidium the Bolsheviks retained a margin of advantage *vis-à-vis* the Left SRs, so that there was never any risk of their losing control of the assembly. True, at one point they were actually outvoted, but the decision was promptly reversed. As a rule resolutions were endorsed with a show of unanimity and any differences of opinion about new laws were settled privately, in commissions set up for that purpose.

For all this dissenters were often able to score telling points in debate. They spoke their minds with a forthrightness inconceivable in such a representative body during any later phase of Soviet history. The exchanges were conducted in a down-to-earth rhetorical style. The delegates would not have appreciated eloquence in the grand manner or recondite literary allusions; their taste ran rather to the cliché or the neat polemical riposte. Sessions were usually held late at night, and this also had its effect upon the quality of the debate. The wonder is that so many revolutionary activists, who had spent all day in physically demanding work, could withstand further hours of nocturnal oratory. But these were stirring times and the CEC was an unconventional parliament by any standard.

Was it peculiarly unique to Russia, a land in which legislative institutions had never prospered? On the contrary: the CEC may rather be said to have set an unhappy precedent. The dictatorships that have proliferated in our time have usually found it worth while to clothe their nakedness by some type of quasi-legislative body, so paying a perverse compliment to the democratic principles they abhor. Such an assembly may be no more than decorative camouflage upon an edifice erected and maintained by force; yet when a crisis breaks and the brittle structure collapses, institutional forms that long seemed to be dead may suddenly take on new life.

The Debate
on
Soviet Power

First Session
27–8 October 1917

[First Part]   7 p.m.

Before the CEC is constituted Kamenev is elected ᵃ⌐provisio-
nal⌐ᵃ chairman and Avanesov secretary . . . After announcing
the agenda drawn up by the Presidium:

1. *CPC Decrees*

KAMENEV informs the assembly of the text of [three] ordinances
issued by the Council of People's Commissars. ᵃ⌐I call upon
everyone to render the new government not just formal but
active assistance, since it faces tremendous tasks and every
effort must be made to implement rapidly the major enactments
of the Second Congress of Soviets of Workers' and Soldiers'
Deputies.⌐ᵃ¹ The government, backed by the broad masses of
soldiers and workers, will find the means of realizing their aspirations. I am sure that the CPC, by maintaining the closest contact with the masses, will fully [satisfy] all needs of the working
class and the revolutionary army. The commissars of Labour,
Posts and Telegraphs, and Transport have already approached
the trade unions representing those who work in these [official]
institutions. They have begun to set up bodies, organized on the
basis of collegiality and equality of rights, to decide any questions that may arise in these ministries. The commissars are putting into practice the principle of coalition, and they therefore
cannot and will not close their doors to those who wish to work
with them on the basis of the principles laid down by the Congress.

2. *Congress of Peasant Deputies*

MILYUTIN, PC of Agriculture, reports that he is proposing to
convoke, as a measure of urgency, a Congress of Peasant
[Deputies] and suggests that a commission be chosen for this
purpose.

A LEFT SR spokesman: I agree that this congress is urgent and suggest that the commission should act in agreement with the left-wing element of the [Executive Committee of the All-Russian] ᵃˈSoviet of Peasant Deputies to ensure that the congress is convoked properly and that it genuinely represents the will of the entire Russian peasantry.ˈᵃ

Resolution approved. A five-man commission is elected, to comprise Spiro, Kalegayev, Vasilyuk, Grinevich, and Muranov. It is instructed to start work immediately, provided, of course, that the question of norms of representation and other technical matters can be settled without any particular trouble.

3. Railwaymen's Union

It is decided to defer the question of the Vikzhel representative's speech at the Congress and his confusion of the facts[2] pending clarification of the results of the talks which Ryazanov is authorized to hold, as a special delegate, with the railwaymen's union [leaders].

4. Actions of the MRC[3]

An MRC spokesman answers an interpellation about the occupation by soldiers of the [Petrograd municipal] Duma [premises]. The MRC has not authorized any such occupation, and if this took place it was evidently due to the outright Black Hundred agitation being carried on in the Duma. For its part the MRC has taken every step to end unauthorized actions by individuals.

5. Situation in the Country

PODVOYSKY reports briefly, whereupon the following resolution is adopted:

To all soviets, to all workers, soldiers, and peasants.

The Second All-Russian Congress of Soviets of Workers' and Soldiers' Deputies, which was held with the participation of [some] peasant deputies in Petrograd on 25 and 26 October, has completed its labours. It has elected a new plenipotentiary directing organ, the All-Russian CEC, to which all the rights of the Congress are transferred in toto. Thereby the powers of the former CEC, elected at the First Congress, have ceased to exist, as have those of all army and provincial commissars appointed by the former CEC. All organizations or individuals sheltering under the name of the CEC but not authorized by the Second Congress are illegitimate and their orders are not to be obeyed.

It is the duty of each comrade to resist all such efforts to spread discord within the ranks of democracy and to weaken our revolution. The CEC insistently requests all soviets to send it information on the state of affairs in their localities and to remain in constant close touch with their central organ.

Comrade workers, soldiers, and peasants! Our revolution is threatened from every quarter. We face tremendously important and difficult tasks. It is your duty to rally round the CEC, the supreme organ of revolutionary democracy, to render it unanimous support, and to help it deepen and strengthen the revolution.

(signed) All-Russian Central Executive Committee of the Soviets of Workers' and Soldiers' Deputies.

6. *Organizational Matters*

A commission, to consist of Avanesov, Sagirashvili, and Levit, is elected to compile and summarize all data relating to the composition and number of participants in the Second Congress. The following [other] commissions are then elected:

Editorial, to consist of five persons;
Convocation of Peasant Congress, [as above, § 2];
Organization: Kurayev, Algasov, Vinter, Gillerson, Bukhartsev;
Compilation of instructions for emissaries to various towns: Belkov, Erman, Smolyaninov.

Consideration of the agenda items relating to workers' control and transfer of land to the peasants and cossacks is deferred until the next session, to be held at 12 noon on 28 October.

Khrispolsky is given the floor to convey an unscheduled message of greetings from the Third Finnish Riflemen's Division.

Finally the names of members of the CEC are read out. There are 62 Bolsheviks, 29 Socialist-Revolutionaries, 6 Internationalist Social-Democrats, 3 Ukrainian socialists and 1 SR Maximalist. The Organization Commission is instructed to report on the question of including representatives from the socialist parties of other nationalities and from military units stationed in Macedonia and elsewhere.

[Second Part]*b*   28 October
*c⌐*Chairman: Kamenev*⌐c*

*a⌐*1. *The Political Situation*[4]

Several reports are delivered on the current situation. Kerensky is said to have only 5,000 cossacks at his disposal. Measures have been taken and reinforcements brought up [to defend Petrograd]. Soviet power has triumphed in all the [provincial] towns of Russia. From Moscow a telegram was received at 4.30 p.m. stating that the staff of Moscow military district has capitulated and that all power has passed to the soviet. The staff was supported only by some French troops present in the city, as well as by some dragoons and by the cossacks. From Minsk it is reported that the local soviet has assumed power without bloodshed. Similar information has been received from Kharkov, Samara, Kazan, Ufa, Mogilev, and a number of towns in the Moscow region.*⌐a*

2. *Actions of the MRC; Press Decree*

*d⌐*KAMENEV: The reports that have appeared in the press about [the condition of] the arrested cadets who have been confined in the SS. Peter and Paul fortress are incorrect. They have been verified personally by the mayor, [G. I.] Shreyder, who has promised to issue a bulletin on behalf of the municipal Duma on this point, but this has not appeared.

A question is tabled regarding the arrest of members of Tsentroflot.[5] KAMENEV calls for their immediate liberation. PROSHYAN suggests the formation of a commission representing the three fractions in the CEC (Bolsheviks, Left SRs, and Menshevik Internationalists) to settle the matter.

LOZOVSKY and STEKLOV raise the question of repealing the [CPC's] ordinance on the closure of newspapers,[6] in view of the statement by the printers' [union] that it will prevent any newspapers appearing so long as this decree remains in force. Steklov is told to inform the printers' union that the question will be settled tomorrow.

OLONETSKY proposes that a permanent commission be set up to maintain contact with the MRC. KALEGAYEV adds that it should have three members and should be given the power to vet the MRC's actions. After some debate a resolution is adopted to detail up to 15^e CEC members charged with transferring the MRC's work to the CEC.⌐^{d}

^{c}⌐URITSKY: The Mensheviks and SRs are carrying on overt Black Hundred agitation in the city and are spreading false rumours about alleged excesses and acts of violence committed by representatives of the new authority. So far as the publication of newspapers is concerned, the MRC has ordered [its agents] to act in accordance with the decree of the CPC.⌐^{c}

NOTES

a *NZ*, 29 Oct.
b No official record has survived of this session, which was, however, reported in *Pr.*, *NZ*, and *ZT* on 29 Oct.; it was presumably held during the previous night. It has been treated here as a continuation of the first ⌐ session.
c *Pr.*, 29 Oct.
d *ZT*, 29 Oct.
e Fourteen members according to *Pr.*, *RG*, and *NZ*; the delegates were 'to carry on organic work' in the MRC and to reorganize it. The nomination of 13 men (Bykov, Goloshchekin, Levin, Galkin, Algasov, Avanesov, Zaks, Fomin, Gzelshchak, Peterson, Peters, Gvozdin, Yevseyev) was reported in *Prot.* for 29 Oct. (p. 10).

Second Session
29 October 1917

[First Part]

Chairman: Kamenev   5 p.m.

1. *Vikzhel's Ultimatum*

KRUSHINSKY: The All-Russian Union of Railwaymen did not have any desire to interfere in the struggle between political parties, but the news that has reached us from Moscow compels us to act. Civil war is continuing in Moscow, where last night two liquor repositories were sacked and a drunken crowd is committing outrages. There is shooting all over the city and many people have been killed and wounded. Therefore the union's Central Committee has adopted the following resolution:

> To all line committees and union branches. To all trade unions. To all soviets ... To the central committees of all political parties ... To all, all, all.
>
> There is no authority in the country, and a bitter struggle is going on to establish such an authority by force of arms. A fratricidal war has begun. At a moment when the people's liberties are menaced by an external enemy, [Russian] democracy is settling its internal feuds by blood and iron. The Provisional Government headed by Kerensky has shown itself unable to retain power. [But] the Council of People's Commissars formed in Petrograd, which rests upon one party alone, cannot gain recognition or support from the country as a whole. It is essential to form a new government that will enjoy the confidence of all democracy and possess the moral force to hold power until the Constituent Assembly meets. Such a government can be formed only by reasoned agreement among all democrats, and definitely not by force of arms. Fratricidal strife has never created and never can

create an authority [recognized] by the whole country. A people that has renounced the death penalty[1] as a means of achieving unity and war as a means of settling international disputes cannot accept civil war as a means of settling its internal differences. A civil war cannot but lead to counter-revolution and benefit solely the people's enemies.

In order to preserve the country and the revolution the Central Executive Committee of the All-Russian Union of Railwaymen has from the start of the present internecine strife observed strict neutrality and declared that the only way to achieve peace within the country is to set up a homogeneous government, to be formed from all socialist parties from the Bolsheviks to the Popular Socialists[2] inclusive. The union's appeal has been welcomed by many public organizations and parties in Petrograd and Moscow. The union Central Executive Committee has declared, and hereby [once again] affirms, that it will allow [use of] the entire railway apparatus only to those who share this platform. It announces to all citizens—workers, soldiers, and peasants—its irreversible decision and categorical demand: stop the civil war immediately and combine your forces to form a homogeneous revolutionary socialist government. The union declares that to enforce its decision it will employ all the means in its power, right up to halting all movement on the railways. This ban will come into force from midnight tonight, 29–30 October, unless by that time fighting has ceased in Petrograd and Moscow. All railwaymen's organizations are advised to take at once every step to enforce the strike and to form strike committees. The union proclaims all those who continue to settle domestic disputes by arms to be enemies of democracy and traitors to the country.

Petrograd, 29 October.

Central Executive Committee of the All-Russian Railwaymen's Union. Chairman: Malitsky. Secretary: Nesterenko.

I should state that, although Moscow is surrounded by [pro-Provisional] Government forces, we shall not allow them to enter either Moscow or Petrograd, since we are opposed to counter-revolution. We are immediately sending a delegation to Kerensky to inform him of our decision. Even if Kerensky were to enter Petrograd, he would have to surrender since the Union of Railwaymen will seal off all access routes to the city. In view of the situation the union invites you to send your delegates to a joint session of the union executive with [representatives of] the socialist parties.

KAMENEV: I am glad that the railwaymen's union resolution recognizes the fact that the government of coalition with the bourgeoisie has collapsed. As regards the formation of a homogeneous socialist government, what matters most is not the personal composition of such a government but recognition of the fundamental [decrees] adopted at the [Second] Congress of Soviets. What we need are not verbal statements but active work. The government must be strong enough to render unthinkable any attempt at counter-revolution, whether this comes from Kornilov or from Kerensky, whose rule we have overthrown. So far as the conference is concerned, we shall all gladly attend in order to set out our platform and [to ensure] that everyone supports, in deeds and not merely in words, the people's demands for peace, land etc. The Central Committee of the RSDRP(b)[3] has already discussed the declaration made by the [Left] SRs and [United] Social-Democratic Internationalists.[4] It has decided that the conference may be attended by representatives of those parties which left the Congress [of Soviets], in proportion to the strength of their fractions there, as well as by representatives of the railwaymen's union and the union of postal and telegraph workers, the army and the peasantry who were unable to attend the Congress. A government formed on the platform of an active coalition will be supported by all of us. Therefore I move that the proposal of the railwaymen's union executive be accepted without debate and that [the CEC] send representatives to the conference.

Motion passed. The following are nominated to serve on the delegation: Ryazanov, Sverdlov, Zaks, Butkevich, Sagirashvili. Resolved: to declare the session continuous.[a]

^b⌐[Second Part]

2. *Inter-party Conference*⁵

KAMENEV: The Mensheviks and SRs have said they will come to an agreement [only] if the Bolsheviks surrender to Kerensky. They want to form a new government that would exclude both the Kadets and the Bolsheviks.

Two proposals were put before the conference: one, [submitted by the Bolsheviks,] to set up a government responsible to the CEC; the other, of which the sense is that we should submit to Kerensky for the sake of reaching a compromise. The Mensheviks and SRs were for the latter proposal, but everyone else was for the first. (No representatives were present from the executive committee of the [All-Russian] Peasant Union.)

The railwaymen's union should decide whose side it is on: that of the Mensheviks and SRs or that of the broad masses in their struggle against counter-revolution. We do not doubt that the railwaymen['s leaders], in so far as they represent working men, will have to turn away from the Mensheviks and SRs and help us in our struggle. The assistance they can render us is immense, for if the railwaymen come over to us, then their whole apparatus can be directed against the counter-revolution. At the conference we were trying to secure an agreement, not with counter-revolutionaries but with the broad mass of railway employees . . .

Our task is to consolidate the alliance between the proletariat and the revolutionary elements which emerged at the conference. The railwaymen's eyes will be opened by Dan's statement that the cossacks who are marching with Kerensky are the most loyal defenders of the revolution. They will understand that these Mensheviks and SRs are halfway to being cossacks and cadets.⁶

The Mensheviks and SRs proposed a three-day armistice. But that is just a trick: they want the workers to return to their homes, and then they will bring in the cossacks. After ten hours of talks it is clear that no agreement is possible. The Mensheviks and SRs just want to give Kerensky time to come to terms with Kaledin⁷ and to draw up his troops, while the workers and soldiers would be disorganized. We said that we would not be party to such a fraud. We said: if you are willing to recognize a workers' and peasants' government responsible to the soviets, say so now, [or else] you are helping Kerensky from within. We are not going to let ourselves be led around by the nose. If no agreement is reached, then there will be a struggle.

A LEFT SR delegate: At the conference of SRs[8] we discussed [the composition of] the government and the exclusion of the Left SRs from the party. By 122 votes to 33 the conference declared in favour of a homogeneous ministry of socialists, including in the first place the Bolsheviks. The government should base [its policy] on the platform of the Second Congress of Soviets. All parties that do not agree to this we consider as belonging to the counter-revolutionary camp.

3. Messages of Support

XIITH ARMY[9] representative: The XIIth Army soldiers' executive committee is digging in and setting up machine-gun posts. If you hear that it is against the revolution, do not be alarmed, for it is isolated. The mass of soldiers are on our side. We shall confront the executive committee with our artillery. On 27 October at Ostrov Kerensky wanted to take control of some troops, but the soldiers decided to arrest him instead. He escaped with some cossack officers, but no one else backed him. The front[-line soldiers] know nothing of the Bolsheviks as a political party. They say: '*we* are the Bolsheviks.' The front is burning with zeal to consolidate soviet power . . .

132ND DIVISION representative: . . . When my comrades saw me off they demanded that here [in Petrograd] everything should be done as was written in the mandate they gave me. If it is not, then the soldiers themselves will take their weapons, board trains, and come here to see that their demands are met.

When the soldiers heard of the insurrection, they were surprised that Kerensky should have fled.[10] The army knows no SRs. It recognizes no one but the Bolsheviks . . .

[Declarations in the same sense are made by spokesmen for the Aviation battalion, the garrison at Shuya, cavalrymen in Novgorod, the 51st division, and elements of the IIIrd and Xth Armies on the Western front.][1b]

NOTES

a This procedural device allowed the session to be interrupted so that the CEC delegates might attend the inter-party conference (Vompe, *Zhelezno-dorozhniki*, p. 23). The second part of the proceedings is reported only in *Pr.* (1 Nov.), where it is not dated. From internal evidence it was apparently held during the morning or afternoon of 30 Oct.

b Pr., 1 Nov.

Third Session
1 November 1917

Chairman: Kamenev

1. *Inter-party Conference*[1]

KRUSHINSKY, for Vikzhel: It is absolutely vital for all the socialist parties to agree on forming a homogeneous socialist administration.

RYAZANOV, reporting on the work of the commission elected at the inter-party conference: No agreement could be reached about the organ to which the future administration should be responsible. The Mensheviks and Right SRs insist on their proposal that a Provisional People's Council should be set up, to consist of 100 representatives from the CEC, 75 from the soviets of peasants' deputies, 100 from the municipal institutions of Petrograd and Moscow, and several from each of the nation-wide trade-union organizations. I pointed out that if the organ controlling the government were so constituted this would reduce the significance of the soviets. I expressed doubt whether the CEC would accept such an arrangement.

KAMKOV, for the Left SRs: From the start the Left SRs have taken the view that the best way out of our predicament would be to form a homogeneous revolutionary democratic government. We realized that only such a union of revolutionary democracy could cope with the counter-revolutionary offensive. We still think that unless such unity is forthcoming the revolution will have to endure bitter trials and most probably will be crushed. Whatever one thinks of the victory over Kerensky, we must recognize that we are presently engaged on at least several dozen internal fronts, and that on either side of the battle line there are peasants and workers who are convinced that they are defending the revolution. This course is leading to utter ruin.

At the present time, when the coalition [with 'bourgeois' parties] has been swept away for ever, all the socialist parties should set aside partisan calculations and close ranks to form a single progressive front. We hold to our view that the soviets are the pivot around which revolutionary democracy can unite. But we attach no significance to the arithmetical proportion of representatives from this or that organization. We have decided to insist that there be 150 soviet representatives [in the future controlling organ]. This is the minimum number that would be fair in view of the central role which the soviets are playing in our political life. The peasant component also ought to be fairly impressive, but this cannot of course be achieved by including fictitious representatives, such as those from the Executive Committee of the Soviet of Peasant Deputies. [a](*Voices*: 'Right!')[a] Therefore we demand that the vast majority of places be allotted to provincial peasant soviets, on the scale of approximately one per province. Further we insist that no more than fifty representatives be admitted from the municipalities. These are the conditions we consider imperative.

But the most important point for us is that, if no agreement is reached, or if the government consists exclusively of internationalists, it will be unable to surmount the enormous difficulties facing the revolution.

VOLODARSKY, for the Bolsheviks: There is scarcely anyone present here who does not want an agreement. But we cannot conclude one at any price. We cannot forget that we are obliged to defend the interests of the working class, the army, and the peasantry. We are told: do not shed blood. Yes, but we should also remember the blood that has been shed on behalf of the workers' and peasants' vital interests. Even though fearing to shed blood, we must not give up positions which have been fought for by hundreds of thousands of workers, peasants, and soldiers.

An agreement must be based on the following principles. The land decree must remain in force: we cannot allow the slightest ambiguity on this point. Similarly, the peace decree must be confirmed by the new government. Nor can we entertain any concessions in the matter of [workers'] control over production. All these principles are fundamental so far as we are concerned.

The commission has said nothing about the programme [of the new government]. We think that agreement is possible and desirable with those parties which accept the fundamental demands that we have indicated.

But who will control the new government? What will be the source of its authority? It has been suggested that a Provisional People's Council be set up. This would be a sort of Pre-parliament,[2] [composed arbitrarily, and] not according to any definite principles. We Bolsheviks cannot under any circumstances accept the creation of such a freak. We protest strongly against inclusion of municipal Duma representatives. We are not of course concerned about numerical proportions: as you know, almost half the deputies to the Petrograd municipal Duma are ours.[3] We reject representation of municipalities on grounds of principle alone. The workers' and soldiers' insurrection was carried out under the slogan: 'all power to the soviets!' There can be no concessions here. By admitting representatives of the Dumas, one would destroy the very essence of soviet power. The CEC is the only source of power[4] and the creation of a new hybrid organ is totally unacceptable to us.

Another basic condition for an agreement is [that the signatories should wage] a merciless struggle against all Kornilovites, among whom we reckon Kerensky too.

We think it essential to enlarge the CEC by adding peasant representatives, but on no account can these be the gentlemen who support Kerensky, Kornilov, and the military cadets, and who are falsely inciting the cossacks to civil war.

I move the following resolution:

Considering an agreement among the socialist parties desirable, the CEC declares that such an agreement can be achieved only on the following terms:
1. Acceptance of the Soviet government's programme, as expressed in the decrees on land and peace and the two drafts [of a decree] on workers' control.
2. Recognition of the need for merciless struggle against counter-revolution (Kerensky, Kornilov, Kaledin).
3. Recognition of the Second All-Russian Congress [of Soviets][b] as the sole source of authority.
4. The government is to be responsible to the CEC.

5. No organizations are to be represented in the CEC which are not present in the soviets.

6. The CEC is to be expanded to include representatives of those workers', soldiers', and peasants' soviets which do not as yet have such representation, as well as of all-Russian trade-union organizations such as the All-Russian Central Council of Trade Unions, the union [i.e. All-Russian Council] of Factory Committees, Vikzhel [i.e. the All-Russian Union of Railwaymen], and the Union of Postal and Telegraph Workers, as well as of the All-Russian Soviet of Peasant Deputies and of those army organizations that have not been re-elected during the last three months, provided that fresh elections are held.

BAZAROV, for the USDI: We are talking here about an agreement, but let us be clear whom it is that we are fighting. Civil war has broken out over recognition of soviet power. If the talks fail, be prepared to yield without a fight, for soon the railways will shut down and life will come to a standstill. This is a much greater danger than Kaledin's campaign. A bloc can be constituted [only] on a basis of equality. Although the Bolsheviks are standing on their principles [the CEC] should state that it alone cannot settle the question as to what kind of government we should have. That government must be responsible to democracy as a whole, and therefore representation of municipal Dumas should be welcomed. Only under such conditions can we [the USDI] remain in the CEC and bear responsibility for all the measures it takes and the political statements it utters [on behalf of] the soviets.

I move the following resolution:

1. The resolution introduced in the CEC by the Bolshevik fraction on 1 November makes a clean break with the fundamental principles underlying the draft agreement worked out at the inter-party conference with the participation of Bolshevik delegates.

2. This resolution not only testifies to the Bolsheviks' [un]-willingness to work towards an agreement on forming a homogeneous democratic government, but is an open challenge to the other socialist parties with which agreement was contemplated.

3. Accordingly, [since] responsibility for continuing the civil war falls upon the Bolshevik party, the USDI fraction declares that in these conditions it considers it impossible to collaborate with the Bolshevik majority in the CEC and leaves the CEC until such time as its majority favours an honest and sincere bloc with the other socialist parties.

KARELIN, for the Left SRs: Volodarsky's resolution is unsatisfactory: it is too categorical, formal, and intransigent. It is impossible to consider the Second Congress [of Soviets] as the sole source of authority because the peasants were inadequately represented there. Even when the CEC has been expanded to include peasant representatives, it will not be the only body to constitute the government. [I agree that] the decrees that have been promulgated [on land and peace] should remain inviolate in their essentials, but from a formal point of view they ought to be confirmed by the new government as soon as it has come into being.

reads the Left SR resolution:

1. The size of the CEC is to be expanded to 150 members.
2. The municipal Dumas are to have no more than 50 representatives.
3. Seventy-five places are to be allotted to peasant soviets: 50 to provincial soviets and 25 to the Executive Committee of the All-Russian Soviet of Peasant Deputies.
[4.] The Left SR fraction proposes that the revolutionary parliament (*Convention*) so formed should base its activity upon the principles contained in the decrees on land, peace, and workers' control passed by the All-Russian Congress of Soviets.
[5.] The Left SR fraction proposes that the CEC choose five members and charge them with the task of securing an agreement on setting up a government in accordance with the above points.

ŁAPIŃSKI, for the Polish Socialist Party:[5] [I am concerned about] the effectiveness of the [proposed] government rather than its juridical basis. The CEC must be expanded. The Bolshevik resolution comes as a bolt from the blue and should be rejected. Every agreement presupposes concessions, and we should [all] make such concessions if an effective compromise is to be reached. I associate myself wholly with Bazarov's statement, but shall make my withdrawal from the CEC contingent upon my party's decision.

AVANESOV: In the elections to the Moscow central municipal Duma,[6] and later in those to the district Dumas, the masses [demonstrated their radicalism]. Why then should we be invited to give more weight to the Moscow central Duma than to the district Dumas, which were formed later, consist of Bolsheviks, and reflect more accurately the masses' mood? Simply because the compromisers are not guided by principles but are engaged in arithmetical calculations in an attempt to substitute their own opinions for those of the workers, soldiers, and peasants.

A previous speaker has noted that they want to resurrect the Pre-parliament, to bury the conquests of the revolution. Why should the insurgent people remain a tiny minority in such a useless assembly[c] while a majority of seats is reserved to deputies from municipal Dumas that are openly supporting the people's enemies? There is no political logic here, as you may judge for yourselves. We have documents proving that the Committee for the Salvation [of the Country and the Revolution][7] is in touch with the counter-revolutionary armies. Delegates from the front have testified that troops were called upon to crush and shoot workers and soldiers in Petrograd. From the first day of the Congress we have pointed out that soviet power must be united. Every day we receive visits from countless delegations. They all favour soviet power. Therefore we are firmly convinced that an agreement will be reached and that it will be reached exclusively on the soviet platform.

RYAZANOV, for ARCCTU: If the Bolsheviks are now governing alone, this is the fault of the Right SRs and Mensheviks, whose actions have been criminal. I detect a great deal of hypocrisy in their statements about the need for unity when at the same time they are doing everything they can to obstruct the revolution.

2. *The 'Gatchina Campaign' and Kerensky's Flight*[8]

VTH ARMY delegate: The salvation committees and Kerensky are spreading false rumours in the army. Kerensky went to the staff [of the Northern front] for talks, but thanks to the courageous and self-sacrificing conduct of Dybenko, who turned up in the cossacks' camp, the latter were persuaded to lay down their arms and to surrender Kerensky. The MRC's actions were crowned with success. The cossacks declared that they had been deceived by Kerensky and sent out telegrams calling for his arrest as a traitor.

DYBENKO [a]reports on his expedition to Gatchina and on the arrest of Kerensky's staff. A sailors' delegation visited the cossack detachments. After they had addressed their representatives a meeting of cossack regiments was called, at which it was decided to hand over Kerensky and to lay down their arms. General Krasnov associated himself with the cossacks' decision.[7a]
reads the text of Krasnov's statement:

Gatchina, 1 November

At about 3 p.m. today I was summoned by the Supreme Commander-in-Chief, Kerensky. He was very agitated and nervous. 'General,' he said, 'you have betrayed me. Your cossacks are saying quite outspokenly that they will arrest me and hand me over to the sailors.'
'Yes,' I replied, 'there is some talk about this. I know they have no sympathy for you at all.'
'But the officers are saying the same thing.'
'Yes, the officers are particularly dissatisfied with you.'
'But what am I to do? I shall have to commit suicide.'
'If you are an honest man you will go to Petrograd at once with a white flag and talk to the MRC as head of the government.'
'Yes, general, I will do that.'
'I will provide you with an escort and ask a sailor to go with you too.'
'Oh no, anyone but a sailor! Did you know that Dybenko is here?'
'I have no idea who Dybenko is.'
'He is my enemy.'
'Well, what of that? If you're playing for high stakes you'll have to give a good account of yourself.'
'In that case I'll leave during the night.'
'That would be running away. Leave calmly and openly, so that everyone can see you are not fleeing.'

'Very well then, but give me a reliable escort.'

'Yes, I shall do so.'

I then summoned Ruskov, a cossack of the 10th Don Cossack regiment, and told him to detail eight cossacks as an escort for the Supreme Commander-in-Chief. Half an hour later the cossacks came to say that Kerensky was nowhere to be found. He had fled, ᵃ⌐disguised as a sailor, in a cab.⌐ᵃ I raised the alarm and ordered a search to be made, as I thought he couldn't have left Gatchina and must be hiding somewhere here. ᵃ⌐When the cossack regimental committees heard that Kerensky had fled they sent out telegrams to all units and to the front stating that Kerensky was no longer commander-in-chief and calling on the army not to carry out his directives.⌐ᵃ

3. Voting of resolutions

For the Bolshevik motion: 38 votes. For the Left SR motion: 29 votes.[9] The former is taken as the basic text. After a one-hour recess, called at the Left SRs' request, the resolution is voted on point by point.

Introductory sentence. Amendment: for 'desirable' read 'essential'. Defeated by 31 votes to 25. Sentence adopted.

Clause 1. Adopted with 2 dissentients.

Clause 2. First amendment: omit all words in parentheses. Defeated. Second amendment: omit 'Kerensky'. Defeated with only 3 in favour. Clause adopted with 2 dissentients and 2 abstentions.

Clause 3. Amendment: omit 'sole source of authority'. Defeated. Clause adopted.

Clause 4. Amendment: for 'responsible to the CEC' read 'responsible to revolutionary democracy'. Defeated by 32 votes to 14. Clause adopted.

Clauses 5, 6. Amendment: to read 'those who left the Congress are to be included in the CEC according to proportional representation'. Adopted. A motion to combine clauses 5 and 6 is adopted.[d]

The resolution presented by Volodarsky for the Bolshevik fraction is adopted unanimously but for 1 abstention.

The USDI fraction leaves the hall.

Resolved: Galkin and Fenikshteyn are to join the CEC's delegation to the conciliation commission [i.e., the inter-party talks].

4. *Appeal for Popular Support*

The following appeal is adopted unanimously but for 2 abstentions:

> The detachments at Gatchina, deceived by Kerensky, have laid down their arms and ordered Kerensky's arrest. Kerensky, leader of the counter-revolution, has fled. The overwhelming majority of the army has declared in favour of the decision[s] of the Second Congress of Soviets and for support of the government it has set up. Dozens of delegates from the front have hurried to Petrograd, which shows that the army is loyal to soviet power. All their distortion of the facts, all their slanders against the revolutionary workers, soldiers and sailors, have not helped the enemies of the people. The workers' and soldiers' revolution has triumphed. The CEC appeals to those isolated military units which follow the counter-revolutionary rebels: lay down your arms at once! do not shed your brothers' blood on behalf of the interests of a band of landowners and capitalists. [The responsibility for] every fresh drop of blood shed will fall upon you. The Russia of workers, peasants and soldiers will curse those who remain even for a minute under the banners of the people's enemies. Cossacks, come over to the victorious people's side. Railwaymen, postal and telegraph employees: rally as one man to support the new people's power.

NOTES

a *NZ*, 2 Nov.

b In the version of this resolution presented by V. M. Molotov to the Bolsheviks' Petrograd committee on 2 Nov., there followed the phrase 'with peasant participation'; clause 5 was omitted. *Pervy legal 'ny*, p. 267.

c literally 'pre-bathhouse' (*predbannaya*): this term had been jocularly applied to the Pre-parliament by Bukharin.

d In its final version clause 5 now began as follows: 'The CEC is to be supplemented—without including organizations not forming part of the soviets—by representatives of those soviets of workers', soldiers, and peasants' deputies not represented in it [and] by proportional representation of those who left the Congress of Soviets.'

Fourth Session
2 November 1917

Chairman: Kamenev   10 p.m.[a]

1. *Muravyev's 'Order no. 1' on the Defence of Petrograd.*[1]

LARIN: In my opinion this order may be seen as an appeal for lynch justice. It is unworthy of an institution such as the MRC. It shows that men can make mistakes and that the most decisive measures must be taken to prevent such errors being repeated in future. I suggest that a three-man special tribunal be set up to verify [such] orders and that in the meantime Order no. 1 be immediately revoked.

AVANESOV: I support this proposal in principle but suggest that we [first] ask the staff [of Petrograd military district] for clarification. I agree that the CEC does have a right of repeal, but this is the only practical step we can take. The document is written by a political illiterate, but there is no evidence of any malicious intent in it.

RYAZANOV: I propose that we address an interpellation to the PC for Internal Affairs regarding this infringement of the rights of the municipal authorities. I consider that not only the point in this decree which Larin mentioned, but the whole document is [politically] illiterate and constitutes a breach of established revolutionary order. For example, commander Muravyev entrusts the security of the city to sailors, soldiers, and Red guardsmen but does not even mention the militia. Furthermore, how can this order in practice [fail to] introduce lynch justice in lieu of [regular] judicial procedure? Why does Muravyev think it permissible to interfere in matters that are within the purview of the PC of Internal Affairs and to issue orders about arrests and searches? [b]⸢From clause 2 we learn that a completely new body, the 'military field staff', exists, whose functions are unknown.⸥[b] It is said here that when premises are searched a member of the MRC should be present, but in view of the [small] size of the MRC what guarantee is there that this rule can be enforced? By issuing this order the commander is infringing upon the competence of institutions to which he is subordinate. Not just clause 3 but the whole order must be revoked.

*b*ℾMALKIN: I propose that the order be annulled and that we pass on to the next business.

SHREYDER: The order takes no account whatever of any kind of legality.

KAMKOV: I agree that the order must be revoked [by] the CEC immediately.

LARIN agrees with these demands.

VOLODARSKY insists that the CEC should propose to the PC of Internal Affairs that the latter revoke the order.ℸ*b*

At the suggestion of one member the debate is closed. Two motions are introduced: (a) to revoke the decree at once; (b) to ask the staff for clarification before taking any decision. After a short procedural debate the CEC resolves by 23 votes to 6 that its decision shall apply to the single instance under discussion and not to the question [of arbitrary actions] as a whole.

LITVIN tables the following motion:

> The CEC considers that Lieut.-Colonel Muravyev's order on the defence of Petrograd should be revoked immediately and requests the PC of Internal Affairs to take such action.

Passed by 28 votes to 3.

LARIN proposes that the CPC be asked to attend all sessions of the CEC, or at the very least [to send] one of the commissars. After a brief discussion the motion is withdrawn. Instead it is agreed that an agenda [for each session] be drawn up at the previous meeting and that this be brought to the commissars' attention.[2]

2. *Inter-party Conference*[3]

MALKIN, for the Left SRs, reads the following declaration:

> Considering that the tactics adopted by the Bolshevik party now in power are leading irrevocably to a schism among the

toiling masses; that the dictatorship of a single political
group, which it has in effect established, will with inevitable
logic bring about severe repression, not only of [members of]
the propertied classes, but also of the masses; that such a
policy has already been put into practice by the 'Council of
People's Commissars' and other executive bodies, in regard to
the press as well as various individuals and organizations;
that this policy is inexorably leading to the ruin of the revolution, and—far from securing further advances for the toiling
masses—is actually exposing the gains they have secured to
mortal danger; that the position of the [Bolshevik] majority
on the CEC in the talks on setting up an all-socialist government is making it impossible for these talks to succeed, and is
thus plunging the country into the abyss of civil war;

the Left SR fraction once again directs the CEC's attention
to the tragic situation that has been created and demands, in
the form of an ultimatum, that the CEC modify its stand in
regard to the conditions for an agreement between all the
socialist parties; and considers that only an immediate con-
solidation of the entire revolutionary front can protect the
labouring classes from economic catastrophe and the growing
menace of counter-revolution.

We are obliged to present this statement in the form of an ultimatum. The news received from Moscow, where our [party]
comrades are fighting on both sides of the barricades, compels
us to return to the question of the kind of government we are to
have. This is not just our right but our duty. We have won the
right to work alongside the Bolsheviks in the Smolny Institute
and to speak from this tribune. We therefore also have the right
to struggle against them if, after a long fractional struggle, they
still refuse [our demands]. At the news that blood is being shed
in the streets all fractional discord should cease and everyone
should rally around a democratically-based government. As the
victors we should act with greater indulgence. We should propose to the democrats terms which they can more readily
accept.

ZINOVIEV, for the Bolshevik CC: Our [Left] SR comrades
should not start criticizing the Bolsheviks at a time when events
in Moscow have taken the turn described to us this morning by

the delegates we sent there. We remind our SR comrades that before we announced the composition of our government we invited them to join it, but they replied that they would only participate in its work [indirectly] and would not join it for the time being.[4]

Zinoviev then reads a statement by the CC, adding that it has not yet been discussed by the Bolshevik fraction [in the CEC]. At the latter's request a one-hour recess is called to discuss the statement.

3.15 a.m., 3 Nov.

KAMENEV reads the following resolution:

The CEC considers it desirable that the government should include representatives of those socialist parties [active] in the soviets of workers', soldiers', and peasants' deputies which recognize the conquests of the revolution of 24/25 October, i.e. peace, workers' control, and arming the workers. The CEC therefore ordains that the talks on [forming a coalition] government should continue and insists on the following terms of agreement:

1. The government shall be responsible to the CEC.

2. The CEC shall be expanded to 150 persons [from workers' and soldiers' soviets].

3. To these 150 delegates of soviets of workers' and soldiers' deputies shall be added: (a) 75 delegates from provincial peasant soviets; (b) 80 [delegates] from military and naval units; (c) 40 [delegates] from trade unions (25 from all-Russian organizations, [selected] proportionately to the number of [branches], 10 from Vikzhel, and 5 from the Union of Postal and Telegraph Workers and Employees); (d) 50 delegates from the socialist [party fractions in the] Petrograd municipal Duma. Not less than half the portfolios in the government shall be allocated to the Bolsheviks. The ministries of Labour, Internal Affairs, and Foreign Affairs shall in any case be reserved for [members of] the Bolshevik party. Control over troops in the Petrograd and Moscow military districts shall be exercised by plenipotentiaries of the Moscow and Petrograd soviets of workers' and soldiers' deputies. The government sets as its task the systematic armament

of workers throughout Russia. It is prescribed that [the delegates to the talks] shall insist on the candidacies of Lenin and Trotsky.

ᶜᶠThe so-called People's Council proposed at the Vikzhel conference is planned to consist of about 420 persons. Of these about 150 mandates would fall to the Bolsheviks. Moreover, there are to be delegates of the counter-revolutionary old CEC, 100 members elected by the municipal Dumas, all of whom would be Kornilovites, 100 delegates of the peasant soviets appointed by Avksentyev, and 80 from the old army committees which no longer represent the mass of soldiers. We refuse to give mandates to the old CEC or to representatives of the municipal Duma[s]. The peasant soviet delegates should be chosen at a peasant congress which we have called and which simultaneously elects a new executive committee. It has been proposed that Lenin and Trotsky should be excluded [from the proposed coalition government]. This would mean beheading our party and we do not accept it. In the last resort we do not see any need to create a People's Council. The workers' soviets are open to all socialist parties, and in the CEC the latter are represented according to their actual relative strength among the masses.ᶦᶜ

STEKLOV: The CEC's delegation should present one resolution, not two. Our opponents are seeking to divide us, but although the Bolsheviks and Left SRs disagree on details they are broadly in agreement. Therefore I suggest to the Left SRs that they vote for the Bolshevik resolution. Such a move would have great moral significance.

KARELIN: The Bolshevik resolution is a step in the direction of an agreement. For this reason we shall vote for it, reserving the right to amend certain details, such as the provision made for peasant representation.

PROSHYAN, for the Left SRs: I propose that the ministry of Agriculture be allocated to an SR.

Adopted unanimously. A five-man commission is elected to continue [to participate in] the talks about composition of the government: for the Bolsheviks—Kamenev, Ryazanov, and Zinoviev; for the [Left] SRs—Karelin and Proshyan.

Kamenev's resolution is adopted. Six votes were cast against it and there was one abstention.

3. Representation of the CEC Abroad[5]

LARIN: I have heard from Azis, who has just returned from America, that even in Stockholm three days ago the peace decree had not been received, and that in general people abroad know nothing about what is happening in Russia. At the Russo-Swedish border British, French, and American officials are still in control, and they are making difficulties for political émigrés returning to Russia. I therefore propose that a delegation[d] be sent abroad from this assembly.

[b][LOZOVSKY: I propose that we should have our permanent representatives abroad for the purpose of [transmitting] information, since it is extremely difficult to communicate by way of England.

SPIRO: Let us not forget that there are already representatives of Russian democracy in Stockholm. We should not squander the CEC's resources. It would be better to use political couriers.

MALKIN: Even in such a question it is clear that we cannot fill the gap left by the collapse of the old state machinery. It is impossible for us to keep western Europe informed of our affairs.[7][b]

AVANESOV: We must also revoke the mandates of the delegates sent by the old CEC, for their policy is out of step with that of the new revolutionary government.

After some discussion it is decided unanimously to set up a Revolutionary Diplomatic Commission with the right not only [to transmit] information but also to conduct diplomatic negotiations, and to ask the PC of Foreign Affairs to work out a draft [instruction] for it.

4. Organization of the CEC

ALGASOV, for the Organization Commission, submits for approval the following draft [statute][6] on the organization of the CEC.

    I. Sessions of the CEC
      1. CEC sessions may be either restricted or expanded. A restricted session is valid if not less than one-quarter of the

members are present. In the absence of a quorum the session is deferred to the next day, when it is valid irrespective of the number of persons attending. An expanded session is valid if not less than half the members are present.

2. The expanded session of the CEC is the organ that directs and guides all its activity. Regular expanded sessions of the CEC are held on the first and fifteenth of each month. A plenary session is held at least once every two weeks.[e]

3. The CEC is called into session as and when required by the Presidium. The Presidium is obliged to call a restricted session upon the demand of [any of] the fractions or of ten members.

4. The fractions are to ensure that their members attend sessions of the Presidium [and] the CEC regularly. Fractions are recommended to give appropriate warnings to those[f] members who without due cause fail to attend two successive sessions of the CEC or its Presidium; on the third occasion they are to be recalled[g] and replaced by the corresponding candidate members.

II. Presidium

5. The Presidium is both a representative and an executive organ. It prepares the necessary materials for CEC sessions, carried into effect its ordinances, supervises the day-to-day work of the CEC's departments, and also takes decisions when it is not possible to convoke the CEC and speed is essential. The size of the Presidium is equal to one-tenth of all members of the CEC. Sessions of the Presidium are held daily and are valid when not less than half the members are present.

The Presidium gives account of its actions daily to the CEC, meeting in restricted session.

III Departments of the CEC

6. To organize and conduct all its work, the CEC sets up departments. These are the operative organs of the CEC. Under guidance from the Presidium the departments conduct all day-to-day business of the CEC, prepare material for decision[s] by the Presidium and by the CEC at its sessions, and give their opinion about matters which confront the Presidium and the CEC in the course of their work.

7. Each department is headed by a commission which directs and co-ordinates all its work. Commission members are nominated by the Presidium and confirmed by the CEC. Commissions have the right to co-opt up to one-third of the members recruited by the commission. The departmental chief (*zavedyvayushchy*) is chosen by the commission. When the Presidium discusses matters concerning any department, members of its commission have the right to participate in its deliberations with a consultative voice.

8. CEC departments are autonomous in regard to matters falling within the scope of their activity. Once a week departments are obliged to give account of their work to the Presidium. The Presidium has the right to veto any ordinance issued by a department. If a difference of opinion arises between the Presidium and a department, the matter is referred for decision to the CEC, meeting in restricted session.

9. Initially the following departments are established:
1) Secretariat; 2) Struggle against Counter-Revolution; 3) Preparation of Constituent Assembly [Elections]; 4) Local Self-Government;[h] 5) Literary and Publishing; 6) Agitation; 7) Inter-City; 8) Automobile; 9) Finance; 10) Editorial; 11) Printing Press; 12) International.

10. Departments keep their own accounts and are obliged to present them for confirmation to the CEC, meeting in restricted session.

IV. Material Situation of CEC Members

11. All members receive maintenance at the minimal rate necessary for their subsistence, which was fixed by the first [-convocation] CEC at the rate of 400 roubles a month. When sent on mission CEC members receive a daily allowance of 10 roubles.

After some discussion the draft is adopted. The following regulations are approved with regard to CEC members' earnings:
1. Members in receipt of a regular income as state, public, or private employees, or of a salary from a labour organization, forego their maintenance allowance from the CEC. If a member's earnings are lower than the established subsistence minimum, he receives the difference.

2. The 400-rouble rate is to be regarded as a subsistence minimum and is fixed provisionally for one month.

It is decided to allocate four places with full voting rights to the All-Russian [Central] Council of Trade Unions;[7] one place with a consultative voice to each nation-wide trade-union organization; and two places with full voting rights to the All-Russian Centre [i.e. Council] of Factory Committees.[8] In regard to representation of national [minority] socialist parties, decision of this question is postponed until it has been examined by the Presidium.

NOTES

a *NZ*, 4 Nov. *ZT*, 4 Nov., gives 11 p.m. and names the chairman as Karelin In *Prot.* the proceedings are given in the following order: items 1, 4, 3, 2.
b *ZT*, 4 Nov.
c *Protokoly TsK RSDRP(b)*, 1929, p. 166. There is no mention in contemporary sources of such a speech, so that some doubt remains as to the veracity of these remarks. The Bolshevik CC minutes were first published at a time when Stalin was anxious to discredit his opponents in the party leadership, of whom Kamenev was one. The editor of the volume claims that Kamenev uttered these words 'in order to preserve an appearance of loyalty to the CC resolution [of 2 November]' and adds: 'however, the sharpness of Kamenev's tone does not alter the fact that the [Bolshevik] fraction [in the CEC] yielded [to pressure by the moderate socialists].' The passage printed, for which no source is indicated, may be an extract from a longer statement.
d *ZT*, 4 Nov.: a delegate.
e The text as published in *Prot.* is corrupt. The preceding two sentences have here been taken from *DSV*, vol. 1, p. 36, where, however, their order has been transposed.
f literally, 'all'.
g *otzyvat'*; *Prot.* erroneously prints *otkazyvat'*.
h *DSV*, vol. 1, p. 38; *Prot.* reads 'self-determination', which may reflect some doubt in the authors' mind whether the right of (national) self-determination should not be extended to regions or localities as well.

Fifth Session
4 November 1917

Chairman: Kamenev   7.30 p.m.

The following mandates are confirmed: Lozovsky and Ryazanov, representing the ARCCTU; Trifonov and Agapov, representing the Macedonian front (provisionally, pending the
Mandate Commission's clarification of the directive given by
the Second Congress of Soviets); Unshlikht, representing the
Polish Social-Democratic Party;[1] Molotov, as replacement for
Smidovich (Bolshevik fraction); and Skrypnik and Antipov,
representing the All-Russian Central Council of Factory Committees. The request for five places with full vote by the Inter-
district Conference[2] is rejected; instead it is allocated one place
with consultative vote.

1. *Freedom of the Press and Responsible Government*

LARIN: [a]At the present moment, on the eve of the elections to
the Constituent Assembly, the situation in regard to the press
needs to be improved. The measures taken against press [free-
dom] could be justified during the actual course of the struggle
[for power], but not now. The press should be free so long as it
does not incite subversion or insurrection. Censorship of every
kind must be completely eliminated. No repressive measures
should be taken except by a special tribunal, whose competence
should extend to all kinds of political repression, arrests etc.
The new government cannot afford to issue any more orders
like the ignorant one signed by Muravyev.

I propose the following resolution:

The CEC ordains:
1. Lenin's[b] press decree is revoked.
2. No acts of political repression may be carried out except by
authorization of a special tribunal, chosen by the CEC in
proportion to the strength of each fraction. The tribunal has

the right to repeal[c] all acts of repression that have already occurred.

AVANESOV: I propose that discussion of this issue be postponed until a decision has been reached on composition of the government.[7a]

[d[MALKIN: The question of press freedom must be examined in the context of the general political situation, considered even more broadly than Larin suggests. We must examine the question of [the powers of] the CPC, which is issuing one decree after another without any sanction by the CEC.

KALEGAYEV: In my view the question of press freedom should be taken separately from that of an agreement [with the socialists on composition of the government], since for a socialist there can be no doubt as to how he should act [on the matter of press freedom].

SHREYDER agrees.

KAMKOV: Either we recognize freedom only in words, or else we are behaving hypocritically. When Bolshevik newspapers were closed down [under previous regimes] we expressed our indignation along with our Bolshevik comrades. No one has yet called for the overthrow of the existing regime, yet press freedom is being infringed without due cause. We are [morally] obliged to rescind these repressive measures, which bring shame on the Russian revolution. I propose that they be so rescinded forthwith.

Avenesov's motion is rejected. By [a majority of] 22 votes it is decided to consider the question of the press together with that of repressive acts in general.[7d]

AVANESOV: The question of press freedom must be seen in the context of the current political situation in the country as a whole. It seems that no one objects to closure of bourgeois newspapers during an insurrection, when fighting is in progress. If this is so, [we must ask ourselves] whether the struggle is indeed over and the moment has come when we can pass on to a normal mode of life. Having silenced the bourgeois press, [the revolutionary authorities] would be very naïve if they were to let slip from their hands such a powerful means of influencing the ideals of all workers, soldiers, and peasants. All these measures are designed to facilitate the creation of a new regime, free from capitalist oppression, in which a socialist press will ensure freedom of speech for all citizens and for all tendencies of thought.

We defend freedom of the press [in principle], but this concept must be divorced from old petty-bourgeois or bourgeois notions of liberty. If the new government has had the strength to abolish private landed property, thereby infringing the rights of the landlords, it would be ridiculous for Soviet power to stand up for antiquated notions about liberty of the press. First the newspapers must be freed from capitalist oppression, just as we have freed the land from the landlords, and then we can promulgate new socialist laws and norms enshrining a liberty that will serve the whole toiling people, and not just capital.

I move the following resolution:[e]

The closure of bourgeois newspapers was not motivated simply by military considerations during the period of insurrection and suppression of attempted counter-revolution, but was an essential transitional measure in establishing a new press regime in which public opinion will not be fabricated autocratically by the capitalists who own the newsprint and printing-presses.

The next measure should be to confiscate private printing-presses and stocks of newsprint, and to transfer their ownership to [organs of] Soviet power in the centre and in the provinces, so that parties and groups may have the technical means to publish [newspapers] in proportion to the number of their adherents.

The restoration of so-called 'freedom of the press', i.e. the return of printing-presses and newsprint to the capitalists, poisoners of the people's consciousness, would be an impermissible capitulation to the will of capital, a surrender of one of the most important strongpoints of the workers' and peasants' revolution, and thus indubitably counter-revolutionary.

Accordingly the CEC repudiates categorically any proposals leading to a restoration of the old regime in press matters and supports the CPC unconditionally against pretensions and intrigues dictated either by petty-bourgeois prejudices or by outright servility to the counter-revolutionary bourgeoisie.[3]

^{d⌐}KALEGAYEV: The way this question has been posed shows that there is a profound disagreement between our position and that of the Bolsheviks. [The latter argue:] previously we defended all civil liberties, but now we are prepared to muzzle our opponents. However, one cannot emancipate society from the fetters of capitalism by taking repressive measures against newspapers. Nor is it possible to carve up freedom of the press like a loaf of bread, allocating so much freedom to each group according to the influence exerted by its ideas. When the Bolsheviks talk of poisoning the people's consciousness by the printed word, they are adopting the viewpoint of [the editors of] *Zemshchina*.⌐^{d4}

TROTSKY: ^{a⌐}One should distinguish between the situation during a civil war and the situation once victory is complete.⌐^a To demand that all repressive measures should be abandoned during a civil war is equivalent to demanding that the war itself should cease. Such a demand could come only from adversaries of the proletariat.^f Our opponents are not offering us peace. No one can provide a guarantee against [a victory of] the Kornilovites. During a civil war it is legitimate to suppress newspapers that support the other side. ^{a⌐}But when we are finally victorious our attitude toward the press will be analogous to that on freedom of trade.⌐^a Then we shall naturally move on to a [regular] regime in press matters. In our party press we have for a long time been accustomed to take a non-proprietorial view of press freedom. Measures taken against [suspect] individuals should also be taken against press organs. We should confiscate and socialize printing-presses and stocks of newsprint ... (*Shouts from the floor*: 'And Bolshevik ones too?') ^{g⌐}Yes,⌐^g all these stocks should be transferred to public ownership. Any group of [workers,] soldiers, or peasants will be able to submit an application for [access to supplies of] newsprint and to a printing-press.

We say that *Novoye vremya*,⁵ which has no electoral support, should not have a single piece of printer's type or a single sheet of paper. Nor should *Russkaya volya*,⁶ so long as it remains simply an organ of the banks, have any right to exist. Such measures should not be continued indefinitely, but neither can we return to the capitalist way of doing things. The transfer of power to the soviets is a transition from bourgeois rule to a socialist system. How was Suvorin able to publish a paper on such a grandiose scale? Only because he had money. Can we permit him and his like to pour out their poison during the Constituent Assembly elections? Such a paper would be bought by only a minuscule section of the population. In general, can one imagine that newspapers should [be allowed to] exist which depend upon the banks rather than upon the people? All the press media should be handed over to Soviet power. You say that [before the revolution] we demanded freedom of the press on behalf of *Pravda*. But then we were living under conditions which were apposite to our programme-minimum; now we are putting forward the demands in our programme-maximum.[7] *a⌐(Applause by soldiers in the audience.)* I see the soldiers are with me. (*Left SR cries*: 'Demagogy!' 'Cirque Moderne!')[8] I used the same language to the crowds there as I am using now; it is not I who speak with a forked tongue.⌐[a, h] When you return—the soldiers to the trenches, the peasants to the villages—you will say that there are two points of view on this question: either freedom for the bourgeois press or confiscation of paper and printing-presses for transfer to the hands of the workers and peasants.

KARELIN: It is a Hottentot morality which holds that it's bad if someone steals my wife but good if I steal someone else's. I say this because Trotsky has been critical of our party. It is surprising that we should hear [such arguments] from a party which itself now enjoys freedom of the press. We cannot have double standards of morality.

But I would rather discuss this question in terms of political expediency. Is it expedient to muzzle the expression of any trend of opinion? History teaches that whenever this is done it only makes such opinions more attractive. Forbidden fruit is sweet. I agree with Trotsky that we have to eliminate capitalist oppression in regard to the press. But the measures [he proposes] are risky. One can attain this objective without muzzling opinion, simply by undertaking a wide range of protective actions in the distribution of material. The [Bolshevik] resolution proposes that parties and groups should have [the right to publish] newspapers in proportion to the number of their supporters, but such calculations will scarcely be practicable. *d⌐*It would be absurd to distribute [opportunities to publish] in proportion to [the strength of various currents of] opinion; this would be like socializing thought itself.[1d]

I should make it clear that in advocating freedom of opinion we do not seek to extend it to the weakest sector [in terms of popular support]. Trotsky alleges that we are arguing from the standpoint of capital. I say that whoever puts the question in such terms is arguing from the standpoint of his own [ministerial portfolio][1i]. Genuine representatives of the people should not be afraid of minority opinions. Such fear betrays an awareness that one's own opinions are weak. 'Who wants press freedom?', Trotsky asks. The answer is: everyone who cherishes the [revolutionary] movement of our people. We think this movement will suffer if we continue to apply the sanctions which at the start we accepted as justified. Moreover, the honour of this movement requires that an end be put to civil war.

LENIN: Karelin assures us that the road on which he stands leads to socialism. But to take this road would be to advance toward socialism hindside first. Trotsky was right: 'freedom of the press' was the slogan under which the cadets mutinied and fighting began in Petrograd and Moscow. This time the SRs are not acting either as socialists or as revolutionaries. [Early] this week the entire telegraph network was in Kerensky's hands. Vikzhel was also on the [Provisional Government's] side. But they did not have the army with them. As it turned out, the army was for us. The civil war, begun by a minuscule group, is not yet over. The Kaledinites[9] are marching on Moscow and the shock battalions on Petrograd. We do not want civil war. Our forces have been very patient. They waited and refrained from shooting. The shock troops fired first, killing three of our men. Krasnov was treated mildly, merely being placed under house arrest. We are opposed to civil war. But if it continues none the less what are we to do? Trotsky was right to pose the question: for whom are you speaking? We asked Krasnov whether he would sign a statement on Kaledin's behalf promising that the latter would stop fighting. But not surprisingly he replied that he could not do so. If the enemy is still in the field, how can we be expected to lay down our arms? When they propose peace terms we shall negotiate. But at present the peace offers are coming from persons on whom the decision does not depend, so they are nothing but fair words. After all *Rech'*[10] is an organ of Kaledinites. We recognize the [Left] SRs' sincerity, but behind them stand Kaledin and Milyukov.

Soldiers! The firmer you stand the more we shall achieve. On the other hand, [if you are soft, our enemies] will say that we are still unsure of ourselves, [pointing to the fact that] we let Milyukov go.[11] We stated earlier that if we took power we would close down bourgeois newspapers. To allow them to exist is to cease to be socialists. Whoever says 'let the bourgeois newspapers publish' fails to understand that we are moving full steam ahead towards socialism. After all tsarist newspapers were closed down when tsarism was overthrown. Now we have cast off the bourgeois yoke. It was not we who thought up the social[ist] revolution—it was proclaimed by the delegates to the Congress of Soviets—and no one there protested at the decree proclaiming it. The bourgeoisie proclaimed liberty, equality, and fraternity, [but] the workers say: 'this is not what we want.'

We are accused of retreating, but it is the [Left] SRs, not we, who are going back to Kerensky. It is said that our resolution contains something new. Yes, of course we are introducing something new, for we are moving on towards socialism. When the SRs spoke out in the First and Second Dumas they too were mocked for saying something new.

Private advertisements must be declared a [state] monopoly. The members of the printers' union [who object to this] are looking at the question purely in bread-and-butter terms. We shall satisfy their [material] desires, but in a different way. We cannot give the bourgeoisie any [opportunity] to slander us. We must at once set up a commission to investigate the connections between the bourgeois newspapers and the banks and to ascertain what sort of 'freedom' these papers enjoyed. It is not freedom to buy up quantities of newsprint and to hire a mass of scribblers. *d*⌐Before [anyone may] start up a newspaper, we shall insist that he prove his independence of the banks. One can hold elections to find out the strength of each party and allocate the technical resources according to the number of votes cast. This will prevent capitalists alone enjoying freedom of the press and flooding the villages with their cheap newspapers.⌐*d* We must get away from the notion that a press dependent on capital can be free. This is an important question of principle. If we are moving towards social[ist] revolution, we cannot reply to Kaledin's bombs with bombs of falsehood. There are of course inadequacies in our draft decree, but it will be implemented by the soviets [flexibly], according to local conditions. We are not bureaucrats and do not want to apply the letter of the law everywhere, like the officials of old. I remember how the SRs used to say that the village is terribly ignorant, that they [the villagers] draw their information from *Russkoye slovo*.[12] It is our fault for leaving the newspapers in bourgeois hands. We have to go forward to the new society and deal with the bourgeois papers in the same way as we dealt with the Black Hundred ones in February–March.

MALKIN: Lenin has no business to allege that we are going to socialism hindside first. Least of all should the charge be levelled by the man who once wanted to advance to socialism by offering his famous 'cutoffs', but who has now wholly accepted our agrarian programme of land socialization.[13]

When this resolution was introduced, we thought that the repressive dictatorship offered us was a result of the panic that seized the Bolshevik maximalists when they found themselves isolated at the moment of their victory. But now Trotsky and Lenin have sought to give this dictatorship an ideological foundation. We firmly repudiate the notion that socialism can be introduced by armed force. In our view socialism is a struggle not merely for material advantages but for supreme human *g⌐moral⌐g* values. The revolution's appeal lies in the fact that we are striving not just to fill our hungry bellies but for a higher truth, the liberation of the individual. We shall win not by closing down bourgeois newspapers but because our programme and tactics express the interests of the broad toiling masses, because we can build up a solid coalition of soldiers, workers, and peasants.

Lenin has told us about slanders put out by the bourgeois press and about Chernov. So what? Has not the truth about Chernov now asserted itself and given the lie to the slanders of the yellow press? We revolutionaries and socialists replied to these lies by telling the truth. *d⌐*The lies of the bourgeois press do not represent an authentic danger to the socialist movement.⁷ᵈ The toiling masses have a reliable compass to guide them: the support of overwhelming numbers of people, who will sooner or later win over the remaining, more backward strata of democracy. ᵈᵣTo be good leaders [we] must first be good politicians, good socialists; at the same time the [mass] movement [itself] is implementing the noble ideals of the labouring people, the bulk of mankind, who are advancing towards socialism.⁷ᵈ

We Socialist-Revolutionaries were once prisoners of tsarism but we were never its slaves, and we don't want to establish slavery for anyone now. We remind the Marxists present that you cannot establish new social relations by decree; they have to be developed gradually, in the process of struggling for socialism. When whole sectors of the nation's economic life are being socialized, when they are being taken over by co-operatives and municipal institutions, one need not fear the bourgeois press. Just let it try to influence the masses: they won't listen! ᵈᵣ'The arm of criticism, not criticism by arms': this should be the watchword in the free Russian Republic.⁷ᵈ Those who feel that defeat is round the corner can scarcely win. You are applying the tactics of the vanquished, not of the victors, for the triumphant proletariat should show magnanimity not only toward its enemies on the battlefield but toward all political opponents, whatever class they belong to. You are dishonouring the socialist movement by depriving it of its moral force.

We propose that the CEC immediately repeal all limitations on press freedom. In vain does Trotsky, referring to the soldiers' applause, tell us that they will not follow us [in such a course]. They applaud him because they are drunk with victory and have lost their reason. At such a moment your tactics may succeed, but once they have sobered up ours will triumph.

A motion to curtail debate is passed. Two resolutions are tabled: Larin's, which fails by 31 votes to 22, and the Bolshevik one, which is passed by 34 votes to 24 with 1 abstention.ʲ

RYAZANOV, explaining his motives for voting against the Bolshevik resolution: I am the representative of [the All-Russian Central Council of] Trade Unions. ᵃᵣI cannot vote for any limitation on press freedom since I believe that even the Anarchists should have the right to express their views.⁷ᵃ _d⌐_At the request of SPIRO⌐_d_ a half-hour recess is declared.

_d⌐_Chairman: Gillerson

PROSHYAN, for the Left SRs: This question is one of acute importance for our fraction. The struggle for press freedom has always been closely bound up with the struggle for socialism. The revolution cannot take a step backward on this matter, covering itself by [offering minority groups] access to technical facilities but in practice prohibiting [them from exercising these rights]. The resolution that has been passed legalizes repression and clearly shows that the Bolshevik members of the CEC are embarking upon a path of terror. This tactic is ruinous for the class struggle and ruinous for the revolution.⌐_d_

Our party has charged me to make the following declaration:

The resolution on the press just passed by the majority of the CEC is a clear and unambiguous expression [of support for a] system of political terror and for unleashing civil war. The SR fraction, while remaining in the CEC, the legitimate [central deliberative] organ of revolutionary democracy, in order to defend the interests of the workers and peasants whom it represents, has no desire to bear any responsibility for this system of terror, ruinous for the revolution, and therefore withdraws all its representatives from the Military-Revolutionary Committee, the staff, and all responsible posts.

NOGIN, given the floor for an urgent statement on behalf of a group of people's commissars, reads the following declaration:[14]

We take the stand that it is vital to form a socialist government from all parties [represented in] the soviets. Only such a government can seal the heroic struggle of the working class and revolutionary army in the October–November days. We consider that a purely Bolshevik government has no choice but to maintain itself by political terror. This is the course on which the CPC has embarked. We cannot follow this course, which will lead to the proletarian mass organizations becoming estranged from those who direct our political affairs, to the establishment of an irresponsible government, and to the annihilation of the revolution [and] the country. We cannot bear responsibility for such a policy and therefore, in the presence of the CEC, resign from our posts as people's commissars.

(signed) V. Nogin, PC of Trade and Industry
          A. Rykov, PC of Internal Affairs
          V. Milyutin, PC of Agriculture
          [I.] Teodorovich, PC of Supply

[The following] adhere to this statement:

          D. Ryazanov
          N. Derbyshev, commissar of press affairs
          I. Arbuzov, commissar of the State Printing Works
          [K.] Yurenev, commissar of Red guards
          G. Fedorov, head of the labour conflict department
          (chairman of the workers' section) in the ministry
          of Labour
Citizen Yu. Larin, commissar, head of department of legislative proposals.

[Addendum:] While adhering to the general appraisal given above of the political situation in regard to the need for an agreement, I consider it impermissible to lay down my responsibilities.
(signed) A. Shlyapnikov, PC of Labour.

An unidentified LEFT SR then reads the following statement:

To the Chairman of the CEC:
The Left SR fraction proposes that the CEC should address the following urgent interpellation to the Chairman of the CPC, Ulyanov–Lenin:
At the Second Congress of Soviets of Workers' and Soldiers' Deputies it was laid down that the CEC is the supreme organ to which the government is wholly responsible. However, in the last few days the government has published a number of decrees which have not been discussed or approved by the CEC. By this procedure the government has taken measures which have *de facto* annulled fundamental civil liberties. We therefore ask the chairman of the CPC:
1. On what grounds were drafts of [these] decrees and other measures not submitted for examination to the CEC?
2. Does the government now intend to desist from the arbi-

trary and completely impermissible practice it has established
of ruling by decree?

(signed) V. Karelin, V. Spiro, A. Shreyder, V. Alexandro-
vich-Dmitriyevsky, I. V. Balashev, Peter Bukhartsev, A. Proshyan, S. Zak, Gr. Zaks.

2. *News from the West*[15]

Before this interpellation is discussed, SOKOLNIKOV takes the
floor to deliver an urgent statement. He reads the following
telegrams received from Stockholm by way of Torneo:

1. [27 Oct.]/9 Nov. French Zimmerwaldians congratulate
Bolsheviks, welcome immediate peace and international
socialism. [Guilbeaux.][k]

2. [28 Oct.]/10 Nov. In reply to inquiry by editors of *Politiken*
Ledebour wires as follows. Lack of information makes it hard
to judge Russian *coup*. In any case Kerensky's fate is clear
proof of harm of coalition with bourgeois parties. Despite his
undoubted personal services in overthrow of tsarism he soon
slid down slippery slope of imperialistic policy and reactionary autocratic methods of government. Soviet's declarations
will aid cause of peace and socialism if transfer of land to
peasants does not lead to partition among individual owners.
Soviet should rally all true socialists to consolidate democratic order. In its efforts towards peace Soviet can rely on
support of fellow socialists in all countries. Ledebour.

3. [31 Oct.]/13 Nov. To Congress of Soviets, Petrograd.
Social-Democratic party of German Austria joyfully greets
Russian democracy on its seizure of power. It expresses complete agreement with your proposal for armistice and peace
talks. On 11th [November N.S.] Viennese workers at vast
meeting on peace proposal demand[ed] immediate armistice.
Appropriate steps will be taken in Parliament. Austrian
proletariat feels indissolubly bound to you in struggle for
speediest democratic peace. Long live International! Telegram from Vienna received in Stockholm by Otto Paul.

4. [1]/14 Nov. Pass to Soviet of Deputies. German Social-
Democratic party sends Russian proletariat heartiest good
wishes on conquest of political power. May it with aid of

proletariat of other countries obtain speedy peace without direct or indirect annexations on either side.
Central Committee.

Zhemchuzhin, commissar at Torneo.

The peace decree, the first act of the new government, has already evoked a response in working[-class] circles in the West. It is especially noteworthy that the Austrian proletariat has embarked upon revolutionary action.

3. *Interpellation on Arbitrary Rule*

LENIN, replying to the interpellation: Let me remind you that in the first days of the revolution the Bolsheviks invited the Left SRs to join the new government, but that they declined because they did not want to share responsibility with their neighbours to the left during these difficult critical days. ⌐In order to exercise control over the government's policy, it is quite sufficient for the CEC to have the right to remove ministers.⌐¹ The new government could not have coped with all the obstacles which stood in its path if it had observed all [legal] formalities. The moment was too serious to brook any delay. We could not afford to lose time smoothing over asperities, for this would only have affected the external trimmings and not the essence of the new measures.

After all, the Second All-Russian Congress of Soviets, too, cast aside all formal considerations when, in a single great session, it adopted two laws of world-wide significance. Let us admit that these laws may suffer from formal defects, considered from the standpoint of bourgeois society: the main thing is that power is in the hands of the soviets, which can correct them as may be required. The criminal inactivity of the Kerensky government led the country and the revolution to the verge of ruin; its delaying policy nearly proved fatal. The new government, by passing laws which meet the aspirations of the broad popular masses, is staking out landmarks along the road to a new way of life. The local soviets may adapt the basic decrees passed by the government, expanding and supplementing them according to their own particular needs. Mass creativity is the fundamental factor in the new society. Let the workers set about establishing workers' control in their factories; let them supply the villages with manufactures in exchange for grain.[16] Not a single product, not a single pound of grain should be left unaccounted for, since socialism is above all else a matter of accounting. Socialism is not created by direction from above. Its spirit is totally alien to that of routine obedience as found in the barracks or in the bureaucracy. Socialism is something vital, the creation of the people themselves.

MIRSKY: I move that for the rest of this session the debate be private.

PROSHYAN: I object. We do not and cannot have any secrets from the people. Our electors ought to know what their chosen representatives are doing.

Motion rejected unanimously.

KALEGAYEV, replying to Lenin for the Left SRs: The fact that the Left SRs are not in the government is one question, the legality of that government's actions is another. The Soviet government ought to keep to the rules laid down by the Second Congress of Soviets. The practice of determining laws in secret and decreeing them autocratically can lead only to the most unfortunate misunderstandings. [¹⌐When decrees are being turned out one after another like fresh loaves from the bakers', contradictions [are bound to] arise which will cause confusion in the provinces.⌐¹] The new laws are not only deficient from an external, formal point of view: they are also mutually contradictory in spirit. For example, the land decree abolished private property in land in perpetuity, but the decree on land committees, which was published shortly afterwards, said nothing about this.[17] This leads to muddle and argument. When these ordinances reach the provinces and come to be interpreted by simple-minded people there will be discord and conflict.

Moreover, however urgent the situation may be the CPC has no right to infringe the rules laid down by the Congress and to act contrarily to their spirit as well as their letter. The government ought to have requested the Congress to give it power to modify the Congress's dispositions. If it failed to do so, it is [acting illegally, just as it is] acting illegally by ignoring the will of the CEC.

[ᵐ⌐A motion to curtail debate is defeated.⌐ᵐ]

PROSHYAN: When I was working in Finland, before coming to Petrograd, I was very much in favour of our party joining the government. But now that I have seen how things are here I have changed my mind. ⌐We are being asked to go back to the old way of doing things: in place of one irresponsible government which led us to the verge of ruin we are being offered another irresponsible government which will finish off the revolution for good.⌐¹ Let us forget about the formal objections. The point is not that the government has broken the law or that it should have to respond to interpellations, but that in the very centre of revolutionary democracy there is disorder, caused by a divorce between the executive authorities on one hand and the central representative organ on the other—the CEC, which does duty for the Congress of Soviets. The Military-Revolutionary Committee is frequently out of touch with the revolutionary staff, the CPC with the Commander-in-Chief,[18] and so on. These lapses and errors can only be of advantage to enemies of the revolution.

It is not because we are addicted to the letter of the law that we insist on the government rendering account of its actions to the CEC. For only if these two organs are in concord can one expect the government to remain loyal to the spirit of the decisions taken by the Congress of Soviets. We have before us the example of the previous coalition regimes. They managed to avoid their formal responsibility to account for their conduct before the CEC, and by doing so they in fact broke the vital link between themselves and the people. This was their basic mistake, the source of their weakness. We warn the new government not to follow blindly along the same path. We do so because we want the new people's government to rest on a solid foundation.

KARELIN: I protest at the abuse of the term 'bourgeois'. It is not only bourgeois governments which need to give account of themselves or to maintain good order in their affairs, even in matters of detail. Don't let's try to cover up mistakes by pinning an unpopular label [on critics]. A proletarian government must also submit to popular control. After all, when a firm is taken over by its workers, they cannot manage it properly without keeping and presenting accounts.

ᴵᴦOur demand for responsible government is being rejected on the simple grounds that this was characteristic of earlier parliamentary regimes. The logical corollary would be to abandon financial accountability as well, as another 'bourgeois' prejudice. Our demand for control [over the government by the CEC] does not stem from any party-political egoism but is a requirement imposed by life itself.

These decrees and draft ordinances which are being cooked up like *bliny* are extraordinarily illiterate, although as yet, thank heavens, literacy has not been declared a bourgeois prejudice.ᵀᴵ This defect will make for a lot of trouble, especially in the countryside, where people are used to interpreting orders from on high literally, ᴵᴦand clashes may even occur there. Thus the government's excessive display of activity, instead of helping the country, will cause it irremediable harm.ᵀᴵ

LEVIN: The soviet which I represent fought hard against the irresponsibility of the previous coalition cabinets. Unfortunately the same light-hearted attitude towards their obligations is being adopted by our present-day Bolshevik leaders, who seem not to realize how serious this matter is.

ᴵᴦMALKIN:ᵀᴵ The reason why we did not join the government was very different from the reason for the resignation of some members of the CPC. We reject the path of experimentation on which the new government has embarked. We want our group, which comprises a significant minority in the CEC, to be able to make its weight felt in the legislative process. Not a single people's commissar has addressed a session of the CEC in an official capacity until today, when some of them announced their resignation. Their departure from the government threatens it with a catastrophic collapse. What steps does Lenin propose to take to avert such an eventuality? He should make his views known on this question, which is of such urgency to us all.

TROTSKY: In Kerensky's day neither the right nor the left wings of the Socialist-Revolutionary party pressed the old CEC to render account of itself. Our Soviet parliament differs from others in that it does not contain representatives of antagonistic classes. Our government is one of the toiling oppressed classes and so has no place for conventional parliamentary machinery.

Procedural rules usually just serve to balance off against each other the opposing class forces represented in the assembly, and to prevent deputies from being influenced by their electors. For when a deputy is asked to do something by the mass [of electors] who voted for him, he can easily reply that he cannot grant their request because of the limitations of parliamentary procedure. But in our system things are different. Our deputies do not need to shield themselves behind formal excuses of this sort. They are linked to their electors by the same kind of bond as exists in a trade union—a bond that is vital and immediate. It is true that we don't have formal guarantees [against abuses of executive power], but in lieu of that our deputies enjoy real controlling authority, for at any moment they may recall the people's commissars. Soviet power is not the result of backstage manœuvres by party leaders, like a French government, for example. Our power expresses the actual will of the organized masses. It may be true that our decrees have some rough edges, but they express a vital creativity that is more important than formal perfection.

Our legislative activity is already yielding results. It has evoked a response throughout Russia and even abroad. The land decree was so well attuned to popular aspirations that it would have been wrong to delay its promulgation by a single day, even if this would have allowed us to improve the wording.

Let those who are tired, who are few in numbers but of high [intellectual] quality, go their own way: we shall continue our march forward without them, holding our heads high. A previous speaker said that the government is facing collapse. It is not collapsing but purging itself. We who remain in it think it would be wrong to make the slightest concession to the bourgeoisie or to the groups of intellectuals who stand in the middle and advocate compromise. If you disagree with us you may recall us, but we shall never voluntarily betray our [revolutionary] line.

LENIN: I shall deal with the concrete charges levelled against the CPC. So far as Muravyev's order is concerned, we only learned of it from the newspapers, since in an emergency the Commander-in-Chief has the right to issue orders on his own authority. This order contained nothing contrary to the spirit of the

new government, but it was phrased in such a way that undesirable misunderstandings could have resulted, and therefore
the CPC has annulled it.

You also criticized the land decree, although it meets the
people's demands. As for the charge of schematism, where are
your own drafts, amendments, and resolutions? Where is the
fruit of your creative thinking? You are free to put forward laws
yourselves, but we don't see any. You call us extremists, but you
are nothing other than apologists for parliamentary obstruction,
for what used to be called chicanery. If you are dissatisfied, call
a new Congress [of Soviets] and act instead of sitting back and
talking about a collapse of the government. Power rests with our
party, which enjoys the broad masses' confidence. It is true that
some of our comrades have taken a stand that has nothing in
common with Bolshevism, but the Moscow workers will not
follow Rykov or Nogin.[19]

Proshyan said that in Finland, where the Left SRs were in
close contact with the masses, they thought it essential for all
left-wing revolutionary socialists to unite. If the Left SRs here
[in Petrograd] do not join us, this simply shows that they have
become divorced from the people, like their defensist predecessors.

RYAZANOV: Let me point out that the CEC delegates who took
part in the talks with [representatives of] the other socialist
parties acted in complete solidarity with the Bolshevik CC.

TROTSKY: The Bolshevik CC is not trying to arrogate all power
to itself. We offered power to the Second Congress of Soviets,
which included some defensist delegates. It is not our fault that
they walked out and refused to go along with the majority. We
responded to Vikzhel's invitation [to attend the conference],
but we cannot afford to sacrifice the new government's programme for the sake of a shadowy agreement [with the democratic socialists].

SPIRO, for the Left SRs, tables the following motion:

The CEC, having heard the explanations offered by the
chairman of the CPC, considers them unsatisfactory.

URITSKY tables a resolution expressing confidence in the
CPC:[20]

The CEC states, in regard to the interpellation that has been presented, that:

1. The Soviet parliament of the working masses can have nothing in common, so far as its procedure is concerned, with a bourgeois parliament, where different classes with antagonistic interests are represented, and where deputies of the ruling class turn procedural rules into a weapon of legislative obstruction;

2. The Soviet parliament cannot refuse the CPC the right to issue, without preliminary discussion by the CEC, urgent decrees within the limits of the general programme adopted by the All-Russian Congress of Soviets;

3. The CEC exercises a general control over the entire activity of the CPC and may replace the government or individual members thereof;

4. The CEC regrets that the Left SRs, who presented the interpellation, have not found it possible to participate directly in the government, and thus in the elaboration of all urgent decrees.

The Left SR resolution is rejected by 25 votes to 20.[n] A discussion follows on whether people's commissars should be allowed to vote. LENIN and TROTSKY point out that at party congresses leaders could do so and that they are bound by party discipline; for this reason they intend to take part in the vote. Uritsky's resolution is taken as the basic text by 25 votes to 23[o] and then, on a roll-call vote, by 29 votes to 23 with 2 abstentions. Subsequently it is voted on clause by clause. Clause 1 is passed without amendment. KALEGAYEV proposes that clauses 2 and 3 be omitted,[p] but this is defeated, in the first instance by 27 votes to 14 [and in the second instance by an unspecified number of votes]. AVANESOV proposes omission of clause 4, but this likewise is rejected. Finally the resolution is approved as a whole.[q]

4. Resignation of the People's Commissars

ZAKS: This step is a sign that their [the resigning commissars'] former comrades in the CPC have set course for a socialist revolution. But if we burn our bridges will we not be entirely isolated? After all, we have won precious little support so far.

Western Europe is shamefully silent. One can't build socialism by decree and by relying solely upon a single party.

LENIN: The phrase 'the west is shamefully silent' is impermissible from the lips of an internationalist. One would have to be blind not to notice the ferment that has gripped the working masses in Germany and the west [in general]. The leaders of the German proletariat, the socialist intelligentsia, consist in the main of defensists, as they do everywhere else, but their proletarian followers are prepared to desert them and to respond to our call. The savage discipline that prevails in the German army and navy have not prevented elements opposed [to the war] from taking action. The revolutionary sailors in the German navy, knowing that their enterprise was doomed to fail, went to meet their fate heroically, in the hope that their sacrifice would awaken the spirit of insurrection among the people.[21] The Spartakus group is spreading its revolutionary propaganda with ever greater intensity. The name of Liebknecht, that tireless fighter for the ideals of the proletariat, is daily becoming more popular in Germany.

We believe in a revolution in the west. We know that this is inevitable, but of course we can't bring it about to order. Did we know last December what was to happen in February? Did we know for sure in September that the next month Russian revolutionary democracy would bring off the greatest overturn in world [history]? We knew that the old government was sitting on a volcano and we could guess from many signs that beneath the surface a great change was occurring in people's ideas. We could feel the electricity in the air, we knew that it would inevitably discharge itself in a purifying storm. But we could not predict the day and hour when the storm would break. It is exactly the same now in the case of Germany. There too the people's sullen discontent is growing and is bound to erupt in the form of a broad mass movement. We cannot decree the revolution but we can at least help it along. We shall organize fraternization in the trenches and help the western peoples to launch the invincible socialist revolution.[22]

Zaks talks about [not] decreeing revolution. But isn't our government calling upon the masses themselves to create a better way of life? The exchange of industrial products for grain and the introduction of [workers'] control and accounting are the beginning of socialism. Yes, we shall indeed establish a republic of labour in which whoever does not work shall not eat.

It is said that our party is isolated, but is this really so? A few individual intellectuals have split away, but with every day that passes we are winning more and more support among the peasants. Only those will conquer and retain power who believe in the people and plunge into the source of popular vitality and creativity.

I move the following resolution:

> The CEC directs the CPC to present at the next session candidates for the posts of PC of Internal Affairs and PC of Trade and Industry, and proposes that Kalegayev assume the post of PC of Agriculture.

PROSHYAN: I again remind the CEC that the Left SR fraction has decided to withdraw its representatives from all Soviet organs.

MALKIN: Our fraction could accept this proposal only if a homogeneous socialist government were formed, the press decree annulled, and the policy of repression abandoned, so that the [inter-party] talks may be brought to a successful conclusion—as the CEC has resolved they should be.

TROTSKY: The Left SR fraction wants the CPC to approve a coalition with Avksentyev and co. [i.e. the Right SRs] and freedom for the press to serve finance capital. But we cannot allow the Left SRs to join the government with [a programme] so hostile to the people. They must [make up their minds:] either to go with Avksentyev or to go with us; ᵐ⌐there is no alternative.⌐ᵐ

MALKIN: Trotsky is putting the question in the form of an ultimatum and so discrediting the CEC's decision, taken yesterday, to continue talks with Gots, Avksentyev, and the rest.

TROTSKY: It is not the individuals as such that we detest, or the groups to which they belong, but rather the tactics they employ. If [the moderate socialists] want to join the soviets we shall be pleased, but we cannot afford to deprive the country of its government while talks are going on—with our consent, incidentally—with the sort of people who incited the cadets [to rise] against Soviet power. If you don't go along with us, just for the sake of the shadow of an agreement, then you are nobodies, mere shadows of Gots and Dan, who are themselves just shadows of the bourgeoisie.

Lenin's resolution obtains 30 votes. The SRs refuse to take part in the vote. ᶦᵣThey also reject the proposal that Kalegayev assume the post of PC of Agriculture.ᵌˡ

NOTES

a *NZ*, 5 Nov.
b *Prot.*: 'the CPC's'; *Pr.*, 5 Nov.: no attribution.
c *Prot.*: 'review'.
d *ZT*, 5 Nov. According to *Iz.* and *Pr.*, LEVIN and POPOV also spoke in the debate, arguing as follows: 'This is a matter of principle. There cannot be a moment when it is permissible to muzzle the press. Unless we want to [rule] at the bayonet-point, this draft must be revoked.'
e The resolution was evidently written by Trotsky, for it is included in his *Sochineniya*, III(ii), pp. 105–6. While it was being read there were ironical interruptions from the Left SR benches: *NZ*, 5 November.
f *NZ* has Trotsky say at this point that when force is used by an oppressed class it is moral, but when used by an oppressor class it is immoral, whereupon the Left SRs interjected 'Hottentot!' The asperities of Trotsky's speech are somewhat attenuated in *Prot.*
g *Iz.*, 5 Nov.
h *Prot.*, *Iz.* have Trotsky refer to support from workers' and peasants' representatives rather than the soldiers present; but the subsequent exchanges bear out the *NZ* version.
i *ZT*, 5 Nov.; *Prot.*: 'his own power'.
j Trotsky, *Sochineniya*, III(ii), p. 403: by 29 votes to 23 with 2 abstentions. Presumably a reference to the roll-call vote held later in the session (see below, p. 86).
k *Prot.*: 'Gilyes'.
l *ZT*, 6 Nov.
m *Pr.*, 7 Nov.
n *Iz.*, *Pr.*, 7 Nov.: 25 votes to 21.
o *Iz.*, 7 Nov.: 25 votes to 24.
p The *Pr.* account is somewhat different: Trotsky is said to have intervened at this point to state that the Congress [i.e. the CEC] had not adopted any written procedural rules and that therefore to reject this clause would be to display lack of comprehension of the essence of Soviet activity; Kalegayev suggested that clause 3 should be omitted as 'an evident truism', whereupon Trotsky argued that it would do no harm to include another reference to the link between the CEC and the CPC.
q *Pr.*, 7 Nov.: 'unanimously'.

Sixth Session
6 November 1917

1. *Organization of the CEC: Departmental Chiefs*

ALGASOV, for the Organization Commission, proposes the following as responsible organizers of departments:[1]

Economic: Milyutin, [Larin][a]
Inter-city: Sverdlov, Algasov
Literary: Steklov, Volodarsky
Agitation and Propaganda: Kakhovskaya,[b] Volodarsky
Finance: Unshlikht, Spiro
Editorial (*Izvestiya*): Zinoviev, Kamenev, Steklov, Malkin[c]
Constituent Assembly Elections: Kamenev, Shreyder
Juridical: Stuchka, Zaks
Municipal: Karelin, Ioffe
Military: Verbo, Yenukidze
Nationality Affairs: Uritsky, Proshyan
International: Zinoviev, Kamkov
Automobile: Sadovsky, Balashev
Domestic: Kirichenko, Dzerzhinsky.

Nominated as secretaries of the CEC: Avanesov, Lesnovsky.

2. *Candidate Members*[2]

AVANESOV proposes, in response to persistent suggestions by the Bolshevik and Left SR fractions, and by individual members, that the CEC statute be supplemented by the following four points to cover substitution of candidate members for full members absent from Petrograd . . .

After a short exchange of views the proposal is adopted with minor amendments in the following form:

1. Each CEC member temporarily absent is replaced during

his absence by a candidate presented by his fraction from its list of candidates.

2. Candidates shall have full voting rights only if the fraction bureau notifies the Presidium of the replacement and if this is confirmed by the CEC [plenary] assembly.

3. [Otherwise] candidates shall have a consultative vote.

4. Not more than half the members of a fraction shall be candidates.

3. *Elections to the Presidium*[3]

The Left SRs state that they will decide tomorrow whether to take part in the Presidium or not. The Bolsheviks elect [as full members] Kamenev, Stuchka, Steklov, Volodarsky, Sverdlov, and Dzerzhinsky; and as candidates Avanesov and Olich.

4. *Elections to the Constituent Assembly*[4]

The question is raised whether measures should be taken, provided that they do not delay convocation of the Constituent Assembly, to allow parties to compile new lists of candidates, since the Left SRs find it hard to vote for the Right SRs whose names are featured alongside theirs in the joint lists.

AVANESOV: Why do not the SRs propose delaying the elections?

LUNACHARSKY: The CPC should know by tonight whether the Electoral Commission ᵈˉwill enter into contact with the government⁻ᵈ or whether it intends to engage in sabotage.

ZINOVIEV: We should not lose sight of the fact that the CPC has already agreed that the elections should take place on the appointed day.

The Electoral Commission is invited ᵉˉto speed up its work on preparing the elections⁻ᵉ.

5. *Inter-party Conference*[5]

KARELIN: The left-wing Mensheviks, who have a majority on their party's CC, have put forward conditions for further participation in the talks. They want freedom of the press to be restored, arrests to cease, and some of those who have been arrested to be released. They refer to this programme as 'the cessation of political terror'. The Popular Socialists and the

Right SRs did not attend the [latest round of] talks. The right-wing Mensheviks, as you know, have come out against an agreement. This means that talks are possible only with the left-wing groups.

ʄʅI consider it would be criminal to make concessions on matters of principle, on the platform [of the proposed coalition government], but I call on the CEC not to make an issue out of the verbal differences that separate the negotiating groups. With every day that passes an agreement becomes more and more essential, since the collapse of the state machinery threatens the country with incalculable hardships.ʅʄ

I propose the following resolution:

> In view of the proximity of the Constituent Assembly elections the CEC considers it essential that freedom of printed and oral agitation be assured, and that those who were arrested during the establishment of the new order be freed unless they represent a security risk.
>
> Directing the CPC to take measures in this sense, the CEC resolves to continue the talks on forming an all-socialist government on the basis of the resolution adopted on 3 November.

STALIN: Karelin should have made it clear in his report that the Mensheviks are demanding the release of everyone who has been arrested and freedom for bourgeois as well as socialist newspapers. I therefore move the following resolution:

> Having heard the commission's report, the CEC resolves:
> [1. to declare] unacceptable the conditions put forward by Abramovich at the conciliation commission [meeting] and printed in yesterday's *Rabochaya gazeta*, i.e. that all those without exception who have been arrested for political offences should be released and that freedom should be assured for the entire press;
> [2.] that the talks should nevertheless be continued on the basis of the resolutions already passed by the CEC, without any additional conditions being imposed.

STEKLOV tables the following motion:

> Having heard the report about the conditions imposed by the right-wing socialists for continuing the talks, the CEC:

[1.] declares that it intends to ensure freedom for the socialist press in so far as it refrains from inciting active measures against the government and the CEC;

[2.] affirms that arrests will be carried out only to protect the people's revolution from aggressive counter-revolutionary acts, and that the question of releasing those already arrested will be settled without delay in the most positive manner except in the case of those individuals whose detention the CEC considers necessary to safeguard the conquests of the revolution.

ᒥsverdlov: The CEC has already passed a resolution on freedom of the press and this is sufficient answer to the Menshevik CC. There is no need for us to revise it.ᒧ

It is decided to call a recess to allow the fractions to consider the resolutions submitted and to try to reconcile them.

After the recess *ᒥKarelin's motion is rejected andᒧ* the following Bolshevik resolution is adopted unanimously but for 5 abstentions:*

In regard to the preliminary conditions put forward by the Menshevik CC, the CEC:

[1.] points out that most of those arrested have already been released and that in future all individuals will be released except those who are a menace to the conquests of the revolution;

[2.] confirms that all newspapers except *Rech'*, *Novoye vremya* etc. may appear freely;

[3.] notes that no order has been given for the arrest of the 'Committee for the Salvation [of the Country and the Revolution]';

[4.] notes that revolutionary order in Petrograd is being assured by the MRC and considers that the municipal Duma cannot be permitted to have any armed detachments at its disposal;

[5.] resolves to continue the talks on the basis of the resolution of 3 November and to complete them as soon as possible. The CEC will be represented at the talks by its previous delegation.

SOKOLNIKOV, replying to a suggestion that he be included in the delegation, declines on the grounds that the Petrograd soviet has just adopted a resolution opposing the agreement.

6. Messages of Greeting

FOKIN, a delegate from the Romanian front,[6] reads the following resolution adopted at a joint meeting:

> Having discussed the situation, we solemnly greet the Petrograd garrison and proletariat, the Petrograd soviet, the RSDRP(b) and the Petrograd soviet of peasant deputies.[7] We declare our solidarity with the transfer of power to a government of soviets. Having learned from the press that the front organizations, ignoring the mood of the mass of soldiers, have expressed on their behalf confidence in the Provisional Government, we protest, for in our view the committees should reflect mass opinion, not the reverse.

A delegate from Vladimir province brings greetings and reports on the situation in that part of the country.

A TSENTROBALT[8] delegate reads the following resolution:

> We representatives of the Baltic fleet, elected at a plenary assembly of Tsentrobalt and all ship committees held on 3 November, have been charged to inform you of our firm opinion about the government.
> We consider that the voice of the navy, which has several times demonstrated its loyalty to the revolution in deeds and not just in words, will only be listened to once the problem of [constituting] the government has been settled.
> And this is what we think: our revolution, which was born as a social revolution, and which ought to give peace to the [warring] peoples, land and freedom to the peasants, and control over production to the workers, should finish off the great struggle against capital once and for all. Eight months of experiment with coalition rule have shown that not all the socialist parties are capable of implementing the programme of peace, bread, land, and workers' control which life itself has put before us. Therefore power should be taken away from those parties [and entrusted to others] who have displayed creative initiative and vitality. This government

should be responsible only to the all-Russian soviet [*sic*] and its CEC. Only such a government will be recognized and supported with all its might by the Baltic fleet.

Long live the power of the soviets of workers', soldiers', and peasants' deputies! Long live the social revolution! Long live the Third International!

(signed) Delegates of the Baltic fleet and its CC

*ᴦ*48TH DIVISION representative: Recently there has been a loss of confidence in the army committee and the senior officers. The instruction which I have brought was compiled before the revolution. It speaks of the army's fatigue, the lack of food and ammunition, and states that the rear units, instead of helping the front, are engaging in anarchy and that the division declares its readiness to combat anarchy.

KAMENEV: A telegram has been received from the XIth Army stating that the troops are starving and that all reserves have been consumed. The position is desperate, but in view of the terrible condition of the country the feeling of responsibility in the army is growing.ᴵᵍ

7. *The Battle for Moscow*⁹

BUKHARIN, who has just arrived from Moscow: Some comrades who call themselves radicals, socialists, and even three-quarter Bolsheviks, like *Novaya zhizn'*,¹⁰ have reported that there have been countless robberies in Moscow, that historical and artistic monuments have been destroyed, *ᵈᴦ*including St. Basil's and other cathedrals in the Kremlin, and that the Nikitsky Gates and [nearby] streets have been burned down.ᴵᵈ The same sort of papers in Moscow reported that in Petrograd the soldiers got drunk *en masse*, that the women's shock battalion had been raped, that the insurrection had been put down and so on. The sole purpose of such reports is to sow dissension among the revolutionary soldiers and workers and to help bring about a victory of the counter-revolutionary bourgeoisie.

I must admit that we were very downcast when we heard that revolutionary Petrograd had been defeated, although the news (like the vicious slander against the insurgents, which we did not believe for a moment) never weakened our resolve to fight on for our ideals to the end. *ᵈᴦ*The truth is that St. Basil's did not suffer at all, or at least only such damage as can quite easily be made good. Two houses, one of them with three storeys, were destroyed near the Nikitsky Gates. One could hardly expect the socialist revolution to be as painless as some popular festival. There was a battle, and a stubborn one.⌐ᵈ

The reason why it lasted so long was not that we were lacking in resolution. It was partly because we were too magnanimous to fight, and partly because the cadets had the chance to train their forces—they could practise firing machine-guns for several hours [a day]—and enough time to make contact with Kaledin. They could organize their field staff in advance, whereas we had to get organized during the actual fighting.

Nevertheless the outcome of the battle was not in doubt. From the first minute the whole of revolutionary Moscow rose up to fight for soviet power. The entire garrison was on our side and we had access to all kind of weapons, even searchlights, 11-inch guns, and some airplanes with which we might easily have destroyed the counter-revolutionaries' headquarters. But the MRC did not show enough initiative in the matter, and this was another reason why the battle was so long drawn out.

The main reason, however, was the treacherous conduct of the Mensheviks and SRs. The Left SRs fought alongside us with exemplary heroism and zeal—⌐ʳfor example, comrade Sablin was wounded in a clash with some cadets⌐ᶠ—but the Right SRs, headed by mayor Rudnev, did everything they could to suppress our insurrection. Let me begin with their tactics in the soviet. In the workers' section we had an overwhelming majority, but the soldiers' section had not been re-elected for about a hundred years and consisted of dentists, chemists etc.—people who had about as much in common with the soldiers as I have with the emperor of China. They opposed us and placed countless obstacles in the way of holding fresh elections, and so we did not have a majority in the executive committee. What did this lead to? They even engaged in espionage, for when we put machine-guns in the windows of the soviet building they telephoned Ryabtsev to inform him of their location. When one of our regiments was ambushed these so-called soldiers' representatives took part in interrogating the prisoners and gave evidence against them. They entered into a real armed alliance with the counter-revolution and fired upon us. Even before that, when we proposed that the soviet should arm the Red guards, they managed to defeat the plan, claiming that if the workers were armed this would lead to conflict with the soldiers.

The falsity of these arguments has been shown by the course of the battle, in which the Red guards fought heroically and gave such valuable assistance to the soldiers, realizing that it would be hard for them to fight alone. But while we were preparing for the struggle these tactics were very harmful. They prevented us from building up the Red guard and improving its organization; but once the insurrection began Rudnev set about forming a White guard, whose members treacherously fired on our patrols from concealed positions during the night.

The battle for Moscow illustrates more clearly than anything else the class significance of the struggle for soviet power. The counter-revolutionary forces here didn't include a single regiment or even a company of soldiers, nor a single workers' detachment, but only White guards and cadets intimately linked to the counter-revolutionary bourgeoisie. They rallied around a salvation committee set up by Rudnev in the Duma... but the soldiers and workers were on our side.

We showed magnanimity towards an enemy who sent clergymen to persuade us to capitulate. While the cadets were firing dumdum bullets at us we refrained from using airplanes against them and even agreed to an armistice. But the armistice was broken by 150 shock troops who were brought into the city contrary to the terms of the agreement and were taken to a secret rendezvous where 150 rifles were waiting for them, whereupon they began to fire at our patrols. Fortunately our soldiers and workers were up to the mark. By their acts of bravery and self-sacrifice they made up for the indecisiveness of our military leaders and brought us victory. For instance, thirty men of the Dvinsk regiment, who shortly before the insurrection had been freed from detention at the soviet's request, ousted 300 cadets from the Metropole Hotel. Two Red guardsmen threw grenades into the enemy trenches and perished in the attempt . . .

We never thought the struggle could be waged without losses, often on a very large scale. *⌐There are thought to have been about 5,000 casualties in Moscow.⌐* We are not afraid of losses, but we do fear diplomats and political tricksters who seek to

annul our heroic victory. ⌐ʳThe news of the collapse of the
Soviet government makes us sad and highly indignant. Those
who leave the battlefield at the most crucial moment are deser-
ters. Those who call for a compromise are like Metropolitan
Platon in Moscow, who came to the soviet and with tears in his
eyes implored us to stop the bloodshed. We think firm measures
are necessary. We have ordered the Duma dissolved and will
not shrink from dispersing it; we're surprised that you haven't
done the same in Petrograd. We shall close all the papers and
won't be put off by cries about freedom of the press. This is the
epoch of dictatorship and we shall sweep away with an iron
broom everything that deserves to be swept away. We have
been saying this for decades and we should not repudiate our
words now, at the moment of victory. The government must be
organized in such a way that a firm majority rests with the Bolsheviks, as the party of the revolutionary proletariat. The
masses insist unanimously on soviet power, for otherwise all the
bloodshed will have been in vain.⌐ʲ

STUKOV comments briefly on Bukharin's report.

SPIRO: I suggest that the CEC send a message of greetings to our
comrade Sablin, who was injured during the fighting in Moscow.

Agreed . . .

NOTES

a Z̧T, 7 Nov.; Prot.: Levin.
b Pr., 11 Nov.: Nikolskaya.
c Z̧T, 7 Nov. confirms Malkin's membership and gives Zak and Kolegayev
  as members of the Economic and Proshyan and Kollontay of the
  Nationality Affairs departments.
d NZ̧, 7 Nov.; Prot., Iz., 7 Nov.: 'will work'.
e NZ̧, 7 Nov.; Prot.: 'to submit a report on the matter'—an unlikely decision. Iz., 7 Nov., adds that a commission on the Constituent Assembly
  elections was now set up, although such a decision had in fact been taken
  earlier: see above, p. 66.
f Z̧T, 7 Nov.
g RG, 7 Nov.
h From Z̧T, 7 Nov., it appears that agenda items 6 and 7 were taken first;

for simplicity's sake we have kept to the order given in *Prot.* and other sources.

i *ZT*, 7 Nov.: by 24 votes to 15.

j *NZ*, 7 Nov., which omits a second tirade against that newspaper (reprinted in *Prot.*), as do we. According to some sources Bukharin here repeated the details given earlier of material damage in Moscow.

Seventh Session
8 November 1917

1. *Chairmanship of the CEC; Procedural Matters*

KAMENEV, ᵃ⌐in accordance with the decision of the Bolshevik fraction,⌐ᵃ resigns as chairman of the CEC.

ᵃ⌐MALKIN,⌐ᵃ for the Left SRs: We express our regret at Kamenev's enforced departure. This is an indication of impermissible pressure on the part of the Bolshevik fraction, and therefore the Left SRs will vote against any other candidate.

SVERDLOV is elected chairman by 19 votes to 14.[1] [After he has announced the agenda] ZAKS proposes that the CEC should meet regularly each day at 3 p.m. This is adopted unanimously. [In response to queries whether a quorum is present, it is stated that] the quorum has been fixed by the statute worked out by Algasov.

Krasikov, Kossior, and Bogdanov are confirmed as members of the CEC from the Bolshevik fraction . . .

2. *Education and Culture*

LUNACHARSKY, reporting on the work of the PC of Education: ᵃ⌐Officials of the central ministry have gone on strike.[2] This is in part to our advantage, since most organs in the central ministry are due to be eliminated and radically altered, and it will be much easier to build everything up from scratch than to have to concern ourselves with old institutions that have had their day.⌐ᵃ ᵇ⌐Much more disturbing is the sabotage [by officials] in the State Education Committee, which under the old dispensation in the ministry worked out a number of valuable draft decrees, which were disregarded by all the ministers except Salazkin—and even he cut down the scope of the committee's proposals. The composition of the State Education Committee is wholly democratic. It includes among its members a number of distinguished and talented pedagogues, and if they are willing to work with the new government we could dispense with ministerial offic[ials] completely and preserve continuity in the work. But there is scarcely any hope that they will do so, at least in the near future. On the contrary, those more likely to collaborate with us are not the democratic intellectuals, who look upon the insurrection as a military conspiracy, but the unprincipled functionaries. Yet the programme which I have outlined is perfectly acceptable to any genuinely democratic teacher.⌉ᵇ ᵃ⌈The All-Russian Teachers' Union³ has adopted a resolution in which it expresses indirect support for my declaration, but which is categorically opposed to soviet power as such.

As far as the former ministry of Court Affairs is concerned, the position is much better. All the officials are thoroughly frightened by the looting which took place during the first days of the revolution. The scale of the robberies from the Winter Palace has been much exaggerated, but all the same it must be acknowledged that about two million roubles' worth of goods disappeared. In the palace at Gatchina less was taken, but even there a lot of valuables vanished.⌉ᵃ ᵇ⌈To preserve these objects, which [are now] the people's property, officials of the old ministry of Court Affairs have been willing to work hand in hand with commissars of the new government, and some of them have had such commissars appointed to [supervise] them.⌉ᵇ ᵃ⌈The other day a conference of artists and archaeologists was summoned. This will discuss my declaration about the future of the former ministry of Court Affairs. When the conference is over the declaration will be submitted to the CEC. It is hoped that in the near future it will be possible to draw up a plan whereby the art treasures of the [Imperial] palaces will be placed at the disposal of the people.⌉ᵃ

Reads a draft decree establishing a State Educational Commission.

MALKIN: I welcome Lunacharsky's action in submitting his draft to the CEC for its approval.

A commission of five (Zaks, Ustinov, Gillerson, Lozovsky, and Volodarsky) is set up to examine the report and to submit its views at the next session.

3. *First Moves in Soviet Foreign Policy*[4]

TROTSKY: Our foreign policy is determined by the peace decree adopted by the Congress of Soviets. The very fact that such a decree was passed came as a surprise to the routine-minded European bourgeois world, where it was at first regarded as a party statement rather than an act of state. It took some time before the European ruling classes realized that they were faced with a proposal from a government representing many millions of people.

In the Allied countries the bourgeoisie has reacted to the decree with the utmost hostility. The attitude of the governments of the enemy countries cannot help but be ambiguous. On one hand they hope that the revolution will increase the anarchy in Russia and improve their military posture. On the other hand, as they begin to understand that the Soviet government is not ephemeral but rests on the support of the broad armed masses, they appreciate that the Soviet victory is an event of immense international significance. In this connection it is worth noting how the Germans responded to the news of our success over Kerensky. Our radio-telegram from Tsarskoye Selo was intercepted by the Austrians, but the radio station in Hamburg jammed it so that its contents should not become known. The ambiguity in Germany's position lies in the fact that as Germans they are pleased but as bourgeois they know they have good reason to be afraid.

The Soviet government has been entrusted with the duty of formulating a proposal for an armistice and for the inauguration of peace talks. But the military and political situation has so far been unfavourable for this step to be taken. Krasnov's troops were at the approaches to Petrograd and one could expect other forces to follow them; a struggle for power was going on in Moscow; and the news from the provinces was uncertain, partly on account of the 'neutral' position adopted by the Union of Postal and Telegraphic Employees.

In western Europe the mood was one of wait and see. There was mistrust of the new Soviet government. The working masses trusted it but were afraid it might not survive. Now our government has established its power in the two capital cities, in many important provincial centres, and over most of the army; it is also winning support from the peasant masses. These are indisputable facts, whatever one may think about the sabotage by leading officials and intellectuals. The CPC is firmly convinced that this sabotage must be broken with the aid of the junior officials, for such saboteurs are agents of the counter-revolutionary bourgeoisie.

Now even the most hidebound European diplomats realize that soviet power will not be defeated in a day or in a week. They can see that the Russian bourgeoisie, for all its tremendous economic might, is politically impotent. They have to reckon with the Soviet government as a fact and to enter into some kind of relation to it. These relations are developing empirically. Agents of the European powers have to deal with us over all manner of practical everyday problems, such as entry and exit visas. So far as political relations are concerned, the attitude of each power varies.

Probably the most hostile is the British government, for the bourgeois leaders in that country have least to lose and most to gain from the war, and it suits them if it drags on. In France most petty-bourgeois democrats are in favour of peace, but they are weak. The government is dependent on the stock exchange. The small shopkeeper is a pacifist who knows nothing about the secret treaties, about the imperialist ambitions for which he is called upon to shed his blood. France has suffered most from the war: she knows that if it continues she will face degeneration and death. The seriousness of the internal situation and the growth of working-class opposition has led to the formation of a ministry under Clemenceau. This is also a response to the emergence of soviet power. Clemenceau is a radical of an extreme Jacobin, chauvinist type. For three years he has been trying in vain to form a ministry. The government he now heads, which contains no socialists and is anti-socialist, is the last gasp of petty-bourgeois French democracy, which is aghast at the establishment of a Soviet government. The French petty bourgeoisie looks upon us as an ally of Wilhelm and perhaps as an enemy of France.

Isolated items of news [b]received through Sweden[b] from Italy tell of the working class there enthusiastically hailing soviet power. For nine months Italy wavered as to which of the belligerent camps she should support, and during this time the

Italian workers had occasion to appreciate the harmful consequences of a coalition with the bourgeoisie. The middle classes
and peasants are also dissatisfied with the war. This creates a
situation in which the protests of the proletariat can find a
favourable response.

The United States entered the war after waiting three years,
and then at the prompting of the stock exchange, which had
made its own sober calculations, ᵃ⌐and not in pursuit of the ideals
proclaimed by Wilson.⌐ᵃ America could not permit the victory
of one coalition over the other. She wants both to be weakened
so that American capital may establish its own hegemony.
Moreover, the arms manufacturers have an interest in the war.
Since it began American exports have more than doubled and
have reached a figure which no capitalist state has hitherto
equalled. Almost all these goods are going to the Entente
countries. In January, when Germany announced unrestricted
submarine warfare, all the stations and harbours were filled
with military supplies. The transport system was disorganized
and in New York there were hunger riots on a scale unparal-
leled here. After that finance capital presented Wilson with an
ultimatum: to find a market for these supplies within the
country. Wilson submitted, and that is why America entered
the war. She does not seek territorial conquests. She can tolerate
the existence of the Soviet government since she is well enough
satisfied if the Allied countries and Germany exhaust each
other; apart from that, America is interested in investing her
capital in Russia.

Germany's internal economic condition makes her half-
tolerate the Soviet government. Her peace proposals are in part
a feeler and are in part dictated by a desire to make the other
side bear the responsibility for continuing the war.

All our information about the impression made in Europe by
the peace decree indicates that our most optimistic expectations
were justified. The German working class understands what is
going on in Russia perhaps even better than the Russians themselves.[5] The actions of the Russian working class are more revolutionary than its consciousness, whereas the consciousness of
the European working class has been formed over decades. The
western proletariat, making a class analysis of the events in
Russia, knows that our revolution is not just a seizure of power

by a group of conspirators with the aid of some Red guards and sailors, as the bourgeois press alleges, but the beginning of a new era in world history. The working class is taking over the state apparatus, and this machinery cannot but serve the struggle for peace. On the historic night of 25 October a mighty blow was dealt against the war. This colossal enterprise, involving many different classes and groups, has been ^{c⌐}undermined^{⌐c}. The European governments are no longer worrying about how they may attain their original war aims but about how they may end the struggle with least damage to themselves. Neither side can hope for victory, and now the working class has thrown its own tremendous weight into the argument. The peace decree is becoming ever more widely known; the war is creaking, and our task is to smash it utterly by making a formal proposal to initiate peace talks.

The secret treaties[6] are in my possession. Neratov and Tatishchev, two senior officials of the ministry, handed them over to me voluntarily—in so far as one can ever say that an agreement is voluntary. These treaties are not [documents] inscribed on parchment but actually consist of diplomatic correspondence in code exchanged between governments. I shall start publishing them tomorrow. They are even more cynical than we expected. When the German Social Democrats get access to the iron safes in which their government's secret treaties are kept, they will no doubt find that German imperialism has been just as cynical and rapacious as that of the Allies.

Today I sent the Allied ambassadors the following document. [*Text follows.*] The PC of War, Krylenko, and the chairman of the CPC, Lenin, have entered into contact with the Supreme Commander-in-Chief,[7] to whom the following communication has been sent. [*Text follows.*] We hope that Dukhonin's reply will be in line with the policy of the Soviet government, but whatever this reply may contain it will not divert us from pursuing the path of peace.

The peace decree is being printed in all languages, above all in German, in Petrograd printing works. We are distributing it in large quantities.

I have ^{d⌐}documents, letters by Kerensky,^{⌐d} showing that Kerensky acted as the agent and subsidiary of Allied imperialism. ^{d⌐}We have broken with this policy for ever.^{⌐d} We are confronting the Allied governments, and also those hostile to us, with the fact that the Russian people and army want to end the war, that we have no imperialistic pretensions, that we are throwing into the waste-paper basket of history all the old treaties which gave us rights over foreign territory, and that we stand for a genuine peace. That is why we are making this formal proposal. All governments are under pressure from their peoples, and our policy serves to increase this pressure.[e] This is the only guarantee that the peace will be an honest one that will lead, not to Russia's ruin, but to fraternal coexistence between her and her neighbours to the west.

The CEC expresses its appreciation of Trotsky's energetic activity on behalf of the struggle for peace.

4. Labour Policy

SHLYAPNIKOV, PC of Labour: [f]I cannot give an account of my work because I have not had a chance to take over the ministry since all the senior officials have gone on strike. I have been told that the ministry's funds are in the municipal Duma and that the officials are not just committing sabotage but are trying to conceal their misuse of these funds, which they managed in a manner that defies all criticism. The ministry faces the task of introducing a social insurance programme. Today the law on workers' control will go into effect.[f8]

It is decided to set up a five-man commission (three Bolsheviks; Kamkov and Zaks for the Left SRs) to draft a decree on workers' control of production.

5. Postal and Telegraphic Services

GLEBOV, PC of Postal and Telegraphic Services: In the provinces the telegraph system is beginning to work again. We are winning over the [employees in the central] post office. After going on strike for three days the telegraph employees have announced that they are willing to resume work.

[b]RYAZANOV, for the ARCCTU, expresses regret at the measures employed by Glebov to combat the Union of [Postal and Telegraphic] Employees.[b]

6. Finance

MENZHINSKY, PC of Finance, reports on the resistance offered by officials to the government's requests for money.[9]

[The following] resolution, drafted by Dzerzhinsky, Stalin and Algasov, is passed unanimously:

The CEC notes that senior officials of the ministry of Finance and the State Bank, who refuse to recognize the Soviet government, are arbitrarily appropriating Treasury funds and providing credit to some [clients] while denying them to the CPC, although such credits are urgently needed to ensure emergency supplies for the front and to carry out the elections to the Constituent Assembly.

Considering that such conduct by senior officials of the ministry, and in particular of the State Bank and Treasury, constitutes criminal sabotage, the very harmful effects of which may be felt by millions of soldiers, peasants and workers and may prevent the Constituent Assembly being convoked on time, the CEC proposes that the CPC immediately take the most energetic measures to liquidate this sabotage by counter-revolutionaries in the State Bank and calls upon all those other employees who are loyal to the people's cause to render the Soviet government every assistance in obtaining the funds it needs for the state to function.

The CEC also sets up a nine-man Finance commission to control the expenditure of funds requested by the CPC, to operate until the Constituent Assembly meets.

The commission, consisting of 5 Bolsheviks and 4 Left SRs, is elected.

7. Abolition of Class Privileges[10]

⌐USTINOV:⌐ The Left SR fraction proposes that [the following] draft decree be published through the CPC:

All class privileges and special rights, along with titles, are abolished for ever in the Russian Republic;

all its citizens shall henceforth be equal in their rights and obligations;

in lieu of the division into social estates of peasants, burghers, merchants, nobles etc. there shall be but one appellation, 'citizen of the Russian republic'. The CPC is requested to take measures to implement this decree immediately and to repeal the relevant articles of the old law.

ᵃ⌐Adopted unanimously.⌐ᵃ

8. *Constituent Assembly*

ZINOVIEV: *ᵃ⌐*I propose that the CEC issue an appeal stating that it considers it essential to carry out the elections to the Constituent Assembly on the appointed day, 12 November. In most electoral districts the elections will be practicable, and in the army they have already begun.

USTINOV: I should like to remind Zinoviev that in a number of provinces it will be impossible to hold elections for formal [i.e. technical] reasons.

STALIN: I have heard privately from the Electoral Commission that elections will not be possible in 40 districts.⌐ᵃ

Zinoviev's resolution is adopted unanimously.

9. *CEC of First Convocation*[11]

LITVIN: I propose that the Presidium demand that the CEC of first convocation surrender its papers to its successor within three days.

Agreed.

10. *Delegation to Moscow Funeral*

Two members are delegated to attend the funeral of victims of the revolution in Moscow.*ᵍ*

NOTES

a NZ, 9 Nov.
b ZT, 9 Nov.
c NZ, 9 Nov.; *Iz., Prot.*: 'killed'.
d Pr., 9 Nov.; *Prot.*: 'a document'.
e Delo naroda, 9 Nov., gives a more forthright version of this passage: 'We are confronting all governments with the fact that we want to end the war. We shall throw all treaties into the cesspit. If the pressure on the western European governments is insufficient, our policy will increase it.'
f Ibid.
g A grant of 500 roubles for this purpose was made at the next session.

Eighth Session
9 November 1917

Chairman: Sverdlov

1. *Partisan Use of 'Izvestiya'*

SHREYDER, for the Left SRs: We protest against the publication in *Izvestiya*, the organ of the CEC, of lists of candidates [in the Constituent Assembly elections] put up by the Bolshevik party. *Izvestiya* should print the lists of all parties in the soviets, as it used to do.

SVERDLOV: The editor of *Izvestiya* should take note of this statement.

*ᵃ⌐*STEKLOV, for the editorial board of *Izvestiya*: *Izvestiya* is the central organ [of the soviets] and in accordance with established convention has not printed any party lists or agitated on behalf of any party. This convention should be maintained in future. The Bolshevik list was printed fortuitously. However, *Izvestiya* has been placed in a very difficult situation. The elections to the Constituent Assembly are due to be held in a few days, and it must tell its readers whom they should vote for. The Left SRs do not have their own list of candidates, but a joint list with the Right SRs. *Izvestiya* cannot call on people to vote for Right SRs, the most ferocious enemies of the revolution. Some way out has to be found, since one can't keep silent about the elections.⌐ᵃ

2. *Situation in Kostroma*

DANILOV, chairman of the executive of the Kostroma soviet: In the provinces we are dealing with a backward mass of people unaccustomed to organization. The factory committees enjoy ᵇ⌐extremely⌐ᵇ little authority; the trade unions are weak; and the same may be said of the party organizations. ᵇ⌐The population has uttered threats against the supply committee,[1] a body which they themselves have elected. As a result those who

worked in such organizations have left them in droves.⁷ᵇ As far
as industry is concerned, ᵇ⌐the situation is critical.⁷ᵇ Many factories will soon have to close down; the Bolshoy factory in
Kostroma has already been shut for over a month. What are we
to do with this mass of starving unemployed? The organs of
local self-government have done nothing and have made no
plans to meet such a contingency.

The supply situation is very serious. Kazan province will not
give us anything; nor will Ufa. Siberia could do so, but the
grain would have to be transported a long way. ᶜ⌐While the
rivers were open to navigation we received nothing from the
producing provinces. Flour is fetching 50 to 55 roubles a pud.
Kostroma province is on the eve of a spontaneous outburst by
the starving masses. The 181st [infantry] regiment has turned
into a drunken mob. Pogroms have begun, with looting of
liquor stores; the next target will be the food supply depots, and
after that the mob will go for the shops.⁷ᶜ The only way out of
the situation is for all democracy to unite. Those who appeased
the bourgeoisie for so long should make some concessions in
their turn, ᶜ⌐but also from our side there should be a maximum
of concessions. If we label various groups of democrats 'counter-
revolutionaries' then democracy will fall apart. We have a duty
to say all this to the people's government, to be sincere and
frank in revealing the critical situation we are in.⁷ᶜ

3. *Supply*

YAKUBOV, reporting on the ᵇ⌐national⁷ᵇ supply situation: ᵇ⌐In
Petrograd⁷ᵇ the situation is very grave. We are only receiving
little more than 12,000 puds [of cereals] a day, but to keep the
[bread] ration at ¼ funt a headᵈ we need 48,000 puds. If this
goes on we shall [soon] have no bread at all in the city.²

Things are also very bad in the provinces of Petrograd, Moscow, Kostroma, Vladimir, and Smolensk. Nor are they any
better in the army. On the Northern front there is enough hard
tack for no more than two days.

The PC of Supply has taken some measures. [Freight trains
in] the Petrograd railway region are being unloaded. This
operation began yesterday and will take a few more days. We
shall at least get some potatoes, if not any grain. ᵇ⌐We have also
discovered two million puds of coal belonging to the Admiralty,

some of which has been requisitioned for industrial use.[1b] Agitators and commissars have been dispatched to the grain-growing provinces to obtain cereals from the peasants. But all these measures are mere palliatives. This problem was bound to arise in such an acute form, no matter who was in power.

[b]The commission [advising] the PC of Supply proposes that the CEC issue a law on confiscating the landowners' grain. We cannot buy it since we have no money and this would take too long. We also need to decentralize the supply organization and to remove all prohibitions on transporting grain from one province to another. On the river Belaya there is a stock of about two million puds of grain, but no barges to move it.

The officials in the Supply ministry do not recognize the new government.[1b] At present there are three organizations concerned with supply matters: our own, the old ministry, and the railwaymen's union. The only course is to concentrate all authority in the hands of the PC of Supply and its [advisory] commission. In order to take over the old apparatus, we must either win the co-operation of the officials or dismiss them. But the latter is impossible, since we would then have none of the information which these officials collect. [Therefore] we have decided to set up our own organizations in the provinces and [through them] to exert pressure upon the centre.[3] There is plenty of grain in Russia: we have to get hold of it and distribute it.

[c]VOLODARSKY: What is the relationship between you and the Supply ministry?

YAKUBOV: Our representative was not allowed into the ministry. For the moment we have decided to leave this question open.[1c]

LUNACHARSKY: I propose that an all-party supply organ be set up, and that an appeal be launched to the entire population to create such a body. The PC of Supply should draft a decree on confiscating the landowners' grain and submit it to the CEC.

SOKOLNIKOV: A five-man delegation should be sent to the Supply ministry to explain to the officials there that they are committing sabotage. Their leaders are clearly trying to provoke hunger riots in the hope of turning the people's anger against the soviets and the CPC. We have to make these officials assist our commissar.

PETROVSKY: The new supply apparatus cannot work without statistics, and these are all in the hands of the old bodies. Hiding these figures is a criminal act and no means should be spared to make these officials work [for us].

DZERZHINSKY: If we agree to carry out a policy of confiscation, this will make it clear that there can be no co-operation with the bourgeoisie.

LEVIN: The whole experience of the soviets with the supply committees showed that concealed sabotage was going on, and this has now come out into the open.

KRASIKOV: Lunacharsky is suggesting propaganda. But if we are in power we ought to make that power manifest by taking measures of a state character, and not confine ourselves to propaganda. We have to apply sanctions against the officials who are committing sabotage. Some of them are actually saying: 'take severe measures against us and then we shall work.' ᵇᵣWe have to set up a revolutionary court which will publicly condemn their anarchic methods of combat.

USTINOV: All the talk about [confiscating] landowners' grain will lead nowhere, for 90 per cent of the harvest is in peasant hands. This is not the way to attain our objectives. Instead of requisitioning we should make use of the old supply apparatus and especially improve the transport system.⁷ᵇ

Resolved: to send a five-man delegation to the Supply ministry to ascertain the position and, together with the commission of the PC of Supply, to persuade the officials [to co-operate]; it is to report and draft appropriate measures.

4. *Education*

ᵇᵣLUNACHARSKY: The commission set up to examine the draft decree on the organization of the Education ministry has approved it subject to minor amendments which I am prepared to accept.⁷ᵇ ᶜᵣTwo of the fifteen [proposed] departments, for school hygiene and school construction, have been added at the suggestion of Ustinov, who was a member of the commission.⁷ᶜ *b*⌐CHIKOIDZE: I object to the idea of appointing commissars to all departments of the ministry. Schools should be treated with particular care, to ensure that their tranquillity is not disturbed and to protect them from experiments. For that reason representatives of the public should be given more weight than appointed officials⌐*b* *c*⌐on the State Educational Commission,[4] which has 15 elected and 15 nominated members.

LUNACHARSKY: I do not insist that the commission be composed as stated in the draft. The number of representatives from public organizations may be increased.⌐*c* *b*⌐The draft proceeds from the principle of public [control], but it is essential to appoint commissars since if we were to wait until the saboteur officials and teachers reorganized the ministry nothing would be done at all. I quite agree that terror is entirely out of place in schools; nevertheless it is not the teachers but public elements who must be in charge of them.

The draft is adopted unanimously.⌐*b*

5. *Congress of Peasant Deputies*[5]

USTINOV: . . . I believe the congress will take place despite the intrigues of the Executive Committee of the All-Russian Soviet [i.e. Congress] of Peasant Deputies. However, these intrigues have led to a terrible muddle in the organizational arrangements. Some of the delegates reported to us on their arrival, whereas others went to no. 6 Fontanka Street, and now some of them are changing camp. A few have even gone to Mogilev, although it should be noted that the Executive Committee's decision to hold the congress there was passed by only 27 votes to 23. At the last moment delegates of the Ist, IVth, VIth, XIth, XIIth, and one other Army arrived, who protested unanimously in writing against this decision. There is accordingly reason to believe that it will be annulled and that the congress will take place in Petrograd, especially since the army delegates have demanded that they be consulted about this. The only argument in favour of Mogilev was that otherwise Gots and Avksentyev could not have taken part, since they risked arrest here.

The commission to organize the congress has done all it can to provide accommodation and food for the delegates, but has met with problems . . . The military hospitals that were used to accommodate deputies to the Democratic Conference and the Second Congress of Soviets have been reserved for the so-called Zemsky Sobor.[6] But the MRC will probably help us obtain the accommodation needed for the representatives of the Russian peasantry.[e]

Replying to questions: Most delegates will undoubtedly support the left. Twenty-seven have so far registered as Left SRs out of about one hundred who have arrived.

[c]⌐The Presidium is charged to appoint a delegation to convey greetings to the congress.⌐[c]

6. *Reform of the Law Courts*

STUCHKA, reporting on draft decrees on abolition of class privileges and on reform of the courts: [b]⌐According to the latter all law courts are abolished. Judges will be popularly elected and will pass judgement according to their [revolutionary] conscience, not the written laws of the old government.[7] These decrees need to be passed as a matter of urgency, since at the moment the courts are continuing to apply the laws of the non-existent Provisional Government. We even have such ridiculous incidents as judges trying to arrest our comrades on the basis of verdicts passed according to the old laws.⌐[b]

NOTES

a *NZ*, 10 Nov. According to *ZT*, at the end of this session Sverdlov stated that in future *Izvestiya* would publish no candidates' lists at all.

b *NZ*, 10 Nov.

c *ZT*, 10 Nov.

d *ZT*, 10 Nov.: 'to maintain the normal ration'.

e The speaker then reports on various administrative details and announces the agenda of the congress.

Ninth Session
10 November 1917

Chairman: Sverdlov

1. A Message from the Trenches

An unscheduled statement is made by a delegate of the 26th Siberian sharpshooters' regiment from the Northern front:

> I have come from the trenches and reflect the genuine mood of the soldiers. When I left there was only enough bread for two days. The soldiers want an end to civil war and a homogeneous ministry; they want bread and peace. If you won't agree to this, the soldiers will bring their demands here at bayonet-point.[a]

2. Congress of Peasant Deputies

USTINOV, reporting: Yesterday there was a [preliminary] conference attended by more than 120 delegates, who decided to convoke the congress in Petrograd, not Mogilev. A telegram in this sense was also received from Chernov. There was some discussion of an appeal to the CPC to guarantee the personal security of Avksentyev, Gots, and Chernov so that they might be able to attend the congress and report to it. Delegates from the peasant soviet in Moscow, dispatched on the initiative of the Moscow Left SRs, are expected to attend. The congress will probably open tomorrow. The delegates' mood is generally to the left.

The CEC elects Ustinov, Zinoviev, and Litvin as its representatives to the congress.

3. The CPC and General Headquarters

LENIN: The complete text of our conversations with Dukhonin[1] has been published and I may confine myself to a few remarks. We were clear that we were dealing with someone hostile to the people's will, an enemy of the revolution. Dukhonin has engaged in various subterfuges and manœuvres to drag the matter out. There was some doubt whether our telegram was genuine, and for this reason an approach was made not to Krylenko but to General Manikovsky. In this way the generals delayed for at least twenty-four hours [action on] such an important question as concluding peace. Only when we said we would turn to the soldiers did Dukhonin himself come to the apparatus. We told him that we wanted him to enter immediately into talks about an armistice, and only that: we did not give him the right to conclude an armistice. This [was] outside his competence, and every step he took in conducting the talks was to be controlled by the people's commissars.

The bourgeois press reproaches us for offering a separate armistice, as if we took no account of the interests of the Romanian army. This is a complete falsehood. We are offering to start peace talks and to conclude an armistice with every country without exception. We have information that our radio-telegrams are reaching Europe. Our announcement of the victory over Kerensky was picked up by the Austrian radio-telegraph and passed on, but the Germans jammed transmission of the message. We can make contact with Paris, and when the peace treaty is ready we shall be able to tell the French people that it is up to them to sign an armistice in a couple of hours. We'll see what Clemenceau will say then!

Our party never said that it could give peace immediately, only that it would immediately propose peace and publish the secret treaties. And this is what we have done: *the struggle for peace* is now beginning. It will be difficult and stubborn. International imperialism is mobilizing all its forces against us, but however large these may be our chances are extremely good. We shall link this revolutionary struggle for peace with revolutionary fraternization. The bourgeoisie would like the imperialist governments to conspire against us.

CHUDNOVSKY, *b*⌐a wounded soldier⌐*b*: *c*⌐I do not doubt the CPC's good intentions, *b*⌐and dissociate myself sharply from malicious critics in the bourgeois camp,⌐*b* but I must say that it has acted in an extremely tactless and light-hearted manner. The appeal to the soldiers to conclude the armistice themselves is a tremendous mistake.⁷ᶜ ᵇˊThe publication of such an appeal can only be attributed to extreme haste. Fraternization, even if 'organized', between units on opposite sides of the line, carried out at the discretion of counter-revolutionary commanders, may be utilized by the Germans to launch attacks on our men.⁷ᵇ ᶜˊIt is quite possible that while one of our regiments is starting to talk about the armistice another one next to it is coming under fire. We have always said that we were against an obsceneᵈ peace. But the step taken by Lenin, Stalin, and Krylenko is making it impossible for our soldiers to fight should the German government not agree to [initiate] peace talks,⁷ᶜ ᵉˊand we should have to continue the war and bring the German proletariat liberation at the point of our bayonets.⁷ᵉ

ᵇˊ*Turning to Lenin*: You as my teacher and I as your pupil know perfectly well that German imperialism may turn out to be stronger than the German proletariat. Entrusting the conclusion of an armistice to the soldiers will not help to bring about a revolutionary peace but will destroy its chances. 'Organized fraternization' is really a sort of 'organized disorganization'. However strong the [soldiers'] organization may be in a particular regiment, the regimental organizations are not linked to one another. Technically it is quite impossible for them to carry on armistice talks on an all-Russian scale, although it is evidently such talks that the CPC has in mind, to judge by its order to General Dukhonin.

I permit myself to make such sharp criticisms of the CPC because I consider it the only [legitimate] authority and I accept all its measures except the latest one. It is only by criticism that mistakes may be avoided.⁷ᵇ

ᶠˊI [also] ask Lenin to confirm or deny whether Colonel Muravyev actually said that 'the war is over'.⁷ᶠ

KAMENEV: Chudnovsky's speech shows that people may misinterpret the people's commissars' appeal to the soldiers about armistice talks. I suggest that the CEC issue an appeal that would correct the errors perpetrated in the CPC's statement. This should make it clear: a) that although the peace talks have been entrusted to the soldiers, the conclusion of peace must be left to the government and be carried out on an all-Russian

scale; b) that one of the conditions of an armistice is a guarantee
that it should not be used [by the Germans] to transfer troops
from the Russian to the French or Italian fronts. This point is
required to prevent French, British, and Italian workers thinking that we are abandoning them [to the Germans]. I suggest
that a commission be formed to draft such an appeal.

LEVIN, for the Left SRs: $^{b\ulcorner}$We likewise welcome the measures
taken by the CPC, but we absolutely reject those against which
Chudnovsky has protested, and for the same reasons that he
gave in such elaborate detail.$^{\urcorner b}$ $^{c\ulcorner}$It was wrong to appeal to the
soldiers to conclude the armistice themselves on an individual
basis. We would have insisted that this unfortunate mistake be
completely eliminated, but since for technical reasons this is not
possible we support the palliative measure proposed by Kamenev. However, the question ought to be looked at in a broader
context. We should make it impossible for such mistakes to re-
cur by ensuring that all similar acts are not implemented until
they have been vetted by the CEC.$^{\urcorner c}$

LENIN: Chudnovsky said he was taking the liberty of making
some sharp criticism of the actions of the people's commissars.
There can be no question whether or not such criticism is
proper. It is the duty of every revolutionary.[2] The people's
commissars do not consider themselves infallible.

Chudnovsky said that we cannot accept an obscene peace.
But he did not adduce a single word or action on our part which
could be interpreted as implying that such a peace is accept-
able^g to us. What we said was: peace can be concluded only by
the CPC. $^{c\ulcorner}$(*Voices from the Left SR benches*: 'by the CEC'.) No, by
the CPC, not the CEC, and this is what we told Dukhonin.$^{\urcorner c}$
When we started to talk to Dukhonin, we knew that we were
dealing with an enemy, and in such cases one cannot delay
action. We didn't know how the talks would turn out, but we
showed resolution: a decision had to be made right away, as we
stood by the [radio-telegraph] apparatus, about what should be
done with this insubordinate general. We didn't have time to
summon the CEC by this apparatus. The CEC's prerogatives
have not been infringed here. In a war one cannot wait to see
what the results of an action will be; we were at war with the
counter-revolutionary generals, and so we turned to the

soldiers instead. We dismissed Dukhonin; but we are not formalistic bureaucrats and know that mere dismissal is not enough. He is going against us, and so we appeal to the mass of soldiers against him and give them the right to take part in the armistice talks—but not to conclude the actual armistice. The soldiers were warned to mount guard over the counter-revolutionary generals.

b⌐One cannot say that the front has been weakened, since after the repudiation of the secret treaties we have all become defensists.⌐*b* I think any regiment is sufficiently well organized to uphold revolutionary order, which is essential. If an act of treachery occurs while the soldiers are negotiating an armistice, or if they are attacked while fraternizing, then it is their duty to shoot the traitors without any formalities.[3] To say that we have weakened our front in the event of a German attack is monstrous. So long as Dukhonin was not unmasked and dismissed, the army could not be sure that it was carrying on an internationalist peace policy. Now the army has that assurance. One can combat Dukhonin only by appealing to the soldiers' sense of organization and to their initiative. Peace cannot be obtained solely from above, but has to be won from below. We don't for a moment trust the German generals, but we do trust the German people. If the soldiers fail to take an active part and allow the peace to be concluded by the respective high commands, it will not be secure. *c*⌐We have appealed for fraternization between regiments, not armies. In the present instance we relied on the military experience of Krylenko, who stated that such fraternization was quite feasible.⌐*c*

I am against Kamenev's suggestion *c*⌐on guarantees against the Germans using the armistice to promote active operations on other fronts⌐*c* not because I think it wrong in principle but because what he is proposing is too weak, inadequate. *c*⌐We have stronger and more effective means of preventing German, French and other imperialists from using the armistice for their own ends. But we cannot speak about them as this would mean telling the imperialists about them.⌐*c* *h*⌐However, in any event a certain length of time will elapse between the drawing up of the treaty and its signature, in the course of which we can undertake the measures necessary to ensure [that the Germans do not breach it]. I am against binding our hands by measures which are too limited in scope and which could weaken our struggle.

In reply to Chudnovsky's question, I declare that Muravyev did not have the right to issue the order that was reported in the press, and that this matter will be investigated.^{7h}

^{cᴦ}KAMENEV: I suggest that a ballot be taken on the question I raised earlier, that the CEC should issue an appeal.

LENIN: I am against issuing such an appeal, but would agree to the setting up of a commission on the armistice provided that its functions and programme of work are not predetermined and that it operates on principles which we decide.^{7c}

KAMENEV [agrees].

Resolved: to elect a five-man commission, its membership to be determined by the two fractions.

LEVIN: ^{cᴦ}I propose the following resolution:

The CEC states that the conclusion of an armistice and of a peace [treaty] are the prerogative of the CEC alone. The CPC is a purely executive organ.^{7c}

^{iᴦ}Speaking on the motives for his resolution, Levin points out that the CPC is showing a tendency to curtail the rights of the CEC.

VOLODARSKY: It is time to stop introducing resolutions for demonstrative effect. These simply obstruct the CPC in its work. The CEC is not the government, but the CPC would not dare to go against its will.

Debate on the substantive issue is curtailed.

VOLODARSKY introduces a proposal, based on what he says is the practice in bourgeois parliaments, that before the Left SR resolution is voted on the members should decide whether or not to put it to the vote.

RYAZANOV: The question should be posed more broadly, as it involves the principle of relations between the CPC and the CEC.

A LEFT SR deputy: So long as this general question is not settled the Left SR fraction will put forward analogous resolutions each time [the matter comes up], in order to emphasize the point that the CPC is solely an executive organ.⁷ⁱ

SVERDLOV: Each fraction and each individual member of the CEC has the right to table this or any other matter for [inclusion in] the agenda.

ᵇ⌐The Left SR resolution is rejected. The Left SRs announce that they will place on the agenda for the next session the question of the relationship between the CEC and the CPC.⌐ᵇ

Resolved: to choose a five-man commission, ᵇ⌐consisting of three Bolsheviks and two Left SRs,⌐ᵇ to draw up the appeal.

4. *CEC's Representation Abroad*

ZINOVIEV, for the International department: This department consists of Kollontay, Voznesensky, Tsyperovich, Kamenev, Ryazanov, Steklov, Nevsky, Chudnovsky and others. The first thing we have to do is to ensure the transmission of news [abroad]; a delegation is superfluous. I propose that Orlovsky be appointed representative in Stockholm.⁴ Axelrod and the other members of the former delegation do not support the new CEC and [their powers] should be annulled. Since the foreign bourgeois press has knowingly reported false information about events in Russia, the CEC decided to send a commission abroad to tell our soldier and worker comrades about the real state of affairs here. Such a delegation should indeed be sent soon, but for the present we may limit ourselves to ʲ⌐sending couriers to Stockholm in a few days' time and⌐ʲ publishing a newspaper in German to make revolutionary propaganda among the German soldiers. This paper will contain only factual material. To set it up an assignation of funds is required.

Resolved: to approve publication of the paper and to assign [the necessary funds], to annul the mandates of the [former] CEC's delegation abroad, and to appoint Orlovsky the CEC's representative [in Stockholm].

5. *Abolition of Class Privileges*

STUCHKA reads the decree abolishing social estates and civil ranks.

The decree is approved ᵏ⌐unanimously⌐ᵏ.

6. *Reform of the Law Courts*

STUCHKA reads a [draft] decree on the law courts.

It is resolved to set up a five-man commission, to be nominated by the fractions, [to examine it].

NOTES

a Prot. mentions that the delegate presented a resolution but does not print the text. *ZT,* 11 Nov., reports that the speaker displayed the rags he wore in lieu of a proper uniform and said: 'unless they are shod, clothed and fed, the soldiers' patience will be exhausted and they will come here to seek out those who are to blame for all their misfortunes.'

b ZT, 11 Nov.

c NZ, 11 Nov.

d RG, 11 Nov.; *Iz.,* 12 Nov. *NZ,* 11 Nov.: 'shameful'.

e Iz., 12 Nov.; this sentence may have been excised from *Prot.* on ideological grounds.

f NZ, 11 Nov.; *Iz.,* 12 Nov., attributes the remark to Ryazanov.

g Lenin, *PSS,* xxxv. 87: 'unacceptable', although the source quoted is *Prot.*; *Iz.,* 12 Nov., also has 'acceptable' which makes better sense.

h RG, 11 Nov. *ZT,* 11 Nov., reports this passage as follows: 'There will be many stages in the negotiations, and the CPC has already discussed what we shall do. After the armistice terms have been formulated we shall immediately inform the French, British, and Italian peoples, and they will be able to force their governments to make the armistice general.' The last paragraph is given in *Prot.* as a separate intervention and is phrased differently: 'Muravyev is no longer Commander-in-Chief and could not issue such an order.'

i RG, 11 Nov.

j Delo naroda, 11 Nov.

k Pr., 13 Nov.

Tenth Session
14 November 1917

Chairman: Sverdlov

1. *Messages of Greeting*

STEMSOV: I represent the 112th division, which is part of the VIIIth Army on the Romanian front. [Describes the growth of 'peasant' organizations in the army and reads the mandate he has brought.] My comrades also asked me to say that their rations should be increased and wherever possible issued in the form of food [rather than cash]. They hear from the villages that their families are starving [and] since the transport system is dislocated little food can be obtained [from home]. At the moment the soldiers' mood is undecided, because various rumours are going round. Everyone wants an end to the war and until then wants the army to be clothed, shod, and fed. We welcome the Bolsheviks' action. All power to the soviets!

VYAZMA SOVIET delegate: The Vyazma garrison, which serves to reinforce the Xth Army, has backed the CEC from the beginning of our revolution. It greets the Bolsheviks and Left SRs, brands the Right SRs, and demands that all land be managed by the land committees before the Constituent Assembly meets. [Describes assumption of power by Vyazma garrison; asks for teachers to be exempted from military duties.] When the army needs reinforcements we shall give them, but we demand that they be clothed, shod, and fed ... We are all exhausted and want an armistice.

SEVASTOPOL delegate: [Describes transfer of power and measures to avert anti-Semitic pogroms and riots at Melitopol and elsewhere.] The Sevastopol garrison, having taken power, demands that the government be organized from all the socialist parties and that it be responsible to the soviet of workers' and soldiers' deputies, for which purpose they should come to Petrograd [*sic*] . . . I greet you as the revolutionary vanguard which is showing the way forward.

35TH CORPS delegate: [Reads mandate; promises support if required.]

13TH CORPS delegate: [Reads similar declaration.]

2. *Workers' Control*[1]

MILYUTIN: I shall not deal with the fundamentals of this question but simply comment on the text of the draft decree, which has been unanimously approved by our commission.

In drafting this law on workers' control we have had to take account of the existing state of affairs. Objections have been raised that we are establishing workers' control without having previously drawn up a general economic plan. But we have been overtaken by events. In practice workers' control has come about in the course of the struggle against sabotage and lock-outs. We have had to co-ordinate the [work of] control [organs] set up in the localities and to draw them into a single stream-lined state apparatus, even at the cost of proceeding in unsystematic fashion. That is why the draft decree on workers' control has been elaborated before one on the economic plan.

Objections have also been raised over the composition of the controlling organ[s]. Some comrades thought that the commission was extending powers of workers' control too far [downwards] and that these powers should be limited. But we proceeded from the principle of control from below. ⌐We based the control apparatus on the local factory committees, so that the higher instances of control will consist of their central bodies [*ob'yedineniya*], filled out by representatives of trade unions and soviets.⌐[a]

There was no disagreement [in the commission] on the functions of workers' control. The third point which aroused objections was whether employers should be bound by the decisions of workers' control [organs] and should have to put them into effect. We have given the employers three days in which to contest such decisions. Our critics argued that if the factory committees act as workers' control organs and their decisions are made mandatory this could endanger the interests of the general economic plan. They suggested that it would be better to make mandatory [only] decisions by the municipal workers' control organs. We countered that unless the lowest organs had such a right the municipal ones would be inundated with complaints which they would be unable to cope with, and the whole machinery would become bureaucratic. This is why we decided that the factory committees' decisions should be mandatory but that entrepreneurs should have three days in which to protest against them, [first] to the municipal organs, and then, if they get no satisfaction there, to the all-Russian workers' control organ. Thus they have nine days in all in which to make such representations.

These were the main points which led to disagreement in the commission. I shall now read the final draft.

Clauses 1 to 5 set out the organizational scheme: at the base are the factory committees, then the municipal bodies, and finally the all-Russian centre, which is already in being and is to include representatives of the CEC and so on.

Clauses 6 to 8 define the functions of workers' control: to supervise [industrial] operations, supply of raw materials, productivity and so on. Labour protection is the function of the trade unions. The controlling organs are to do this not just by visual observation but by inspecting the firm's books and correspondence.

Clause [10] establishes criminal responsibility [for offences against the decree]. This is very important, for we view workers' control as part of the general state economic plan, and naturally any infringement of this plan makes an offender liable to criminal proceedings.

Clause 12 gives the All-Russian Council of Workers' Control the right to decide, by issuing instructions, all manner of practical questions arising from implementation of this measure.

Clause 13 establishes a close tie between the control organs and those to be established for managing or regulating the economy, [especially] the [Supreme] Economic Council.

Clause 14 annuls all previous legislation.

Our project co-ordinates existing practice and makes possible a further development of workers' control. [To harmonize] this with regulation of the economy is a difficult and complex task, and we need an apparatus which will perform its operations efficiently.

^{a⌐}ZAK: I distinguish strictly between two types of control: workers' control for combating sabotage by industrialists and unofficial lockouts, and state control designed to regulate the entire economy. The national economy is an extremely complicated mechanism, and to regulate it requires vast erudition. For this reason we should set up an apparatus comprising the best scientists, economists, financial experts, and technologists. The apparatus that is proposed here does not meet these demands. It does not correspond to the objectives which the draft itself sets as those of workers' control. But the apparatus we are offered is quite suitable for the more modest task of combating sabotage by industrialists, and since at the moment the struggle against such abuses is proceeding with great ferocity the draft should be made law at once—except for clause 1, which sets forth the aims of the organization; this needs to be amended.

A draft law on regulation of the entire economy needs to be worked out in the near future. This matter must be approached with all due earnestness ... Regulation is possible given the present-day concentration of industry, for large corporations are actually capitalist regulatory organs. But we must on no account confuse the two types of control, for this can only create the impression that we ourselves are unclear about the innovations we are making.⌐^a

LOZOVSKY: The main defect of this draft is that it is inadequately integrated with [measures for] regulating the economy. It distributes [authority to] control production too widely, instead of concentrating it at the centre. In making factory committees' decisions mandatory upon employers, it does not specify what kind of decisions are involved. From the actual practice of these factory committees we know that sometimes workers and employers reach agreements which conflict with the general class [interests] of the proletariat. They may show more concern for their own factory than for the community as a whole. For this reason the junior control organ[s] should act within the limits of instructions issued by the All-Russian Council of Workers' Control.

This must be made categorically clear, so that workers of a particular enterprise should not get the impression that it belongs to them. This is all the more necessary since decisions contrary to the interests of the broad working masses may be taken by, for example, employees of the State Bank ... or private banks, who likewise according to this decree have the right to take decisions mandatory upon their employers. The phrasing used in clauses 1 and 8 could lead workers to think that workers' control is the beginning of socialism, whereas everyone knows that control over production is by no means the same thing as socialization of the means of production.

*⌐As a convinced trade-unionist I propose that in all the control organs increased weight be given to the trade unions, organized according to the production principle, and that the control apparatus be as centralized as possible. In the draft presented by the commission I detect a deviation in the direction of Anarcho-syndicalism. If we give broad powers to the factory committees after several branches of industry have been nationalized we shall paralyse the whole state economic plan.⌐ᵃ

For these reasons I, as representative of ARCCTU, was unable to vote for the draft as proposed. It goes without saying that the trade unions will enter the organizations to be set up under this decree, in order to make the control system correspond to the interests of the working class.

FENIKSHTEYN, AVANESOV, and SHLYAPNIKOV counter the arguments of Lozovsky and Zak. [Speeches not recorded.]

*⌐MILYUTIN: I do not recognize that there are two types of control. The draft before you is only part of a general scheme of economic regulation. This is clear from clause 1, where it is stated that this apparatus is set up 'in the interests' of regulating the economy, not 'with the object' of doing so. In reply to Lozovsky, I should like to say that the local cells will implement the general state plan in conformity with ordinances handed down to them by higher instances [in the control apparatus].⌐ᵃ

ZAKS proposes an amendment to clause 1: 'control is instituted to combat sabotage and lockouts'. [Rejected.]

LOZOVSKY moves an amendment [to clause 13: 'junior organs to act within instructions']. Rejected.

RYAZANOV proposes that clauses 2 and 4 be reversed and that clause 2 be amended to read: 'organs of control are elected institutions . . .' Rejected.

In clause 6 the word 'norms' is substituted for 'minimum' [to read: 'control organs are to establish production norms'].

The draft as a whole is passed with 24 votes in favour and 10 abstentions.[b]

3. Armistice Negotiations

KARAKHAN [reports briefly on his direct-wire conversation with Dvinsk about the initiation of armistice talks with the German high command]. (*Applause.*)

4. Partisan Use of 'Izvestiya'

A LEFT SR delegate submits an interpellation, signed by Kakhovskaya, Kotlyarevsky, and Melkov, to the editors of *Izvestiya* asking them why, [contrary to] a promise by one of the editors in the CEC and in the department concerned, *Izvestiya* nevertheless published appeals to vote for list no. 4 [Bolshevik]. If this was done at the behest of the Petrograd soviet, the Left SRs will table a resolution affirming that the latter cannot override decisions of the CEC.

[a]STEKLOV, editor of *Izvestiya*: The appeal was published at the behest of the Petrograd soviet, of which body *Izvestiya* is also the official organ. When the Left SRs made their first interpellation on this subject they did not insist that the CEC make a ruling [against publication of such appeals].

KALEGAYEV: I admit that we made a mistake in not demanding such a written document. We were content with the verbal explanation given by the editor.[7a]

SPIRO presents a motion that *Izvestiya* should not publish electoral appeals on behalf of the Bolsheviks. Rejected.

SOKOLNIKOV tables a resolution:

Since the Left SR fraction, while protesting against the publication of the Bolshevik list in *Izvestiya*, did not introduce a list of its own, the CEC considers the matter closed.

Approved.

NOTES

a *ZT*, 16 Nov.
b *NZ*, 15 Nov.: 11 abstentions. *ZT*, 16 Nov.: 23 votes in favour, 11 abstentions.

Eleventh Session
15 November 1917

*ᴬᵣ*Chairman: Sverdlov   1 p.m.

SVERDLOV: Yesterday a recess had to be called so that negotiations could take place with the presidium of the [Second Extra-
ordinary] Congress of Peasant Deputies about merging our
executive committees.[1] This merger, and the expansion of the
CEC, have been approved at meetings of the [two] fractions. I
am confident that the question will also be settled affirmatively
at fractional meetings in the peasant congress, so that we may
simply confirm, without debate, the decision reached at the
meeting of the two presidiums. I shall now announce the terms
of this agreement:

> The CEC shall be constituted as follows: 108 representatives
> [each] from the CEC of soviets of workers' and soldiers'
> deputies and from the peasant congress, on a parity basis; 100
> representatives of the navy and army; 35 representatives of
> the trade union[s, plus] 10 from Vikzhel and 5 from the
> [Union of] Postal and Telegraph [Employees].

I repeat: since this decision has not been questioned in the
fractions, we have only to confirm it. The point is that the
presidium of the peasant congress needs to leave immediately
for that congress, so that the decision may be confirmed there as
well, and that the unification of all revolutionary democracy
may thus come to pass.

The agreement is approved without debate.

SVERDLOV: Before closing the session, allow me to express the
assurance that this union will lay a solid basis for agreement
among all the toiling classes of Russia. The ceremonial joint
session of the [expanded] CEC will open at 6 p.m. in the Hall of
Fame.ᵀᵃ

6.25 p.m.

SVERDLOV opens the joint session of the CEC, the peasant congress and the Petrograd soviet.

ZINOVIEV: ᵇ⌐Today, instead of our routine business, we are holding the first ceremonial session of the CEC of Soviets of Workers', Soldiers' and Peasants' Deputies.⌐ᵇ The agreement was reached already yesterday between the presidiums, and today has been confirmed by the executive committees on the following terms (*reads the text*). All these groups are united on the platform of the Second Congress of Workers' and Soldiers' Soviets. [This is] the plenipotentiary representative [assembly] of revolutionary democracy. ᶜ⌐(*Applause.*)⌐ᶜ . . . For the first time our slogan, 'power to the soviets of workers', soldiers' and peasants' deputies', is really being implemented.

7.15 p.m.

ᶜ⌐The peasant deputies enter and are greeted by an ovation.⌐ᶜ Sverdlov [reopens the joint session].

SPIRIDONOVA ᶜ⌐(*Applause*)⌐ᶜ: Comrades, you all feel as I do the great significance of the moment we are now living through.[2] A grandiose event of world-wide import is taking place. We are laying the foundations for the liberation of labour. We do so by rallying around our red banners which bear, written in blood, the great words of fraternity among peoples, among toilers. This fraternity, this liberation of the world, we . . . are carrying through not just for ourselves but for all mankind. To achieve this great task our national efforts are insufficient. We need a world-wide union of all the unhappy, suffering, and oppressed. This is what the word 'International' means: a world-wide union whose nucleus we are creating here. The Russian peasant should know that, unless he links his destinies to those of the Russian worker, of the workers and peasants of France, England, Austria, and Germany and all other countries, he will not win freedom, equality, or even that plot of land he needs so urgently to survive. He should know that on his way to land and freedom he will meet a world-wide army of capitalists and usurious landlords, hardened in cruelty and ready for a bloody struggle . . . Finance capital is the same in all countries . . .

The bourgeoisie and ruling classes have always tried to poison the consciousness of the toilers by national chauvinism . . . but the hard-bought lessons of the war have shown the labouring peoples the true way to happiness and liberty. This way we are now pointing to our brothers in western Europe.[d] Let them thirst for freedom and strive to achieve people's power as embodied in our soviets . . . Never in history has the world faced such vast perspectives or have so many millions been mobilized to attain their ideals. Western Europe knows only groups of revolutionaries, of high quality but weak in numbers, who were eventually conquered by the massed enemies of the people. The revolution will not be defeated even by famine and economic chaos. We are marching forward to a bright future, despite the bitter struggles that lie ahead . . . We shall attain our ideals not just through hatred but also through feelings of pity for all who suffer and love for all who are oppressed. For our ideals we shall give everything, our lives and even perhaps our honour. [e⌐We must cast off the last traces of slavery in our psychological outlook. We must eliminate hatred among ourselves and direct our enmity solely against our enemies. We must develop mutual respect and tolerance towards our comrades in the struggle. We must cleanse our souls as we approach the great kingdom of socialism that awaits us. We must become better, purer, more sincere, so that no one should dare say that our insurrection is bringing forth hatred and evil. Upon the ruins of the old society there is being born, hidden from our eyes, a new society of justice and love. The triumph of the International is near. Moved by justice and love, the soviets are bringing [their ideals] to all peoples of the globe. Long live the fraternal union of workers, soldiers, and peasants! (*Stormy ovation.*)⌐e]

TROTSKY, for the Petrograd soviet: In this hall, which has witnessed the work of the Petrograd soviet, I am privileged to welcome our dear guests. From the moment you entered this building you became the absolute masters of Russia's life. Nothing can stand in the way of the concentrated will of such broad masses of people, for here peasant, worker, and soldier have stretched out their hands to one another to defend the conquests of the revolution. (*Stormy applause.*) . . .

The Petrograd soviet has been accused of raising the question of power without waiting for the all-Russian congress [of soviets]. But if it had not done so Kerensky would have surrounded the congress with cadets and cossacks . . . We have overthrown Kerensky . . . and say to the Russian worker and peasant: 'Come and take the power that is yours.'

Our comrades in Petrograd and Moscow did not die in vain, for the news is going out by radio-telegraph all over the world that the German authorities have agreed to conclude an armistice on all fronts.[3] If the bloodthirsty Kaiser and his generals, whose chests are covered with decorations won for their martial deeds, have entered into talks with ensign Krylenko, this is not out of sympathy—if they had their way, they would strangle revolutionary Russia—but only because ⌐the Russian revolution has put its boot on the chests of the possessing classes all over Europe.⌐ It has shown the way out of the endless war and so forced [the Germans] to forget our military defeats, our economic disintegration, and the cursed legacy of tsarism. The Kaiser treats us as equals because he knows that if he does not do so the German workers, soldiers and peasants will rise in revolt and reply with a wave of indignation that would prove fatal to him.

The Allied diplomats have not replied to the proposal of the Russian people.[4] Let the press spread the news of what is happening here so that they may see that we are indeed speaking for the entire people. We are not asking for recognition of soviet power, for an entire people does not need to have its power recognized. The question we are putting to them is: shall millions of peasants and workers spend a fourth year in the trenches? Tomorrow there will not be a single worker or soldier on either side who will not know that on 19 November the representatives of all peoples will have the chance to conclude a general peace. If on that day talks between all the belligerents do not begin, and the armistice terms are signed by only some of them, the French and British peoples will know that the fault is not ours. In our talks with those who do respond to our outstretched hand of peace we shall discuss the terms of a general peace, and when this becomes known in a few weeks a wave of popular indignation will compel [the Allied governments] to join us. Then the world will understand that we have never betrayed the French or British peoples, but that the [real] traitors are their ruling classes, who are afraid lest their peoples compel them to render account for the millions of lives they have thrown away and the milliards they have wasted. We have published the secret treaties and in this way have helped the peoples to press for these accounts to be settled in the same way as we have settled ours with Nicholas II, Milyukov, and Kerensky.

[c]⌜This war will give birth to a new [race of] men who will not give mercy to their enemies. In this hall we take an oath to the toilers of all countries that we shall remain at our revolutionary posts until the end. If we are overcome, then it will be while fighting for our banner. Together with our peasant brothers let us repeat the oath we took on 25 October, that if need be we shall die together. But then we had only a half-chance of victory, whereas now the peasants are with us and our forces have multiplied tenfold. We are on guard in the struggle for land and liberty for the peasants, workers' control for the workers, the democratization of the army for the soldiers, and peace for all mankind. (*Ovation.*)⌝[c]

KRYLENKO: [g]⌜I greet the peasant delegates in the name of millions of soldiers who, despite frightful conditions, despite cold and mud, are continuing to do their duty in the trenches. On their behalf I voice their hopes, which we fully share . . . Our comrades in the trenches are thirsting for peace. Kerensky deceived them for months with talk about the value of their self-sacrifice, but it is we who took the first steps toward peace.⌝[g]

[c]⌜The delegation I sent was given instructions only to approach the German high command on the Eastern front with an offer to enter armistice talks.[5] An answer was received even before the twenty-four-hour term had expired. It said that the Commander-in-Chief of the Eastern front had been empowered by the Supreme Commander-in-Chief to open negotiations. In our proposal we spoke of an armistice on all fronts. We have therefore done everything to show that we are not seeking a separate armistice. But if the Allies do not reply affirmatively before 19 November, then we shall ask [ourselves]: are we to be

cannon-fodder for the Anglo-French imperialists or should we decide our own fate? Dukhonin and some of the commanders are sabotaging and concealing the peace that is being brought about. My task is now to ensure that this lair of generals is rooted out. (*Stormy applause.*) I have told them that anyone who hinders the cause of peace, whoever he may be, will be arrested. Now, fully aware of my responsibility for uttering these words, I declare that if they stand in [our] way the blood will be upon their heads. *ᵍ(Stormy applause.)ᵍ* I shall not withdraw. The cause of peace is in the people's hands. Its success depends on our readiness for battle and our revolutionary consistency. Let Dukhonin and those with him know that we shall spare no one who stands in our way. (*Stormy applause.*)⌐ᶜ

DYBENKO: ᵃ⌐In the name of the Baltic fleet I greet our peasant fathers . . . [Recalls the fleet's role in the insurrection.] Now we have to fight on another front: to defend the Finnish people from the Finnish bourgeoisie.[6] Previously we were kept short of provisions, but now, as we behold our peasant fathers, we put our trust in their support. On this solemn occasion the Baltic sailors declare that they will not set foot on dry land until the people's cause has triumphed.⌐ᵃ

ᶜ⌐KRUSHINSKY, for the Union of Railwaymen, reads a declaration demanding a united revolutionary front. In view of the merger between the workers', soldiers' and peasants' soviets, the railwaymen's union considers it possible to enter the CEC on the following platform: the government to be responsible to the soviets, workers' control, transfer of land to the peasants, a speedy peace and convocation of the Constituent Assembly on the due date.[7] At the present moment, when revolutionary democracy has united, the railwaymen will do their best to end the disruption of rail transport. As from today the entire army of railwaymen will be at the service of revolutionary democracy.⌐ᶜ

ᵃ⌐LUNACHARSKY, for the Bolsheviks: Throughout the revolution the Bolsheviks who returned from exile, hard labour, or emigration continually called for all power to pass to the soviets. We warned that the coalition ministry was but a mask for the bourgeoisie . . . and spoke of the need for workers' control of production and distribution . . .

The Russian revolution will either flow beyond Russia's borders and ignite all Europe or else it will in the last resort be throttled . . .

The movement of 25 October marks the beginning of a new social era. It was a convulsion of the Russian people . . . who are overcoming the crisis well and are entering upon a broad path leading to freedom for the toilers . . .

Our enemies said we would be alone, but the Constituent Assembly elections have shown that the Bolshevik party is the strongest one in Petrograd.[8] They called our legislative acts mere pieces of paper, but they are attracting the attention of the entire world. They said we would be isolated internationally, but in fact soviet power has been recognized by representatives of almost all neutral countries.[9] Even the German Kaiser has been compelled to accept our proposal for an armistice, not because he is fond of us but because he knows that his own people is thirsting for peace. Now we are confident that our slogans and tactics are correct . . . Long live the social revolution that began on 25 October.[7a]

PROSHYAN, for the Left SRs: [Describes the growth of the peasant movement since 1905 and criticizes the Right SRs.] There is a legend about a popular folk hero who gained strength by touching the earth, so that to overcome him his enemies had to tear him from the soil. Today the Russian revolution has touched earth and become invincible. We believe that the link between peasant and proletarian will not be a temporary one.

SAGIRASHVILI, for the United SDs: Now that the people have won this victory we insist on union among all socialist parties. We were obliged to leave the CEC because such a union did not come about, partly due to the Bolsheviks' irreconcilability. Now that union has been achieved we are returning to the CEC [r]to support its policy of peace, and we hope that the armistice will lead to the desired result. Now all those who left the Congress [of Soviets] should return [to the CEC] to accomplish the tasks facing revolutionary Russia.[7c]

PLATONOV, for the Black Sea naval congress. [Message of greetings.]

BROŃSKI,[h] for the Polish SDs: It would be an historic injustice if at this historic moment the voice of the Polish proletariat, your ally in the fight against tsarism, were not to be heard. The Polish workers are combating German imperialism across the front line, and when the armistice is signed they will be the first to stretch out their hands to you in the common struggle for peace and socialism . . .

SKRYPNIK reads a resolution adopted at the Fifth All-City [Petrograd] Conference of Factory Committees:[10]

> After discussing the present situation and the composition of the government, the conference endorses whole-heartedly the resolutions and decrees of the Second Congress of Soviets and [the Extraordinary Congress of] Peasant Deputies . . . condemns all vacillations and deviations by individual groups . . . and requests the CPC to take the most resolute measures to overcome the ruinous strike by senior officials, who have sold out to the bourgeoisie. The conference categorically repudiates any agreement with the bourgeoisie or with petty-bourgeois compromising and treacherous parties, whatever socialist labels they may disguise themselves with, and recognizes only the coalition of the toiling masses . . . in the struggle for socialism.
>
> Long live the Russian and world socialist revolution!
> Long live the revolutionary International!

IZMAYLOVSKY [Guards] regiment delegate: [Condemns the Right and Centre SRs.]

STASHKOV, of the Presidium of the Peasant Congress:[11] ᶜᵀ(*Cries of 'Long live the village'; ovation.*)I bring greetings and a bow from the peasants, who think that all power should rest with the soviets.ᵀᶜ We used to live not in the light but in some kind of coffins, as it were, like corpses. But those who fought for the people suffered more than we did. They were put in chains and rotted in prison. This is a great day. On the way from Fontanka to Smolny I didn't walk: I flew! I cannot describe my joy. ᵍᵀThe slaves have vanished;ᵀᵍ the gates of hell have been sundered by the blows of truth; ᵍᵀand the light is victorious.ᵀᵍ I congratulate you all on the resurrection to a new life in freedom. Long live the revolution! Long live land and liberty!

LOZOVSKY, for ARCCTU: When I saw on the tribune today a

grey-haired old peasant, I said to myself: how great is Russia, if the flame of enthusiasm burns not only in young hearts but in old ones as well. Now we have to create a new [system of] values . . . We have to send grain to the front. The economy is ruined; we have to get it going again by our united efforts.

Turning to the Allies' policy: I recall that Paul Lafargue said somewhere: 'The revolution will break out in France once Russia refuses to pay her debts.' The French bourgeois are afraid of losing their capital in Russia, of losing the sheep they have shorn for decades. The bourgeois are weakest in their pockets: to make them dance, one has to hit them there. We can say to them: 'If you do anything against the Russian revolution, your milliards in Russia will be finished.'

The trade unions face the colossal problem of demobilization, and a plan for this must be worked out at once.

TRIFONOV, from the Macedonian front: [Calls for the return of these troops to Russia so that they may join in the struggle.]

REINSTEIN, delegate of the American Socialist Labor Party:[12] [Emphasizes the significance of the merger.]

[Other speakers are representatives of the 1st Turkestan corps, of sick and wounded soldiers in Petrograd, and of the Red guards. Messages of greeting are read out from 73 other organizations or groups.]

SVERDLOV moves the following resolution:

> The All-Russian CEC, the Extraordinary Congress of Peasant Deputies, and the Petrograd soviet of workers' and soldiers' deputies confirm the decrees on peace, land and workers' control adopted by the CEC.
>
> ⌐The joint session expresses its complete confidence that this union of workers, soldiers, and peasants, this fraternal union of all toilers and exploited, having consolidated the state power it has seized, will for its part take all the revolutionary measures necessary to hasten the transfer of power to the toiling masses in other more advanced countries, so as to secure the victory of a just peace and socialism.
>
> Long live the revolutionary union of workers, soldiers, and peasants!⌐ⁱ

SPIRIDONOVA moves that a commission be set up to draft an

appeal to the world's peoples that they should call for an immediate peace.

Approved. Stalin, Sokolnikov, Volodarsky, Malkin, and Kamkov are appointed to the commission. The session closes with singing of the *Internationale* and *Marseillaise*.

NOTES

a *Iz.*, 16 Nov.
b *Pr.*, 17 Nov.
c *NZ*, 16 Nov.
d *ZT*, 16 Nov., renders this passage: 'Now our path is becoming straight again. Our task is to stir up (*raskachivat'*) the workers in other countries. We must strike at their hearts, setting them on fire and making them thirst for struggle against the bourgeoisie for the happiness of mankind. We have enough strength for this.'
e *ZT*, 16 Nov.
f *NZ*, 16 Nov.; *Prot.* gives a milder version.
g *ZT*, 17 Nov.
h Pseudonym of Warszawski (Warski); given correctly in *Iz.*, 17 Nov. *Prot.*: Wroński (name of a PPS activist).
i *Iz.*, 17 Nov.; text in *Prot.* corrupt.

Twelfth Session
17 November 1917

Chairman: Sverdlov   1 a.m., 18 Nov.

1. *Dissolution of Petrograd Municipal Duma*[1]

SPIRIDONOVA introduces the following emergency statement:

Since the dissolution of the Petrograd municipal Duma was not discussed in or sanctioned by the CEC, the Left SR fraction declares the CPC's decree to be an inappropriate, crude, and mistaken political measure [such as is] impermissible in future, since the CPC is responsible to the CEC. It declines to bear any responsibility for this [measure] but, considering that, whatever the line taken by the CPC, it is absolutely necessary for the country to have without delay a government ⌐responsible to the CEC⌐, the Left SR fraction considers it necessary to take part in setting up such a government responsible to the CEC and in the organs of such a government.

KRUSHINSKY: ⌐The decree on dissolution of the Duma has come as a complete surprise to us. It is a breach of the agreement previously arrived at. Any agreement involves two partners, each of whom assumes certain obligations. In this case one partner, the Bolshevik fraction, does not wish to assume any such obligations, as is evident from the manner in which this decree was issued.⌐ ⌐We were a party to the agreement because we were afraid of [a breakdown of] the transport system, yet today two railwaymen have been arrested.⌐ ⌐I consider most of these repressive acts unnecessary. They only show lack of confidence in our strength. The dissolution of the Duma has been followed by another example of tactlessness: closure of certain newspapers for printing the laughable appeal issued by ministers of the last cabinet,[2] those miserable men of the past whose action deserves only ridicule.

Vikzhel considers that the question of dissolving the Duma should be reconsidered at a plenary session of the CEC at which army representatives are also present; in the meantime the decree should not be put into effect.⁷ᶜ ᵃᵣAll extraordinary terroristic measures must be repealed and in future a state of exception of any kind must be imposed only with the consent of the CEC.⁷ᵃ ᶜᵣWe are only remaining in the CEC because we know how urgent it is to try to normalize the country's situation so far as may be possible, and because the catastrophic state of the transport system is likely to become even worse [unless the CPC changes its policy].⁷ᶜ

KRAMAROV, for the United SDs: ᵃᵣIf acts of this kind by the CPC continue, we shall be faced with a Bonapartist regime, an autocracy of the CPC. The latter is completely divorced from the CEC. It acts in an arrogant manner. Its members behave like usurpers⁷ᵃ ᶜᵣand make the central [soviet] organ a laughing-stock by presenting it daily with new *faits accomplis*.⁷ᶜ ᵃᵣIt is rumoured that the dissolution of the Duma was motivated by actions of certain of its members. Even if such actions did occur, one cannot hold the other members responsible for them, and the dissolution of the organ itself cannot thereby be justified.

I also protest against the closure of newspapers, likewise carried out behind the CEC's back. I support Krushinsky's statement. If the CPC continues to pursue a policy of 'what's good for me is good for everyone else', it is impossible to think of agreement.

This statement is greeted coolly. Sverdlov does not open a debate on the matter but proceeds to the next item of business.⁷ᵃ

2. 'Constitutional Instruction' on Relations Between the CEC and the CPC

SVERDLOV reads the following 'constitutional instruction':[3]

1. According to the resolution of the Second All-Russian Congress [of Soviets], the CPC is[d] responsible to the CEC.
2. All legislative acts, as well as ordinances of a major general political character, are submitted for examination and confirmation by the CEC.
3. Measures of struggle against counter-revolution may be carried out by the CPC directly, on condition that [the CPC is] accountable [for them] to the CEC.

4. Once a week each member of the CPC renders a report to the CEC.

5. Interpellations by the CEC must be answered immediately. Interpellations are considered valid if they are supported by 15 members of the CEC.

I propose that this be adopted without debate.

Agreed. It is then voted on by paragraphs. Paragraph 1: approved with 1 abstention. Paragraph 2: approved with 3 abstentions. Paragraph 3:

KRUSHINSKY moves an amendment:

that the introduction of a state of exception in particular localities may be introduced only on the initiative of the CEC.

SVERDLOV: This is out of order.

Amendment rejected. Paragraph 3 adopted with 1 dissentient and 14 abstentions.

The instruction as a whole is passed with 5 abstentions.

3. *Changes in the CPC*[4]

The following changes are accepted:

1. The PC of Agriculture is to be allotted to [a member of] the Left SR party.
2. The Left SRs are to introduce their representatives into all the directing boards (*kollegii*) attached to the CPC.
3. The Bolsheviks are to have their representative in the PC of Agriculture.

SVERDLOV: This does not rule out future changes in the composition of the CPC. I have indicated only those that have been agreed.

NOTES

a *NZ*, 19 Nov.
b *Pr.*, 19 Nov.
c *ZT*, 19 Nov.
d *Pr.*; *NZ*; *ZT*; *DSV*, vol. I, p. 102: 'wholly responsible'.

Thirteenth Session
21 November 1917

Chairman: Sverdlov   5.30 p.m.

1. *Dissolution of Petrograd Municipal Duma*

ᵣKRAMAROV⁻¹*ᵃ*, for the United SDs, tables the following inter-pellation:

> On 16 November the CPC issued a decree on dissolution of the Petrograd municipal Duma. This decree was issued without previous examination and confirmation by the CEC. In view of the major general political significance of this measure, we the undersigned CEC members table an interpellation on this matter to the CPC.
>
> (signed): Avilov, Stroyev, Zaks, Kramarov, Levin, Katel, Verbo, Sagirashvili, Trifonov, Zhilinsky, Kryuchkov, Bulochnikov [and four others whose signatures are illegible].

KATEL proposes that this be taken as the first item on the agenda.

ᵃᵣThe chair rejects the plea of urgency and the matter is postponed. The same action is taken in regard to an interpellation by Ryazanov about illegal actions by the MRC.⁻¹*ᵃ,ᵇ*

2. *Policy Statement by the PPS–Lewica*

ŁAPIŃSKI reads the following declaration:

> In view of the merger of the Executive Committee of the Congress of Peasant Deputies with the CEC, which has created new conditions of work within the latter for fractions which are in disagreement with this or that feature of the policy adopted by the people's commissars, the PPS has instructed me to return to the CEC in order to defend in it the principle that the government should be genuinely responsible to organized revolutionary democracy, and also to struggle for a democratic peace by methods calculated to

awaken the revolutionary energy of the European peoples
and to prevent the possible indirect strengthening of Austro-
German imperialism.

Considering that civil war within democracy inevitably
threatens to undermine the revolution, and should on no
account be motivated by a desire to achieve socialism immediately in the country's present condition, I shall in particular fight for the peaceful transfer of power to the Constituent Assembly and for restoration of the soviets as active
organization[s] of the advanced and really revolutionary
elements among the people; and I shall oppose . . . rule by
terror, which can but corrupt those who apply it, above all
the working class, and so weaken the government, which
seeks a firm foundation in the broad popular masses.

3. *Decree on Right of Recall (Re-election)*[1]

LENIN ^{c⌐}*(Applause)*^{⌐c}: The question of re-elections is one of
implementing democratic principles properly. In all advanced
countries it is customary for elected persons alone to speak the
language of state legislation. The bourgeoisie has deliberately
not allowed people the right to recall [their deputies], the right
to exercise effective control [over them]. However, the right of
recall runs like a red thread through all the revolutions of history.

Democratic government exists, and is accepted [as such]
wherever a parliamentary order obtains, but this right of representation is limited by the fact that the people can vote only
once every two years. It often happens that they elect deputies
who help to oppress them, for they have no right to prevent this
by getting rid of such deputies. However, in countries which
have maintained the old revolutionary traditions of their forma-
tive period, as in certain Swiss cantons and American states, the
democratic right of recall has remained in being. Every great
revolution clearly compels the people to go beyond simply
utilizing existing legislation ^{d⌐}and to create appropriate new
laws.^{⌐d} Therefore, on the eve of the Constituent Assembly, we
need to revise the electoral rules.

The soviets have been created by the working people themselves, by their revolutionary energy and creativity. This alone
guarantees that they work wholly to satisfy the interests of the

masses. Each peasant who sends [deputies] to a soviet may recall them. This is the real popular significance of the soviets.
Under the previous system the dominant position was held by
various parties. The last shift of influence from one party to
another was accompanied by a revolution, and a fairly turbulent one at that. If the democratic right of recall had been in
effect, it would have been enough to exercise that right [for the
change to occur peacefully].

We talk about liberty. The pseudo-freedom that existed before was freedom for the bourgeoisie to dupe [the electorate]
with the aid of its moneybags, freedom for it to exercise its
strength with the aid of this deceit. We have finally broken with
the bourgeoisie and with this kind of freedom. The state is a
repressive institution. Previously the entire people was oppressed by a handful of individuals with fat purses; we, however, want to turn the state into an institution for enforcing the
people's will. We want to organize violence in the interests of
the toilers.

Not to apply the right of recall to the Constituent Assembly
would be to fail to exercise the people's revolutionary will and
to usurp the Constituent Assembly's rights. We have a proportional system of representation, which is indeed extremely
democratic. To introduce the right of recall into such a system
is a bit difficult, but these difficulties are purely technical and
can be quite easily overcome. In any case there is no contradiction at all between proportional [representation] and the right
of recall.

The people vote not for individuals but for a party. There is
a great deal of party feeling in Russia, and [each] party has a
certain political image in the voters' eyes. For this reason every
schism within a party must lead to chaos unless the right of
recall is provided for. The Socialist-Revolutionary party enjoys
great influence. But after the electoral lists were compiled it
underwent a schism. It is not possible to change the lists; nor
can one postpone [convocation of] the Constituent Assembly.
Thus in fact the people have voted for a party which no longer
exists. This is evident from the left-wing stance taken by the
Second [(Extraordinary)] Congress of Peasant Deputies. The
peasants were deceived, not by individuals but by the party
schism. This state of affairs needs rectification. We have to

implement democratic principles directly and at once. This means introducing the right of recall.

There is reason to fear that we shall be faced with election [results] that are false [to the voters' true sentiments]. But there is no need to be afraid of the results if the right of re-election is introduced, for the masses have shown a high degree of consciousness, as is evident if one compares the revolution of 1905 with that of 1917.

The people have been told that the soviets are plenipotentiary organs. They have believed this and have put these powers into effect. We have to go further in the direction of democratization by introducing the right of recall. The right of recall should be given to the soviets, for they are the most perfect exemplars of the idea of the state, of compulsion. In this way power can pass from one party to another bloodlessly, by means of re-elections.

KARELIN: Lenin's [measure] corresponds to the socialist minimum programme. I endorse it whole-heartedly, speaking for myself as well as for the Left SR fraction. It is natural and inevitable. However, it is a long way from the enunciation of a principle to its implementation in practice. *⌐The draft is more of a newspaper article than a legislative enactment.⌐* One should not sweep aside formal [rights] which often play a big part, and an honourable one too. We should approach the question of the Constituent Assembly cautiously, in order not to disturb the normal course of its labours, all the more so since the masses place such trust in it. With our system of proportional representation it would be extremely difficult to introduce the right of recall. Two amendments would be necessary: the first to institute a second round of elections, when certain representatives who had been elected in the first ballot would be eliminated; and the second to institute a referendum on each occasion, in which the whole population would be entitled to take part, since it is the entire electorate which enjoys voting rights.

⌐AVILOV: I consider the decree impermissible on grounds of principle and inexpedient politically, for it seeks to undermine in advance the authority of the Constituent Assembly, to which all power in the country should belong.⌐

ŁAPIŃSKI: If the right of recall is applied to the soviets, in view of the passivity displayed by much of the electorate only a certain group would take part in the re-elections, which would thus not reflect the views of the electorate as a whole. I agree with Karelin's proposed amendment.

RYAZANOV: I do not believe that the Constituent Assembly can be democratic, since the election campaign was carried out under the aegis of the former ruling parties and the constituency boundaries were fixed by the Kadets. The right of recall is a welcome, if inadequate, measure which will make good some of these mistakes and injustices. If we had it already, the municipal Duma, a centre of counter-revolution, would simply have dissolved itself.[e]

KRAMAROV: Lenin's plan is a military ruse. It skirts the real question, which is whether sovereignty over Russia is to be exercised by Lenin and his comrades or by [the Constituent Assembly]. It is an attack upon the latter. It is designed to stir up people to use their right of re-election in such a way as to strengthen the Bolsheviks.

TROTSKY: The objections that have been raised to the draft decree are not based upon principle but have an opportunist character. Kramarov calls it a military ruse, but if it leads to greater democracy, if it places the Constituent Assembly in direct, permanent touch with the people, then the more such ruses we have the better. The way he puts the matter, it would appear that the more democratic [the electoral system] is, the more sympathy there will be for the Bolsheviks.

The Constituent Assembly should be convoked in such a manner that the people should not be obliged[f] to end its existence by an act of surgery, by dissolving it. If the Kadets were to have a majority—which is unlikely: I am using this just as an example—then of course the Constituent Assembly would not be given power. The right of recall gets round this problem in a painless manner.

We want to give the people the opportunity to cast their votes in accordance with the law. [But we know that] in a revolutionary era the people are learning every day, and often they hate what [they wanted] the day before. Therefore the people must be given the power to control their representatives by exercising the right of recall.

Karelin's amendment [designed to ensure] uninterrupted

continuity [of representation] is perfectly acceptable to us. But his amendment on introducing the right of recall by means of a referendum puts the matter in the wrong way. [There is no need for such a referendum because] the soviets have already organized one-third of the population—that is the first point; and secondly because a decision by a soviet [can be overturned] if re-elections are held.

AVANESOV reads the draft decree. Amendments are proposed. The principle of the right of recall is adopted with 2 dissentients and 1 abstention.*g* By 67 votes to 59 it is decided to pass the [draft] decree to a commission, along with the amendments, as material [for a compromise text]. The following are elected to the commission: Sverdlov, Steklov, Avanesov, Chudnovsky, Karelin, Kamkov, and Malkin.

4. *Reform of the Law Courts*[2]

STUCHKA reads the draft decree.

It is proposed, and agreed, that this be passed to the same commission and that a recess of two hours be called, after which the final text of both decrees be approved.

Session resumed.   2 a.m., 22 Nov.

The decree on the right of recall is adopted unanimously, but [confirmation of] the decree on reform of the courts is postponed to the next session owing to the lateness of the hour.

NOTES

a *ZT*, 22 Nov.
b *Pr.*, 22 Nov., and *Iz.*, 23 Nov., report at this point, in lieu of the above, a protest by Katz (United SD) against an account in *Iz.* of his party's tactics in the CEC. The text of this interpellation is given separately in *Prot.* (p. 77).
c *Iz.*, 23 Nov.
d *Pr.*, 22 Nov.; followed in Lenin, *PSS*, xxxv. 110.
e According to a report in *Noch'* (the short-lived successor to the moderate socialist *Den'*), cited in *Bulletin de la Presse*, p. 2090 (22 Nov.), Ryazanov went on to protest against infringements of press freedom.
f literally: 'should be unable to'.
g *Pr.*, 24 Nov.: unanimously but for 2 dissentients.

Fourteenth Session
24 November 1917

Chairman: Sverdlov   9 p.m.

1. Procedural Matters

Kalegayev's appointment as PC of Agriculture is unanimously confirmed.

ᵃᴦᴀᴠɪʟᴏᴠ: I wish to register a protest against the practice of complementing the CPC by [nomination of] representatives of [the two major] fractions, instead of reconstructing it on the principle of proportional representation of all groups taking part in the work of the CEC.⁷ᵃ

The composition of the Credentials commission is confirmed as follows: Strunin, Selivanov, Medvedev, Pluzhnikov, Gusev; candidate member: Smirnov.

Lists of deputies replacing absent colleagues in each fraction are read out and approved.

2. Brest-Litovsk Armistice Negotiations[1]

SVERDLOV: The chair proposes that the report be heard jointly with the Petrograd soviet in the Hall of Fame.

Rejected by 78 votes to 68.

IOFFE delivers a brief report.ᵇ

Delegates from the Petrograd soviet arrive and ask that the report be heard at a joint session. This is agreed to, and the CEC moves to the Hall of Fame.

KAMENEV: ... Our delegation went [to Brest-Litovsk] to ascertain the terms on which an armistice could be brought about on all fronts and a peace congress of all belligerent countries held. Unfortunately from the first papers we set eyes on after our return I see that the campaign of slander and rumour launched

against us is still going on. We promised to inform you of everything and are publishing the minutes of the proceedings as well
as the radio-telegraph tapes, so that you can judge for yourselves each step we take. Tomorrow two general staff officers
will bring the minutes here and I swear that they will confirm
everything I tell you here today.

The composition of our delegation broke with all old-fashioned notions as to how international negotiations should be
conducted. We sent to the talks not diplomats but five representatives of political parties and four representatives of the
classes in power: a peasant, a worker, a sailor, and a soldier.
The delegation was complemented by a commission of experts
from the military and naval general staff. Such a delegation
could be dispatched only by a revolutionary country which has
nothing to hide and knows that peace can be brought about
only by the efforts of the peoples themselves. The composition
of the German delegation was quite different. Its powers were
attested by Hindenburg and Holtzendorff; the authority to
conduct the talks was given to [Prince] Leopold of Bavaria,
Commander-in-Chief of the armies on the Eastern front; in fact
the negotiations were carried on by his chief of staff, Major-
General Hoffmann. The Austro-Hungarian, Bulgarian, and
Turkish armies were also represented.

The powers given to the delegations were as different as their
composition. The Russian government regards the armistice as
the first step to peace. We can only accept an armistice that is
the prelude to a general peace which will render impossible any
resumption of hostilities. We considered ourselves bound to discuss not just the technical military arrangements but also the
political platform of the forthcoming peace. The opposing delegation's powers extended solely to military questions. This
difference accounts for the arguments that took place.

We had three sessions. At the first [on 20 November] the
Russian delegation stated that it had come to place on a proper
footing the forthcoming negotiations for a general peace without
annexations or contributions, on the basis of national self-
determination. We had come to negotiate such a peace and no
other; and for this purpose we were willing to discuss the terms
of a general armistice on all fronts, both Russian and Allied.
The German delegates replied that as military men they were

not empowered to negotiate political questions, but said they
were confident that the statements by Kühlmann and Czernin,
the German and Austrian ministers of Foreign Affairs, were
sufficient proof that their governments were willing to negotiate
on the platform of the Russian government.[2] They could give
no further reply to our statements.

We answered that Kühlmann's and Czernin's speeches did
not state that their *governments* accepted the Russian people's
peace formula, but that we were certain this would be accepted
by the *peoples* of the belligerent countries. We went on to state
that . . . we were prepared to proceed to the next question, and
proposed that they, following our example, approach all the
powers not represented at the talks and invite them to join in.
They reiterated that this was a political question outside their
competence.

At this we called for a recess. When the talks were resumed
[on 21 November] we stated that, although the German delegates were not empowered to issue such an appeal, they were
nevertheless obliged to transmit it to their governments, and
that only pending their reply were we willing to proceed to
discussion of the next point, the terms of the armistice. (*Reads
text of this declaration.*)

The object of our statement was to show people in the Allied
countries and in Germany that we had come to Brest not to
compromise with German generals but to appeal over their
heads to German workers, so that they might add their voice to
ours in the struggle for a general peace . . .

When we were asked what our armistice terms were, we
stated them. It has been falsely reported in the press that Germany was the first to set forth her armistice terms, and that
these were based upon her estimate of the military capacity of
each side . . . Our terms were:

1. Russia wants the armistice to last long enough for the
peace congress of all peoples to assemble.
2. The armistice should not be utilized by Germany to move
troops from one front to another.
3. Germany should evacuate the Moon Sound islands, which
are not to be occupied by Russian forces during the armistice.

The second point is clear and comprehensible: we are concluding an armistice and fighting for peace without betraying the workers and peasants in uniform of any country, and we therefore seek guarantees that the armistice will not be exploited to the disadvantage of the Allied peoples. The third point, about Dago and Oesel, has puzzled some bourgeois journalists, who cannot comprehend the grandeur of the gesture being made by the Russian people in concluding peace. On one hand they slanderously assert that we went 'to beg peace from the Germans' and on the other hand claim that our terms are too stiff for them to accept. This is contradictory and mendacious... Our revolutionary honour led us to put forward the demand for non-transfer of troops; the interests of the revolution led us to demand evacuation of the Moon Sound islands, [occupation of] which threaten[s] Petrograd, centre of the Russian and world revolution. This danger was pointed out to us by our commission of military experts.

When these points were set forth, the German representative stood up and declared that such terms could only be presented to a defeated country ... But General Hoffmann did not take account of the fact that although Russia may be militarily weakened she is capable of unleashing enough revolutionary energy to threaten German imperialism from within as well as from without. These terms will be interpreted by all peoples as [essential to] peace, and therefore they are immutable. Hoffmann does not see that our strength lies not in bayonets but in the revolutionary enthusiasm of those who see us as fighters for peace among all nations.

Yet after making this statement he proposed that each of our conditions be examined in turn; he criticized them in general terms and set forth Germany's own conditions, which we then asked to have in writing. We decided that the moment had come for us to [return to Petrograd and] ask the Russian people for further instructions. The point of the matter is that in reply to our demand for a general armistice Germany has proposed a separate one from the Black Sea to the Baltic ... (*Reads statement requesting a recess.*) Our demand for a recess [on 22 November] came as a surprise to the Germans, who expressed regret (quite sincere, I believe) at our departure. They agreed to postpone the negotiations for one week.

The fact that we have proposed a general and not a separate

armistice cannot but assume great significance in the eyes of the belligerent peoples. During the week that lies ahead the governments, parliaments, press, and parties of these countries should state whether they wish to take part in these talks, in which revolutionary Russia is defending not its egoistic interests but principles dear to all democracies . . .

The Central Powers' delegates tried to propose[c] a separate armistice in another form. They stated that they could but bow to the wishes of the Russian delegation and suggested concluding an armistice for one week. We answered that we were not empowered to conclude one that was not general. We said we could only sign an agreement on the cessation of military activity which would just formalize the existing situation on the Eastern front. This we have done. The agreement has been published. It contains a ban on movement of units of divisional strength and upwards [unless] such dispositions were made prior to 22 November. The conference broke off on [the understanding] that it would resume to discuss a longer armistice to allow for convocation of the peace congress.

After the talks had been suspended the German delegation proposed that we hold a session of a semi-official character, in which minutes would be taken but anything said would not bind either party; in this session they invited us to express our views about the German proposals. We did not reject this invitation but warned that whatever we said would be published. Our object in attending this session was to ensure that the German people knew of our criticisms of the German peace [sic] terms.

I shall deal here only with those points that have political significance, leaving the senior military expert[3] to comment on the others.

The first point is about not transferring troops to other fronts. We insist that the [enemy] forces on the Russian front not be diminished. Not a single soldier or gun should be transferred to another front. The Germans said: 'We guarantee that the forces on the Russian front shall not be increased.' But this was not enough for us. Finally the Germans agreed not to transfer troops. I repeat: they are not bound by this promise, but their attitude shows how far they are willing to go, not because the generals want to [please us] but for other reasons.

The second point deals with fraternization between soldiers

on either side of the front. In putting forward this point we knew it would be unacceptable to the German generals. Its purpose is to create such amity between their soldiers and ours that, should the generals seek to continue the war after the armistice, the soldiers would resist this. In the end they conceded that such a point should figure in the agreement on a long-term armistice.

Finally we stated that revolutionary propaganda should be admitted into Germany and other belligerent states. The German delegates said they could not discuss this, but that they thought their government would willingly permit such literature to be dispatched to England, Italy, and France, but that it would firmly oppose its distribution within Germany . . .

We left [Brest-Litovsk] with an armistice proposal which could be the beginning of the peace that revolutionary Russia has proposed. ᵈ⌐We do not nurture the hope that the German generals will sign this armistice.⌐ᵈ My impression is that Germany is willing to make very great concessions to get a separate peace; but that is not what we have been negotiating for . . . We consider that the Russian revolution has brought a glimmer of light in the darkness, for the German people know that our representatives proposed not some secret treaty but peace without annexations or indemnities on the basis of self-determination. And these terms are now being discussed all over the world by every soldier and every worker . . . When they know of our terms they will say that our demands are also theirs . . . From the minutes of our negotiations they will be able to judge who is right: those who have proposed a general peace or those governments that are trying to hinder one. (*Applause.*)

ᵃ⌐ALTFATER describes details of the German draft and the amendments made to it by [the Russian] delegation.⌐ᵃ

The CEC returns to its hall.

LARIN proposes that the debate [on this matter] be postponed until the next session, and that the CEC now turn to other important business.

Agreed.

3. *Ukrainian Trophies*[4]

LUNACHARSKY makes an unscheduled statement:

The staff of the Ukrainian military council has approached the PC for Nationality Affairs, Stalin, with a request that it be given certain museum relics. These objects are of little value from an artistic point of view. They are simply testimony to the fact that when the Russian people took possession of the Ukraine they also took some trophies. Now that the principle of national self-determination has been proclaimed, such trophies from the distant past serve to symbolize the oppression of one nation by another and besmirch Russia's freedom. They consist of cannon, ceremonial staffs (*bulavy*) and banners. I propose that these trophies be given to the Ukrainians and that a ceremony be arranged [to honour] this practical [sign of] fraternity between peoples.

UKRAINIAN MILITARY COUNCIL representative: The Ukraine was a free republic at a time when many peoples did not even dream of such a form of government. We Ukrainians do not need these cannon [for making war, but as a symbol of independence].

LUNACHARSKY moves a resolution in this sense.

Adopted without debate, with 3 dissentients and 10 abstentions.

4. *Dissolution of Petrograd Municipal Duma*[5]

KARELIN: The Left SRs consider that the CPC's decree dissolving the Duma clearly contravenes the constitution adopted by the CEC, which regulates the relationship between it and the CPC . . . We do not contest the decision in principle, for we take the view that the Duma has become divorced from the mass of voters and therefore should be re-elected. We therefore propose a resolution of which the first part repeals the decree as an illegal act and the second part indicates that the CEC thinks the Duma should be dissolved and appoints elections within the shortest possible time, not later than 27–28 November. A favourable atmosphere should be created for the electoral campaign, with full freedom of agitation, both written and oral. (*Reads the resolution.*)

AVILOV, for the United SDs: We agree with the first part of the resolution. But if the CPC has broken the constitution, how can the Left SRs declare their full solidarity with the CPC in its dissolution of the Duma? This act, coming as it does a few days before the opening of the Constituent Assembly, is senseless and politically inexpedient. One cannot agree with the proposition that the Duma should be re-elected just because its composition does not accord with the transient mood of the masses: in that case, what would the ruling parties do if a majority of voters were to support the Kadets? The Constituent Assembly election results in Petrograd have shown that the voters are fed up with the Right SRs, Mensheviks, and Kadets; but if they were later to move to the right, the Bolsheviks would have to declare that these election results [also] no longer correspond to the voters' present mood. In political life one cannot be guided by the electorate's transient moods. Besides this, the way in which the dissolution was carried through, by Red guards, is impermissible.

KRAMAROV: I shall only be convinced that the Duma is counter-revolutionary if this is proven by documentary evidence.

STEKLOV: There are two aspects to this question, one formal and the other substantial. As regards the first, the decree dissolving the Duma was issued before the CEC adopted its constitution, and therefore cannot have breached it.[6] At the present critical moment, when our enemies are trying to weaken soviet power and to split the Bolsheviks from the Left SRs, Karelin should not provoke a crisis of authority over such a minor issue.

As regards the substance of the question, the counter-revolutionary nature of the municipal Duma needs no documentary proof. It is clearly hostile to soviet power. [Mayor G. I.] Shreyder himself said, when interrogated, that he represented the Duma in the notorious Committee for the Salvation of the [Country and the Revolution, which one might better call a committee for salvation of the] counter-revolution and for strangling the country. I am surprised that CEC members should differ over the question of sovereignty of the soviets at a time when this is under attack and when appeals are being made to disobey soviet power.

... CEC members should control the CPC's actions and ask for explanations of its conduct when this is called for. We are

not among those who will support the existing government unconditionally in everything it does. But this action gives no
ground for criticism.

When the Duma was elected the question of recognizing or
not recognizing soviet power had not arisen. Now it has been
placed on the agenda by the Duma itself. Let the electors themselves give their answer. Those who argue that the dissolution
of the Duma is a clear breach of democratic principles have forgotten, if they ever knew it, the basic principle of a democratic
election. It is obvious that if an elected body differs from its
electors and opposes them, the representatives themselves, if
they are honest, ought to wonder whether they should continue
in office or should rather submit to another popular vote. The
municipal Duma did not follow this course but instead engaged
in politics. We condemn it not for that but for opposing the will
of the majority of the population. The Duma was undoubtedly
a party to the cadets' rising, to Kerensky's campaign, and to the
sabotage carried on by civil servants; only a blind man could
insist on documentary proof of this criminal and counter-revolutionary activity.

It is said that dissolution of the Duma will have catastrophic
effects upon the supply situation by creating confusion among
different agencies active in this domain. But we have asked
[members of] the municipal administration and the supply
board to remain at their posts. If there is any trouble here the
fault will lie not with the CPC but with those who are ready to
sacrifice the people's interests to help their saboteur friends.

KARELIN: In principle I agree that the Duma was mistaken to
involve itself in counter-revolutionary politics, but I stand by
the first part of my resolution.

STEKLOV clarifies a phrase in his speech and presents the following resolution:

Taking into account that:
1) after the October insurrection the municipal Duma came
out against the clearly expressed will of the majority of revolutionary democracy in general and of the majority of the
population ⌐of Petrograd⌐ in particular;
2) that when the Duma was elected . . . the question of recog-

nition or non-recognition of soviet power had not been posed, but that the Duma itself ^{e}⌐by its policy⌐^{e} has now posed it;

3) that the Constituent Assembly election results have shown that its composition is totally out of line with the mood of the people;

4) that the decree dissolving the Duma was passed before the CEC adopted the constitution;

the CEC confirms the CPC's decree and ordains that new elections be held on 27 and 28 November.

Karelin's resolution is put to the vote and receives 85 votes; Steklov's receives 84.^{f}

KHARITONOV proposes a roll-call vote, which is then taken. In the roll-call vote 88 votes are cast for Steklov's resolution and 85 for Karelin's. The former is taken as the basic text.

FLEROVSKY moves an amendment: to strike out clause 2.

Rejected.

AN UNIDENTIFIED member moves an amendment: to declare the CPC's decree revoked.

This receives 84 votes;^{g} Steklov's resolution receives 85 votes.

KHARITONOV proposes a [stylistic] amendment to clause 2.

STEKLOV raises no objection.

Agreed.

KRAMAROV proposes that a point be included in the decree dissolving all city-ward Dumas. On the demand of CEC members this proposal is entered in the minutes.

Steklov's resolution is voted on as a whole and approved.

NOTES

a $\mathcal{Z}T$, 25 Nov.
b This factual but colourless report anticipated the principal one given by Kamenev. It was ignored by all newspapers except $\mathcal{Z}T$, 25 Nov., and has been omitted here.
c *Iz.*, 26 Nov.; *Prot.*: *prolozhit'* for *predlozhit'*.
d *Iz.*, 26 Nov.; *Pr.*, 26 Nov.; evidently suppressed from *Prot.*

e Iz., 26 Nov.

f The ensuing recess is reported in *Delo naroda*, 26 Nov., which adds that it was called at the behest of the Bolsheviks; both they and the Left SRs used the opportunity to mobilize their supporters.

g Prot.: 'a majority of 84'. By 'Steklov's resolution' is presumably meant: 'against the amendment'.

Fifteenth Session
25 November 1917

Chairman: Avanesov   9.30 p.m.

AVANESOV presents the agenda.

KARELIN proposes that first place be given to the arrest of members of the Constituent Assembly Election Commission.[1]

AVANESOV and LARIN oppose this. The Presidium's agenda is endorsed by 92 votes to 76.

1. *Armistice Negotiations*

ŁAPIŃSKI, for the PPS: *⌐*I should like to point out a number of mistakes made by the Russian delegation to the armistice talks. It was a serious error not to insist on an exchange of prisoners of war.[2] Our soldiers in enemy hands have to exist in frightful conditions. It is imperative to demand the speedy return of all of them, and not just of a number equivalent to that of German prisoners in Russia.

The demand for non-transfer of enemy forces to other fronts is badly formulated. The German transport system is in perfect condition and enables the German [high command] to send wherever they want the enormous reserves which they have in the immediate rear as well as in the interior of the country. Therefore we should demand that no transfers whatever of troops or artillery be made during the armistice period.

The delegates had no right to accept such a short term for the armistice as twenty-eight days, for already [in the peace resolution adopted] at the Second Congress of Soviets the limit was put at three months. The congress proceeded from the consideration that it was vital to give the working class in the belligerent countries the chance to develop an intensive struggle for peace, and this can be done only if the breathing-space at the front is fairly lengthy. After all, a separate armistice and a separate peace are regarded by all of us as extreme measures, and we are obliged to do all we can to give the [western European] proletariat time to organize. The Germans want a short armistice period and a separate peace with Russia as soon as possible, so that they can throw twice as many troops against the Allies.[3] Our delegates failed to insist on a longer period. It is true that each side may ask for an extension, but at any moment Germany may refuse such an extension and resume military action. She wants a short term so as to keep us in a state of continual terror.

Our semi-official spokesmen are deceiving themselves in claiming that Germany's consent to an armistice is the result *inter alia* of popular pressure within the country. This is not true. It is precisely the German *imperialists* who want a separate peace with Russia. They know that later they will not be able to satisfy their appetites and are therefore trying to seize as much as they can [now]. For more than six months the Germans have been talking of their readiness to recognize the right of national self-determination, but by this they mean only self-determination for the nationalities subject to Russia. It is therefore monstrous naïvety on the part of Bolshevik semi-official spokesmen to claim that the German imperialists have renounced annexations. Our interest is that German imperialism should not emerge as the victor, for this would mean the collapse of all hopes for revolution in Europe. We should not console ourselves with illusions. Our delegation seems to have behaved in front of the German generals much as it is wont to behave in Smolny: making speeches and taking minutes. It forgot that these speeches and minutes are not reaching the German proletariat, or that they will reach it only in a year's time, when German scholars will be teaching their students the history of the present war.

I call upon our delegation to behave with more dignity. Never will the revolutionary Russian people support German imperialism. On no account will we betray the European proletariat. If we stop talking like people who are mortally scared and ready to accept with trembling hands whatever the Hofmeisters give us, and instead behave like representatives of a great revolutionary country, then the Germans will be obliged to take account of our demands. When they seek to turn the

Russian revolution to their own advantage, we should let loose our cannon. To do this it is necessary to preserve at least a small well-disciplined army which could remain in the trenches and back up our demands. Two to three million able-bodied soldiers should be kept back when the army is demobilized and be entrusted with the defence of revolutionary Russia.

In future the delegation should receive its mandate not from the CPC but from the CEC.

LINDOV, for the United SDs: The talks have begun; the way is open to peace—but are these negotiations being conducted in the spirit that animates [true] internationalists, left-wing Zimmerwaldians who refused to go to Stockholm to talk to Scheidemann? Alas, these representatives of the revolutionary workers, peasants, and soldiers have begun to talk not to the German proletariat but to the German generals. When the latter said they had no power to negotiate a general peace, what did our delegates do? Walk out, break off the talks and appeal to the revolutionary proletariat? No: they stayed on and discussed technical military details. But during the course of these talks they remembered they were revolutionaries and made the ridiculous suggestion that the German generals should allow our revolutionary brochures to be distributed. One might as well have asked Nicholas II's gendarmes to distribute our proclamations. The German generals replied that they were willing to distribute our literature, but on the French and British fronts.

We began the talks to compel the belligerents to make peace. But what will the German Social Democrats think when they hear that extreme left-wing Russian revolution[aries] are talking not to [Friedrich] Adler but to their worst enemies, the German generals?

I blame the Bolsheviks for not having waited for convocation of the Constituent Assembly, which alonè is empowered to undertake a liquidation of the war. (*Ironic catcalls.*)[1a]

MSTISLAVSKY, a member of the [armistice] delegation, for the Left SRs: It would be important for us in the future to have the views of CEC members. I do not deny that there were minor defects and instances of brusqueness in the delegation's work. We must do everything to eliminate them, as we have a serious and responsible task to fulfil. I am sorry that what we have heard today has not been well-founded criticism but mere quibbling. It is said that we talked to the German generals, but we did so only about technical questions; there was no social contact, as the published record makes clear: to maintain the contrary is to spread a deliberate untruth. The CEC should set up a commission to draft a mandate to guide us in our work; this should be presented for confirmation to [a plenary assembly of] the CEC.

SOKOLNIKOV: The delegation could not have raised the question of an exchange of prisoners, for this would clearly be to Germany's advantage. As far as the non-transfer of troops to other fronts is concerned, we got our way. The German workers and soldiers will be kept informed of all details of the course of the peace talks. The German government will be unable to keep the proceedings secret from the people.

YEZHOV, a soldier (United SD), speaks mainly about reorganization of the army and a partial demobilization designed to strengthen its military might.

CHUDNOVSKY: Such questions should not be discussed in the CEC but in some smaller and less public body consisting of persons competent in such matters.

NIKITIN, for the Left SRs: [speech not recorded.]

SELIVANOV, for the SR Maximalists: Neither the coalition government, nor, probably, the Constituent Assembly could give the peace question the priority it deserves.

DYBENKO: [reviews the Provisional Government's record on the question of peace.]

BARANOV, chairman of the First All-Russian Naval Congress: (reads a resolution passed at this congress.) The mutiny in the German navy belies Lindov's claim that the German people are doing nothing to bring about peace. The navy trusts the [armistice] delegation even though it has no mandate from the CEC. We shall not trust the future Kadet[-inspired] Constituent Assembly in this matter. It is said that we need a strong armed force: we do have one, in the navy, which is ready to combat the [German] imperialists as well as our own counter-revolutionaries. The whole fleet will rise up as one man and die for the cause of socialism.

KAMENEV: We are accused of not having included an exchange of prisoners in the armistice terms. We did think of doing so, but [as yet] we are only negotiating an armistice and have no guarantee that the present German government might not use these millions of able-bodied ex-prisoners of war once again in a military capacity. ᵇˡThis would be madness on our part at a time when the Allies are not represented at the talks and would give the Germans a very strong advantage over them.˥ᵇ If Liebknecht were in power in Germany, we would release them.

Łapiński was wrong in asserting that we have allegedly agreed that the Germans may transfer some troops to other fronts. The German delegation resisted this point at first but then conceded it. If anyone is bothered by the fact that only formations of divisional strength or larger are mentioned, we have the assurance of our military experts that the Germans always move their forces in units of that size. Of course, such an obligation is inadequate and needs to be controlled.

Łapiński also criticized the term of the armistice, which we proposed should last for six months but which we finally agreed to fix at twenty-eight days. This is long enough to call a congress of all peoples to make peace. To prolong it would be to give the imperialist [Allied] governments the chance to drag out [their reply] and so would mean keeping the troops in the trenches for several more months. In twenty-eight days the diplomats will not have enough time to knit their intrigues, but this is quite long enough to call a peace congress. The three months which were specified in the peace decree will have elapsed by the end of the term we have agreed to, since the talks are due to resume on 2 December. Moreover, the twenty-eight-day armistice can be automatically prolonged unless either side objects.

The Turkish representatives wanted us to agree to withdraw Russian and Turkish forces from Persia.⁴ We replied that it was impermissible for the government of the Russian republic to maintain troops in a neutral country such as Persia, but that we would negotiate their withdrawal not with Turkey but with the government of a free Persia. We shall negotiate about neutral countries not with the belligerent powers but with the neutrals themselves: such an attitude has never before been adopted in such negotiations.

In regard to Łapiński's remarks about Kurland, the German Kaiser was being hypocritical when he spoke of liberating [Kurland,] Lithuania, and Poland from tsarism. But now that the Russian republic has granted the Ukraine and Finland the complete right to separate,[5] who will believe the German generals when they claim that they are defending the peoples [of the occupied territories] from revolutionary Russia? This advantage has been knocked from their hands. Poland, Lithuania, and Kurland can state that they don't need German bayonets to help them separate [from Russia].

Lindov's speech was insincere. If his party were in power, it would have acted in the same way. He criticizes us but does not offer any alternative road to peace. He refers to the Constituent Assembly, but if that body knows no more what to do than Lindov does it won't give us peace either.

He ridiculed us for demanding that our revolutionary literature be distributed in Germany. Yet it *is* being distributed: we have just heard from the representative whom we left behind in Brest that German soldiers there are reading the appeal signed by members of our government. In this appeal the people's commissars state that if the German soldiers go to the aid of revolutionaries in their rear the Russian soldiers will not attack. This appeal is being distributed in millions of copies. The Germans have sent a semi-official protest against it, arguing that it represented interference in their country's internal affairs, warning us what might happen if our hopes for revolution do not materialize, and stating that it threatened the peace talks. In reply I affirm that revolutionary Russia has assumed no obligations other than those in the armistice agreement, i.e. not to shoot at German soldiers; we have done this precisely in order to interfere in Germany's internal affairs,[6] to arouse among German soldiers that urge for peace which German generals regard with horror as revolutionary. Now that they have begun to negotiate with the Bolshevik party [*sic*], they cannot hope to be insured against [the effect of] the millions of revolutionary leaflets with which our pockets are stuffed, and will be compelled to continue the peace talks none the less.

ᶜᵋNor is it true that the delegation was too loquacious. Our longest intervention lasted no more than three minutes . . .

Karakhan's telegram shows that the course of the talks will

not be hidden from the German working people. This telegram ought to put a stop once and for all to unjustified reproaches that we are negotiating with imperialists, for now everyone can see that the German people will send to the peace congress not generals or admirals but their real representatives: workers, soldiers, and peasants.[7c]

ŁAPIŃSKI, making a personal statement:[d] As one of the founders of Polish social democracy and of the Zimmerwald conference, I do not deserve to be charged with undermining the Russian revolution. I advise the assembly to hear out quietly those who do not agree with the majority and not to hurl such accusations at them.

A BOLSHEVIK deputy tables the text of an appeal to the peoples of the world [to press their governments to join in the peace talks and to send their own delegates].

The appeal is adopted with 2 dissentients and 2 abstentions, and is passed to a commission for final editing.

The Presidium is charged with drawing up a mandate for the [armistice and] peace delegation, to be submitted to the CEC for confirmation.

2. *Supreme Economic Council*[7]

BUKHARIN reads the [draft] statute of the Supreme Economic Council.

KATEL protests against adoption of this statute and insists on a coalition with groups engaged in trade and industry, since otherwise the country is doomed to suffer economic catastrophe.

SKRYPNIK replies to Katel and urges that the statute be confirmed.

SHREYDER points out that at the [Extraordinary] Congress of Peasant [Deputies] it was decided to participate in the SEC on [parity?][e] principles, and proposes that the statute be referred to a commission. This should not delay matters for more than a day.

Agreed by 76 votes to 51. It is decided to hold a special session on 27 November at 4 p.m. to discuss this question and none other. Subsequently this is amended to allow other matters on the agenda to be discussed.

KARELIN, for the Left SRs: I propose that at the present session the question of arrests and press [censorship] be discussed.

AVANESOV: Although Karelin has no right to make such a statement, the Bolshevik fraction bureau requests a recess of half an hour to discuss the situation.

After 15 minutes AVANESOV makes the following statement:

> Since the meeting has decided to close and to hold the next session on 27 November . . . and to discuss all matters on the agenda then; [and] since Łapiński has been given the floor for a personal statement, which is invariably done only at the end of a session;
>
> the Bolshevik fraction considers that Karelin's proposal is out of order and that the session should close; but in order not to give the impression that we are sabotaging [discussion of] the question of the press and of arrests we consider it possible to stay simply to hear the interpellation on this question and to place the matter on the agenda for the next session.

The Left SR interpellation is read and the session closed.

NOTES

a *NZ*, 30 Nov.
b *Iz.*, 28 Nov.; evidently suppressed from *Prot.* on political grounds.
c *Iz.*, 28 Nov.
d According to *Iz.*, 29 Nov., this statement was made later in the session.
e Word missing in *Prot.*

Sixteenth Session
27 November 1917

Chairman: Sverdlov   7.25 p.m.

SVERDLOV announces the agenda. Item 1: mandate to the [armistice and] peace delegation. Item 2: decree on the Supreme Economic Council.

AVILOV: I propose that the question of the arrest of *ᵃ˹*Groman and*˥ᵃ* the Supply Commission be included.

LOZOVSKY: I propose inclusion of the question of the demonstration [planned for] 28 November.[1]

SPIRO: Let us cease this discussion and proceed to a vote.

The agenda proposed by the Presidium is confirmed.

HÖGLUND, greeting the CEC in the name of the Swedish Radical party: All eyes of the revolutionary element of the European proletariat are turned towards Russia, where the Russian proletariat faces problems of world-wide significance.

1. Armistice Negotiations

[SVERDLOV] reads a telegram received [from Karakhan at Brest-Litovsk] by Trotsky, PC of Foreign Affairs:

> After a long discussion which made it necessary to interrupt the proceedings to communicate with their governments,[b] the delegation[s] of Germany, Austro-Hungary, Bulgaria, and Turkey have agreed to accept our formulation of the point about the [non-]transfer of enemy forces from the Eastern to the Western fronts.[2] The precise text is as follows:
>   The contracting parties obligate themselves until 30 December 1917 (12 January 1918 [N.S.]) not to carry out any operational military transfers from the front between the Baltic and Black Seas except those which have already begun at the moment of signature of the present agreement.

We consider it useful to publish this communication both in Russia and for [transmission] abroad by radio-telegraph.

(signed) L. Karakhan.

SVERDLOV reads the following mandate for the delegates leaving for Brest to conduct the [armistice and] peace talks:

> The CEC approves the actions of the delegation carrying on preliminary negotiations for a general armistice in Brest-Litovsk and confirms the delegation's powers to continue the negotiations and to undertake, on the basis of the decisions of the [Second] All-Russian Congress of Soviets of Workers' and Soldiers' Deputies and of the [Extraordinary] All-Russian Congress of Peasant Deputies, all steps necessary to achieve an armistice as rapidly as possible in order to struggle for a general peace, on a democratic foundation, between the [belligerent] peoples.

The resolution is adopted without debate, 2 delegates dissenting and 4 abstaining.

2. *Supreme Economic Council*

MILYUTIN reports on the work of the commission organizing the SEC and proposes that the draft statute which it has worked out be taken as the basis [for the final text], that a [new] commission [be] chosen on a parity basis to complete the drafting, and that the decree be published immediately.

The proposal is endorsed unanimously.

3. *Arrest of Supply Chiefs*[3]

[A LEFT SR representative tables the following interpellation:]

> The undersigned CEC members address to the CPC, and in particular to the PC of Internal Affairs, the question: on what grounds and on whose authority were arrests carried out to-day of members of the council elected at the Moscow congress of supply organizations and a number of employees of the supply department?
>
> (signed) Avilov, Łapiński, Lindov, Katel, Yezhov, Planson, Krivoshein, Kovalev, Stroyev, Zhilinsky, Pryanichnikov, Aleksandrovich, Zak, Matusov, Shaposhnikov

SPIRO: I propose that discussion of this matter be deferred until

28 November, since most members of the [Left] SR fraction have to take part in the [Second (Regular)] Congress of Peasant Deputies.

Approved with 6 dissentients.

LOZOVSKY: I propose that the Presidium be charged to take all measures, as a matter of urgency, to ensure immediate release of the arrested members of the supply [board].

ZHILINSKY: I propose that the CEC [itself] adopt an ordinance on immediate release of [these men].

Motions rejected. Lozovsky's resolution is adopted, as is also a proposal by Avanesov that all decrees received by the Presidium be passed to the appropriate commission for immediate examination and that the Presidium be empowered to set up as many commissions as may be needed, on a proportional representation basis.

4. *Organizational Matters*

A spokesman for the Credentials commission makes a statement on the replacement of eight Left SR members and the receipt of a request by cossack forces[4] for five seats.

On the second point three proposals are made: to confirm the Credentials commission's decision; to defer a decision until 29 November; to approve the request in principle, but to decide the number of seats at the next regular session.[c]

[Decision not reported.]

After the session closed the Presidium received two statements, one submitted by Zhilinsky and the other by Trifonov, and a draft decree on railwaymen's wages submitted by Krushinsky.[d]

NOTES

a Iz., 28 Nov.

b Text in *Prot.* garbled.

c Iz., 28 Nov., attributes the third proposal to Chudnovsky.

d Zhilinsky's statement was as follows: 'I recommend that the CEC discuss the procedure for holding its sessions and propose that certain days be set aside for plenary sessions (three to four a week); that the agenda be published in *Izvestiya* on the previous day and on the day of the session itself; and that the other days be reserved for sessions of commissions, to which all pending legislation should be referred, as Lozovsky proposes.' Trifonov's statement (not printed in *Prot.*) related to representation of Russian forces on the Macedonian front.

Seventeenth Session
1 December 1917

Chairman: Sverdlov $^{a\lceil}$12 a.m., 2 Dec.$^{\rceil a}$

HÖGLUND [greets the assembly in terms similar to those of his speech on 27 November].

KOLLONTAY [replies].

VINOGRADOV^b offers greetings from the socialist [i.e. re-elected] Petrograd municipal Duma.

1. *Supreme Economic Council*

MILYUTIN reports for the commission set up to examine the draft decree. [Speech not reported.]

$^{c\lceil}$LEVIN argues that the Supreme Economic Council should be subordinate to the CEC rather than to the CPC. Only if it is built up from below will it be able to combat economic chaos and be ensured against making mistakes which are [particularly] impermissible in the economic field.$^{\rceil c}$

$^{d\lceil}$LENIN: The Supreme Economic Council cannot be reduced to [the role of] a parliament, but must be a militant organ of struggle against the capitalists and landowners in economic [life], just as the CPC is in politics.$^{\rceil d}$

$^{c\lceil}$TROTSKY: The council should be attached to the CPC, since the latter is the supreme organ of government.$^{\rceil c}$

$^{d\lceil}$AVILOV: I support the [Left] SR amendment. The SEC will take important measures affecting the economic life of the country, and these should not be left to the discretion of the people's commissars.$^{\rceil d}$

[Shteynberg, Mstislavsky, Selivanov, Repinshteyn [Reinshteyn?], Katel, Moiseyev and others take part in the ensuing debate, but none of their speeches have been recorded.]

The Left SR amendment is rejected by 161 votes to 104. The decree is approved but for 12 dissentients and 2ᵉ abstentions.

2. Railwaymen's Wages¹

SENYUSHKIN, for Vikzhel, reports: This draft [ordinance] is based on a scale worked out at the All-Russian Congress of Railwaymen in Moscow. All employees are divided into 14 categories with wages ranging from 75 to 300 roubles a month; cost-of-living allowances have been fixed on a scale ranging from 210 roubles a month in the Petrograd area to 80 roubles in Siberia and the Far East.

ᶜ⌐This decree is being submitted to the CEC at a time when the railwaymen are on the verge of a work stoppage. I insist that it be confirmed at once. The government of workers, soldiers, and peasants must confirm it: the railwaymen's hopes rest entirely with you, and they expect your decision today.⌐ᶜ

ᵈ⌐A LEFT SR member proposes that the two types of payment be merged, so that the most junior employees [in the Petrograd region] should receive 285 roubles and the most senior ones 585 roubles a month.

A BOLSHEVIK member proposes that the rate for the lowest-paid workers should be increased to 325 roubles and that for the highest-paid lowered to 485 roubles.⌐ᵈ

The draft ordinance is adopted ᶜ⌐without debate⌐ᶜ and is passed to an editorial commission for revision prior to publication ᶜ⌐within 24 hours⌐ᶜ.

3. Outlawing of Kadets²

ᶜ⌐SHTEYNBERG: The Left SRs have tried to take account of both the political and the formal [juridical] aspects of this decree. We think that if its object is to combat counter-revolution then one should not [be diverted from this aim] by a casual episode. There is no place in the class struggle for arbitrary repressive measures. One should fight by isolating [one's opponents] socially, not by technical means. The Soviet government should not apply the old outdatedᶠ methods of Kerensky. What does it mean to declare the Kadet party 'enemies of the people'? Is anyone who wears a black cloak to be an enemy?

This decree shows political weakness and loss of nerve, not strength. We demand that the revolutionary struggle be waged openly and honestly. The CEC should know who exactly is its foe and who its friend. The decree suggests a willingness to disrupt the Constituent Assembly, and we announce that we are categorically opposed to such a step. We are equally far distant from both sides and consider that each of them [i.e. the Kadets and the Bolsheviks] is making the same mistake. The Constituent Assembly should be subjected to the same test as was given to the coalition [Provisional] government. If it struggles against soviet power then it will destroy itself.

I should like to point out that for very many years the socialists taught the Russian people [to respect] the Constituent Assembly, and that the October insurrection likewise took place under this banner.[3] On behalf of my fraction I insist that the assembly be called, in its [full] complement as [elected], and that it be presented with the questions of peace, land, and [workers'] control. We must not give the counter-revolutionaries this trump card but must strike the weapon from their hands. We must merge the Tauride Palace with Smolny, and let the people decide how this may best be done.[7c]

LENIN: If one takes the Constituent Assembly out of its [present] context of a class struggle which is turning into civil war, then there has never been an assembly which expressed more perfectly the people's will. But one cannot live in a world of fantasy. The Constituent Assembly has to act in a situation of civil war started by the bourgeoisie and the Kaledinites. First they tried to drag out the struggle in Moscow; then there was Kerensky's unsuccessful attempt to move troops against Petrograd; after that came the fruitless effort to organize the counter-revolutionary senior army commanders; and now they are trying to raise a revolt on the Don. This is bound to fail, because the toiling cossacks are opposed to the Kaledinites.

We are reproached for persecuting the Kadet party. But one cannot distinguish between class struggle and [the struggle against] political opponent[s]. When it is said that the Kadet party is not a strong force, this misrepresents the facts. The Kadet Central Committee is the political staff of the bourgeoisie. The Kadets have absorbed all the possessing classes; elements to the right of the Kadets have merged with them and support them.

It is suggested that we convoke the Constituent Assembly as it was [originally] devised. No, gentlemen, I beg your pardon! It was devised [as a weapon] against the people. We carried out the revolution in order to obtain guarantees that the Constituent Assembly would not be used against the people, that these guarantees would be in the government's hands. In our decree we gave a precise answer on this point. Don't try to read what is in our hearts: we are not concealing anything. We have said that when 400 deputies assemble, we shall convoke the Constituent Assembly. It is not our fault that the elections were held later than the day initially appointed. In some places the soviets themselves fixed the polling day later. Since the elections took place at different dates [in various regions], we had to fix the number of deputies that would suffice for the assembly to open.

An attempt was made to open the Constituent Assembly [by direct action of the deputies present], taking advantage of the fact that this number had not been legally prescribed. What position would the government have been in if it had permitted this to happen? The Soviet government acted correctly in ordaining how many deputies should be present for the assembly to be legitimate. This we have done. Whoever disagrees must criticize the decree; but if instead of [straightforward] criticism we hear only hints and general speculation, then we shall ignore them.

When a revolutionary class is waging war against the possessing classes that resist it, then it must suppress this resistance; and we shall suppress the possessors' resistance by all the methods which they used to suppress the proletariat; other methods have not yet been invented.

You say that one should isolate the bourgeoisie. But the Kadets, hiding behind the slogan of formal democracy, the slogan of the Constituent Assembly, are in fact initiating civil war. They say: 'we want to sit in the Constituent Assembly at the same time as we wage civil war'—and you reply with talk about isolating them! ᶜᴵt is ridiculous to stop at measures of isolation. The bourgeoisie is using its capital to organize counter-revolution and to this there can be but one reply: prison! That is how [the Jacobins] acted in the great French revolution: they declared the bourgeois parties outside the law.[1c]

We are not persecuting[g] people simply for formal breaches [of the law]; we are bringing forward a direct political charge against [an entire] political party. That is what the French revolutionaries did, too. This is our answer to those peasants who elected deputies without knowing whom they were voting for. Let the people know that the Constituent Assembly will not meet in the way that Kerensky hoped. We have introduced the right of recall, so the Constituent Assembly will not be the sort of gathering which the bourgeoisie dreamed of. Now that the convocation of the Constituent Assembly is but a few days away the bourgeoisie is organizing civil war, stepping up acts of sabotage, and wrecking the armistice. We shall not allow ourselves to be deceived by formal slogans. They want to sit in the Constituent Assembly and organize civil war at the same time. Let [our critics] examine our charges against the Kadet party in substance; let them try to show that the Kadet party is not a staff for waging civil war—a war they know will be hopeless and will drown the country in blood. Shteynberg did not try to prove this [was not so]. He forgot everything that has been discovered about the links between the Kadets and Kornilov.[4] It was not we but Chernov, one of our political opponents, who discovered this link. It is suggested that we should [arrest only] the ringleaders, but we shall not drop the political charge levelled against [the Kadet party as] the directing staff of a whole class and substitute for it a mere hunt for a few individuals.

As for the objection that the Bolsheviks were themselves once proclaimed enemies of the people, this was only a threat; [in fact our opponents] did not dare to do this. We told them then: 'If you can do it, try to tell the people that the Bolsheviks as a party, as a tendency, are enemies of the people.' But they didn't dare. They just arrested individuals and slandered us. We told them: 'you cannot declare us enemies of the people, for you have not the shadow of a case in principle against the Bolsheviks; you can only spread slander.' Our accusation against the Kadet party will put an end to such petty methods of conducting a political struggle. We shall tell the people the truth, that its interests are superior to those of [any] democratic institution.

There is no cause to go back to the old prejudices which made
the people's interests subject to formal democracy. The Kadets
scream: 'all power to the Constituent Assembly' but in fact this
means 'all power to Kaledin'. We have to tell the people this
and they will back us.

h⌐TROTSKY, making an unscheduled statement: On the night of
[30 November to] 1 December a sharp conflict occurred between the Russian and German delegations at Brest over the
question of [a pledge] not to transfer troops from the Eastern to
the Western front. The Germans rejected [our] demand and
proposed that during the armistice there should be no transfers
of units of divisional strength or more. The Russian delegation
stated that this was unacceptable and referred the matter to the
CPC. Lenin and I told the Russian delegation to insist on
acceptance of its demands. I have just received a telegram to the
effect that the Germans have accepted this point. Since this is
the most essential point in the entire armistice negotiations, I
can inform you that the armistice is a *fait accompli*.⌐*h*

d⌐ŁAPIŃSKI: The terror which the CPC is applying against the
Kadets will in the nature of things be extended to parties standing to their left. The Constituent Assembly will be disrupted
and with it the most noble aspirations of the people. Let me
point out that all is not well as regards the most urgent matter
of the moment, namely the conclusion of peace. There is nothing to show that the German proletariat is preparing to act
against its government or that a democratic peace is a real
possibility. If the broad masses do not obtain peace, or the land
either, they will turn against us.⌐*d*

h⌐TROTSKY: Russia is completely split into two irreconcilable
camps, that of the bourgeoisie and that of the proletariat. Between them are the Left SRs, who have yet to find their feet and
are vacillating in a petty-bourgeois funk which leads them to
obstruct the CPC's class struggle. There is nothing immoral in
the proletariat finishing off a class that is collapsing: that is its
right. You wax indignant at the naked terror which we are
applying against our class enemies, but let me tell you that in
one month's time at the most it will assume more frightful
[*groznye*] forms, modelled on the terror of the great French
revolutionaries.[5] Not the fortress but the guillotine will await

our enemies.⌐*h* *d*⌐(*Cries from the left*: 'Your attitude to us is the same as Bleykhman's!')⌐*d* *h*⌐We have to drag along behind us [as if] on a lassoo that party [the Left SRs] which keeps one ear cocked to whatever Chernov is saying, while Chernov is looking at Avksentyev and the latter is listening to Milyukov.⌐*h*

c⌐MSTISLAVSKY, for the Left SRs: It is not for the Left SRs to listen to reproaches from Trotsky or anybody else about their [alleged] 'petty-bourgeois' character. On the contrary, it is precisely this point that divides the Left SRs from the present Bolshevik leaders. It is no accident that Lenin and Trotsky should continually refer in their speeches to the great French revolution—a revolution that was bourgeois and petty-bourgeois in character. They do not realize that they are entangling themselves in the deepest contradictions here. They talk of a 'socialist' revolution yet in practice they are trapped in the narrow ring of purely bourgeois forms of political revolution. This is what gives the Left SRs the right to affirm that by thoughtlessly forcing [the pace] of revolution the Bolsheviks are taking the wrong road. Instead of making use of the freedom of action that has been granted them to undertake creative organic work, so establish new forms [of social life], the Bolsheviks, to quote Trotsky, are 'struggling to gain control of the state apparatus'. But in a situation where the class struggle has been sharpened to the point of bloodshed it is impossible to win command of the levers of the old state mechanism; indeed, this is unnecessary in so far as our revolution is a socialist one.

The only result of this 'struggle to gain control of the levers', to which Lenin and Trotsky give the form of political terror, is to distort the very essence of the class struggle, to make it degenerate into civil war, a war that is not justified by objective circumstances. Among the measures they take so blindly are repressive acts against the Constituent Assembly and the Kadet party as a whole. The Left SRs can never approve such measures, precisely because we are faithful to our notion of the class character of the revolution. The more acute the tension in the class struggle, the greater the assurance with which we can call the Constituent Assembly, for the less danger there will be of it diverting the people from accomplishing their social tasks by empty talk of 'the general national interest'. On the other hand, the CPC's fear of the assembly and of the Kadets, evident from its latest decrees, displays a bourgeois conception of revolution: the Bolsheviks are socialist in words, but their political practice is thoroughly bourgeois.

This difference prevents the Left SRs from following in the wake of the policy adopted by the ruling party. We agree with the Bolsheviks in our analysis of the essence of the current revolution as a social one, and we stand firmly for soviet power, but we differ sharply from them in our view of the practical tasks to be accomplished, of the tactics suited to the present moment. In these critical times we do not consider ourselves entitled to separate ourselves from the mass movement, as the socialist parties of the right and centre have done. We [are determined to] share the people's difficulties and dangers. Faced with the fact of Bolshevism, which was not our creation, we shall exert all our efforts to minimize the harm it is doing to the revolutionary cause and to make use of it in the service of that cause. Whenever the occasion arises, before their intentions have become reality, we shall raise our voice in warning and try to prevent them taking the false step they have in mind. That is what we are doing today, with special vehemence and insistence, since the Bolshevik leaders are about to make a very big mistake.

In these protests Trotsky detects a lack of courage. In his view we are too prone to look back. On the contrary: if anything, we are looking too far ahead. We see that this great movement is taking the wrong road. And if we do not abandon the masses at this grim moment, but try instead to direct the movement back on to the right road, this is because it is our duty to fight alongside the people and not to forsake them even when they are on the wrong track. In such a matter we shall not listen to any voices calling to us from the other camp but shall hearken solely to the voice of our revolutionary conscience. (*Applause.*) I table the following resolution:

Recognizing that the toiling masses can only define their attitude to the Constituent Assembly once that body has defined its own attitude to the questions of peace, land, government and workers' control; recognizing that any [measure] designed to prevent convocation of the Constituent

Assembly, and to an even greater extent any efforts to disrupt or to dissolve it before it meets, will sow confusion among the toiling masses and give the bourgeoisie a dangerous weapon for its counter-revolutionary agitation; the CEC re-asserts to the CPC, for its unfailing compliance, [its will] that the Constituent Assembly should meet freely, in the presence of [all] its constituent elements, both socialist and bourgeois;

recognizing further the necessity for fierce and merciless struggle against counter-revolution, however, the CEC permits the arrest of individuals or groups [of deputies] only on the basis of sufficient well-founded data leading to criminal prosecution.

In virtue of this, that part of the decree of 28 November which contradicts the principle indicated is hereby repealed. Furthermore, noting that this decree, like many others of general state significance, was published contrary to the statute of the CEC, without its sanction and even without its knowledge, the CEC ordains that in future only those governmental acts of general state character which have been confirmed by the CEC in plenary session shall have binding force.

[A spokesman for the PPS and for the Menshevik Internationalists follow. Neither speech has been recorded.][1]

SHTEYNBERG: It would be stupid to maintain that we are arguing in defence of the Kadets. Lenin and Trotsky are like the Right SRs and Mensheviks, enslaved by the idea that it is necessary to fight the Kadets. I call on our Bolshevik comrades to free themselves from their nightmare about Kadets. I should also like to point out that if decrees were passed through the CEC the people's commissars would not be obliged to squirm as they do.

In my view we should seek to turn the Constituent Assembly into a revolutionary Convention.

It is not true that you have to drag the Left SR party behind you [as if] with a lassoo; it is rather that the Bolsheviks are dragging the revolution behind them. We have always been with the people, and shall work together with the Bolsheviks, but for this [collaboration to succeed] the two parties' views need to be fairly close.[7c]

By 150 votes to 98 with 3 abstentions[j] the CEC adopts the Bolshevik formula for moving on to the next business [and resolves as follows]:

1. The CEC considers that the CPC's decision to convoke the Constituent Assembly once there are present in Petrograd 400 deputies who have shown their credentials is the most expedient way of ensuring that the assembly is convoked at the earliest moment.

2. Having heard the explanations given by CPC representatives of the decree declaring the Kadets to be a party of enemies of the people and authorizing the arrest of members of the directing organs of this party and supervision of it by the soviets; the CEC reasserts the need for the most resolute struggle against the counter-revolution headed by the Kadet party, which has launched a cruel civil war against the very foundations of the workers' and peasants' revolution.

[3.] The CEC assures the CPC also in future of its support [for measures taken] along these lines, and rejects the protests of political groups whose vacillations undermine the dictatorship of the proletariat and poor peasantry.[k]

4. Unemployment Insurance[5]

Without debate, and even without a preliminary reading, the decree on unemployment insurance is passed to a commission, which is given the right, provided there are no disagreements within it, to work out, together with the Presidium, the final text of the decree and to pass it to the CPC for publication and implementation.

NOTES

a *Novy luch*, 3 Dec., which adds that 250 persons were present. This was therefore a plenary session. Gorodetsky, *Rozhdenie*, p. 207, notes the presence of army delegates, presumably elected according to the terms of the 14 November compromise. *Delo naroda*, 3 Dec., puts the opening half an hour earlier.

b *ZT*, 3 Dec.: Vinokurov.

c *ZT*, 3 Dec.

d *NZ*, 3 Dec.

e *ZT*, 3 Dec.: 22 abstentions.

f literally: 'rusty' (*zarzhavlennye*).

g *Prot.* and *Pr.*, 6 Dec.: 'persecuting' (*gonim*). In Lenin, *PSS*, xxxv. 136 the phrase is softened to 'pursuing' (*lovim*).

h *Delo naroda*, 3 Dec.

i *Delo naroda*, 3 Dec., adds that Selivanov (SR Maximalist) intervened at this point and asserted that 'no one needs the Constituent Assembly, which will be an assembly of criminals.'

j *NZ*, 3 Dec.: 150 votes to 99. *Delo naroda*, 3 Dec.: 150 votes to 104 with 22 abstentions, the mover of the resolution identified as Fenikshteyn.

k Printed separately in *Prot.*, which also gives the text of four interpellations, whose signatories are not listed. One requested that the CPC render account of the general political and economic condition of the country; another that it fulfil its obligation to give an account of its work weekly to the CEC; the other two inquired the reasons for the arrest of Constituent Assembly deputies and for persecution of the press.

Eighteenth Session
8 December 1917

Held in the Aleksandrinsky Theatre conjointly with the CPC, delegates to the Second All-Russian Congress of Peasant Deputies, the Petrograd soviet, Petrograd district soviets, the Petrograd municipal Duma, regimental committee representatives, the CC and Petrograd committee of the RSDRP(b) and the Left Socialist-Revolutionary party, the [Central Council] of Factory Committees, trade unions, and other labour organizations.

[Chairman: Sverdlov]

SVERDLOV: *⌐This session is being held on the initiative of the CEC and is devoted to the question of the armistice[1] and [the continuing struggle for] a general fraternal peace.⌐*a

At the beginning of the war the internationalists were but a tiny handful of individuals who opposed the European war [as] the fruit of the capitalist system; but now vast masses of people follow our lead. The greatest stimulus to this involvement of whole peoples in the anti-war movement was provided by the February revolution in Russia. At the present time dissatisfaction with the war is spreading ever more widely in all belligerent countries. The day is not far distant when these masses will conclude a peace that will constitute the climax of the age-old struggle between labour and capital, a struggle that is assuming ever more tangible forms. *b⌐I invite the meeting to endorse the following slogans:⌐*b

Long live the general peace!
Long live the Russian revolution!
Long live the International!
Long live the fraternal union of all peoples!

(*Prolonged applause.*)

SPIRIDONOVA, for the Left SRs:*c* . . . *a⌐The internationalists of all lands have been striving to bring about an armistice on every front. We have proceeded from the theory that when an army ceases to fight, even for a moment, the soldiers awake from the nightmare of warfare; that a reaction occurs in their minds and it becomes psychologically impossible for the war to go on.

We want all armies to stop fighting, so that there will be a [universal] sentiment that it would be impossible to resume hostilities. We are holding out the keys to peace on every front. Yet everything which our revolutionary government does is subjected to the most merciless and unjust criticism from every quarter.

You, comrades, know what war is like. You are also familiar with every word spoken and every step taken in the peace negotiations. We Left SRs support whole-heartedly the peace policy of the people's commissars. (*Stormy applause.*) We differ from our Bolshevik comrades on some technical questions, but in this matter we are at one with them.

Despite their stubborn struggle the internationalists of all countries have so far had very little success. It is our duty to force a breach [in the war]. We must act with profound faith [in our ultimate victory].

Long live soviet power!
Long live fraternity among all peoples!
Long live the International!

(*Stormy, prolonged applause.*)[7a]

TROTSKY (*applause*):[d] . . . In 1914, when war broke out, I had two conversations that were characteristic. I asked the German [b]ᴦSocial Democraticᒣ[b] deputy Molkenbuhr[e2] how long he thought the war would last. He replied that two to three months would suffice: the German armies would exert considerable pressure upon Russia, strike two or three mighty blows against France, and victory would be theirs. Then I talked to a French socialist who said much the same thing: France had thrown back the Germans in the battle of the Marne and would press on to the Rhine; meanwhile the Russians would threaten Berlin and that would be enough to bring the war to an end. Indeed, at that time anyone who dared to suggest that the war would last a year or more was taken for a madman. The enormous masses of manpower and military equipment which the European powers had amassed seemed sufficient guarantee that the war would not go on for long.

But now it is four years since mankind has been trying to escape from the vicious circle of endless slaughter. The war has shown what mighty feats men can accomplish, what terrible sufferings they can endure; but it has also shown how much barbarism there still is in modern man. Never has technical progress reached such heights as at the present time: men can conquer space by the radio-telegraph; they can rise into the skies in airplanes, unafraid of the elements—while on the ground, up to their knees in mud, other men look through field-glasses [at the enemy] under the watchful eye of [officers belonging to] the ruling classes and do their dreadful, disgusting work. Man, the lord of nature, sits in this slaughter-house, espies another human being through his binoculars, as if through the peephole in a prison door, and considers him his booty. That is how deep man has sunk in this war. One cannot but be ashamed of humanity, which has progressed through so many stages of cultural development—Christianity, absolutism, parliamentary democracy—and has given birth to the idea of socialism, yet has enslaved itself to the ruling classes and is killing wildly at their command. And if this war should end with a victory for imperialism, if people return to their hovels to live off the dregs left them by the bourgeoisie, then mankind would be unworthy of all the intellectual efforts made on its behalf over thousands of years. But that shall not be, that must not be. (*Stormy applause.*)

At the Zimmerwald conference we, the internationalists, were but a tiny group of thirty, mercilessly hounded by the chauvinists of all countries. It seemed as if we were the last relics of a great chapter [in human history], and that the entire socialist movement had been drowned in this nationalist blood-bath. But we received a letter from Karl Liebknecht, whom the German tyrants had imprisoned in a fortress, in which he wrote that we should not be put off by the fact that we were so few in number; that he was sure our labours would not be in vain; that although individuals could easily be done away with the people's faith in revolutionary socialism could not be annihilated. And in saying this he was not deceiving us, for with every day that passes his expectations are coming to pass. I invite you to join with me in proclaiming: Long live our friend Karl Liebknecht, valiant fighter for socialism! (*Stormy applause; voices from the hall*: 'We demand freedom for Liebknecht and Fritz Adler!') . . .*f*

Turning to our own struggle for peace, we may regret that matters are not moving as swiftly as we would like; nevertheless *eppur si muove*: there is no cause for despair. In Russia, in young, uncultured and backward Russia, where the weight of tsarist arbitrariness was felt most oppressively, the revolutionary struggle broke out before it did in other countries. We were the first to act. But the reasons which led our people to enter the struggle are present in all countries, irrespective of [differences in] national temperament, and sooner or later these causes will produce corresponding effects. The fact that during the war we overthrew the tsar and the bourgeoisie, that in a country of 180 million people power has been assumed by those who not long ago were dismissed as a little band [of nonentities]—this fact is of world historical significance and will always be remembered by workers in every land. The Russian people, which has rebelled in the country that once belonged to the gendarme of Europe (as Nicholas [I] was once respectfully called), declares that, together with its brothers-in-arms in Germany, Austria, Turkey and elsewhere, it wants to speak not in the language of cannon but in the language of international solidarity among working people. It has announced loudly to the entire world that it does not need conquests, that it does not seek to infringe anyone else's possessions, but that it seeks only the fraternity of peoples and the emancipation of labour. This fact cannot be driven out of the minds of all those who are groaning under the heavy burdens of war, and sooner or later these masses will come to us, will hold out to us their helping hand. And even if we suppose that the people's enemies should defeat us, that we should perish, be trodden on and turned into dust, nevertheless the memory of our existence will be handed down from generation to generation and will incite our children to carry on the fight. Of course our position would be much better if the European peoples had risen together with us and if we had to talk not to General Hoffmann and Count Czernin but to Liebknecht, Clara Zetkin, Rosa Luxemburg, and others. But that has not yet come to pass and that is not our fault. Our brothers in Germany cannot accuse us of conducting talks behind their backs with their accursed enemy the Kaiser. We are treating him as a foe, as a tyrant for whom we preserve undying hatred.

The armistice has made a breach in the war. The gunfire has ceased and everyone is nervously waiting to see how the Soviet government will deal with the Hohenzollern and Habsburg imperialists. You must support us in treating them as foes of freedom, in ensuring that not one iota of this freedom is sacrificed to imperialism. Only then will the German and Austrian peoples thoroughly appreciate our aims. Unless the voice of the German working class makes itself heard peace will be impossible. But I think that we have crossed the Rubicon and that there can be no return to the past. We are becoming more and more convinced that the peace talks will be a powerful weapon in the hands of [other] peoples in their struggle for peace. If we are mistaken, if Europe continues to remain as silent as the grave, and if this silence gives Wilhelm the chance to attack us and to dictate his terms to us, terms that would insult the revolutionary dignity of our country, then I am not sure whether, given our shattered economy and the general chaos (the result of the war and internal strife), we could fight. I think, however, that we could do so. (*Stormy applause.*) For our lives, for our revolutionary honour, we would fight to the last drop of our blood. (*Fresh outburst of applause.*)[3] The older age groups, the fatigued, would not go into battle. But we would say that our honour was in danger; we would sound the call and would raise an army of soldiers and Red guardsmen, strong in its revolutionary enthusiasm, which would fight for as long as it could. We have not yet played our last card.

Our enemies and the 'Allied' imperialists should realize that we did not overthrow the tsar and the bourgeoisie in order to kneel before the German Kaiser, to bend our heads before foreign militarists and to beseech them for peace. If they offer us conditions that are unacceptable, which contradict the principles of our revolution, we shall present them to the Constituent Assembly and say: decide. If the Constituent Assembly accepts them, the Bolshevik party will relinquish power[g] and will say: find yourselves another party prepared to sign such conditions, for we Bolsheviks (and I hope the Left SRs too) call upon everyone to wage a holy war against the militarists of all countries. (*Loud continuous applause.*)

If, owing to the economic ruin, we are unable to fight, if we are forced to renounce the struggle for our ideals, we shall say to our comrades abroad that the proletariat has not abandoned the struggle but only postponed it, as it did in 1905 . . .

That is why we are not pessimistic or down-hearted about the peace talks. However much bourgeois newspapers may fume that by engaging in such talks we are harming the interests of democracy, we shall not stop doing what we are doing, for [our aims] are not those ascribed to us by these liars and slanderers. They call us traitors to the peoples of Britain and France on the grounds that the Germans will transfer fresh forces from the Eastern front and hurl them against the Allies. But as you know the Russian delegation insisted forcefully that the German general staff should not move soldiers from the Russian to the Western front. General Hoffmann protested strongly and tried very hard not to accept this point, but we stood our ground and [the clause about] not transferring troops is now being implemented.[h] (*Displaying two maps of the Western front in September and October*:) from these maps it is clear that during these two months a lot of men were shifted from our front to the West. But we were not in power then and were not negotiating peace.

Nor did we give in when the Germans demanded that we cease making propaganda among their troops. We replied that we had come to Brest to talk to the German generals about ceasing military action, not about revolutionary propaganda. Our real negotiations are with the German peasants and workers in uniform. [b⌐](*Displaying a copy of the newspaper* 'Die Fackel' *designed for German soldiers*:)⌐[b] this is the paper that will carry on a different sort of negotiation, in which we shall develop an authentically popular diplomacy, a diplomacy of the trenches. I think that in such negotiations we shall acquit ourselves honourably. (*Loud applause.*)

[i]I pass on now to the policy of the western imperialist powers [as reflected in] their press and to the recent statements by Lloyd George and Noulens. At the moment we are closer to the French and British peoples than we were before. In all countries we have both friends and mortal enemies. As an illustration of this let me cite the correspondence between Colonel Kalpashni-

kov and the head of the American Red Cross mission, Anderson.[4] On the night of 7/8 December Colonel Kalpashnikov, who was supposed to take an American Red Cross train to Jassy, was arrested. Some time ago [Robins][j] came to me in Smolny and asked that such a train, containing ambulances and passenger cars for the Romanian front, be allowed through without hindrance. We promised our assistance. But some time ago we heard that these cars might land up not in Jassy but on some internal [i.e. civil war] front, most likely on the Don. I therefore turned to Colonel Robins, Anderson's deputy, and suggested that the dispatch of the cars be temporarily halted. During the search of Colonel Kalpashnikov's [apartment] the following documents were seized:

i) a letter [of 6 December] from Kalpashnikov to Anderson in which the former complains that Robins is preventing him from doing his job and that he will probably be unable to leave with the cars because the whole train and he himself are about to be placed under arrest by the Bolsheviks;
ii) a telegram from Anderson to Kalpashnikov dated 5 December: 'Do everything possible to take all cars, whether assembled or not, to Rostov-on-Don by first possible train';
iii) a certificate [dated 19 November] given to Kalpashnikov by Francis, the American ambassador, stating that 72 ambulances and eight light trucks are destined for the American Red Cross mission in Romania, and asking everyone to help Kalpashnikov get these cars to Jassy.

Thus all the threads in this affair lead to the American ambassador, Francis. This Sir Francis has been the most taciturn of all the [Allied] diplomats since the insurrection. Apparently he has been consistently and firmly following the principles laid down for diplomats by Bismarck: 'speech is silver but silence is gold.' But Sir Francis ought at long last to abandon his silence and give his explanation about the affair revealed by the documents which I have read to you. Let Sir Francis give us a little of his silver eloquence. (*Laughter.*)

It is time for the representatives of all foreign powers to realize that we are not so weak as to let them tread on our toes with impunity. We say this to all of them, German and Austrian diplomats included. If they think that just because they are foreign representatives they can secretly subsidize Kaledin under cover of the Red Cross, then they are mistaken. From the moment that their role in assisting the counter-revolutionaries becomes known to us, in our eyes they are no more than private individuals. They will be crushed under the boot of the revolution, which will bring its full weight to bear upon them. (*Stormy applause.*)[k5]

The bourgeoisie is rich in gold and dollars, which serve it as a means of oppression. We do not have such resources, but our position is just as strong, for we have the sympathy of the masses and our socialist principles. [b⌐In the affair of Chicherin and Petrov[6] we have already had occasion to show the British ambassador that we have our revolutionary dignity. We do not act at the behest of the Anglo-American bourgeoisie; our hands are clean, and in the struggle for our principles against all kinds of imperialists—not only the Germans but also Messrs. Clemenceau, Lloyd George, and the rest—we shall either conquer or perish. (*Stormy applause, turning into an ovation.*)⌐b]

Everyone should know that we shall not submit to the Anglo-American bourgeoisie ... If necessary we shall shed the last drop of our blood in the struggle for our revolutionary dignity, for our honour, for peace, freedom and fraternity among all peoples. (*Stormy, sustained applause, turning into an ovation.*)

MOISEYEV, for the United Internationalists: If everything turns out the way Trotsky has suggested, our party can but approve and welcome the CPC's policy. [l⌐But we are afraid that a Bolshevik peace may turn out to be a separate peace at the expense of Russia's interests.⌐l]

[The speaker then reads a declaration on behalf of his party, the text of which has not been preserved.]

[l⌐In addition, on my own account, I should like to register a protest against Bolshevik policy in regard to the Ukraine, which is leading to a fratricidal civil war.[7] (*Whistles, derogatory cries.*)⌐l]

KOLLONTAY, for the Bolsheviks: If anyone had prophesied a year ago that any party would compel the imperialists to negotiate an armistice, that party would have been generally blessed. Now we see that an armistice has been brought about by the efforts of the revolutionary workers, soldiers, and peasants. What satisfaction must fill our hearts at the thought that at least on one front, after 42 months of warfare, there will be a peaceful Christmas, free of the terrible knowledge that every minute blood is flowing somewhere or other—not in the sacred cause of the proletariat but in order to strengthen the hold of the bourgeoisie.

But if the peoples admire the courageous actions of the people's commissars, their enemies clench their teeth, knowing that these actions will never be forgotten so long as history is written.

The war split the socialists into three groups. One group, the social patriots, betrayed their principles and helped the war effort. A second group hated the war and fought for peace, but thought that tyranny could be overthrown by a stroke of the pen. But there was also a third current: the revolutionary internationalists. Although few in number, men like Trotsky, Lenin, and Karl Liebknecht took the revolutionary road. Long before 1914 we warned that if [the imperialists] launched a war to satisfy their insatiable appetites this would lead not only to chaos, hunger and howls of distress but also to the beautiful spectre of world revolution [sic]. What we prophesied has come to pass, although things are even worse than we anticipated. The revolution was fated to begin in the country where suffering and oppression were worst: in Russia, where the March revolution brought a tremendous step forward. It was not difficult to overthrow the moribund tsarist government and to give power to the bourgeoisie. We received liberties of a kind, but the workers and peasants did not feel they had been freed and the old spirit of officialdom remained alive. In the ministries, for instance, one found the same people, with the same functionaries' psychology, the same subservience and bureaucratism, although these people made a pretence of being revolutionaries.

Only now is there a new creative spirit to be felt. The first to come out with criticism were the Bolsheviks. We revolutionary internationalists said that the war had to be brought to an end. This was impossible so long as Kadets and defensists were in power. But the people have succeeded in suppressing the war by giving power to the soviets. The [revolution] for which we were condemned as madmen and traitors has come to pass. But we are still surrounded by enemies with whom we must do battle. The civil war was inevitable. It will not finish until soviet power is consolidated.

The greatest thing we have done is to show the [other] peoples of the world that a socialist revolution is not something for the distant future but has already begun here in Russia. The imperialists of all countries . . . spread lies about us, and this makes difficulties for the world protest [movement]. We have to send our delegates abroad and put a spark to the tinder-box. That is why we call ourselves internationalists. We are working not just for Russia but for the world proletariat. And we believe that the revolutionary torch raised above Russia will ignite the flame of revolution all over the globe.

KARELIN, for the Left SRs: A great change has been accomplished. [But] the victorious Russian revolution faces tremendous tasks. In celebrating our initial success we should not forget that securing an armistice and a peace is only the first step along the road upon which we have been launched by the revolution. Three terrible years of war have done enormous damage to the fabric of human civilization. The success of the revolution has been achieved at a heavy price.

The fundamental question of the Russian revolution is that of land. The only way to solve it is by socializing the land, allowing the mass of the people full autonomy of action.

Our resources are not so great that we can afford to neglect any instrument—such as the Constituent Assembly, for example. This body must either carry out the people's will or else it will be by-passed. Of course there are other approaches than through the assembly, but I repeat that we are too weak not to utilize all the means available. It is more than a matter of land and peace. Having secured the armistice and cried 'long live peace!' we shall still have to lead the socialist revolution and re-establish fraternal relations among the world's toilers.

ZINOVIEV: There was a moment when Herzen, one of the greatest and most intelligent of men, felt obliged to exclaim: 'I am ashamed to be a Russian.' This was a time when the Poles were being savagely repressed and an omnipotent tsarism was crushing the national rights and dignity of all the peoples inhabiting Russia. But ᵐ⌐that time has passed. Our people has done everything [possible] in this direction, and we are approaching⌐ᵐ the moment when each people in Russia will establish its [mode of] life solely according to its own wishes.

Now every honest Ukrainian ought to say of himself what
Herzen once said. We have seen who is benefiting from that
game of neutrality which the Rada is trying to play. ⌐We had
assumed that the Rada would let us have 100,000 soldiers to put
down General Kaledin, but instead⌐¹ they let cossacks through
to the Don while denying our troops the right to go to the aid of
our brothers. As a result Rostov has become a sea of blood. The
Rada knew this [would happen] and as if in mockery of common sense declared Kaledin's movement one of national self-
preservation.[8]

We knew our path would not be strewn with roses, but we did
not expect a blow from this quarter. Eight months should have
been enough to teach the Rada unforgettable lessons: it ought
to have realized that the interests of the Ukrainian people can
be satisfied only by union with the Russian working class. Instead it tried to remain friends with Kerensky even when he was
preparing to put its members on trial, when he was arguing
with it over [which] provinces [should belong to an autonomous
Ukraine], and when Nekrasov, who was then in charge of
nationality affairs, literally put the knives on the table.[9] Even
after this the Central Rada did not take a step towards [the
Bolsheviks, who would soon form] the people's government.

When [we] invited the Rada to take part in the armistice
talks it refused, but Ukrainian soldiers forced it to send its representatives to the delegation.[10]

The other day, at the Menshevik conference, Liber said that
the Russian delegation's misfortunes arose from the fact that it
consisted of soldiers. But we say that this is a guarantee of victory, since the soldiers are a bridge between town and country,
and it is the integral character [of the popular movement] that
will make the revolution invincible. The same thing applies to
the conflict with the Rada. Our regiments in the Ukraine were
disarmed during the night and expelled from the territory like
beggars without any preparations being made for them or any
rations provided. They naturally bear a great grievance, not
against the Ukrainian people but against the Rada. The
Ukrainian soldiers and peasants who want to settle the land
question in the same spirit as we do will compel the Rada to
turn towards us. If, contrary to our expectations, such a rap-
prochement does not occur the reason must be sought in the

following [circumstances]. We are guilty[n] only in that the Great
Russian peasant has taken little interest in the national question.
We have redeemed [this] sin by granting full freedom of self-
determination. But self-determination for the Ukrainian people
is not, of course, self-determination for counter-revolution.

We say to Ukrainian democracy: if you do not want bloodshed to occur among brothers, send your representatives so that
we may come to terms. Surely you must understand that we
value the blood of sailors and soldiers more highly than Kaledin
does?

These are not just local [squabbles]. We know that behind
Kaledin stands international capital. This was clearly shown by
the documents which Trotsky read out. The bourgeoisie is
offering the Rada its services in order to get it to attack us. If the
Rada were able to see beyond tomorrow and were really concerned about the people's interests, after its experiences with
Kerensky and Milyukov it ought to avoid quarrelling with us.
I propose that we make a last effort—maybe it is not yet too late
for this—to appeal to the Ukrainian people. (*Reads the text of
such an appeal*:)

To the Ukrainian workers, soldiers, and peasants.
To the entire Ukrainian people.
Brother Ukrainians! The enemies of your freedom and ours
want to divide us. The Central Rada has gone over to the
enemies of Soviet power in Russia . . .
It is conducting negotiations with the Kornilovite Kaledin . . .
It has fallen by night upon the revolutionary Soviet armies,
disarmed them, and expelled them from Kiev. This is a challenge to the working class of all Russia . . .
Brother Ukrainians! You are being told that we are infringing [the right of] the Ukraine to exercise self-determination.
That is a lie . . .
Sensing the Central Rada's treason, all the black crows of
counter-revolution are gathering in Kiev. The imperialists of
all countries are pinning their hopes on the Rada . . . Parties
and leaders which yesterday were suppressing the Rada are
today conspiring with it against Soviet power . . .
Demand immediate re-election of the Rada! Demand the
transfer of all power in the Ukraine to soviets of workers',

soldiers', and peasants' deputies! Let Ukrainians predominate in these soviets. Let Soviet power become established in the Ukraine as well ... Socialism is imminent. All mankind is about to be freed from oppression of every kind, that of nations included.

For your freedom and ours! For victory of the workers, soldiers and peasants! For socialism!

The appeal is approved by acclamation.

PROSHYAN, on behalf of the Presidium, reads the appeal addressed to the toiling masses of all countries:

[Recapitulates the Soviet government's position in the armistice talks.]

The joint session appeals to the German workers: you ... should support by every possible means the Russian people's struggle for a just general peace ... and prevent the imperialists from disrupting the talks that have commenced. Do not let them tell you that only by continuing the war can the French and British governments be persuaded to make peace. The same arguments are being used by the British, French, and American imperialists to their peoples ...

Workers of France, Britain, and Italy, peoples of long-suffering Serbia and Belgium! You too must raise your voices ...

We, representatives of the toiling masses of Russia, cannot on our own give you a general peace. You must demand that your representatives also take part in the talks ...

We want a just democratic peace. But we shall get this only when the peoples of all countries dictate its terms by their revolutionary struggle, when they send to the peace conference not representatives of capital and militarism but representatives of the masses ...

Long live the international revolutionary struggle of workers, soldiers, and peasants!

Long live socialism!

The appeal is approved by acclamation.

The session closes with singing of the *Internationale*. Then, at the suggestion of one delegate, a funeral hymn is sung to honour those workers, soldiers, and sailors who have just lost their lives in Rostov fighting the armies of the Kornilovite Kaledin.

NOTES

a ZT, 9 Dec.

b NZ, 9 Dec.

c NZ, 9 Dec.: for the Second Congress of Peasant Deputies. Spiridonova was chairman of this assembly, and this attribution is more plausible. The introductory passage of her speech, dealing with the war, has not been recorded.

d Text also in Trotsky, *Soch.*, vol. III(ii), pp. 211–17 (where however explanatory notes nos. 168–200 have not been printed, evidently due to a printer's error).

e *Prot.*: 'Molkenburg.' NZ: 'Molkenbruck.'

f *Prot.* notes briefly that Trotsky went on to speak of the activities of other internationalists, including Adler, Höglund, and Luxemburg.

g Literally, 'will go away' (*uidut*).

h *Prot.* omits the 'not', clearly a misprint.

i See E. Sisson, *One Hundred Red Days*, pp. 152–5, for a fuller (but not necessarily more accurate) version of Trotsky's speech recorded by A. Gumberg, Raymond Robins's assistant and interpreter.

j NZ: 'Anderson.' Presumably a slip either by the speaker or the reporter, for Anderson remained at Jassy throughout this period.

k Gumberg's stenographic notes, as reproduced in Sisson, op. cit., p. 155: 'private counter-revolution[ary] adventurers and the heavy hand of the revolution will fall upon their heads!' In Francis's report of the speech (*FRUS* 1918: *Russia*, vol. I, p. 321) the threat is slightly toned down: 'is no more an Ambassador but an adventurer and the heavy hand of the revolution will deal with him.' The version given in Kalpashnikov's memoirs (p. 75), said to have been taken from *Izvestiya*, is inaccurate. According to this account Trotsky said: 'if I do not get satisfaction I shall not hesitate to take extreme measures and wipe out all the Americans and foreigners who dare to plot anything against the liberties so dearly bought by us for our country.' In W. Hard, *Raymond Robins' Own Story*, p. 118, it is stated that the audience responded with shouts of 'Arrest Francis! Hang him! Shoot him!'

l *Nash vek*, 9 Dec. These few remarks are all that survives of Moiseyev's speech. ZT (9 Dec.) promised a follow-up report on the latter half of the session, but this did not appear; evidently it was crowded out of its columns by reports on the Ukrainian crisis.

m *Iz.*, 12 Dec.; text in *Prot.* is corrupt.

n *Iz.*, 12 Dec.; *Prot.*: 'not guilty', which makes no sense. Zinoviev's argument, which here has been rendered scarcely intelligible by compression, is as follows: while the main responsibility for the tension lies with the Rada government, a subordinate factor is national chauvinism among the Great Russians.

Nineteenth Session
12 December 1917

Chairman: Sverdlov   9.40 p.m.[a]

1. Re-election of Presidium

SVERDLOV: Since the Presidium was elected a number of events have taken place which have completely altered the composition of the CEC. It has been enlarged to include 108 representatives of the All-Russian Congress of Peasant Deputies and is thus at the present time the central executive organ not only of the soviets of workers' and soldiers' deputies but also of those of the peasants. For this reason the Presidium considers that it should be re-elected by the CEC on the same basis as that on which the original Presidium was formed, namely by choosing one member for each group of 15 deputies. If a group less than 15 strong wishes to take part in the election, it is of course entitled to unite with other groups.

DZEVALTOVSKY, for the Bolsheviks: Since the Bolsheviks have 175 votes in the CEC we delegate to [serve on] the Presidium the following 12 persons: Sverdlov, Avanesov, Fomin, Zinoviev, Steklov, Shchukin, Olich, Peterson, Bruno, Litvin, Medvedev, and Badayev; as candidate members we nominate Volodarsky, Preobrazhensky, Chudnovsky, Gzelshchak and Plaksin; and as secretary Avanesov.

A LEFT SR spokesman: We delegate Natanson, Spiridonova, Kamkov, Ustinov, Mstislavsky, Malkin, and Levin; and to the Secretariat Smolyansky, with Sapozhnikov as his deputy.

A UNITED SD spokesman: We also have 15 members in our group, and so delegate to the Presidium Moiseyev, with Zhilinsky as his deputy.

The list of nominations is approved unanimously.

2. *Interpellations and Procedural Matters*

KARELIN, for the Left SRs, ᵇ⌐in an unscheduled statement⌐ᵇ: I wish to state our reasons for submitting an interpellation to the CPC about the conflict with the Rada.

ᶜ⌐In our relations with the various national entities included within our republic, we must adopt the same approach as we do in foreign affairs, that is to say an internationalist one. The struggle which is being planned against bourgeois elements in the Rada makes sense only if it is waged from within [the Ukraine]. Proceeding from this consideration, the Left SR fraction considers that the Ukrainian question should be handled with the utmost caution.⌐ᶜ We should not rely on the military forces present [in the Ukraine] or on the chance of a military victory. Yet relations between the CPC and the Ukrainian Rada have taken a turn which makes it likely that one side or the other may commit some irremediable [error].

At the moment we are going through a period when the [minority] peoples of Russia are awakening from the interminable oppression inflicted upon them under tsarism and are beginning to feel their way towards the ideal of complete national self-determination. In this period of their [national] development it is particularly easy to divert them from the right road by some wrong-headed or careless measure. The use of armed force may play a fatal role in this connection. It is only from within [each nation] that one may wage a struggle against the bourgeoisie, against all the excesses of imperialism, annexationism, and chauvinism. Our internationalist principles oblige us not to make it harder for Ukrainian workers, soldiers, and peasants to struggle against the counter-revolutionary forces.

I therefore ask [members of] the CPC to explain their conduct in this question today, as a matter of urgency. If for some reason they cannot do so, then they should reply at the next session on Thursday [14 December].

SAGIRASHVILI, for the United SDs, registers a protest against the failure to convoke the CEC for two weeks[1] and against the CPC's practice of deciding matters of exceptional importance without consulting the CEC. ᵇ⌐This infringes the statute. The

Presidium . . . did not put the Ukrainian question on the agenda for today.⁷ᵇ

SVERDLOV: The Presidium has received three ᶜ⌐written⁷ᶜ interpellations: on the Rada, on the Constituent Assembly and on railwaymen's wages.ᵈ ᶜ⌐The third of these was received at the last meeting.⁷ᶜ The question about the Constituent Assembly concerns the date when it will meet, its rights, and the CPC's attitude towards it; the first signatory is Avilov. As regards the first interpellation, before the session began, ᶜ⌐at the request of the Left SR fraction,⁷ᶜ I asked the CPC whether it could respond today but received the following reply:

1. For various technical and political reasons the CPC cannot today give an account of its relations with the Ukrainian Rada. This will only be possible at the next session, when the interpellation about the Constituent Assembly will also be answered.

2. The decree on railwaymen's pay has not been issued because the editorial commission presented it in ragged form and the CPC could not examine it until 7 December. Only yesterday was agreement reached about implementing the measures detailed therein, subject to the proviso that the decree be resubmitted to the CEC for further examination in the light of the new circumstances that will become apparent at the congress of the [All-Russian Union of] Railwaymen,² as well as in the light of the views now arrived at concerning nation-wide pay scales. Ordinances to this effect have already been passed to the printers and will probably be published tomorrow.

I therefore recommend that this interpellation be withdrawn ᶜ⌐until the next session, when it will be taken as the first item. (Agreed.)⁷ᶜ I should like to point out that the CPC has the right to return decrees that have been passed by the CEC for its re-examination, ᵉ⌐and only if they are adopted a second time do they acquire force of law and have to be carried out.⁷ᵉ

AVILOV: I protest against this new method of legislation by means of 'clarifications' made by the Presidium. Once decrees have been passed by the CEC they have the character of legislative acts and must be published immediately by the CPC. The

CEC's constitution makes no provision whatever for the return of decrees for reconsideration. On behalf of the United SDs I protest strongly against such attempts to alter the established relationship between the CEC and the CPC ᵉ⌐and I propose that the CEC pass a motion of censure upon the chairman and the Presidium for this infringement of our rights and di gnity.⌐ᵉ

KRUSHINSKY: It seems to me that the CPC's new attitude on the question of raising railwaymen's pay is due to sheer misunderstanding. When the decree was discussed in the CEC almost all members of the CPC were present, yet none of them objected. Indeed, how could they object when the railwaymen are receiving such miserably low wages: three, four, or five roubles [a day] for work which in other branches [of industry] is remunerated at a rate of fifteen to twenty roubles. ᶠ⌐Leaving aside this relative injustice, it is clear that when nation-wide pay scales are drawn up the railwaymen should not find themselves in an exceptional situation, even if this should mean that their wages are lowered.⌐ᶠ³

AVANESOV, in his capacity as secretary of the CEC, comments on the technical difficulties that have arisen from the fact that the decree was submitted by the editorial commission in improper form. It is wrong to blame the CPC for changing the text. The decree has been passed [to the printers] in the same form in which it was received from the editorial commission, ᶜ⌐and will appear tomorrow, but with an addendum by the CPC.⌐ᶜ The delay arose exclusively on technical grounds and not because the CPC was trying to ᶠ⌐alter its relationship with the CEC⌐ᶠ.

ᶜ⌐The other interpellations will be placed on the agenda of the next session.⌐ᶜ

SUKHANOV, on the question of the agenda: I agree with Sagirashvili's protests against the failure to convoke the CEC for two weeks during which time the CPC has carried out a number of most important measures. It has initiated peace negotiations, although the CEC has had no part in elaborating the fundamentals of [our position in] the talks. A number of steps have been taken in regard to the Rada, although this question is one of the most vital in the revolution. In addition the CPC has introduced censorship in Moscow and declared a state of siege in Petrograd.⁴ ᵉ⌐(*Bolshevik cries*: 'Sabotage!' 'Obstruction!')⌐ᵉ

All these moves have been made behind the back of the CEC, in contravention of its constitution, which specifies that the CPC should render account of its actions once a week. I therefore propose as the first point in today's agenda [a motion] that the CPC render an account of its actions during the last fortnight, ᵉ⌐[particularly of its conduct in] the peace talks. In no country in the world can the monarch alone determine the terms of peace: yet that is what the Russian delegation in Brest-Litovsk is doing.⌐ᵉ

KALEGAYEV: I do not understand why these charges are being levelled against the CPC when sessions of the CEC are convoked by its Presidium, not by the CPC. No doubt the Presidium had its reasons for acting as it did. In any case the CPC is not guilty of all mortal sins, as is being suggested here.

ᵇ⌐AVILOV, demanding the floor on a point of order: I insist that the people's commissars should reply at once to the interpellation on the Constituent Assembly.

Demand rejected. KRAMAROV [interjects]: Long live autocracy!⌐ᵇ ᵉ⌐(*Bolshevik laughter.*)⌐ᵉ

SVERDLOV, ᵍ⌐from the chair, tells Kramarov to be quiet, or else measures will be taken against him.⌐ᵍ

Sukhanov's motion is rejected, as are all others to include in the agenda matters that are the subject of interpellations.

3. *Changes in Composition of CPC*⁵

SVERDLOV reads out a list of changes in the composition of the CPC:

PC of Justice: Shteynberg.
PC of Local Self-Government: Trutovsky.
[Joint] PC of Military and Naval Affairs, with a full vote: Mikhaylov.
PC for Protection of Property of the Republic: Karelin.
[Joint] PC for Internal Affairs, without portfolio but with a full vote: Algasov.

ᵇ⌐I propose that the list be endorsed without a vote. (*Cries from the hall*: 'Who introduced this list?', 'Let's discuss it!')

SUKHANOV, on a point of order, after a long argument with the chair: The head of the present government has made no report on this question and the CEC does not know the grounds for this crisis in the Bolshevik government or its reasons for abandoning the principle of single-party rule and entering into a coalition with the [Left] SRs. By not debating this question and not demanding that the CPC render account of its actions, the CEC is burying the principle of soviet power and affirming the autocracy of the CPC, so deceiving the trust placed in it by the representatives of the workers, soldiers, and peasants.⌐b

c⌐KRASIKOV, *from his place*: Our programme remains the old one!⌐c

SVERDLOV, continuing: I move the following addition to the statute of the Supreme Economic Council:

> The CEC ordains that the PC for Organization and Regulation of Industry be appointed chairman of the SEC. [V. V.] Obolensky is appointed PC for Organization and Regulation of Industry.

These proposals are voted on [together] and approved but for 2 dissentients and 9 abstentions.*h*

b⌐AVILOV, explaining his vote, expresses solidarity with Sukhanov's views and protests against interjections by Bolsheviks who identify any criticism of the CPC as sabotage.⌐b

4. *Civil Marriage and Divorce*6
STUCHKA reads the [draft] decrees.

On behalf of the Bolshevik and Left SR fractions it is proposed that the decree[s] be accepted in principle without debate and that[they] be passed to the Presidium for final editing and publication. Any amendments are to be submitted to the Presidium in writing. There shall be only one speaker for and against the decree, whose speeches shall be of limited duration.

The proposal is accepted, 4 members dissenting and 8 abstaining.

The following amendments to the decrees are submitted:

> 1. That part of the draft dealing with divorce makes this possible only for those with means. Divorce will be impossible for those who cannot maintain children from a previous

marriage as well as from their present one unless the state pays for maintenance and education of these children. A democratic divorce law should cater to the *demos*, not to the bourgeoisie.

2. Omit the word 'only' from the phrase: 'Only civil marriage is henceforth recognized in the Russian Republic'.

3. [Add:] The decree is to come into force on 1 January 1918.

4. Omit the phrase prohibiting marriage between cousins, whether related by blood or not. They are free citizens.

5. Omit from clause 10 the word 'illegitimate'.[i]

6. With reference to clause 2: Those wishing to marry should be required to present a medical certificate for the information of their partner; [failure to do so] should not be a bar to conclusion of the marriage.

7. In lieu of publication in the official gazette (clause 5) substitute: publication in a local newspaper, specified by the organs of local self-government, [within] one year.

8. Reword preamble as follows: 'The Russian Republic henceforth recognizes civil marriage' and add: 'Marriages concluded by religious rites are considered valid only once they have been registered.'

All amendments except that submitted by Kharitonov are rejected. By a unanimous vote, but for 7 abstentions, the decree is passed to the Presidium for final editing and publication.

5. *Soldiers' Greetings*

[A delegate of the 32nd Kremenchug infantry regiment reads a message of support, dated 8 December, signed by the chairman and secretary of the regimental MRC.]

NOTES

a *NZ*, 14 Dec.: 'Held in the Hall of Fame owing to the large number of persons present'. This was therefore a plenary meeting.

b *NZ*, 14 Dec.

c *ZT*, 13 Dec.

d *ZT*, 13 Dec., omits the first item and lists food supplies in Petrograd as the second. This question is also mentioned in *Nash vek*, 13 Dec., but does not seem to have been discussed.

e *Nash vek*, 13 Dec.

f *Pravda*, 14 Dec.

g *Delo naroda*, 13 Dec. According to *Prot.* at this point he announced the agenda, but this was probably done before Sukhanov spoke to it. This agenda had nine items, of which the first were decrees on civil marriage and divorce, sickness insurance, and the prohibition of private ownership of urban buildings. It did *not*, however, include the point actually taken next, despite its significance. The latter is included in the list given in *ZT*, 13 Dec., but this mentions only the first two of the nine items recorded in *Prot.*

h *Delo naroda*, 13 Dec., reports only a vote on the changes in the CPC, in which 6 members are said to have abstained.

i The text of the draft as printed in *Prot.* substitutes for this term (*nezakonnorozhdenny*) 'out of wedlock' (*vnebrachny*).

Twentieth Session
14 December 1917

Chairman: Sverdlov   10.30 p.m.[a]

[b]SVERDLOV proposes that Trotsky's report on the peace negotiations be taken as the first item on the agenda, followed in turn by the interpellations tabled on the Rada, the Constituent Assembly and so on.[b]

[c]SOKOLNIKOV requests that the question of nationalizing the banks be taken first.

SUKHANOV supports the agenda proposed by the chair.

LEVIN[d] suggests that the issue [of bank nationalization] be referred to a special commission, which should decide the matter by accelerated procedure.

AVILOV supports this proposal.

The CEC decides to accept Sokolnikov's request[c] [b]by an overwhelming majority, only the United SD members objecting.[b]

1. Nationalization of Banks[1]

SOKOLNIKOV: In all countries, even the most democratic, power lies with the bourgeoisie, which keeps the labouring classes under the heel of capital. If we restricted ourselves to taking political action against the bourgeoisie and did not strike at the economic [basis] of its strength, we should find ourselves back in the grip of those who were vanquished by the October insurrection. There are many ways in which one can strike such a blow. Throughout the country people are [taking over] the forces of production and reconstructing them on new principles. Whole industries are being nationalized from below. We have to strike a blow from above as well. At the summit of our economic system stand the banks: an omnipotent force, a mighty fortress defending the rule of finance capital.

Some time ago the State Bank passed under the people's control. This obliged us to define our attitude to the private banks as well. Our policy was to restrict their activities and to bring them under [workers'] control. But this control showed itself to be unworkable, since it did not prevent the bankers from carrying on their business. Some banks refused to accept this control and would not supply any information. Those that did produced only worthless data, for accountancy is a kind of fraud which the banks have developed to a fine art. Only a blind man could have been satisfied with this information, for all its apparent accuracy. Left SR and Bolshevik bank employees have told us how these accounts were prepared. All the figures were simply invented and bore no relationship to reality. The resources [ostensibly] allocated to business enterprises, which should have eased the country's economic situation, went into the pockets of people close to the banks. We have received information that the banks are financing the struggle against our government. The State Bank is passing money through the private banks to subsidize [the bank employees] in their sabotage, upon which the bourgeoisie is pinning all its hopes. ^{e⌐}That is to say, the existing means of control are inadequate and we have had to reconsider the situation.^{⌐e}

Just as we are restructuring the political order in the interests of the workers and peasants, so likewise we must effect a decisive change in its financial order. This reform points directly to the achievement of socialist revolution.[2] It is not as brutal as it may seem at first sight. Owing to the lack of currency in circulation the banks have had to slow down their operations. We have put a stop to their speculative dealings and they are dying of their own accord. This means that our measures will not lead to a catastrophe. The State Bank is continuing to perform a number of important functions, ^{e⌐}such as paying the labour force, and this activity must be expanded into other areas as well.

These are the considerations which have led the CPC to proceed with nationalization of the banks.^{⌐e} Of course the question at once arose of protecting the interests of small savers, of those who entrusted the fruits of their labour to the banks by purchasing small amounts of securities. We announce here and now that we intend to guarantee their interests in full measure.^f

But a different policy will be adopted towards members of the wealthy classes who for so many years robbed and exploited [the people] in the most shameless fashion and so accumulated their millions. We declare that from today their capital is national property.

It is not possible today to pass a comprehensive decree defining the principles on which the State Bank is to merge with the private banks into a single Bank of the Russian Republic. The draft before you contains only instructions and directives as to the first steps that need to be taken. Later on a draft decree will be submitted on verification of bank safety deposits. The new millionaires who earned their fortunes in a particularly unsavoury way by speculation during the war did not put them into their current accounts but placed them behind barred steel doors guarded by hired bank employees. That is where they have secretly hoarded their criminally acquired gold, in ingots and in coins. We must authorize the CPC to carry out a very strict verification of the contents of these safety deposits so as to bring these hoards out into the daylight. The gold which ought from the start to have been deposited in the State Bank will be taken there. We shall render them that service and open current accounts for them there. When each safety deposit box is examined its owner will of course be present with his key; if he does not appear, that will be proof that the documents it contains are too disreputable and that he is afraid to expose [himself] to public condemnation. The boxes belonging to persons who do not appear will have to be opened in their absence and their contents confiscated on behalf of the people as a whole.

*[KRAMAROV, *interjecting*: After this verification will the contents of the boxes be distributed among members of the CEC?]*

SOKOLNIKOV, *continuing*: The passage of this decree will place the emancipation of labour on a sure footing. It will complete what was begun in the October days and will hold aloft the banner of socialism—a banner which will, I trust, never be lowered. (*Reads the [draft] decree.*)[h]

SVERDLOV: The Presidium proposes that the debate be curtailed and that one orator be allowed for each fraction, who may speak for 15 minutes.

TRUTOVSKY, for the Left SRs: There can be no doubt that we are here 'expropriating the expropriators'. We are prepared to back our Bolshevik comrades in every way. $^{c\Gamma}$(*Applause*.)$^{\daleth c}$ We see clearly that there is no other course but to socialize³ the means of production and finance at the present time, when the tensions of the capitalist system have reached an acute pitch and all its burdens are being borne by working people.

However, in putting this decree into practice we must be extremely careful. $^{i\Gamma}$The CEC should settle this question only in principle, leaving the practical measures to be worked out in a commission in which specialists should take part.$^{\daleth i}$ $^{c\Gamma}$I am afraid lest hasty action should damage the complex [economic] mechanism.$^{\daleth c}$ $^{i\Gamma}$I warn you that implementation of this decree will lead to an intensification of the sabotage carried on by public employees.$^{\daleth i}$ $^{c\Gamma}$I state further, in the name of the Left SRs, that we cannot agree with the way this question is being decided. It should be discussed [first] in a special commission. We propose that such a commission be set up at once and deliver its opinion within the shortest [possible] delay.$^{\daleth c}$ $^{i\Gamma}$So far as the decree on verification of safety deposit boxes is concerned, we have no objection.

AVILOV: I agree that such a complex question as nationalization of the banks should first be discussed in a commission to which competent [experts] should be invited. I warn the assembly that the CPC will not succeed in implementing these measures. If the commissars have not been able to cope with the State Bank or establish control over the private banks, how will they be able to manage such a complex apparatus as these banks control?^{j} This decree is bound to fail. The approach being taken is primitive, as if everything could be solved by a single blow of an axe.$^{\daleth i}$ $^{g\Gamma}$(*Interjections*: 'We'll get the diamonds too!' 'But what shall we really do with the jewels we find in the safes?' 'They will also be put on account in the State Bank.')$^{\daleth g}$ $^{i\Gamma}$The banks in the provinces will not submit to it and it goes without saying that nationalization will completely destroy the value of the rouble on foreign exchanges, reducing it to zero.$^{\daleth i}$

LENIN: The last speaker tried to frighten us by saying that we are heading for certain ruin, for the abyss. But this intimidation is nothing new for us. The newspaper *Novaya zhizn'*, which reflects the views of that speaker's group, wrote before October that nothing would come of our revolution but pogroms and anarchic riots. For this reason [I affirm that] statements to the effect that we are on the wrong road are simply reflections of bourgeois psychology, from which even those who have no personal axe to grind cannot free themselves. (*A United SD deputy*: 'Demagogy!') No, this is not demagogy, but your constant talk about us wielding the axe certainly is.

The measures foreshadowed in the decree are the only way to assure real control. You say that the [economic] apparatus is very complex and fragile, that the question is not a simple one: but all this is elementary and familiar to us all. If this truth is being [reiterated] just to delay socialist initiatives, then our answer is that those who say such things are demagogues, and harmful ones at that.

We want to make a start on the verification of safety deposits, but are told on the authority of erudite socialists that these contain nothing but documents and securities. If that is the case, what is so bad if they are verified by the people's representatives? If that is the case, why do these selfsame learned socialist critics go into hiding? In all our debates in the [CEC] they keep on saying that they agree with us but only in principle. This is the characteristic response of bourgeois intellectuals, of compromisers of every hue, who ruin everything with their continual agreement in principle but disagreement in practice. *ᵍᴦ*Sokolnikov, who spoke as *rapporteur* on this matter, is a very competent person in financial matters. He has a lot of practical experience and even has scholarly works on the subject to his credit. Consequently we are not solving this question by taking an axe to it, [as has been asserted].*ᵀᵍ* If you are so skilled and experienced in everything, why do you not help us? Why do you do nothing but sabotage us on our difficult path?

You proceed from a correct scientific theory, but for us this theory gives grounds for confidence in the actions we undertake, not mortal fear as to their outcome. Of course any beginning is difficult, and we often have to deal with delicate matters, but we have coped with them in the past, are coping with them at the present, and shall cope with them in the future. If theoretical literature served only to delay [action], to make people afraid to innovate, then it would be worthless. *ᵍᴦ*(*A voice*: 'Down with science!')¹⁹ No one except the Utopian socialists ever held that one could succeed without [meeting] resistance, without a dictatorship of the proletariat, without laying an iron hand on the old world. In principle you too have accepted this dictatorship, but when this term is translated into Russian—it is called 'an iron hand'—and is applied in practice you issue warnings about how complicated and delicate matters are. You persist in refusing to see that this iron hand creates as it destroys. If we move on from principles to action, that is undoubtedly a point in our favour.

In carrying out control of the banks we [first] summoned the employees and worked out with them a system of measures to which they agreed: there was to be full control and accountability, and [in return the banks] would get loans [from the State Bank]. But some bank employees had the people's interests at heart and told us: 'you are being deceived; hurry up and cut short their criminal activity, which is designed to do you serious harm.' And we quickly responded.

We know that this is a complicated measure. None of us, even trained economists, will set about implementing it [alone]. We shall call upon specialists in this field, but only once we have the keys [to the banks] in our hands. Then we shall even be able to hire ex-millionaires as consultants. Whoever wants to work [for us] will be accepted gladly, provided that he does not try to turn every revolutionary initiative into a dead letter: we shall not fall for this trick. The term 'dictatorship of the proletariat' is a serious one on our lips, and one we intend to implement.

We wanted to collaborate with the banks; we gave them credits to finance [business] enterprises, but they carried on sabotage on an unheard-of scale, so that we have been compelled by experience to implement control in different ways.

The Left SR speaker said that they would vote for immediate nationalization of the banks in principle, so that the practical measures could be worked out as soon as possible later. But this is a wrong approach, for our draft does not contain anything more than [general] principles. [The details] will be discussed afterwards by the Supreme Economic Council. Failure to approve the decree now will allow the banks to do all they can to disrupt the economy seriously. The decree must be put through without delay, or else we shall perish at the hands of those who oppose and sabotage [our policy]. (*Applause, turning into an ovation.*)

SELIVANOV, for the [SR] Maximalists: Once again members of the *Novaya zhizn'* group are trying to scare us as they did before the revolution of 25 October. At that time they reproached us for our ignorance and suggested we turn to experts in international law such as Milyukov; now they want us to turn to specialists in banking. We should ignore this intimidation and make good the error we committed on 25 October, for which we are now paying dearly. If we had nationalized the banks then, [Russian] finance capital would have been unable to organize the revolts of either Kaledin or Dutov.[4] We defeated our enemies in October but instead of disarming them we simply took away their digging tools, so that now they can fire at us with all their weapons.

There are two sorts of people: those who are continually urging delay and those who get things done. If we had followed *Novaya zhizn'*'s advice and had postponed the October revolution, we should not now be rejoicing at the news of an imminent peace. We ought to listen less to the ravens croaking in *Delo naroda* and *Novaya zhizn'*. We know that nationalization of the banks will affect the interests of international capital, as Avilov points out, but the same was true of nationalization of the land. Are we then to renounce this too? . . . [k]If one cuts down a tree one should fell it at the base, or else it will be dislodged by the wind and will fall and crush us all. I support immediate nationalization of the banks.

SOKOLNIKOV, *summing up*: The [Left] SRs seem confused. The decree presented by the CPC is only a declaration of the principles [underlying] the nationalization and an explanation of them for the broad masses. It is nevertheless necessary to make these principles known, for if the CEC does not sanction them the government will have to consider whether it should not[1k] return the keys of the banks and safes to the bourgeoisie. Those bank officials who are Left SRs do not share this point of view and are amicably working alongside us, whereas those who support *Novaya zhizn'* are actively organizing sabotage in the private banks. I don't see how Avilov can assert that there is no cash in the safe deposits. For example, bank employees have discovered that just yesterday one bank director deposited in a safe a suitcase containing twenty million roubles.

As for the international implications of this measure, I should add that the Crédit Lyonnais, the [largest] organization of French capital in Russia, adopted the most conciliatory attitude of all the banks with which we have had to deal. The foreign capital[ists] feel the mighty force of the Russian revolution too keenly to try to resist it. It has been said here that we are approaching the complex and highly developed banking system with saw and axe; but the *Novaya zhizn'* people are using needle and thread to sew up the old rags of the bourgeois order . . . We shall cope with this task just as we managed the colossal job of taking over the State Bank. About a thousand of our men are employed there now, and in its provincial branches work is going on under the supervision of soviet-appointed commissars. We have completely mastered this key to [control of] the economy, and this initial success will enable us to launch an attack on the private banks. The junior employees, who are genuine proletarians, are with us as usual, and we shall continue our work in the private banks with their assistance. Today we sent our commissar to Moscow to enforce the bank nationalization decree there, and now we are taking the same steps on an all-Russian scale.

BUKHARTSEV, for the Left SRs: We shall vote in favour of the decree.

AVILOV, for the United SDs: We shall abstain.

SUKHANOV, [for the Menshevik Internationalists]: Although I support nationalization of the banks in principle, I shall vote against the decree because I do not think the CPC is capable of implementing this measure.

The decree is adopted ⌐against 5 dissentient votes and⌐ 5 abstentions.

2. *Brest-Litovsk Peace Negotiations*[5]

TROTSKY (*greeted by an ovation which for a time prevents him from speaking*): [In connection with the Central Powers' reply to the Soviet proposals] I recall that last year Bethmann-Hollweg, the German Chancellor, stated that the war map should be the basis of the peace talks. As socialists and internationalists we were then deeply convinced that history would come up with many other maps than this one. Our hopes have been borne out, for at the present time the delegations of Germany and her allies have abandoned the idea of using the war map; they have acknowledged that this card cannot be played any longer. This is of course not the result of any idealistic evolution in [the minds of] the Prussian generals and *Junker* now in power. In addition to the factor of the military victories on which German imperialism [was counting] last year there are now the factors of economic chaos, general starvation, and the social discontent and conflict to which this gives rise. And so those [war] maps played the historical role we predicted. They led to a collapse of the hopes entertained by the nationalists and strengthened the influence exerted by the socialists over the proletariat, which at the beginning of the war had not yet been able to withstand the fateful nationalistic poison being spread by the bourgeoisie . . .

Imperialism is bankrupt even in a purely military sense, for three and a half years of warfare have shown that the victory for which the imperialists yearn will not and cannot come about. This is why the world revolution is deepening with every day that passes and why it has already succeeded in Russia. On the contrary: these maps—of the international war and also of the internal struggle—will determine [the outcome of] that frightful game which the imperialist bourgeoisie began with such criminal light-heartedness. And precisely the *German* bourgeoisie, which in its rapacity is the most sober-minded and realistic detachment of international capital, has not failed to take account of the all too obvious change in the relationship of historical forces, and has abandoned its most stoutly held advance position. It has declared that it is prepared to evacuate its forces from the occupied [regions of] northern France, Belgium, Romania, Serbia, Poland, Lithuania, and Kurland, and that it is prepared to offer these peoples the right to complete and unfettered self-determination. Thus Germany has accepted wholly the condition set by the [Second] Congress of Soviets. But it takes a different view of those territories it robbed decades ago, which in our eyes are still stolen property. The German, Turkish, Austrian, and Bulgarian bourgeoisie have decided to return what they have seized during the present war,

but they are asking us not to make them liquidate the results of
their earlier robberies. Even our enemies [in the Entente], who
so recently prophesied that the German diplomats would not so
much as talk to us but would make war against us instead, now
see that the German proposal is a tremendous success for our
policy, one which they did not expect at all.

We stand by our earlier demands for [recognition of the right
to] complete national self-determination and for the correction
of every historical injustice perpetrated until the present time.
Only he stands firm who asks [for more], who takes account of
more or less favourable combinations of circumstances. We are
calculating[m] all the advantageous and disadvantageous aspects
of our situation—but at the same time we stand solely by our
principles; since these principles do not change, so likewise our
demands do not change.[6] The fact that we do not haggle, that
we are defending the truth (and the truth alone) to the bitter
end, makes us the strongest of all the parties involved or likely
to become involved in the peace talks. [The experience of] our
first step, when invincible Germany, in its first diplomatic bout
with us, was obliged to withdraw from its advance positions,
confirms the correctness of our stand—for truth is on our side,
whereas all they have is the brute force of Prussian militarism.

Even if it were just a matter of physical force, even then Germany could not stand by her demands as confidently as we do.
She would have to take account of the fact that she is only one
link (albeit the strongest) in a chain of alliance[s] embracing
Austria, Turkey, and Bulgaria; and since the strength of a chain
is measured by the strength of its weakest link, not of its strongest, Germany would willy-nilly have to put herself on the same
level as her allies, which are half-crushed by the effects of the
war. As it is she is obliged to yield not only to [the moral force
of] our truth but to the weakness of Austria, Turkey, and Bulgaria, as well as to her own economic chaos and the threat of
revolution it conjures up, which menaces the very existence of
the bourgeois order.

We understood this when, directly after 25 October, we put
an end to the cowardly and feeble policy which made our great
country a miserable appendage of the imperialist West.[7] From
that very moment when we threw in the face of our allies the
robber treaty concluded with them by the tsarist government,

and showed that we recognized only one unwritten treaty, but a sacred one, that of international proletarian solidarity, . . . we gave the Russian revolution an immense appeal. It is exerting an increasingly hypnotic effect upon the proletarian masses in the west. There the bourgeoisie is still powerful politically, and especially psychologically, owing to the slander and lies spread by a press which is completely under its control, yet the people already know that the Russian revolution has been victorious and that Germany has recognized this victory.

Thus there are now two platforms on which the peace talks may be conducted: ours, which calls for renunciation of all conquests, present or past, and the German one, based on a readiness to abandon only what has been seized during the last war. Our allies will either have to adopt one of these two platforms or else put forward one of their own. If they adopt ours, if England grants Ireland freedom of self-determination, if Clemenceau grants self-determination to Madagascar and Panama,[8] then we shall give them a whole-hearted welcome and will work alongside them in fraternal solidarity [to achieve] the self-determination of these peoples, as well as of Alsace-Lorraine, German and Austrian Poland, etc. Our position is one of principle; that is why it is the most lofty, the noblest. For bourgeois diplomacy these negotiations are like a trial in which it is the accused under cross-examination. As we see, the German delegation has already acknowledged this and is trying to mask its past crimes by democratic phrases. But we shall ruthlessly tear off this mask and expose to the world its political nakedness—just as we shall eventually compel also the American, British, and French bourgeoisie to make plain their real aims and intentions. There are already signs that our tactic of arousing the international proletariat is having a big effect upon [these powers]. (*Reads a recent telegram from France about the Conference of Trade Unions.*)[9] The whole imperialist bourgeoisie has been given a ten-day term in which to think matters over. During this period it will be under heavy pressure from below. This pressure may be strong enough to force it to come over to our side; in any case, whatever it does, we have decided to renew the peace talks after the ten days have elapsed.

AVILOV: How do you interpret that passage in the German reply where the Quadripartite Pact powers state that they cannot enter into unilateral obligations without guarantees that Russia's allies will recognize the peace treaty and take part in the talks?

TROTSKY: This passage does not allow of any ambiguous interpretation. It means that, if Russia concludes a separate peace with Germany, Germany's obligations towards our allies will not extend to her future peace.[10] Germany is offering a deal. She is aiming a loaded revolver at those of her enemies that refrain from taking part in general peace talks. Of course she will try to falsify these obligations, but it will be the task of revolutionary democracy to keep on exposing this falsification. However, at the present time German diplomacy cannot say to us [plainly]: unless France is present at the talks, we shall not give up Kurland and Lithuania to Russia. It does not utter such threats. What the Germans essentially want is to restore the *status quo ante bellum*. This in itself is the greatest condemnation out of its own mouth of imperialism and materialism, for after 42 months of warfare it can propose nothing better than to turn back the clock to where it was at the beginning.

Nor are our allies capable of proposing any other peace programme.[11] Their governments are exhibiting a pathetic and shameful confusion. At this great historic moment they can think of nothing better to do than to discuss whether the Soviet government may send its diplomatic couriers to Italy by way of Britain. History will not forget this shameful behaviour, nor the French and American imperialists' wager on Kaledin. We shall defeat this [manœuvre] as we have all the others. We have had a report that in Kharkov the Ukrainian soviets of workers' and soldiers' deputies have met [in congress] and declared themselves to be the central revolutionary authority in the Ukraine. Meanwhile the cossack [forces] are dissolving, and our troops are continuing to concentrate on the front against Kaledin. Soon we shall witness the defeat of the counter-revolutionaries.

SHTEYNBERG: This is the first big success for our diplomacy since the revolution began. Despite the enthusiasm [unleashed by] the October revolution, when we sent our delegation to the enemy camp we were not sure whether it would hold aloft the banner of the revolution. Each step it took and each word it uttered were eagerly followed not only by our [friends]*ⁿ* but also by our opponents on the right. *ᶜ⌐*Today we affirm that the delegation was on the right track.*⌐ᶜ* Whatever may happen in future, there can be no return to the past. The question of peace has ceased to be an abstraction and has assumed concrete shape. Spirit has triumphed over matter, the revolution over imperialism. Unarmed, we entered the enemy camp and spoke not as equals but as superiors. A mortal blow has been inflicted upon imperialism. The German generals are bowing their heads before the slogans of the Russian revolution. This shows that in Germany a mood of indignation and insurrection has developed. We were convinced that this would occur in all the belligerent countries. Now we have to awaken the slumbering forces of socialism and recreate the international socialist front. We have to lay the foundations of the Third International. Long live the Third International! *ᶜ⌐(Loud applause.)⌐ᶜ*

I move the following resolution:

> The CEC notes with satisfaction that a mighty blow has been dealt against the strongest citadel of world imperialism. German militarism has retreated before the Russian revolution. Let us also pay our respects to it, conscious of the ever-growing movement [of revolt] among the long-suffering peoples.
> But world imperialism seeks to ease its [internal] tensions by [repressing] the people. World democracy must prevent this by exerting pressure upon all governments.
> Welcoming these successes achieved by our delegation at Brest-Litovsk, the CEC urges ever more decisive measures to rally the socialist front for peace.

The resolution is passed unanimously but for 1 abstention.

ZINOVIEV: I propose that on Sunday 17 December a grandiose peace demonstration be held throughout Russia.

Approved unanimously.

3. *Conflict with Ukrainian Rada*[12]

STALIN *ᵒ⌐(Applause)⌐ᵒ*: It may seem strange that the CPC, which has always resolutely defended the principle of self-determination, should have come into conflict with the Rada, which likewise proceeds from this principle. In order to understand the cause of this conflict, one must examine the Rada's political physiognomy. It proceeds from the principle of a division of power between the bourgeoisie on one hand and the proletariat and peasantry on the other. The soviets repudiate such an arrangement and give all power to the people, excluding the bourgeoisie. That is why the Rada opposes the slogan 'All power to the soviets' (i.e. to the people) and instead calls for 'All power to the organs of local self-government in town and country' (i.e. to the people and the bourgeoisie).

It is said that the conflict arose over self-determination, but this is not the case. The Rada has proposed that a federal structure be established in Russia. But the CPC goes further than the Rada, [conceding] even the right of secession. Consequently the disagreement between the CPC and the Rada is not about that.

The Rada is also completely wrong in maintaining that the disagreement is about centralism [on our part]. Regional centres modelled on the CPC in Siberia, Belorussia, and Turkestan[13] have asked us for directives, and the CPC has replied: 'you yourselves are the government in your areas, work out your own directives.'

In reality the disagreement between the CPC and the Rada has come about over the following three questions:

The first is the concentration of Ukrainian units on the southern [part of the] front. It is doubtless true that national units are best suited to defend their own territory. But at the present time our front is not constructed according to the principle of nationality. The restructuring[p] of the front according to the nationality principle would lead to its complete annihilation, given the chaos on the railways. This would undermine the cause of peace. The Ukrainian soldiers have shown themselves more sensible and more honest than the General Secretariat, for most of them have shown no desire to submit to the Rada's orders.

The second question is the disarming of Soviet forces in the Ukraine. By disarming Soviet forces the Ukrainian Rada is defending the interests of the Ukrainian landlords and bourgeoisie and dealing a blow against the revolution. Its actions in this regard differ in no whit from those of Kornilov and Kaledin. There is no need to add that the CPC will combat this counter-revolutionary policy of the Rada by every means.

Finally, the third question is that of refusal to allow Soviet troops to pass through [the Ukraine] to fight Kaledin, around whom all the counter-revolutionary forces of Russia are rallying. The Rada justifies its action by its [desire to remain] neutral towards Kaledin['s cossacks], who are [allegedly exercising the right of] self-determination. But here the Rada is substituting Kaledin's autocracy for self-determination by the toiling cossacks. By refusing to let Soviet forces through the Rada is helping Kaledin move troops northwards. Simultaneously cossack forces are being freely permitted to pass through to the Don. At the moment when our comrades are being shot in Rostov and the Don basin the Rada is preventing us from going to help them. I need not say that this treacherous conduct by the Rada cannot be tolerated.

The CPC cannot refrain from struggling against Kaledin. This counter-revolutionary nest must be liquidated. This is inevitable. If the Rada prevents us moving against Kaledin and shields him, then our blows against Kaledin will fall upon its forces. The CPC will not shrink from a resolute struggle against the Rada, since it knows that the latter is in secret alliance with Kaledin. The CPC has intercepted a coded telegram from which it is clear that the Rada is directly linked with the French mission [in efforts] to delay conclusion of peace until the spring, and through the French mission it is linked to Kaledin.[14] This alliance is directed against peace and against the revolution. It must and will be destroyed.

We are reproached for being too resolute in our policy towards the Rada. But it is this resolute policy which has opened the eyes of Ukrainian workers and peasants to the Rada's bourgeois nature, ⌐as is evident from the information we have just received by telegraph to the effect that power in the Ukraine has been transferred to the Ukrainian congress of soviets in Kharkov, which has declared itself the supreme organ of authority in the Ukraine.⌐ ⌐(Applause.)⌐

KRYLENKO ⌐(Applause)⌐: ⌐The entire policy of the Rada has been aimed at disrupting the peace [talks] and has already had unfortunate consequences by disorganizing the front, causing hundreds of thousands of men to go hungry.⌐ ⌐(Reads a report on the supply situation in the army.) These are the figures of the

military supply authorities, who [are inclined to] paint the
picture unduly dark . . . , but the closure of the access routes
[from Siberia] through Chelyabinsk and from the Ukraine
threatens our armies with total starvation.⌐l ⌐qThe front is
living from hand to mouth. Even before the conflict began with
the Rada the least disruption of normal supplies threatened to
lead to starvation. Now Kovalevsky, the Rada's Supply minister, is refusing to allow food and fodder to be sent to the Northern and Western fronts unless they are paid for in gold specie.[15]
If this threat is carried into effect there will be a catastrophe.⌐q

   ⌐cNor has the Rada yet replied to Trotsky's invitation to send
delegates to the peace talks. When I, as Commander-in-Chief,
issued a categorical demand [to this effect], Petlyura replied
with a long-winded explanation, the sense of which was that the
Soviet government was entirely to blame since it allegedly did
not want to recognize the Rada's authority and should have
joined with Kaledin's counter-revolutionary forces in saving the
country.⌐c

   ⌐qLet me give you some details about the way in which
forced Ukrainization of the army has disorganized the front.⌐q
⌐l(*Reads text of agreement of 6 November between Dukhonin and the
Rada about Ukrainization.*) This reform was to have been put into
effect gradually and according to plan. It would have led to a
systematic weakening of the front. When I assumed the post of
Commander-in-Chief the Rada took urgent measures to put the
plan into effect as quickly as possible. Petlyura sent a number of
menacing telegrams,ʳ culminating in a demand for a separate
Ukrainian front combining the South-western and Romanian
fronts.⌐l ⌐qDespite repeated proposals on our part that the Rada
should send its representative to General Headquarters, where
he could work together with me in regulating the movements of
Ukrainian units, it has not yet sent anyone; meanwhile these
units have been encouraged to engage in spontaneous acts [of
violence]. They have seized trains and moved them off in
various directions, completely disrupting the transport system,
which was already in a parlous state. The Rada has issued
orders which have led to a complete breakdown of communications between GHQ and the Western and South-western
fronts. Three armies of the South-western and Southern [i.e.
Romanian] fronts have refused to submit to Petlyura's authority

and he has taken harsh measures against them. He has suggested that they be withdrawn from the front, but this is categorically opposed by GHQ as it would do irremediable harm to the front and to the country as a whole. [These] armies are obeying GHQ's orders, but Petlyura has decided to starve them out by refusing to supply them with grain, fodder etc. (*Reads documents in support of this contention.*)⁷ᵃ

ᵗᵣ(*Reads the Rada's reply to the CPC.*) After we received this message I could but recognize that the Rada had declared war on the CPC. From a number of telegrams it is clear that it has been carrying on the most desperate agitation, consisting of lies, hypocrisy, deceit, provocations, and chauvinism. As a result there have been chauvinistic [i.e. Russo-Ukrainian] clashes, fortunately few of them. Everywhere there is an atmosphere of hostility; units are disarming each other, tearing up railway tracks and blowing up bridges. The lengths to which the Rada is willing to go in this provocation is evident from an order by the Commander-in-Chief in Odessa, who has given all non-Ukrainians three months' leave, playing on the soldiers' fatigue in the hope of bringing the railways to a standstill and reducing the effectives at the front. I have been obliged to halt the process of Ukrainization and to restrict it by imposing certain conditions, in the first place recognition of soviet power, but I have also had to dissolve certain regimental soviets (*rady*).⁷ˡ

ᵃᵣIf the Rada does not stop its policy of rallying all the counter-revolutionary forces under its aegis then we shall have to use all [available] means against it, not shrinking from bloodshed.⁷ᵃ

A BOLSHEVIK member moves the following resolution:

> Having heard the replies given by Stalin and Krylenko for the CPC to the interpellation about [its relations with] the Rada, the CEC expresses complete approval of its resolute policy towards the bourgeois Rada.

ᵃᵣMOISEYEV, for the United SDs: This guillotining of debate on our interpellation has the effect of nullifying it. I propose that discussion of our interpellation be deferred until the next session, when orators for each fraction should be given an opportunity to respond.

This proposal is rejected, whereupon Moiseyev tables a second motion:[7][q]

> The CEC considers that the CPC acted incorrectly in arbitrarily declaring war on the Ukraine behind the back of the CEC and in not reporting the existence of a state of war to the CEC.

This motion wins only 3 votes in favour and is rejected. The Bolshevik resolution is adopted with 2 dissentients.

NOTES

a *NZ*, 15 Dec.; *ZT*, 15 Dec.: 10 p.m.
b *Delo naroda*, 15 Dec.
c *ZT*, 15 Dec.
d *NZ*, 15 Dec.: Moiseyev.
e *Pr.*, 16 Dec.
f The variant in *ZT*, 15 Dec., is less liberal: 'In regard to them the Soviet government is not of course contemplating any infringement of their property.'
g *Nash vek* (a hostile source), 15 Dec., which adds: 'This remark is ignored by the speaker and most of the audience, which for once were paying close attention to the speaker's words.'
h *ZT*, 15 Dec.: and the decree on verification of safety deposits.
i *NZ*, 15 Dec.
j literally: 'represent'.
k *Iz.*, 17 Dec.; text of this passage as given in *Prot.* is corrupt.
l *Iz.*, 17 Dec.
m *Prot.*: 'intriguing' (*intriguyem*).
n *Prot.*: 'enemies'.
o *Pr.*, 19 Dec.
p *Pr.*, 19 Dec.; *Prot.*: 'structure' (*postroyka*).
q *NZ*, 16 Dec.
r According to *ZT*, 15 Dec., Krylenko read out details of these exchanges, which have not been preserved. Much of his speech is also reproduced as an appendix to *Prot.* (pp. 159–60).

Twenty-first Session
19 December 1917

(Held jointly with the Petrograd soviet (600 persons) and the Demobilization Congress (300 persons); 350 members of the CEC are present.)[a]

Chairman: Sverdlov   7.30 p.m.[b]

1. *Peace Negotiations: Delegation's Report*[1]

KAMENEV (*Applause*): The armistice agreement included a clause to the effect that talks on peace were immediately to follow. As you know, the Russian delegation considers these negotiations an urgent and serious matter, and therefore we saw no reason to delay the initiation of talks on a general peace. We began by setting out definite and precisely formulated principles on which, in our view, a general democratic peace could be concluded. It was clear merely from the composition of the Central Powers' delegation that the governments of Germany, Austria, Turkey, and Bulgaria were eager to emphasize the seriousness of their intentions. For our part we went to Brest[-Litovsk] determined to conclude, not a separate peace, but a general democratic peace in the interests of liberating the toiling masses of the entire world.

Such a peace must be based on the resolutions and decisions of the Second Congress of Soviets, and in our six-point declaration we did no more than elaborate on these principles. We said that all conquered and occupied territories must be evacuated immediately and that the peoples which had been deprived of their independence during the war should get it back again: this applies to Belgium, Serbia, Romania, Montenegro, and Greece. In the third[c] point of our declaration we categorically demanded that the enslaved and robbed peoples be given the right of self-determination, up to the right to secede from the states that had [annexed] them, and that national minorities be given the right of territorial–cultural autonomy. We stated that all colonial peoples, all the peoples of Africa and Asia, should have the same wide-ranging independence as the liberated peoples of Europe. The Russian revolution does not draw any distinction, or allow any distinction to be drawn, between the peoples of Europe and those of Asia and Africa where freedom is concerned. Nor will the Russian revolution accept [imposition of] any contributions, any obligatory commercial treaties, any exploitative economic relationships. Such were the general principles contained in our delaration.

The Central Powers' delegations were slow to give a definitive and precise reply. Our bourgeois press lost no time in starting a new campaign against our policy on this account, alleging that some kind of secret negotiations were going on in Brest, that we were engaging in concealed bargaining. But we knew well why the other side was delaying its response. Although Germany has not quite lost hope of leading her people into new military adventures, Turkey and the other states have abandoned such ideas. Undoubtedly there were tensions and disputes between them once we had posed the question of annexations and contributions so forcefully. During these [private] talks certain members of the opposing delegation[s] convinced the others to accept [their draft] reply. This has been published in all the papers and so I shall not read it. For us in the delegation the important thing about this reply was that the Germans recognized that 'the basic principles of the Russian delegation may be made the basis of negotiations for a general peace.' This we regarded as a major victory for the October revolution. By accepting this declaration the German imperialists were obliged to expose before the whole world the foul acquisitive aims they were pursuing in this war.

We took only three hours, not three days, to give our answer.[2] In it we said that in their declaration we discerned a number of skilfully contrived passages and loopholes designed to permit the imperialists to carry out their plans of conquest. The Germans and Austrians are refusing to give their [subject] peoples the right of self-determination, of independence. This destroys absolutely [the value of] their recognition of a peace without annexations. Therefore their statement that 'the Russian revolution does not have the right to interfere in the destinies of other peoples'[d] shows that they [wish to] go on exploiting and oppressing other peoples. We insisted firmly that our demands be granted in full, since in our view the German reply nevertheless contained grounds for continuing the talks among all belligerents.

After three years of warfare it is not so easy as some people think to obtain peace. But it is the task of the Russian revolution to expose the imperialists of all countries before their peoples, and in this regard we have won a major victory, for by exposing the belligerent powers' annexationist plans we are bringing nearer the day when bayonets will give way to diplomats' pens. Our reply ended with a request for a ten-day recess in the talks, so that the peoples and governments of France, Britain, and other countries could become acquainted in detail with our declarations and finally come to a decision one way or another.

In their reply the Central Powers' representatives agreed to the ten-day recess and proposed that we [first] hear their proposals in regard to [e]⌈certain very important points of interest to both sides. At [the next] two official sessions we heard these statements, which were⌉[e] concerned with formulating the relationship between Russia on one hand and Germany and Austria-Hungary on the other after peace has been concluded. The main proposals fall into two categories: first, economic and juridical relations, and second, political, involving territor[ial changes].

The bourgeois press has always been shouting that the revolutionary government was prepared to enslave Russia economically[3] to get an immediate peace, but at Brest we told the German bourgeoisie clearly that our foreign trade policy was based on the principle of complete economic equality [i.e. reciprocity]. And it must be said that, contrary to these press reports, in reply to our declaration Germany did not dare to claim any special advantages or privileges over those of other nations trading with Russia. Germany hopes that natural conditions, her geographical proximity, will give her a favourable position, [so that she does not need] any formally agreed [special] rights.

The German delegation stated that it was prepared to accept any one of three methods [of proceeding]. It was ready to restore the old commercial agreement of 1904 for one year, until a new treaty was concluded; [e]⌈to establish⌉[e] a system of free trade; or to agree at once to a 'most-favoured nation' system for one year, ᵉ⌐whereby the ships and [other means of] transport of each country would enjoy reciprocal privileges.⌐ᵉ It stands to reason that we expected such proposals from a bourgeois government. But the point to note is that they contain no demand that German exports and imports be given privileges.

To these proposals we responded by pointing out that at present Russia is undergoing a mighty upheaval that will result in a new economic order, and that we could not permit the application of principles contrary to those of socialism at a time when we are introducing control over industry, nationalizing the banks, and restraining the greed of private entrepreneurs; consequently German imports would have to be subject to state control and regulation.[4] Even after this reply the [spokesmen for the] German bourgeoisie, contrary to the affirmations of the Russian bourgeois press, did not dare to demand privileges. So far as particular problems [in this area] are concerned, we decisively rejected the notion of renewing the commercial agreement of 1904, even for a brief period, as well as the notion of signing treaties with Germany and Austria granting them most-favoured nation status. We declared that this would mean realizing the imperialistic aims of the *Mitteleuropa* [concept],[5] designed to wage economic war after conclusion of peace. We said that we rejected this not only for practical reasons but also on grounds of principle, since we were opposed to any economic war, whether planned by the Allies at their Paris conference or by [the partisans of] *Mitteleuropa*.

Let me pass on to the question of the occupied territories. We proposed to the Germans that they remove all their armies behind their old frontiers and allow all [other] peoples to decide their future by a [plebiscitary] vote. In reply the German diplomats came up with a clause which needs to be studied carefully. They said that they were not willing to evacuate all the territory their armies had occupied, but that they would divide it into two parts. From one part, Belorussia and Volhynia, the German armies would withdraw, but as for Poland, Lithuania, ᵉ⌐Kurland, and part of Estonia⌐ᵉ the population had allegedly already declared for secession from the Russian state, and therefore Germany did not find it possible to evacuate her troops.

This ambiguous and devious formula is a product of the

struggle going on between two currents in Germany's ruling groups. One group holds that all the territories occupied by Hindenburg's soldiers should be retained. The other group, the advocates of a covert and veiled annexation, has to reckon not only with the Hindenburg party but also with the masses of workers and soldiers who are eager for peace. The evacuation of Poland and Lithuania would undoubtedly lead to an upsurge of the revolutionary movement among the masses in those countries on the Russian model; that is why the Germans want to keep their troops there. ᵉᵣThey are motivated purely by class interest.ᵀᵉ

This raises the question whether a German corporal would be present to control [the referendum at which] the Polish, Lithuanian, and other peoples decide their fate. Should the great Russian revolution give the German imperialists the right to supervise the way in which the Polish and Lithuanian workers, peasants, and soldiers win their independence and settle their destinies? Or should we summon all our available forces and unflinchingly resist such an infringement of the rights of the Polish, Lithuanian, and Latvian proletariat and peasantry?[6]

Article 2 in the German terms is in flagrant contradiction with the principle of national self-determination. This is now the main point at issue between us. The Germans claim that they have received letters and resolutions from a number of villages in which the inhabitants say they would like to be under German protection, and that there have even been requests for them to establish such a system forthwith. Indeed, they add that such requests have been addressed to them by inhabitants of places they have not yet occupied. But of course all such decisions and demands stem from privileged groups of the population, from those who believe that German military might is the basis of a legal order, a stronghold against the insurrectionary slogans coming from Russia.

Thus the question is completely clear. This is not a national but a class problem: shall the toilers of the occupied regions be given the chance to choose freely between the principles of the Russian revolution and the bourgeois order of Germany? We are within our rights in turning to the German soldiers and asking them if they want to be tools of Baltic barons and Polish bourgeois, to help them torture their peoples to maintain their power. If^f we asked the Polish, Lithuanian, and Latvian peasants whether they are willing to exercise their right of self-determination under the control of the German imperialists or whether they [would prefer to] march under the banners of the Russian revolution, I have no doubt that they would as one man all cry out that they trust only the great Russian revolution, the liberator of peoples, $^e\lceil$despite the letters and resolutions received by the Germans.$\rceil^e$

Now that the Germans have turned the self-determination principle from a formula for national liberation into a disguise for annexation, now that its class nature has been exposed for all to hear, [we state that] we are not willing to defend a territorial border that has resulted from military conquest,^{g} but exclusively the limits within which the Russian revolution expands. For our revolution has come about solely to defend the interests of workers and soldiers all over the world.

Accordingly we have made the following counter-proposal to the German [draft of] article 2:

Art. 2. In full accord with the public statement[s] by both contracting parties that they have no plans of conquest and desire to conclude a non-annexationist peace, Russia withdraws its troops from the occupied regions of Austria-Hungary, Turkey, and Persia and the Quadripartite Alliance powers withdraw theirs from Poland, Lithuania, Kurland, and other regions of Russia.

In conformity with the principles of the Russian government, which has proclaimed the right of all peoples inhabiting Russia without exception to exercise [the right of] self-determination even up to secession, the population of these regions shall be given the possibility, within an exactly defined period in the very near future, to decide in complete freedom whether they wish to join another state or to form independent states. When this [vote is being taken] the presence in the regions where self-determination is proceeding of any troops other than those of the nationality concerned, or local militia, is impermissible. Until this question is decided the administration of these regions shall be in the hands of democratically elected representatives of the local population. The period [within which] the evacuation [shall be carried out] is to be determined by a special military commission, having regard to circumstances, [i.e.] to the beginning and course of the armies'[7] demobilization.

There is no doubt that, if Germany should now make so bold as to send her armies against revolutionary Russia, her aim would be to liquidate completely the freedom of Poland, Lithuania, and a whole number of other countries. This would be the spark that would finally touch off the explosion and overturn the whole edifice of German imperialism. We are certain that Germany will not dare to attempt this, for if she did we would eventually secure a peace, no matter what the obstacles—but then the peace talks would be not with the representatives of German imperialism but with the socialists by whose efforts the German government would have been overthrown. Our dispute with the German imperialists must be settled by revolution.[h]

Finally I should explain that after we heard [the text read out of] article 2 of the German terms, we declared that we could not enter into a detailed discussion of the other points until this matter was finally settled, but would simply report these points to the revolutionary Russian people. (*Reads these articles.*) The German terms [include] a demand that Germans living in Russia receive back the land taken from them. To this we replied that we had confiscated all the landowners' property and were not prepared to make an exception for anyone, least of all for German landowners. As a result the Germans had to add a clause to their text stating that they recognized the nationalization carried through as a result of the revolution. Their [draft of] article 9 now reads:

All landed property, mines, businesses, and partial [ownership] rights are returned to their proprietors in so far as this property has not been taken over by the state according to the recent Russian legislation.

In connection with article 13 [dealing with the release of internees] we demanded the liberation of everyone imprisoned in all countries for their active struggle for peace. Kühlmann objected that he did not know which countries were referred to, and when we mentioned Liebknecht he said that he was not empowered to answer this question but hoped it would be settled satisfactorily. We paid no attention to this statement since Liebknecht will be liberated only by the [German] revolution.[8]

The floor is given to representatives of the All-Army Demobilization Congress now taking place in Petrograd. [Declarations of support[i] are made by speakers for the following units: Yaroshevsky (XIIth Army), Belenky (Ist Army), Livshits (Vth Army), Konstantyev (Reval front), Bykov (IInd Army), Sokolov (IIIrd Army), Zamyatinsky (South-western front), Komissarov (VIIth Army), Kolesnikov (XIth Army), Groman (Special Army), Khobotov (IVth Army), Malishchevsky (VIIIth Army), Kruze (IXth Army), Trifonov (Russian troops in France and Macedonia), Kalegov (Western front).]

KASHGAROV, for the Petrograd soviet: I assure our soldier comrades that everything will be done here to improve the supply situation at the front. If necessary we shall send men from the rear to relieve those now in the trenches and shall entrust the safety of the revolution in the interior of the country to the revolutionary Red guards.

BARANOV, chairman of the All-Russian naval congress,[9] for the Russian navy: The fleet wholly supports the Soviet government and is inspired by complete readiness to fight with all its might for the slogans advanced by the revolution. The Russian navy will not depart from the principles of revolutionary socialism but will hold aloft its banners until the end before [the onslaught of] German imperialism. (*Stormy applause.*)

[j]MOISEYEV, for the United SDs: Today is the first occasion when the question of concluding peace has been posed seriously, and now we should discuss the peace terms in a business-like manner. We are all convinced that with things as they are on the [various] fronts Germany can no longer hope to engage in overt aggression, in the political subordination of foreign territories, but this does not mean that she is willing to abandon economic exploitation of the regions she has occupied by carving them up into autonomous states. Germany wants a general peace, not just a separate one with Russia, and therefore in renouncing annexations and contributions she has made an essential qualification: that these terms are only binding on her if the Allies join in the talks that have been initiated. In the face

of this fact it is our duty not to meet all the Germans' demands, not to agree to all the terms they put forward.

The sorry state of the front means that the rear should do all it can to help, and [in the first instance] cease the civil war which is the prime cause of the difficulties our soldiers confront.

The German government has refused to issue passports to the German delegates who had been authorized to make contact with socialists in other countries. It has prevented *Die Fackel* from being distributed at the front. Three hundred German socialists have been arrested for making propaganda for peace. We should react to all this in a resolute manner and also exert our influence on the Allied countries.

The Germans have refused to allow Russian officers to control the movement of German troops [to the interior], saying that this demand is a sign that we distrust their word.

The German [soldiers] are short of food, but the exchange of foodstuffs all along the front, in accordance with the armistice terms, [is unwise] at a time when we ourselves are starving. We are only giving the Germans the chance to get the grain we need in return for their [surplus] commodities.

The main tasks facing us are to convoke an international socialist conference, to supply the front with the material it needs, to liquidate the civil war, and above all else to convoke the Constituent Assembly as soon as possible. (*The speaker is constantly heckled with cries of*: 'Saboteur!', 'Go to the defensists!', *etc.*)⁷ʲ

KAMKOV, for the Left SRs (*Ovation*): We are not at all surprised by Kamenev's statement that the German delegation was proving stubborn over the question of national self-determination, on which we have strongly insisted and will continue to insist. It would be hard to believe that the German imperialists would capitulate at once before [the eyes of] the whole world and say that our demands are acceptable . . . even to the Hindenburg clique.

The hue and cry raised in the bourgeois press is designed to minimize the extent of our success in getting Germany to accept the Russian revolution's peace formula and to impede our further efforts in the struggle for peace.

In the German terms the point about self-determination is

formulated in an ambiguous way designed to conceal the most cynical annexationist aims. But if we nevertheless continue to insist on unconditional acceptance of our principles, it is because we represent a force which the imperialists have to take seriously. Our force does not lie in bayonets but . . . in the sympathy of Europe's toiling masses. I agree that it will now be less easy than it was for the German imperialists to move troops against us, . . . for Hindenburg will come up against German democracy, at the price of whose blood he wants to ensure that German feudal lords can dominate Lithuania, Poland, Estonia and so on. Such an attempt will blow up the powder keg on which the German imperialists are sitting.

. . . We support whole-heartedly the refusal of our peace delegation to compromise with the German imperialists. Our road is the only correct one to victory over imperialism. (*Loud applause.*)

TROTSKY [e]⌜(*Ovation; some stand; the chairman has difficulty in restoring order before he can speak*).⌝[e] On that very same day when in Brest the commission of representatives of Russia, Germany, and Austria-Hungary was beginning its work, the press here was full of news and speculative gossip [k]⌜about some peace talks that were allegedly taking place in Petrograd⌝[k]. I shall therefore have to begin by setting out our position correctly.

A tremendous fuss has been created over the arrival [in Petrograd] of a German delegation.[10] I may say that this does not consist of 500, or even 150, men armed from head to toe or about to be so equipped by the PC of Foreign Affairs, as some newspapers have suggested. Nor are we concluding any secret treaties with this delegation. I inform the press, including those [correspondents] here today, that the delegation consists of 25 members, accompanied, by thirty servants and orderlies—they still have orderlies—making some sixty persons in all. Nobody who has read the papers is unaware that according to the armistice terms it was decided that commissions should meet in Petrograd to facilitate the possible return of civilian prisoners and hostages and to ease the lot of prisoners of war. The whole world knows about this and the newspapers inform their readers of it: only the Russian press has not heard of it and persistently keeps on talking about secret treaties.

We began our meeting with this delegation by protesting against the arrest of 300 revolutionary socialists in Germany. Count Mirbach, who is at present spending some time on the red-hot soil of our capital, replied that he had come on a specific mission and was not empowered to answer our protest. History has thought fit that to end the slaughter we should have to talk to German and Austrian imperialists and feudal lords. This is not our doing: it is [a circumstance] imposed upon us by History. We do not forget that on the other side [of the front] our revolutionary blood-brothers have been arrested, and we hope that soon they will be our partners [at the bargaining-table]. *j⌐Our moral justification lies in the fact that we are arresting our own representatives of feudalism and capitalism.⌐j The German and Austrian feudal representatives who visited our Smolny Institute could see Red guardsmen marching away Russian feudal lords and bourgeois. If they had protested against this, we should not have taken refuge behind [diplomatic excuses] but would have looked them squarely in the eye and said: yes, we *are* doing this and we consider we have a right to do so because when the proletariat arrests [members of] the élite it is casting off oppression, whereas to arrest Liebknecht and other revolutionaries is to trample on the people's rights. We do not for a moment forget what divides us from members of the delegation; we speak to them as strikers do to capitalists. During a strike there comes a moment when the strikers put their terms to the other side, but in doing so they do not cease to feel themselves a revolutionary force. In our case, too, this will not be the final agreement: we believe that we shall negotiate that agreement with Karl Liebknecht, and then we shall remake the map of Europe, together with its peoples, to ensure complete self-determination and the final liquidation of oppression on earth.

*j⌐It is characteristic that those who reproach us the most severely for talking to German imperialists are those who themselves were lackeys and obedient servants of Allied imperialism. Today⌐j I received information from a most official source that an extremely well-known patriot, a defender of the Constituent Assembly, approached a neutral diplomat and asked him to tell the Germans that he was willing to offer his services to carry on peace talks with their delegation on the basis of the Soviet formula.[11] ᴶ⌐These unemployed 'diplomats' are awaiting the moment when we, remaining loyal to our banners, tell the Germans that we shall make no further concessions; then they will appear and say 'we will make them'. I am sure that if by some miracle the Kadets and Right SRs were to be in power now, they would quickly conclude a shameful peace to free their hands in order to shore up a bourgeois order in Russia.⌐ᴶ

In Germany, alas, there is less freedom of speech than there is in Russia, where nothing is concealed from the people . . . Despite the fact that German imperialism is doing everything to hide the truth and prevent our ideas penetrating, there was never so strong a bond of solidarity between [our] peoples than there is now, when the war has brought about a complete divorce between the masses and their leaders. We have already got rid of our top people [*verkhushka*]. When we arrest exploiters, people who ruin the economy for their own profit, we are freeing the working people for creative labour; but when they put in prison those who produce wealth and their leaders they are cutting the ground from beneath their own feet.

At the present stage of the peace talks which Kamenev was speaking about, even if the terms put before us do not correspond to our aims, and we reject them, we nevertheless feel that we are stronger now than we were before the talks began. ᴶ⌐We shall tell the German soldiers, through the newspapers which we are distributing on their side of the front, the whole truth about why we do not see eye to eye with the representatives of German imperialism.⌐ᴶ Tomorrow we shall state openly [at the talks] that we cannot accept the suggestion that the principle of national self-determination be implemented in the presence of armed troops. In saying this we shall be supported by the Polish workers. If Poland is prevented by German armed might from determining her fate as a whole nation, then the more its body is tortured the more its spirit will be with us.

Later on our talks will be held in a neutral country, where they will become the property of the whole world and all toiling people will be able to find out what they [the Germans] want and what we are doing. ᴶ⌐Neither the Germans nor the Allies inform their peoples fully about the course of our negotiations. Not all our proposals are reported. Today I learned that Clemenceau has again refused to issue passports to French socialists of the Tsereteli stripe. We must ensure that all peoples are properly informed.⁷ʲ We must conduct our revolutionary policy with firmness, for we are the fortress of revolution and a fortress must be strong.

Our comrades from the trenches have just told us how unbearably hard their life is at the front, how hungry and ill-clad they are. But there are [enough] supplies in our country: we are [merely] going through a period of unheard-of chaos and disorganization. Many aspects of our life need an organizer's hand.¹² In every sphere a thin stratum of intellectuals has betrayed the people that nourished it and whose interests it was [morally] obliged to serve, and has devoted all its knowledge and willpower to the task of destroying and disorganizing the country as much as possible. And when I hear these reports by front-line soldiers I say to myself: we have been too condescending towards these criminal saboteurs. (*Applause.*)

On the eve of the October days we swore that we would tear the clothes off the bourgeoisie, take away the bread from the rear and send it to the men in the trenches. The time has come to do this. We must enforce revolutionary workers' discipline upon the upper strata throughout the country. We promise the front-line soldiers' representatives all possible aid. We say to them: tell [your comrades] in the trenches that the difficulties of the moment are but the birth-pangs which the motherland must go through in order to bring forth a new free and beautiful life.

Hold on for this essential last minute. Let the German soldier know that we have a new army without chiefs, without punishments, one that is not driven forward by the [officer's] baton; that on our side of the front each soldier is a citizen filled with revolutionary consciousness; and that such an army is capable of accomplishing [great deeds]. It is manning the forward trenches of the world-wide revolutionary movement. Its banners are those of world-wide liberation of the toilers, and no one shall tear them from its hands. Long live the revolutionary army! Long live the revolutionary navy! (*Stormy ovation.*)

ʲ⌐IOFFE: [States that he is a member of the Demobilization Congress but is speaking on behalf of the Mensheviks.]⁷ʲ ¹ʳWe have been proved wholly correct in our forecasts that the Germans would not accept democratic peace terms. It seems to me that when the Russian delegates asked Kühlmann why Lieb-knecht had not been released, he ought to have replied: 'Physi-cian, heal thyself!' Instead of protesting at the arrest and im-prisonment of Liebknecht and other German Social Democrats, you ought to be protesting at the arrest of Rozanov, the man who travelled all over Europe on behalf of Russian democracy to arrange the Stockholm conference. (*Uproar, applause.*) You ought to be protesting at the [order for the] arrest of the man who for eight months withstood accusations of internationalism, the man who enjoys the support of many millions of peasants, V. M. Chernov. (*Tremendous uproar, applause.*)⌐¹

SVERDLOV, from the chair: I apologize for giving the floor to a Menshevik and for not silencing him immediately. Erlich went abroad on behalf of the defensist soviets.[13]

KAMENEV, concluding the debate: I should like to answer the questions that have been raised.

So far as the exchange of prisoners of war is concerned, this question cannot be settled before conclusion of a peace treaty, for [otherwise] the return to Germany of several million healthy soldiers by such an exchange would enable her to use them on the French and other fronts, which of course we could not accept.

There are unconfirmed reports that Serbia and Romania would like to join the peace talks but are being held back by Britain and France.

To the question 'when will peace be concluded?' I reply: it will be concluded, of course, but no one can say even approxi-mately how long [negotiations will continue] since everything depends on how the international situation develops in the meantime, what position France, Britain, and other countries adopt, ⌐and whether Poland, Kurland, and Lithuania will be allowed to exercise the right of self-determination without Ger-man troops being present. We shall not give in on this point. When Czernin told me that Britain would never accept self-determination [for her colonies], I countered: 'don't speak for Britain but for Austria-Hungary.' Later Kühlmann rejected the right of the peoples of Austria-Hungary to self-determination. He was speaking with the lips of Clemenceau, who would say the same to us if he were at the bargaining-table.⌐ʲ

As regards distribution of revolutionary material on the German side of the lines, I recall that on my return from Brest I had to pass through a sector held by the Vth Army. I noticed that they received several bundles of *Die Fackel* daily, each of which contained 100,000 copies. Our soldiers said that all this literature went over to the German trenches. Of course the German authorities have not authorized this material to be distributed, but we could hardly ask the Germans to authorize us to make revolution in their country!

Let me conclude by expressing the assurance that the watchwords of the Russian revolution will evoke a warm response in the hearts of the toiling masses of all countries and that the revolutionary movement which is already beginning in all belligerent states as a result of three years of imperialist war will sooner or later bring down the European absolutist governments and open the door widely to creative action by all peoples.

The following resolution is passed unanimously:

Having heard the report of the peace delegation, and wholeheartedly approving its actions, the joint session of the CEC, the Petrograd soviet and the All-Army [Demobilization] Congress resolves:

The first programmatic statement by the representatives of the Quadripartite Alliance in Brest recognized the principle that peace should be concluded without annexations or contributions. This acknowledgement paved the way for further talks on a general democratic peace. However, already in this statement the German representatives refused to recognize the right of self-determination for those oppressed nationalities and colonial peoples seized before the war of 1914 ... The statement by the Austro-German delegation setting forth its practical conditions for peace in the east does even further violence to the idea of a just democratic peace. The gist of it is that the Austro-German government [*sic*] is refusing to pledge itself to withdraw its troops immediately and unconditionally from the occupied regions of Poland, Lithuania, Kurland, and parts of Livland and Estonia. A genuine free expression of the popular will of Poland, Lithuania, Kurland, and all other occupied regions is impossible so long as foreign troops are maintained there and those elements of the population that have been evacuated are not returned. The delegation's statement that the population of those areas has already expressed its will is clearly groundless. These peoples could not express their will so long as these occupied regions were in a state of siege and subject to military censorship. Any documents to which the German government might refer could in the best of circumstances only express the will of various privileged groups and not of the popular masses of those territories.

We declare: the Russian revolution remains faithful to its international policy. We stand for genuine self-determination for Poland, Lithuania, and Kurland. We shall never accept as justified the imposition of any alien will upon any people. The Russian workers' revolution has fulfilled its duty before the peoples of the whole world. The government of workers and peasants has published the secret treaties and it is prepared to evacuate immediately all territories occupied by Russian armies during the war. It is offering all peoples inhabiting Russia, without exception, the right of complete self-determination even up to secession without any military pressure on its part. But it demands the same from the other side.

We appeal to the [British,] French, Italian, and Serbian workers. The governments of your countries have not taken that step towards peace which the governments of [the] central Europe[an states] have been obliged to take. Your governments have not yet stated their war aims and are dragging out the war by all manner of truths and untruths. Your governments are not taking a single step to meet the peace programme of the Russian revolution. Your governments do not want to abandon the treaties they concluded, in secrecy from their people[s], with the former tsar Nicholas II. Make your countries join at once in the peace talks on the basis of the statements by the Russian delegation in Brest!

We appeal to the peoples of Germany, Austria-Hungary, Bulgaria, and Turkey. Under your pressure your governments have been obliged to accept verbally our slogan of peace without annexations or contributions, but in practice they are trying to carry on their old policy of conquest.

Remember that now more than ever it is for you to determine whether a really democratic peace will be concluded in the near future. The peoples of the whole of Europe, exhausted by this unexampled bloodletting, are looking to you. You will [surely] not allow the German and Austrian imperialists to wage war for the purpose of enslaving Poland, Lithuania, Kurland, and Armenia. The workers' revolution calls upon the labouring classes of all countries to rise in revolt.

[Addendum:] The joint session insists that in future the peace talks be held in a neutral state and instructs the CPC to take all measures to effect this.

NOTES

a Sisson, *One Hundred Red Days*, p. 191 : 'some 800 present'.
b *ZT*, 20 Dec.
c *Pr.*, 20 Dec.: 'fourth'.
d This sentence does not occur in the text of the Central Powers' reply as given in the Russian edition of the minutes.
e *Pr.*, 20 Dec.
f In *ZT*, 20 Dec., the following passage is rendered still more forcefully: 'I am sure that the Russian representatives are the genuine representatives of the Polish workers and the Lithuanian and Latvian peasants, and that the latter would unanimously admit that they would trust the Russian revolution to defend their right to self-determination.'
g literally: 'a geographical line that has resulted from historical acts of violence'.
h *ZT*, 20 Dec., places here the passage on p. 227 beginning: 'We are within our rights . . .'
i Not printed: as reproduced in *Prot.* (pp. 165–6) and in the press, these statements followed a stereotyped pattern, with references to the conditions in which the soldiers were obliged to exist and expressions of willingness to fight the Germans (notably by spokesmen for armies on the Northern and Western fronts); representatives from units in the south announced support for the CPC's policy towards the Ukrainian Rada.
j *NZ*, 21 Dec.
k *ZT*, 21 Dec.
l *Delo naroda*, 20 Dec.

Twenty-second Session
22 December 1917

Chairman: Sverdlov   9 p.m.

1. *Recognition of Finnish Independence*[1]

STALIN: The other day Finnish representatives approached us with a request to recognize immediately the complete independence of Finland and to confirm the fact of its separation from Russia. In response the CPC ordained that this request should be granted at once and decided to issue a decree on the complete independence of Finland, which has already been published in the newspapers:

> In response to the Finnish government's appeal for recognition of the independence of the Finnish Republic, the CPC, in full agreement with the principles of [the right of][a] nations to self-determination, ordains: The [following] proposal is to be put before the CEC:
> a) to recognize the Finnish Republic as an independent state;
> b) to organize, in agreement with the Finnish government, a special commission consisting of representatives of both sides to work out the practical measures arising out of Finland's separation from Russia.

The CPC could do nothing else but issue this declaration,[b] for if a people, through its representatives, categorically demands from [the previously sovereign] authority[c] recognition of its independence, a proletarian government, proceeding from the principle that nations should be granted the right to self-determination, must go all the way to meet [the demands of] Finland.

The bourgeois press asserts that we are bringing about the country's complete collapse and have 'lost' a whole number of countries, including Finland. But we could not 'lose' Finland, comrades, because it was in fact never our property. If we held back Finland by coercion, this by no means meant that we had acquired it.

We know full well how Wilhelm is 'acquiring' whole states by violence and arbitrary actions, and what sort of foundation this is laying for [future] relations between people[s] and [their] oppressors.

The principles of Social Democracy, its slogans and aims, consist in creating the long-awaited atmosphere of mutual confidence among peoples. Only on this basis can we realize the slogan 'Proletarians of all lands, unite!' All this is familiar and nothing new for us.

But if we look more closely at Finland's acquisition of independence we shall first of all discover that in practice the CPC has involuntarily given freedom, not to the Finnish people, but to the Finnish bourgeoisie—which, by a strange turn of events, has received independence at the hands of Russian socialists. The Finnish workers and Social Democrats have found themselves in a position where they have had to receive their freedom not directly from the hands of socialists, but with the aid of the Finnish bourgeoisie. We regard this as a tragedy for the Finnish proletariat, and cannot help observing that it was only their irresolution and incomprehensible cowardice that prevented the Finnish Social Democrats from taking decisive steps to seize independence themselves from the ruling bourgeoisie.

People may curse the CPC, may criticize it and oppose it sharply, but there is no one who could call [its members] hypocrites who do not fulfil their promises, for no power on earth could compel the CPC to renege on its promises. We have shown this by the fact that we reacted with complete impartiality to demands for independence even by bourgeois, and at once proceeded to publish the decree on Finland's autonomy. May Finland's freedom finally give complete independence to the Finnish workers and peasants and create a firm basis for eternal friendship between [our] peoples.

*d⌐*SVERDLOV: I propose that the CPC's decree on granting independence to Finland be confirmed without debate.⌐*d*

*e⌐*MOISEYEV: The question at the moment is not one of Finnish self-determination, for this self-determination has already taken place. It is only one of sanctioning it *de facto*. This sanction can be given only by the All-Russian Constituent Assembly, not by the CEC. In this connection I move that a debate be opened on this matter.⁻ᵉ ˢ⌐ (*Laughter*.)⌐ˢ

Motion rejected by a large majority.

PROSHYAN, for the Left SRs: The Left SRs have always warmly supported the idea of complete self-determination of peoples, and have always stood guard over [the interests of] the workers and peasants. In the name of the Left SRs I greet the Finnish proletariat and associate myself with the CPC's decision.

The declaration is adopted with 4 abstentions ᵉ⌐and a Bolshevik amendment:

> That the Russo-Finnish commission to be set up should include representatives of the Finnish working class as well as of the Finnish government.⌐ᵉ, ᵍ

2. *Convocation of Constituent Assembly*²

SVERDLOV reads the following decree, adopted by the CPC on 20 December:

> Whereas there is still no quorum for the Constituent Assembly, even if the figure [is broadened to include] those deputies who have not presented their mandates [for registration] according to the established procedure;
>
> whereas many of the deputies who arrived in Petrograd have [since] left for the provinces;
>
> whereas there is uncertainty about the date when the Constituent Assembly is to meet;
>
> whereas it is possible at the present time, owing to the progress of the elections, to determine more or less at which moment after the [Christmas and New Year] holidays a quorum will be attained;
>
> the CEC appoints 5 January as the opening day of the Constituent Assembly, provided that a quorum of 400 [deputies] is present.

The decree is adopted with 2 abstentions.

3. *Convocation of Third Congress of Soviets*³

After a brief debate . . . the floor is given to Zinoviev.

ZINOVIEV: Bourgeois newspapers of every hue will no doubt

again assert that in convoking a new Congress of Soviets we are seeking to counterpose the soviets, our revolutionary organs, to the notorious Constituent Assembly. Naturally we by no means wish to conceal the truth, and in saying this the bourgeois writers are partly correct. ^e⌐According to the statute we would not be obliged to hold congresses of workers', soldiers', and peasants' deputies until three months [have elapsed] after the Second Congress, on 20 January. But we deliberately propose that the convocation of these congresses be advanced by two weeks so that when the Constituent Assembly meets the opinion of the oppressed classes on the most important questions of the day may be represented. Our opponents, from Mensheviks and Right SRs to right-wing Kaledinites, have unanimously put forward the slogan 'All power to the Constituent Assembly!' But this slogan conceals a different one, 'Down with the soviets!'⌐^e This explains the wild delight with which all the right-wing papers, up to the filthy fly-sheets of Suvorin, endorse it.

None [of us] has ever concealed or intends to conceal the fact that we counterpose the soviets to the Constituent Assembly. May I remind you that not long ago, when *Izvestiya* was under Menshevik editorship, there was some talk about doing away with the soviets; it was said that the soviets were just timbers for constructing revolution, and that [later] they would have to be eliminated. And today ^e⌐in *Delo naroda*⌐^e Chernov again declares that the soviets are only the light cavalry of the revolution, whereas we are firmly convinced that they are the long-range artillery that can guarantee its safety. Without the soviets the victory of proletarian revolution is unthinkable. ^h⌐We say: the soviets are the new word which our revolution has given to the whole world.⌐^h They are a great new historical phenomenon. However much bourgeois hangers-on may try to turn back the clock they will not succeed. If they were consistent and honest they would announce openly for all to hear that the Constituent Assembly's purpose is humbly to hand over the keys [of the revolution] to the capitalists, who are at present trying to destroy everything the soviets have done for the people.

^h⌐We are told that elections to the soviets are not conducted rigorously enough. Chernov holds it against the soviets that only the most active elements [of the population] take part in elec-

tions to them, whereas in the Constituent Assembly elections [everyone down to] the least old woman is involved. But this is a splendid compliment to the soviets, citizen Chernov! Yes, the soviets do consist of those who want to fight, who are ready to smash the old [society] and construct a new life. In a transitional revolutionary period it is precisely such organizations that should have the last word.[h]

In the duel between the Constituent Assembly and the soviets we see a historical struggle between two revolutions, one bourgeois and the other socialist. The Constituent Assembly elections are a reflection of the first, February revolution ... Are there any bourgeois representatives here who would dare to claim, hand on heart, that the overwhelming majority of peasants back the right-wing elements rather than the Bolsheviks and Left SRs? The victory of the left is readily apparent. At all the provincial peasant congresses, at every village meeting, it is clear that the peasants are adhering to the revolutionary workers' movement.

'All power to the Constituent Assembly!' means 'All power to Messrs. Rudnev and Avksentyev!' Whoever asserts the contrary, that we won't have to pull the assembly towards the soviets by its eyebrows, [or] that they can work together, is taking the simple way out.[4] Let those who are desperately fighting for the Constituent Assembly recognize soviet power and there will be no conflict.

In satisfying the popular demand for the right to [recall and] re-elect [deputies to the Assembly] the revolutionary government was simply defending the elementary requirements of the revolution. The right of re-election must be upheld by every means. Why are [our opponents] so afraid of re-elections, whereas we are not? You know why: because you (*turning to the right-wing members*) represent the revolution's past; you are dreaming that in a year or two some Rudnev or other may assume full power, put his feet on the table and make a mockery of the peasants' and workers' [aspirations].

It is a big question whether the Constituent Assembly [deputies] will hear the distant thunder of the socialist movement, whether they will understand that the soviets are our temple, that they have entered into every pore of our being and will die only with the revolution. The soviets have outlived their defensist phase; they rose up against the Kerensky regime; and now they have entered upon the phase of great constructive work. You say that only over your dead bodies shall anyone infringe [the rights of] the Constituent Assembly. We say that your programme can be implemented only after the soviets have been destroyed, which of course shall never come to pass since the people will never permit anyone to destroy this foundation-stone of the proletariat's impending independence. This was made clear at the Second Congress of Soviets, at the last [Second (Regular)] Congress of Peasant [Deputies],[5] and at the railway-men's congress. If the Constituent Assembly should stand in the way of revolutionary development it will be paralysed by the will of the proletariat.

I move the following resolution:

The Constituent Assembly is due to open on 5 January. The parties of open and concealed counter-revolution, the Kadets, Mensheviks, Right SRs, Kornilovites, and the officials who are committing sabotage are all aiming to turn the Constituent Assembly into a stronghold of the rich against the poor . . . These calculations are based on the fact that the Constituent Assembly was elected in conditions highly unfavourable for a genuine expression of the people's will, at a time when the Kerensky government was mercilessly persecuting all revolutionary organizations of workers, soldiers, and peasants, when constituency boundaries were defined quite arbitrarily, when the revolutionary parties' voting papers were not delivered to the villages and so on. The counter-revolutionary elements are seeking to exploit for their anti-popular ends the fact that the elections took place at a moment when large masses of peasants in the remoter provinces had not yet understood the significance of the October revolution and were even un-aware of it, and were therefore obliged to vote for lists [of candidates] drawn up long before the October revolution, which reflected a grouping of political forces that has been radically altered by the revolution of proletariat, army and advanced peasantry. The Constituent Assembly as at present composed is lagging a whole epoch behind the development of events and reflects the bourgeois revolution much more than the workers' and peasants' revolution of October.

The All-Russian Congress of Peasant Deputies showed quite convincingly that the Right SRs, who claim a leading role in the Constituent Assembly, clearly do not express the mood of the genuinely toiling elements of the peasantry . . . The bourgeois and compromiser parties seek to counterpose the Constituent Assembly to soviet power, the creation of the working classes. The CEC considers it necessary to offer determined resistance to this anti-popular scheme. The Constituent Assembly can only play a beneficial role in developing the revolution if it takes a stand, resolutely and without equivocation, on the side of the toiling classes against the landowners and bourgeoisie, consolidates soviet power, ratifies the decrees on land, workers' control and nationalization of the banks, recognizes the right of all peoples of Russia to self-determination, and supports the present policy of the soviets designed to bring about a speedy democratic peace.

The CEC considers it essential that the soviets should with all their organized might support the left wing of the Constituent Assembly against the right-wing bourgeois and compromiser half,[6] and for this purpose ordains:

The Third All-Russian Congress of Soviets of Workers' and Soldiers' Deputies shall meet on 8 January and the Third All-Russian Congress of Peasant Deputies on 15[i] January. To implement this decision the CEC charges its Presidium to set up appropriate Organization Bureaux for convocation of both congresses.

PROSHYAN, for the Left SRs: We are living through an era in which we are breaking with all the traditions and principles of the old bourgeois order one after another. It stands to reason that these breaches are costing us dear. They are initiating a long destructive process. Yet acute labour pains are inevitable in a revolutionary epoch when a new state order is being born.

We are now on the eve of a serious new breach. Given the class composition of the Constituent Assembly as elected, it will undoubtedly present us with a complex conflict. We should look truth straight in the eye and recognize the acuteness and painfulness of the problem. Until the last few days we SRs stood up in defence of the Constituent Assembly as a popular representative institution. We defended it until real life faced us with the prob-

lem of our political survival. We were not being hypocritical,
we were not lying, when we defended the assembly. Individual
representatives of [our party]^j may have lied but the party as a
whole cannot of course be reproached for this. If we have now
changed our position in regard to the Constituent Assembly,
this question which so agitates [democratic] politicians, this is
because many different and mutually incompatible interests are
involved here. Real life is more intransigent than political
dogma. Its logic is more merciless, and saner, than that of any
political programme. It is this reality which is compelling us to
follow in its wake, to hearken to its voice, and to act in each
instance as expediency demands, as reality dictates.

What do we mean by 'reality'? There is no doubt that we are
experiencing a social revolution. The development of this revolution requires an executive power capable of reconstructing
political life on socialist lines. The Constituent Assembly cannot
assume such authority. It will not consolidate the socialist revolution . . . We need have no illusions that, with its semi-bour-
geois composition, it will sympathize with the goals of the
October revolution, which has created a totally new form of
authority, that of the soviets . . . Executive authority, as a
weapon of struggle, must remain with the revolutionary people
. . . The people have entrusted authority to the soviets, which
are not mere trade organizations, as many people claim, but the
sovereign bodies of the workers and peasants who are struggling
against capitalism.

Even before this struggle has been won the soviets are con-
fronted with the Constituent Assembly. We say that, if the
assembly declares war on the sole organs of revolutionary
authority, . . . we shall not abandon our positions and allow the
soviets to be torn from the people's hands. Those who are undermining the soviets and the conquests of October under cover of
the slogan 'All power to the Constituent Assembly!' should bear
in mind that the soviets will not yield, that they will perish only
with the revolution itself.

There is not much time left before the assembly meets. This
will be the last test [of strength]: two organs, each concerned
with fundamental questions of our political life, will meet [side
by side]. Which of them will stand the test? If the Constituent
Assembly . . . does not recognize soviet power . . . , conflict is

inevitable. Undoubtedly those who have suffered defeat over the war, whose land policy has proved a fiasco, and who have shown themselves bankrupt as statesmen, will suffer yet another defeat over the Constituent Assembly. Let them in their intransigence and stubbornness force us to fight them: we are not afraid. The soviets, victorious in every clash with counter-revolution, will pass this test too and will successfully finish off the struggle for fraternity among peoples and for socialism. (*Applause.*)

ᵉʳSUKHANOV: Representatives of both fractions have spoken about the Third Congress of Soviets and the role of the Constituent Assembly. I recall that at the beginning of the revolution, when Lenin and Trotsky were still abroad, they denounced the assembly as a liberal scheme which had no place in the Russian revolution. As soon as he arrived Lenin proclaimed that we do not need a parliamentary republic or any other form of government except a soviet one. But afterwards they began to take a different line. One of the slogans of the October insurrection was the immediate convocation of the Constituent Assembly, [the elections to] which, the Bolsheviks maintained, were being disrupted by the bourgeoisie and by Kerensky. After the October revolution a new campaign began against the Constituent Assembly. It was declared to be incompatible with the 'dictatorship of the proletariat', but so far they have hesitated to get rid of it openly. This reflects irresolution in the policy of the CPC, [some members of] which consider the Constituent Assembly a reactionary institution but want to keep it in reserve so that they have something to fall back upon. They have resurrected the 'in so far as' formula[7] and are prepared to keep the Constituent Assembly not as a sovereign institution but as the servant or office-boy of the soviets. To make the Constituent Assembly a sort of 'Prussian globe' is not only a sign of irresolution but also hypocritical.

If we were really now establishing a dictatorship of the proletariat and implementing socialism, a Constituent Assembly would indeed not be necessary. But irrespective of the question whether the time has come for socialism, the CPC is a government that is incapable of carrying out any kind of policy. What we have is not a [genuine] dictatorship of the proletariat but a malicious caricature of one. Soviet power has led to chaos in every sphere of the economy. It is ruining every aspect of [social] life with its struggle against 'counter-revolution', in which it is displaying both cowardice and pig-headedness (*samodurstvo*). Having taken fright at a few harmless intellectuals in the municipal Duma, the government has destroyed the latter's supply organization. In trying to carry through democratic principles by wielding a club, the government is paralysing the activities of schools, hospitals, theatres, and other institutions which do no one any harm and are actually necessary [to society].

Persecution of the press, arrests and terror have reached a point of complete irrationality. I recall the scene when Chernov was arrested in the courtyard of the Tauride Palace on 4 July and Trotsky declared this a senseless and criminal act, saying that Chernov had been arrested by a dozen miscreants (*negodyai*) who had nothing in common with Bolshevism. I don't know which authorities have now issued an order for the arrest of Chernov, Tsereteli, Dan, and other socialist leaders who have no other weapon than the spoken and written word. Probably such a senseless and criminal step could again be decided by a dozen miscreants. (*Disturbance in the hall. The speaker is called to order and obliged to end his speech.*)[k]

We are now confronting the greatest dangers from without and from within. The war is not over and we do not know when it will end. There is a risk that the country will be carved up between the enemy powers and the Allies. In such a situation our only salvation is in a united democratic front such as we had in the days of the Kornilov affair, when the danger dissolved like a puff of smoke. The most important thing for us now is to have a government which could save the country. The present government is incapable of doing this. It does not know how to build, only how to destroy. Remember what it has done with the law courts, the banks, and municipal self-government: everything has been destroyed. We need a government which would unite all the forces of democracy. [The source of] such a genuine government can only be the Constituent Assembly, which must therefore be convoked in conditions which would enable it to do its job as a sovereign institution and form a government capable of rescuing the country from the perils it faces.[le]

ʲ⌐Zinoviev's resolution is adopted as a basis of discussion.⌐ʲ

ᵉ⌐TRUTOVSKY tables an amendment:

The Constituent Assembly should annul the state's [foreign] debts out of practical considerations.⁸

KHARITONOV opposes the amendment.⌐ᵉ

ⁱ⌐AVANESOV: The question of annulling [state] debts ought to be settled by the Soviet government and the Constituent Assembly should only confirm that decision.⌐ˡ

ᵉ⌐MOISEYEV, also opposing the amendment: This is too serious a matter to be decided in this way. It would present a challenge to the imperialists, who would exploit it in order to take repressive measures against Russia. Most Russian securities [abroad] are held by French workers and democrats who would become fierce foes of Russia.

The amendment is rejected.

MOISEYEV moves an amendment:

to remove from the resolution all reference to the Constituent Assembly.

The amendment is rejected. The Bolshevik resolution is passed except for 2 dissentients and 2 abstentions.⌐ᵉ

4. *CEC's Representation Abroad*⁹

ᵉ⌐SVERDLOV moves the following resolution:⌐ᵉ

To establish close ties between all toiling elements in western Europe, [the CEC resolves] to send a delegation to Stockholm. This delegation is charged with taking every step to prepare convocation of [a fourth] Zimmerwald–Kienthal international [socialist] conference and to organize a Soviet Information Bureau in Stockholm.

ᵉ⌐MOISEYEV moves an amendment:

In view of the failure to clarify the question of the conclusion of peace, the CEC charges the CPC to supply the front with everything it needs and to send reinforcements at once.

The amendment is rejected.⌐ᵉ

Sverdlov's resolution is passed. The Presidium is charged with the task of choosing the delegation and determining its character.

5. *Appointments*

The appointment of Proshyan as PC of Posts and Telegraph is confirmed.

⌠6. Sickness Insurance[10]

The decree on sickness insurance is adopted.⌡*

NOTES

a The word *prava* was omitted from the text as published in *Pr.*, 23 Dec., but it occurs in the original document, now preserved in the archives of the Finnish ministry of Foreign Affairs: Syukiyaynen, *Revolyutsionnye sobytiya*, p. 154.

b *Pr.*, 23 Dec. (and Stalin, *Soch.*, vol. IV, p. 22): 'could not but proceed in this manner'—a happier rendering which eliminates the confusion between the terms 'decree' and 'declaration'.

c The same source omits this phrase (*ot vlasti*), so eliminating the ambiguity arising from this phrase, as printed in *Prot.*, which could be regarded as acceptance of the view that the Soviet government was heir to the sovereignty previously exercised by the tsars.

d *Nash vek*, 24 Dec. According to *Prot.* (p. 175) the question was opened to debate (by the chair); but this would have eliminated the need for Moiseyev's request (not reproduced in this source).

e *NZ*, 24 Dec.

f *Nash vek*, 24 Dec.

g The words 'and representatives of the Finnish working class' were added after 'government' in the excerpt from the CEC's minutes that was forwarded to the Finnish authorities: Syukiyaynen, *Revolyutsionnye sobytiya*, p. 155.

h *Iz.*, 24 Dec.

i Dated according to contemporary newspaper sources. The date of the convocation of this congress was subsequently brought forward to 12 January, for reasons of political tactics, and this date was given in *Prot.*, where (p. 177) the words 'and representatives of the land committees' are added after 'Peasant Deputies'.

j Literally: 'the given political camp'.

k According to *Nash vek*, 24 Dec., Sukhanov's speech was frequently interrupted by jeering.

l *Delo naroda*, 23 Dec.

Twenty-third Session
29 December 1917

Chairman: Sverdlov   ᵃ⌐8.30 p.m.⌐ᵃ

1. *Food Supply*[1]

SHLIKHTER, for the PC of Supply: ᵃ⌐When the Supply ministry
came under Soviet [control] on 21 November the officials proclaimed [a campaign of] sabotage which had a pernicious effect
on the food supply. The PC of Supply had but one[b] course of
action: to apply repressive measures against the saboteurs and
to form a new staff of supply workers. We also had to take
repressive measures against the so-called 'council of ten', which
did all it could to step up the sabotage, to disrupt the supply
mechanism, and to increase the chaos; everyone knows about its
proclamation calling for a strike. In my view the tactics we have
adopted towards the sabotaging officials have been very mild.

[In the provinces] supply work has gradually been passing
into the hands of the local soviets. Siberia, Russia's granary, has
come over to the side of soviet power. Kursk is another area
whence we can obtain grain. At the moment we do not have
enough men:⌐ᵃ ᶜ⌐in the ministry about 300 people are working,
as compared with 1,500 before the insurrection, and they are by
no means experienced,⌐ᶜ ᵃ⌐but I am sure that those whom we
are recruiting will justify our hopes.

I should point out that the [amount of] grain [available] is
entirely adequate and that we are not facing the terrible famine
with which bourgeois and right-wing socialist newspapers are
continually trying to scare us. It is just a matter of organizing
its transport. Here I should stress the tremendous damage that
the so-called 'bagmen'[2] are doing to efforts to bring some order
into the transport system. These soldiers turned merchants are
constantly travelling about on the railways and taking up all
available space. I shall soon lay before the CEC a specific proposal on measures to deal with this trade.

I may add that the PC of Supply has taken over from the army quartermaster's branch all its stocks of manufactured goods for dispatch to the countryside where they will be exchanged [for food]. In conclusion I state once again that we are not facing any kind of peril in regard to the procurement of food supplies.

PROSHYAN: Since the report is solely of an informative character I propose that it be adopted without debate.⁷ᵃ

ᶜᵣKRAMAROV: I move that Shlikhter's report be declared unsatisfactory, since he has not yet presented to the CEC the basic principles of his policy in the matter of food supply.

Motion rejected.⁷ᶜ Proshyan's motion is passed.

2. *State Control of Publishing*³

POLYANSKY, for the PC of Education: ... The entire responsibility for enlightening the masses has fallen upon public cultural organizations, which have unexpectedly come up against a serious obstacle in their work: speculation by booksellers and publishers. The excessively high price charged for books is putting a brake upon all their activities. (*Reads a [draft] decree on state [control of] publishing, which he presents for the CEC's confirmation.*)

SUKHANOV: In this decree I note that two completely different matters have been confused. One is the popularization of [scholarly] and literary works, i.e. state publishing in the limited sense of this term; the other has to do with inheritance law. As regards the latter I do not see why the rights of legal heirs are recognized at all. This completely contradicts the general policy of the CEC and the CPC, which is based on the assumption that we are at present undergoing a socialist revolution. I therefore move that this 'counter-revolutionary' decree be rejected and that copyright earnings not be made hereditary.

VOLODARSKY ᵈᵣ(*ironically*)⁷ᵈ: I completely agree with the argument of the United SD representative and likewise consider that that part of the decree which permits the transmission of copyright earnings to authors' heirs should be rescinded. ᵉᵣThe CPC should be charged with drawing up a decree abolishing authors' rights altogether and looking after [the welfare of] the most deserving popular writers.⁷ᵉ

ZAKS: In drafting this decree the State [Education] Commission found itself divided: a minority took the view [that has just been expressed]. The majority opinion was based on the consideration that copyright earnings are not an important source of income for those entitled to them and that, like other inheritance income, they could be justified on the grounds that this would serve the general interest of the community and that the recipients would show a due sense of moral responsibility.ᶠ I myself shared the minority viewpoint.

POLYANSKY: I move that we do not hold up the business of establishing a state publishing house but pass the decree as presented.

The decree, with an amendment tabled by Volodarsky on behalf of the Bolsheviks, is adopted unanimously and passed to the Presidium for editorial revision.

3. Supply: Interpellations

SHLIKTHER: ᶜᴦIn reply to Kramarov, I should point out that my report was of an informative character only. The basic principles of the CPC's supply policy will be presented later. (KRAMAROV, from his seat: 'We've been waiting for a month and a half!')ᴨᶜ
The PC of Supply will soon become a separate section of the Supreme Economic Council, since its work is closely connected with the problem of supplying the villages with industrial products and obtaining such goods for distribution to the peasants. At present the commissariat is about to send 120 wagon-loads of manufactured goods—footwear, metal objects, and the like— to the grain-growing areas. ᶜᴦFor each yard of cloth the peasants will be asked to supply ten puds of grain, and the difference will be made up by cash payments. In this way we shall get the amount of grain we need. In pursuit of this policy the PC of Supply has deprived Petrograd, Moscow, and [other] cities of manufactured goods that are very badly needed there.ᴨᶜ
As regards the state of food supplies [bound] for Petrograd, at the moment we have 300 wagon-loads of grain, ᶜᴦwhich is enough for nine days,ᴨᶜ and another 200 wagon-loads are on their way from Vologda by rail. The position is so favourable that we could raise the bread ration already now, but the Cen-

tral Supply Board is afraid of dislocations on account of the winter weather, for example snowdrifts, and therefore considers it more expedient not to rush such a measure.

(*In reply to a question about famine in Pskov province.*) Eighteen provinces have approached the PC of Supply with appeals to send them grain as soon as possible. We have directed them straight to the grain-growing regions so that they may get the grain more quickly. Probably Pskov province was one of those that sent such a request.

On the subject of relations between the commissariat and the Ukrainian Rada, I should prefer to enter into close contact with the Kharkov government. Five to six days ago we sent a representative there with special powers and a large sum of money. We are fully capable of engaging in commercial relations with the Rada, but for political reasons we are holding back.

ᶜᴦ(*In reply to an interpellation about squads of men at railway stations who requisition small amounts of food . . . from passengers as they arrive.*) These detachments are under instructions to confiscate food only where they suspect that it is being brought in for speculative purposes. We shall take energetic measures to stop soldiers and others sending out parties of men to nearby provinces to get food for speculative purposes.ᵀᶜ

4. *Suppression of Law Courts*[4]

SHTEYNBERG: ᵈᴦTwo basic principles will underlie the organization of the new revolutionary system. So far as possible, judges will be elected and they will render judgement freely according to their discretion.ᵍ These two principles should not be seen as [manifestations of] arbitrariness. The PC of Justice is seeking to establish courts of law which will administer justice simply, so that there will be no need to resort to appeal procedure.ᵀᵈ This decree is merely concerned with final liquidation of the [pre-] revolutionary law courts. Later a decree will be presented on the organization of the new system. ᵈᴦA whole range of hearings will be eliminated. Trials of political offenders will cease for good; courts of appeal will be abolished, leaving only courts of cassation; and all cases [due to be heard] by the former naval tribunals will likewise be dropped for ever.ᵀᵈ Judges will be subject to recall as soon as they lose the confidence of their electors. The courts of cassation will become involved only if a judge's verdict is in evident contradiction with the established norms of justice. (*Reads the decree.*)

⁀ᵈALGASOV: I propose that the decree be adopted without debate and sent to a commission for final editing.

Agreed over the objections of KRAMAROV, who protests: The CPC is relying on the CEC as if it were a 'voting machine'!

5. *Welfare*⁵

KOLLONTAY: In this ministry only the senior and middle-ranking officials engaged in sabotage. The work of our commissariat never ceased, since we were helped by the junior employees, of whom there are a great number, not one of whom went on strike.

We need to set up a large number of departments and to turn the State Welfare Committee into a Committee of Social Welfare in line with the practice in all European countries.⌐ᵈ

ᵉ⌐We have discovered a number of abuses in various foster homes, nurseries, and so on . . . One of our most urgent tasks is to set up homes and hostels which would prepare young citizens to fight for our ideals. We shall liquidate the Institutes for Noble Ladies which served only to fit girls to marry into the aristocracy. All monasterial property must be confiscated. A beginning has been made on this in Moscow, where contact has been established with junior employees in the monasteries, who have formed a soviet. This is collecting information on behalf of the CPC about all the monasteries' treasures, which must be enormous. However, the black clergy has learned of this. I shall shortly submit to the CPC a draft decree abolishing monasterial property and turning it over to the state.⌐ᵉ

NOTES

a *ZT*, 30 Dec.
b *ZT*, 30 Dec.: 'two courses'; the alternative is, however, not stated here.
c *NZ*, 31 Dec.
d *ZT*, 31 Dec.
e *Nash vek*, 31 Dec.
f Tentative reading: the text here is garbled.
g *sud po svobodnomu sudeyskomu usmotreniyu*: perhaps a version of the phrase 'according to their revolutionary conscience'?

^aTwenty-fourth Session
3 January 1918

Chairman: Sverdlov ^b⌈11.10 a.m.⌉^b

A message of greetings is read from the First All-Russian Conference of the Social-Democratic Party of the Kingdom of Poland and Lithuania.

1. *Ultimatum to Romania*[1]

SUKHANOV: In the last few days the CPC has decided on measures of tremendous importance, [notably] the ultimatum to Romania. The conduct of the Romanian leaders is beneath contempt, but the CPC's actions should be repudiated for there are other means of combat other than those it has adopted. The personal immunity of a diplomatic envoy has always been respected and this principle should be maintained. These measures could endanger the cause of peace, which has never seemed so close as it does now. I move that the agenda be amended to include a report by the CPC on this matter.

Motion rejected.

2. *Measures Against Constituent Assembly*[2]

SVERDLOV: The CPC decided to convoke the Constituent Assembly on 5 January. At present it is expected to meet on time. As regards the procedural arrangements, it is thought that it will be opened by a representative of soviet power. The Bolshevik and Left SR parties have agreed that a declaration [of allegiance] to soviet power will be read from the tribune, and that this should form the basis of the assembly's work. (*Reads this document, entitled 'Declaration of Rights of the Toiling and Exploited People'.*)

The text is approved by acclamation. ^c⌈(*A Menshevik–Internationalist deputy interjects*: 'What a stupid comedy!')⌉^c

Also approved is the following ordinance:

^d⌐On the basis of all the conquests of the October revolution, and in conformity with the Declaration of Rights of the Toiling and Exploited People, adopted by the CEC on 3 January, all power in the Russian Republic inheres in the soviets and in soviet institutions. For this reason any attempt by any individual or institution to appropriate any function of state authority will be regarded as a counter-revolutionary act. Any such attempt will be suppressed by all the means at the disposition of soviet power, including the use of armed force.⌐^d

^a⌐The chairman reads an order signed by Uritsky addressed to the commandant of the Tauride Palace, instructing him to prevent any crowds gathering and to control entry into the building. This is approved by acclamation.⌐^{a,} ^e ^c⌐[Also] approved is a Bolshevik resolution on the procedure to be followed in electing the Presidium of the Constituent Assembly. This is to consist of 16 persons, chosen proportionately to the strength of parties in the assembly.

KRAMAROV, explaining the motives for his vote: I am not speaking in order to convince you, for one can only talk to you with sticks.

Protests by Bolshevik deputies. The chairman proposes that Kramarov be suspended for one session. Shouts of: 'Exclude him!' A Left SR delegate: 'A verbal reprimand would be sufficient.' Kramarov explains his remark, softening its asperity. The chairman states that he will administer a reprimand.⌐^c

^a⌐3. *Annulment of Public Debts*[3]

BOGOLEPOV introduces a decree annulling Russia's state debts.

TRUTOVSKY: We think this decree should be passed and acted upon. It is time to implement the resolutions of Zimmerwald and Kienthal. We are the first [country] to fulfil our obligations in this regard. We understand full well that this decree administers a sharp blow to the capitalist system. There is a difference between a state declaring itself bankrupt and a state annulling its debts. In the first case it recognizes that it cannot pay what it owes; in the second case it says that it will not pay, so challenging the bourgeois order. Of course there will be difficulties. The bourgeoisie of all countries will rally all the more solidly against us, but despite this we of the new world throw down the gauntlet to the old.

The decree is adopted unanimously and passed to the Presidium for final editing.[7][a]

NOTES

a   *ZT*, 5 Jan. The last two sessions of this convocation were omitted from *Prot.*
b   *ZT*, 4 Jan.
c   *Novy luch*, 5 Jan.
d   *Pr.*, 4 Jan.
e   *Iz.*, 5 Jan., reports that two delegates voted against and that one abstained.

^aTwenty-fifth Session
6 January 1918

Chairman: Sverdlov   11.30 p.m.

1. *Shooting of Persons Demonstrating in Support of the Constituent*
   Assembly[1]

SVERDLOV: Today's emergency session has been called to consider the dissolution of the Constituent Assembly. I propose the
following agenda: confirmation of the CPC's decree on the dissolution; incorrect compilation of party lists in the Constituent
Assembly elections.

RYAZANOV, on a point of order: I protest in the strongest terms
against yesterday's bloodshed, when peaceful demonstrators
were fired upon. I demand that the CEC suspend its sessions
until the Third Congress of Soviets, which should consider
whether the CPC acted correctly in permitting such excesses,
and I further demand that a commission be set up at once to
investigate these events.

SHTEYNBERG: As PC of Justice, I support this proposal for a
commission of inquiry. Yesterday's incident has made everyone
rather excited. When I went round all the places where clashes
occurred I discovered that only minor injuries had been caused.
However, this morning [in the CPC] I insisted that an investigating commission be set up, and I repeat this demand now.

The proposal is adopted unanimously. The commission is to
consist of seven persons, chosen by the fractions, to whom trade-
union representatives are to be added. It is to be organized by
the Presidium.

2. *Dissolution of Constituent Assembly*[2]

LENIN (*Sustained applause*):^{⌐a,} ^b ^c⌐The conflict between soviet
power and the Constituent Assembly was foreshadowed by the
whole history of the Russian revolution, faced as it is with the

unheard-of problems of reconstructing society on socialist lines. After the events of 1905 there could be no doubt that tsarism was at its last gap. Only the backwardness and ignorance of the countryside allowed it to climb back from the abyss. In the 1917 revolution the party of the imperialist bourgeoisie [i.e. the Kadet party] has been turned by force of circumstance into a republican one, and democratic organizations have emerged in the form of soviets. These were created as early as 1905: already then socialists realized that their appearance signified something entirely new in the history of world revolution. The soviets, created by the people entirely on their own [initiative], are a form of democracy that has no equal in any other country.

The [February] revolution brought forth two forces: the masses, who united for the purpose of overthrowing tsarism, and the organizations of labouring people. When I hear enemies of the October revolution crying how impossible of realization, how utopian, the ideas of socialism are, I generally put to them the simple and obvious question: 'what are the soviets?', 'what led to the emergence of these popular organizations, which have no parallel in history . . . ?' And to this question none of them has ever given me, or could ever give me, a definite answer. Their stubborn defence of the bourgeois order leads them to oppose these mighty organizations, the like of which no revolution hitherto ever witnessed.

Whoever is fighting the landlords joins the soviets of peasants' deputies. The soviets are made up of all those who want to engage in creative work instead of idling. A network of them has spread over the whole country. The denser this network becomes, the less chance there will be for exploitation of working people, for the existence of soviets is incompatible with a flourishing bourgeois order. This explains all the contradictions into which bourgeois representatives fall. They are struggling against our soviets solely in order to advance their own interests.

The transition from capitalism to socialism involves a long and bitter struggle. Having overthrown tsarism, the Russian revolution has inevitably gone further. It could not limit itself to ensuring the victory of a bourgeois [order], for the war imposed untold sufferings upon the people, and their exhaustion created conditions in which social revolution could break out. There is accordingly nothing more ridiculous than to assert that the deepening of the revolution, the growing indignation of the masses, has been stimulated by a single party, by a single individual, or—as [our enemies] scream—by the will of some 'dictator'. The revolutionary conflagration has come about exclusively as the consequence of the incredible sufferings to which Russia has been subjected by the war. This relentlessly forced working people to choose: either to take a bold, desperate and fearless step [forward] or else to perish, to die a hungry death. *d*⌈(*Applause.*)⌉*d*

The revolutionary [impulse] expressed itself in the creation of soviets, bastions of the revolution of labour. The Russian people have made a gigantic leap from tsarism to soviets. This is an incontestable and unprecedented fact. At a time when in all [other] countries bourgeois parliaments, inhibited by the limitations of capitalism and [respect for] property, have never given any support to the revolutionary movement, the soviets, stoking the fires of revolution, are imperiously telling the people to fight, to take everything into their hands, to organize themselves.

No doubt all manner of mistakes and blunders will be made in the course of deepening this revolution, called into being by the mighty soviets. But it is no secret that every revolutionary movement is invariably accompanied by chaos, destruction, and disorder. Bourgeois society involves war and slaughter too, and it is this which has so accentuated the conflict between the Constituent Assembly and the soviets.

Those who keep on telling us that we used to defend the assembly but are now 'dissolving' it have no sense and are just uttering empty phrases. Formerly, we preferred the Constituent Assembly to tsarism, to the republic of Kerensky, but as the soviets developed [we saw that] they, as revolutionary organs of the entire people, were incomparably superior to all parliaments anywhere in the world. I stressed this point already in April.[3] The soviets, by effecting a radical breach in bourgeois and landlord property, by assisting the insurrection which finally swept away all traces of the bourgeois order, pushed us on to the course which led the people to build their lives for themselves.

We have set about this great [task of] construction, and we are right to have done so. The socialist revolution cannot be

served up to the people in a neat, smooth package. It is inevit-
ably accompanied by civil war, by sabotage and resistance.
Those who assert the contrary are either lying or blind.[e]
(*Stormy applause.*)

The events of 20 April,[4] when the people—independently,
without any orders by 'dictators' or parties—manifested their
opposition to the compromisers' government, demonstrated
already then the feeble basis on which bourgeois [power] rested.
The masses sensed their own strength, and to please them, or
rather to deceive them, there began that celebrated ministerial
leapfrog [of the first coalition]. But the people saw through this,
especially once Kerensky, who had in his pockets the secret
robber treaties with the imperialists, launched the offensive.
The people gradually came to understand that they were being
deceived by everything the compromisers were doing. Their
patience began to run out, and the result of all this was the
October revolution. The people learned from their experience
of tortures, death sentences and mass shootings. It is no use
assuring them that the revolt of the labouring people is the work
of the Bolsheviks, or of some kind of 'dictators'. This is clear
from the schism apparent among the masses at their various
congresses, conferences, meetings and so on. As yet the people
have not finally assimilated the [lessons of the] October revolution.

This revolution showed in practice how they should proceed
in taking the land, the natural resources, the means of transport
and production, into their hands, into the hands of the workers'
and peasants' state. 'All power to the soviets!' was our slogan.
That is what we are fighting for. The people wanted the Constituent Assembly convoked—and so we convoked it. But they
at once realized what this notorious Constituent Assembly
amounted to. And now we have fulfilled the people's will by
[transferring] all power to the soviets. We shall crush the saboteurs.

When I left Smolny, pulsating with vitality, and went to the
Tauride Palace I felt as though I were amidst corpses and life-
less mummies. The enemies of socialism used every available
means in their fight. They resorted to violence and sabotage;
they even exploited knowledge, humanity's great pride, against
the labouring people. They were able to delay the advance to-

wards socialist revolution, but they could not halt it and they never shall. For the soviets are too strong: they have begun to smash the antiquated foundations of the bourgeois order, not in a gentlemanly fashion but in the [rough] manner of proletarians and peasants.

The transfer of all power to the Constituent Assembly [would be] another compromise with the pernicious bourgeoisie. The Russian soviets place the interests of the toiling masses much higher than the interests of the treacherous conciliators, who have donned a fresh disguise. The speeches of Chernov and Tsereteli gave off a mouldy smell. These politicians of bygone times are still whining about stopping the civil war. But so long as Kaledin exists, so long as the slogan 'All power to the Constituent Assembly!' masks the slogan 'Down with soviet power!', civil war is inevitable, for we shall not for anything in the world surrender soviet power! (*Stormy applause.*)

And when the Constituent Assembly announced its readiness to postpone once again [decisions on] all the urgent issues presented to it by the soviets, we answered: there is not a moment to lose. And so by the will of the Soviet government the Constituent Assembly, which refused to recognize the people's power, has been dissolved. The general staff of the Ryabushin-skys has been defeated. If the latter resists, this will only lead to a new upsurge of civil war. The Constituent Assembly is dissolved and the revolutionary Soviet Republic will triumph, cost what it may. (*Stormy applause, turning into a prolonged ovation.*)⌐c

ᶠ⌐STROYEV, for the United SDs: The dissolution of the Constituent Assembly seems to me a dizzying jump into the unknown. I remind the Left SRs that not long ago they were numbered among defenders of the assembly. Too soon have they shed this 'illusion', and in so doing also their [allegiance to their] red banners and to political liberty. On the basis of the Constituent Assembly it would have been possible to unite the whole of revolutionary democracy. This course is no longer possible. As late as November the Bolsheviks were also in favour of broadening the basis of the revolution, but now they have betrayed this principle.⌐ᶠ

ᵇ⌐Yesterday red banners were being snatched from the workers' hands. One more illusion is being done away with. The respect for socialist banners reddened with proletarian blood . . . (*Cries of 'That's enough!' Uproar.*) I am used to speaking against noises like these. I made speeches despite [interruptions] by the Black Hundreds . . . and should like to think that now I am under the protection of the red flag. (*Tremendous uproar. The chairman calls on the speaker to refrain from such comparisons.*) The Bolsheviks who control the government failed to carry out the will of the Second Congress of Soviets, . . . which resolved to call the Constituent Assembly, not to dissolve it . . . (*Cries and hisses in the hall.*)⌉ᵇ

ᶠ⌜Amidst the commotion Stroyev tries to continue his speech but is forced to leave the tribune.⌉ᶠ ᵇ⌜[Before doing so he reads a resolution which ends as follows:]

> . . . The Constituent Assembly alone is capable of uniting all parts of Russia to end the civil war which is accelerating the country's economic ruin and to solve all the essential questions raised by the revolution . . . In view of this the CEC resolves that the CPC shall enable the Constituent Assembly to continue its labours without interference, and that a new government shall be formed in agreement with the assembly's socialist majority.⌉ᵇ

ᶠ⌜SELIVANOV, for the SR Maximalists: Once again we have heard from this tribune the whining of the United SDs. We still remember what they said about our October revolution, and then about nationalization of the banks. They keep on repeating themselves and threatening us with every kind of misfortune. I call on the assembly to ignore the whining of these petty-bourgeois intellectuals and to carry on with the revolution.⌉ᶠ ᵍ⌜Now that the Constituent Assembly has at last been closed down, Russia will march ahead rapidly to a Soviet Republic of Labour (*Applause.*)

RYAZANOV, explaining his vote: We are taking an extremely serious step which affects not just Russia but the whole world proletariat.⌉ᵍ ᶠ⌜I never made a fetish of the Constituent Assembly but I believe that, having convoked it, we should have given it time to show its true face. This was not done. In a single day the people could not assess its [value] or compare their own opinions with its performance.⌉ᶠ ᵍ⌜Before dissolving the assembly we should have shown that it had to be dissolved by

confronting it with the Third Congress of Soviets and letting the
people decide between them. For this reason I shall vote against
the [motion approving] dissolution of the Constituent Assembly.⁷⁹

ᵇᴬVILOV: Lenin talked exclusively about the superiority of the
soviet form of organization but failed to say why the Constituent
Assembly did not reflect the people's will . . .⁷ᵇ

ᵃᴷARELIN, greeted by stormy applause, reads the text of the
decree.⁷ᵃ

ᶠᴿSUKHANOV, given the floor for an amendment: It is false to
assert that the Constituent Assembly refused to acknowledge the
conquests of the October revolution, and I suggest that this
passage be omitted from the resolution—as well as the immediately following passage, namely the approval given to the dissolution. (Cries of indignation; laughter.)⁷ᶠ

ᵍᴿLOZOVSKY, supporting the amendment: The CEC has committed a tremendous mistake, indeed a crime, in voting in
favour of the decree, for in so doing it has assumed the function
of the [rightful] legislative organ. It is also wrong to say that the
people have seen the assembly's real face, since not even Petrograd, let alone Russia, has had a chance to take proper stock of
it.⁷⁹

ᶠᴿThe amendment is rejected.⁷ᶠ ᵍᴿThe resolution is put to the
vote and passed with 2 dissentients⁷⁹ ᶠᴿand 5 abstentions.⁷ᶠ

3. *Incorporation of Radical Constituent Assembly Deputies into the CEC*

ᶜᴿAs Karelin ascends the tribune KRAMAROV calls out: 'Bolshevik lackey!' Storm of indignation in the hall. The chairman demands that he retract the expression. When he merely modifies
it the chairman excludes him from the session, adding that the
Presidium will consider his misconduct.

KARELIN: Kramarov's remark applies to the whole Left SR
fraction, not just to myself, and I bear him no personal grudge—
although it was ill-mannered. I oppose his exclusion since in a
class organization such as the CEC we should preserve comradely relations.

   I propose that those Bolshevik and Left SR deputies to the
Constituent Assembly who walked out of that body be invited

to take part in the work of the CEC, as this will improve our liaison with the provinces.

An UNIDENTIFIED member moves that the same right be extended to the national-minority deputies who walked out.

Resolution adopted unanimously, except for the United SDs, who take no part in the vote.⁷ᶜ

NOTES

a *ZT*, 7 Jan.
b *NZ*, 9 Jan. Cited from excerpts in B & F, pp. 380–4.
c *Pr.*, 9 Jan. (text of Lenin's speech also in Lenin, *PSS*, xxxv. 238–42).
d *Iz.*, 7 Jan.
e lit.: 'in a case'—an allusion to a pedantic character in a Chekhov story.
f *Pr.*, 10 Jan.
g *ZT*, 9 Jan.

Notes to the Minutes

1 *The Second Congress of Soviets* was the deliberative assembly which conferred an appearance of democratic legitimacy upon the Bolshevik regime (see Introduction, p. 22). It was called under pressure from those soviet organs which had passed under Bolshevik control during the summer and autumn, notably in the Petrograd region and at the front, despite opposition by the moderate-controlled Central Executive Committee of the first convocation, set up in June. The congress held two sessions, during the nights of 25–6 and 26–7 October. The Bolsheviks claimed 390 out of approximately 650 delegates; some contemporary estimates give them a lower proportion. Party affiliations were still fluid, and a number of delegates changed their mind during the congress. There was a clear majority in favour of 'soviet power', but most delegates understood this to mean setting up a coalition government of all 'revolutionary democracy' (i.e. the socialist and other left-wing parties represented in the soviets), rather than one composed exclusively of Bolsheviks.

The moderate socialists' withdrawal from the congress, in protest against the Bolshevik insurrection, eased their rivals' task. At the first session the congress had resolved to take power; what this meant in practice became clear at the second session, when it was asked to endorse the all-Bolshevik Council of People's Commissars (CPC). By this time the delegates' enthusiasm had been aroused by adoption of two historic decrees on peace and land. The final act of the congress was to elect a new CEC of 101 members, whose party affiliation is given here (p. 41). It was stated that the CEC might be enlarged later to accommodate representatives of other (especially peasant) soviets that had not sent deputies to the congress, as well as of those parties or groups that had withdrawn. It was understood that such persons would be committed to support the Bolshevik-inspired programme adopted by the congress.

The three ordinances issued by the CPC on 27 October, and here presented to the CEC for its approval, dealt with local government organs' powers in the field of supply, the holding of elections to the Constituent Assembly on the appointed day, and restrictions on the press. The last of these was to arouse considerable opposition: see below, p. 272.

2 *Vikzhel*. The Central Executive Committee of the All-Russian Union of Railwaymen, best known by its Russian acronym Vikzhel, was elected at the union's constituent congress, held in Moscow from 15 July to 24 August. It had 40 members, of whom 14 could be characterized as moderate, 15 as left-wing and 11 as 'centrist'. In October the committee's chairman was A. L. Malitsky (PSR); its secretary, Nesterenko, had no party affiliation. The breakdown of the transport system in the autumn of 1917 gave the union leaders considerable political weight. They were anxious to avoid a polarization of left-wing opinion, which in their view could lead only to civil war and still greater anarchy, to the detriment of working people in general and railwaymen in particular.

On 26–7 October at the second session of the Second Congress of Soviets a Vikzhel representative overcame Bolshevik efforts to deny him the floor and set forth briefly the union's viewpoint that power should rest with a coalition of socialist parties responsible to 'revolutionary democracy' as a whole. Simultaneously Vikzhel announced that, pending establishment of such a regime, all orders on the railways should be obeyed only if they were authorized by Vikzhel, which was taking over the Transport ministry. The union's pressure compelled the Bolsheviks to enter into talks with the moderate socialists on a political compromise (see below, pp. 275, 278, 288).

3 *Military-Revolutionary Committee* (*MRC*). This *ad hoc* executive organ of the Petrograd soviet was the chief instrument employed by the Bolsheviks to effect their insurrection in the capital. The idea of establishing such a committee originated with the Mensheviks (9 October), but the initiative soon slipped from their

hands. The MRC's statute, devised by Bolshevik leaders active in the garrison, was approved by the soviet executive committee on 12 October and by the plenum four days later, but the MRC did not actually meet until 20 October. Its leaders skilfully camouflaged their insurrectionary purpose behind a flood of rhetoric directed against the Provisional Government and the moderate socialists, depicted as 'counter-revolutionary'. The MRC ran its affairs as an informal collective, the leading roles in its five-man bureau being played by L. D. Trotsky, N. I. Podvoysky, and V. A. Antonov-Ovseyenko; some prominent activists, notably P. E. Lazimir, were left-wing SRs. About 200 persons were actively associated with the MRC's activities, which mainly involved rallying soldiers, sailors, and armed civilians to its authority in readiness for the *coup*.

After overthrowing the government the MRC remained in being until 5 December as one of the chief decision-making centres on the insurgent side. It concerned itself with security matters, i.e. the suppression of real or suspected centres of anti-Bolshevik activity in the capital. Although the MRC was still formally responsible to the Petrograd soviet, in practice it took its cue from the Bolshevik CC, and its authority rivalled that of the CPC. The arbitrary acts perpetrated by bands of armed men operating under the MRC's aegis aroused much public dissatisfaction and alarm, even in circles close to the new regime, as is evident from this brief exchange.

On the Petrograd municipal Duma, see below, pp. 282, 336.

4 *Political Situation on 28 October.* These reports (delivered, according to *Znamya truda*, by L. B. Kamenev and A. V. Lunacharsky) were inaccurate in several particulars, since the new regime was all but isolated from its supporters in the provinces, not least as a result of action taken by communications workers.

The forces at the disposal of prime minister Kerensky, who on 25 October had left Petrograd for the headquarters of the Northern front in quest of loyal troops to suppress the insurgents, were much slighter than the Bolsheviks thought. On their operations, see below, p. 284. In Moscow the agreement reached on 28 October was conditional, and fighting soon flared up again; the city did not pass under Bolshevik control until 2 November: see below, p. 311. There is no truth in the allegation that foreign troops were involved in the battle for the city.

In the provincial towns mentioned (to which the *Znamya truda* report adds Orel) it was often some time before the local soviet, or more accurately a body acting in its name, could make its claim to power effective. In particular the Bolsheviks did not establish themselves in Orel until 1 November, in Minsk until 12 November, in Mogilev (the seat of GHQ) until 18 November, and in Kharkov until 10 December. In Kazan, on the other hand, a localized clash between troops loyal and disloyal to the Provisional Government ended in a victory for the latter as early as 25 October.

5   *Tsentroflot* was the acronym for the Central Committee of the All-Russian Navy. This body was set up at the end of June 1917 by the CEC of first convocation, with the sailors' section of the Petrograd soviet as its nucleus. It comprised elected representatives of all ocean-going fleets and inland waterway flotillas. The chairman was M. N. Abramov, a right-wing SR, of the Arctic Ocean fleet; all but six of its members were non-Bolshevik. During the 'July Days' Tsentroflot attempted to buttress the authority of the Provisional Government and the CEC against strong pressure by radicalized sailors of the Baltic fleet, whose loyalties lay chiefly with their own fleet committee, known as Tsentrobalt (see below, p. 310). Tsentroflot reluctantly acquiesced in the government's measures designed to bring Tsentrobalt to heel, but this turned opinion among the sailors against it. The radicals held that Tsentroflot had forfeited all right to be represented at the Second Congress of Soviets, at which it claimed 6 of the 40 places allocated to naval representatives. The Baltic sailors' delegation to that assembly, led by N. A. Khovrin, was advised by Podvoysky of the Petrograd MRC to liquidate Tsentroflot (recent Soviet accounts attribute this advice to Lenin).

On 26 October Tsentroflot rallied to the Committee for the Salvation of the Country and the Revolution (see below, p. 283), which gave its enemies a convenient pretext to act. Guards were posted at the doors of its conference room and some of its members detained. Some ships' crews protested and on 29

October the MRC ordered the arrested men to be released; others were, however, sent to Kronshtadt as a punishment. Sixteen men took the insurgents' side. Tsentroflot was replaced by a Naval Revolutionary Committee headed by I. I. Vakhrameyev, which helped to stiffen Bolshevik resistance to Krasnov's advance on Petrograd and then, with the aid of some sympathetic officers, gradually imposed its authority on the Naval ministry. At the end of November it convoked an All-Russian Naval Congress (see below, p. 397) to sanction 'democratization' of the fleet.

6 *Press Decree; Union of Typographical Workers.* During the Petrograd insurrection MRC activists took several measures to muzzle press organs deemed hostile to 'soviet power'. In response to protests from various quarters, notably by the printers and journalists immediately affected, the CPC issued an edict, signed by Lenin on 27 October and published in *Pravda* the following day, stating that only those newspapers would be closed down which called for open insubordination to the government, incited their readers to criminal acts, or 'slanderously distorted the facts'; prohibitions, whether temporary or permanent, were henceforth to be authorized solely by the CPC; the decree was to be repealed once normal conditions had been restored. An accompanying clarification promised that once the new order had been consolidated a 'broad and progressive' press law would be issued, providing for 'the fullest freedom within the limits of responsibility before the courts'. Some leading Bolsheviks evidently took these promises seriously, but others, including Lenin, undoubtedly put tactical calculations first: they were anxious to mollify the opposition at a critical moment and to delude it as to their party's real intentions with regard to press freedom and other civil liberties under a 'proletarian dictatorship'. This objective was, however, not attained. Protests continued and the issue soon helped to provoke a breach within the Bolshevik leadership.

The Union of Typographical Workers was one of the oldest and most firmly established trade unions in the country. The printers were noted for their superior educational and cultural standards, which enabled them to appreciate the benefits of press freedom: more was involved here than mere concern for their own livelihood, as some of their critics suggested (cf. above, p. 74). On 27 October delegates from several printing establishments resolved 'not to help the MRC in its efforts to crush freedom of speech, which we consider the greatest good of a free people'. On the following day the union executive called a meeting of delegates who voted 173 to 60 in favour of a resolution in the same sense and later approved strike action, if necessary, in support of their principles. At the union's second all-Russian conference (14–21 December) the maximalist parties (Bolsheviks, PLSR) secured the allegiance of 22 out of 96 delegates; many printers favoured the Mensheviks. The union's decentralized structure left much autonomy to regional branches in such centres as Moscow, Kharkov, and Odessa.

Yu. M. Steklov was appointed editor of *Izvestiya*, official organ of the CEC.

SECOND SESSION

1 *Abolition of the Death Penalty.* Capital punishment was a serious moral and political issue for most Russian revolutionaries. Abolished by the Provisional Government on 12 March, it was subsequently (12 July) reintroduced for certain grave crimes or acts of insubordination by front-line soldiers, but the public outcry was so great that the measure was seldom enforced. The socialist parties agitated for abolition of the death penalty at the front, and on 25 September Kamenev declared before the Preparliament that this should be the first act of a Soviet government. One month later he had an opportunity to fulfil his promise. On 26 October the Second Congress of Soviets, acting on his motion, passed an edict in this sense. Lenin is known to have been extremely angry when he learned of this step, since he believed that maintenance of the death penalty was essential to protect the new regime's security. He wanted the decree to be immediately rescinded, but since the other Bolshevik leaders felt this would make an unfavourable impression the matter was left in abeyance. Execution of real or alleged 'counter-revolutionaries' became a commonplace in 1918.

2 *Popular Socialists.* The Popular Socialist party (*Narodno-sotsialisticheskaya partiya*), the most moderate Populist group,

originated in 1906. Led by a group of widely respected intellectuals (A. V. Peshekhonov, N. F. Annensky, V. A. Myakotin, S. P. Melgunov), it had relatively little mass following. The phrase 'from the Popular Socialists to the Bolsheviks' (either inclusive or exclusive of the latter) became current at this time as a synonym for the entire 'revolutionary democracy'. The moderate socialists saw such a government as the sole alternative to Bolshevik dictatorship and civil war.

3 The *Central Committee of the RSDRP(b)* had met earlier in the day to discuss Vikzhel's ultimatum. It decided unanimously that the basis of the government should be broadened and that its composition might be modified. To this end the Bolsheviks were to take part in the proposed inter-party conference. Their Central Committee (CC) was represented by G. Ya. Sokolnikov and Kamenev. (D. B. Ryazanov, another prominent Bolshevik, attended on behalf of the CEC.) Their conduct at the talks was circumscribed by certain other decisions taken at this session of the CC, although these were not free from ambiguity and did not amount to formal instructions. This point was to lead to trouble later when Lenin, who was not present at the CC meeting, and other 'hard-line' Bolsheviks sought to interpret the decisions in a more restrictive spirit and charged their more moderate colleagues with disloyalty.

These decisions were as follows. The new broadened government was to be 'created' (i.e. approved) by the CEC and was to be responsible to it. It was to endorse the decrees on land and peace adopted at the Second Congress of Soviets (i.e. not to abandon the essentials of the Bolshevik programme). A commitment in favour of a coalition embracing all the socialist parties up to and including the Popular Socialists (see n. 2) was defeated by 7 votes to 4; but each party to the talks was to have the right to challenge nominations made by others. (This presupposed that the delegates would discuss the personal composition of the future cabinet.) The CEC was to be expanded to include representatives of the moderate socialist parties and of the trade unions; nothing was said, however, about including or excluding representatives of local self-government organs.

4 The *United Social-Democratic Internationalists* (USDI: *Ob'yedinennye sotsial-demokraty-internatsionalisty*) were a small group of

non-Bolshevik left-wing Marxists, ideologically close to but organizationally distinct from the Menshevik Internationalists who followed the lead of Yu. O. Martov; the main personalities in the group were N. N. Sukhanov, V. A. Bazarov, and V. A. Stroyev. They were sometimes known as *Novozhintsy* after the newspaper *Novaya zhizn'*, which they helped to publish. This organ, among whose editors was Maxim Gorky, took a critical stand towards both the Bolsheviks and their principal opponents on the left, the official Mensheviks and SRs. The USDI delegates at the Second Congress of Soviets did not follow their former comrades' lead in walking out of the assembly. Like the Left SRs (see n. 8), they accepted the principle of 'soviet power' but interpreted it in a generous manner, hoping to preserve civil liberties and to reserve to the Constituent Assembly the ultimate decisions on Russia's future. The homogeneous all-socialist government for which they strove was to implement the soviet movement's programme (a general democratic peace, land reform, workers' control) but avoid harsh terroristic measures.

The declaration issued by these intermediate groups (which included the Polish Socialist Party as well as the two named here) was printed under banner headlines in *Novaya zhizn'* on 29 October.

5   *Inter-party Conference.* Kamenev's account of the first session of the inter-party conference suggests disappointment that the negotiations had not led to agreement with the moderate socialists on the Bolshevik CC's terms (see n. 3). He was no doubt aware of Lenin's attitude to the talks, which the Bolshevik leader was soon to make explicit, and was anxious to assure his listeners that the Bolshevik negotiators' stand had been reasonable yet firm. Since no other speaker reported on the matter, those present were unlikely to contest his account which, though partisan, was not factually incorrect.

So far as the course of the talks can be reconstructed from the contemporary press and other published sources (a detailed account, evidently compiled for Vikzhel, remains in Soviet archives), it appears that the first meeting, held during the evening of 29 October in the Transport ministry building where Vikzhel had established its Petrograd headquarters, was attended by 26 persons representing eight political parties and nine other organizations. Kamenev invited the other socialists present to join the Bolsheviks in implementing the programme announced at the Second Congress of Soviets. This suggestion was rejected by the SRs and Mensheviks, who thought it morally wrong and politically inexpedient to collaborate with those who had usurped power on the eve of the Constituent Assembly elections and thereby made civil war all but inevitable. Confident that the insurgents would soon be defeated by the forces which Kerensky was gathering on the Northern front, the Menshevik leader F. I. Dan put forward stiff terms for a compromise. First there must be an internal armistice: all military units in the Petrograd region were to be placed under control of the municipal Duma; the insurgents were to disband the MRC and issue an appeal against violence; and the arrested Provisional Government ministers were to be freed. In return he offered an undertaking that Kerensky's forces, when they entered the capital, would refrain from reprisals or provocative acts. A new government would be set up in agreement with Kerensky which would exclude both 'bourgeois' (i.e. nonsocialist) elements and Bolsheviks. Its task would be to convoke the Constituent Assembly, transfer ownership of the land to the land committees, and approach the Allies with a proposal for immediate peace talks—in effect to implement much of the Bolshevik programme while denying them any share in its implementation. Such a demand made sense only on the assumption that the Bolsheviks' collapse was imminent.

The centre and left-wing SRs, Menshevik Internationalists and USDI (see n. 2) took a less intransigent stand, although their position was not identical with that of the Bolsheviks, as Kamenev here suggests. For the Left SRs Malkin suggested an arrangement which would give the Bolsheviks 40 per cent, the moderates 40 per cent, and the intermediate (Internationalist) groups 20 per cent of the seats in the government and the CEC. He evidently hoped that this would give his own group a dominating position.

Although the Bolsheviks rejected these proposals, they did participate in the work of a seven-man commission set up by the conference to study them. After sitting through the night the commission failed to reach any agreement. The four non-

Bolsheviks insisted on an immediate armistice, which the three Bolsheviks (Kamenev, Ryazanov, Sokolnikov) refused. It was at this point that Kamenev returned to report to the CEC. (The fact that he, rather than Ryazanov, the CEC's official delegate, reported, reflected his senior status in the party; Ya. M. Sverdlov, the other Bolshevik nominated by the CEC, does not seem to have attended.)

6 On 29 October *military cadets* (*yunkery*) tried to seize control of certain points in the capital with the object of deposing the Bolshevik government. They were acting in response to advice given by the PSR leader A. R. Gots and other moderate socialists on the Committee for the Salvation of the Country and the Revolution (CSCR: see below, p. 283). The operation was badly planned and within a few hours the cadets had been shelled and intimidated into submission, with some loss of life. Cossacks were the principal element in the small task force being organized by Kerensky and General P. N. Krasnov (see below, p. 284).

7 *Kaledin.* Forces under the command of General (and Don Cossack ataman) A. M. Kaledin were the first to offer serious armed resistance to the Bolshevik take-over. On 25 October Kaledin formed a regional government and in the next few days sent troops to occupy Rostov-on-Don and some mining centres in the Donets valley, where they engaged locally-recruited militia bands (see below, p. 295). There was no time for Kerensky to come to terms with Kaledin, since the former's troops were defeated on 30 October.

8 *Conference of SRs.* This was the first meeting of the group which came to be known as the Party of Left Socialist-Revolutionaries (PLSR). The left-wingers in the PSR were particularly strong in the Petrograd region, not least among the garrison troops. By 10 September they had won control of their party's committee in the capital, which claimed 45,000 members; their leading activists were B. D. Kamkov, M. A. Spiridonova, and M. A. Natanson. On 25 October, at a caucus meeting of SR delegates to the Second Congress of Soviets, a vote on the party's attitude to the crisis went 92:60 in favour of the left. The next day the party CC summoned those who had taken part in the 'Bolshevik adventure' to leave the MRC; the

order was ignored, whereupon the left-wingers were expelled from the PSR 'for gross breach of discipline' (27 October). The schism forced the radicals to formalize their existence as a separate party.

9 *XIIth Army*. Of the three armies on the Northern front the XIIth was the closest to Petrograd and had been severely affected by revolutionary agitation. The soldiers' executive committee (Iskosol) backed the moderate socialists, which lost it support among the troops. When news of the Petrograd insurrection was received, units of Latvian sharpshooters and other radicalized troops staged demonstrations and took over the military communication network to prevent hostile moves against the capital. This report somewhat exaggerates the men's commitment to the new regime, for at a congress of XIIth Army soldiers at Wenden (Cēsis) on 28 October the radicals secured only a slender advantage (248:243), and for this reason decided to join Iskosol in order to subvert it from within. Power finally passed into their hands on 14 November.

The 132nd infantry division formed part of the Xth Army on the Western front.

THIRD SESSION

1 *Inter-party Conference*. On 30 October the conference had marked time while both Bolsheviks and moderate socialists awaited the outcome of the fighting between the MRC's forces and those mustered by Kerensky and General Krasnov (see n. 8). By the evening it became clear that the latter were in retreat. This news softened the attitude of some of the moderates towards the proposed agreement.

The session of the conference held during the night of 30–1 October opened with an exchange over an order issued by the MRC for arrest of the PSR leaders A. R. Gots and N. D. Avksentyev, who were associated with the Committee for the Salvation of the Country and the Revolution (see n. 7)—an organization which the Bolsheviks considered counter-revolutionary, but which was one of the bodies participating in the conference. Martov, the Menshevik Internationalist leader, won general support for a resolution condemning the resort to 'political terror', i.e. the use of physical force against political opponents. On the main question under discussion Dan now suggested that the Mensheviks might participate on certain conditions in a broad socialist coalition government to *include* Bolsheviks. The PSR spokesman, however, reiterated his party's demand for a three-day armistice, during which time a socialist ministry should be formed. Kamenev repeated his opposition to the armistice proposal and added that changes in the composition of the government could only be made once the Bolsheviks' prospective partners had formally adhered to the 'platform' of the Second Congress of Soviets.

Since no agreement seemed possible on this point, the negotiators moved on to discuss the composition of the deliberative organ to which the new government was to be responsible. The idea was mooted that the CEC should be broadened into a 'People's Council' (*narodny sovet*), to include representatives of the (moderate) CEC of first convocation (see below, p. 320), certain municipal Dumas and leading trade unions. A commission was set up to explore this proposal.

By the time this commission met, on the evening of 31 October, the Mensheviks had made their stance more explicit. Their Central Committee, which had met that morning, by a one-vote margin passed a resolution (published in *Rabochaya gazeta*, 1 November) to the effect that, since all other considerations should yield to averting bloodshed within 'revolutionary democracy', the talks should continue with a view to forming a homogeneous socialist ministry 'from the Popular Socialists to the Bolsheviks': the intention was evidently to include the latter party.

A compromise now seemed possible. The moderate socialists suggested that the People's Council should have 420 seats distributed as follows: 100 from the two CECs, chosen by mutual agreement; 100 from the peasant soviets; 100 from local self-government organs (75 from Petrograd and 25 from Moscow; they could choose provincial municipal representatives if they wished); 80 from revolutionary organizations in the army and navy; and 40 from the trade unions. This was expected to give a rough balance between political forces favourable and unfavourable to the insurgents.

When the delegates turned to the composition of the government, a deputation of workers from the Obukhov factory appeared, whose spokesman declared: 'Finish your talks as soon as possible. Don't you see that a bloodbath is starting, that bayonets are clashing? In the working-class areas there are already cries of "To hell with your leaders, Lenin, Kerensky, Trotsky, they'll be the death of us!" ' This seems to have injected a sense of urgency into the discussions. The names of Avksentyev and V. M. Chernov were put forward for the post of prime minister, but neither was acceptable to the Bolshevik negotiators. When the latter were asked who their candidates were, they intimated that they would not insist on retaining Lenin as premier. They then went on to discuss candidates for various other posts in the cabinet, and indicated that Trotsky would not have to remain as PC of Foreign Affairs.

Meanwhile the hard-line Bolsheviks were not inactive. Lenin seems to have disapproved of the talks from the start, but he did not command solid support for his stand in the party's Central Committee. Moreover, as long as the outcome of the insurrection was still in doubt it would have been foolhardy for him to press his views on his colleagues. On 31 October his natural distrust of Vikzhel's mediation efforts was intensified by a report that the union was refusing to allow detachments of sailors to be sent from Petrograd to help the insurgents in Moscow. He turned to the party's Petrograd ('Peterburg') committee, which took a more intransigent stand than its CC, and urged it to agitate among the rank-and-file railwaymen for immediate re-election of the union executive. That afternoon G.E. Zinoviev, addressing the Petrograd soviet, stated that the proposal for an internal armistice was regarded in Smolny as a hostile manœuvre and that it could be accepted only 'once the enemy has been rendered harmless'; in the meantime military measures were to be vigorously prosecuted. The outcome of the battle, he declared, would determine the fate of the talks.

On 1 November Lenin addressed the Petrograd committee in person. The minutes of this meeting have not been published, but it is known that he sharply attacked his 'soft-line' colleagues on the CC. Having won support for his stand in this quarter, he convoked an 'expanded' session of the CC, attended *inter alia* by five members of the Petrograd committee whose presence would bolster his position. F. E. Dzerzhinsky led the verbal onslaught on the Bolshevik negotiators at the talks. Trotsky said that the Bolsheviks should have three-quarters of the places in the CEC; that Duma representation could be permitted only once these bodies had been re-elected; and that Lenin must remain head of the government. Lenin himself was even more explicit. He wished to break off the talks, or at least to continue them only 'as diplomatic cover for military action'. The moderate Bolsheviks argued that the talks were only exploratory and that the CC should stick to the concessions it had already agreed on. Ryazanov held that the masses would fight only to defend the soviets, implying that they would not support a single-party dictatorship.

A proposal to break off the talks received only four votes. It was decided instead to take part in the talks that day 'in order finally to expose the insubstantiality of this attempt [at compromise] and to cease once and for all any further talk of a coalition government'. Passed by 9 votes to 4 with 1 abstention, this was a victory for Lenin—but one obtained only at the price of a schism in the Bolshevik leadership, as the next moves were to show.

The spirit of this decision is truly reflected in the resolution which Volodarsky immediately afterwards presented to the CEC.

2 *Pre-parliament.* In maximalist circles the term 'Pre-parliament' had become synonymous with ineffectual talk in lieu of action.

The Provisional Council of the Russian Republic, to give it its proper title, was a deliberative assembly called into being on 19 September to bolster the Provisional Government's authority pending elections to the Constituent Assembly. It had nearly 500 members, representing various political parties and public organizations. The Bolsheviks were initially divided in their attitude to the Council. On 21 September the CC resolved (by 9 votes to 8) to boycott it, but this decision was reversed at an ensuing party conference. At the single preliminary session held on 23 September a Bolshevik resolution was rejected. When it met in full session on 7 October Trotsky delivered a stinging denunciation of the Pre-parliament, whereupon the Bolshevik delegates withdrew: the gesture had a sensational impact and helped to weaken such authority as the assembly possessed; it continued its deliberations ineffectually until 25 October, when it was dispersed by the insurgents.

3 *Petrograd Municipal Duma.* This local government body, inherited from the Imperial regime, was re-elected twice during 1917 on a progressively broadened franchise. At the second poll, held on 20 August, the Bolsheviks increased their representation from 37 to 67 deputies, becoming the second largest party in the Duma after the PSR, with 75 deputies; it was to this party that the mayor, G. I. Shreyder, belonged. For the Duma's role during and after the insurrection, see below, n. 7.

4 Evidently an error due to ellipsis in transcription. According to Bolshevik theory the source of sovereignty in the Soviet system lay with the Congress of Soviets, whose powers were exercised on its behalf when it was not in session by the CEC. (The real source of authority, of course, was the party's Central Committee.)

5 The *Polish Socialist Party* (PPS: *Polska partia socjalistyczna*), founded in 1893 by J. Piłsudski, S. Wojciechowski, and others, placed national independence in the forefront of its programme and was at first cool towards collaboration with the Russian Social Democrats, suspected of hidden chauvinistic tendencies. After a schism in 1906 the left-wing elements in the PPS sometimes used the name PPS-Lewica to distinguish themselves from Piłsudski's followers, who claimed the party's title. Some members of the former group found themselves in Russia in 1917, and played an active part in radical politics. Their line was close to, but not identical with, that of the Bolsheviks. The less extreme members of the group tempered their commitment to international revolution with the hope that this would lead to an independent socialist Poland. On the question of revolutionary terrorism the PPS activists in Russia took a stand similar to that of the Menshevik Internationalists and the USDI. In 1918 most members of the group joined the SDKPiL.

6 *Moscow Municipal Duma.* In Moscow the municipal elections, held on 25 June, were better organized than those in the capital. The PSR emerged as the clear winner, the Bolsheviks being relegated to fourth place. Although the leftward drift was less

marked here than in Petrograd, in September, when elections were held to city-district (*rayon*) Dumas, the Bolsheviks won the support of 50·9 per cent of the electorate. City-district Dumas were set up in several large cities in 1917, and vied for influence with the district soviets.

7 The *Committee for Salvation of the Country and the Revolution* (*CSCR: Komitet spaseniya rodiny i revolyutsii*) was an umbrella organization which sought to co-ordinate opposition to the Bolshevik take-over by moderate left-wing elements. It was formed at 3.30 a.m. on 26 October, shortly after the fall of the Provisional Government, at a meeting of the Committee of Public Safety in the Petrograd municipal Duma. (This committee had come into being five days earlier to prepare for an expected German attack on the city, but had soon assumed a more explicitly political function.) Both committees consisted of representatives drawn from a large number of public organizations. In the case of the CSCR three men were delegated by each of the following: Petrograd municipal Duma; CEC of first convocation; Executive Committee of the All-Russian Soviet of Peasant Deputies; Menshevik and PSR fractions at the Second Congress of Soviets; Central Committees of the Mensheviks (RSDRP) and PSR; the All-Russian Union of Railwaymen; the Union of Postal and Telegraph Employees; and the Provisional Council of the Russian Republic ('Pre-parliament'). Also represented were the Popular Socialists, the USDI, the All-Russian Union of Co-operators, the Central Committee of the All-Russian Navy (Tsentroflot) and several front-line army organizations.

This list gives a misleading impression of the committee's actual strength, which was in practice confined to Petrograd and its environs, although 'salvation committees' of similar composition came into being in several provincial centres which tried to maintain contact with the parent body and to perform an equivalent role in local affairs.

The CSCR issued a number of appeals and proclamations condemning the insurrection as an 'adventure' and calling on the population not to obey orders by the Bolshevik authorities. Its leaders at first hoped that Kerensky's task force would restore order 'by methods that would safeguard the interests of democracy', i.e. without any excesses likely to encourage the centre and right. The failure of the 'Gatchina expedition' (see n. 8) and the collapse of the inter-party talks left the organization bereft of any realistic policy. On 8 November the Mensheviks announced that they were curtailing their participation in its affairs and on the next day it was suppressed by the MRC on the grounds that it had supported bank employees in their passive resistance to the new government (see below, p. 318).

Despite this move many members of the CSCR remained at liberty. At least one further statement appeared in its name. Its functions were to some extent assumed by a somewhat less representative (but equally ineffective) body known as the Union for the Defence of the Constituent Assembly.

8   *The 'Gatchina Campaign' and Kerensky's Flight.* The first round in the Russian civil war (26 October–1 November) anticipated in microcosm its final outcome three years later. During the night of 24–5 October, as the insurgents were taking over the capital, A. F. Kerensky, prime minister and Supreme Commander-in-Chief, called for troops to be sent from the front to relieve the beleaguered Provisional Government. Some hours later he left Petrograd to expedite their dispatch; but on reaching Pskov, headquarters of the Northern front, he was told by the Commander-in-Chief, General V. A. Cheremisov, that no forces could be spared and that he had ordered a halt to such troops movements as had begun. In common with many other senior officers, Cheremisov was alarmed by the spread of pro-Bolshevik and anti-war sentiment among his men and feared that any armed intervention on behalf of the government would provoke civil war at the front, so making it impossible to resist the Germans. He wired his subordinate commanders: 'political strife in Petrograd should not affect the army, whose task is to maintain its present positions and to preserve order and discipline.'

Kerensky encountered a more positive response from General Krasnov, commander of the 3rd cavalry corps, a predominantly cossack formation which had supported Kornilov against the government in August and had then been dispersed to various points in the region, partly from fear of its 'counter-revolutionary' potential and partly to strengthen morale in non-cossack units. Neither Krasnov, a convinced monarchist, nor his officers had much respect for Kerensky, whom they held responsible for the dissolution of the army; but they feared the Bolsheviks more. A task force (*svodny otryad*) was swiftly created, consisting of about 700 cossacks (in ten squadrons) and a few guns; it was later joined by an armoured train, but disposed of no infantry other than some cadets, who could not be committed to offensive action.

This force made its way with difficulty by rail from Ostrov (Pskov province) to Gatchina, a former Imperial residence twenty-six miles from Petrograd, which it occupied without resistance, and on 27 October moved on to Tsarskoye Selo. However, the impetus behind the operation was already flagging and the Bolshevik MRC had time to organize the capital's defences. On 29 October it crushed the attempted rising within the city by several hundred military cadets, on whose support the attackers had been reckoning. On 30 October a hastily assembled force, consisting mainly of sailors from the Baltic fleet and some Red guards, beat off a small-scale assault on the Pulkovo heights, on the outskirts of the city. Krasnov, who had exhausted his ammunition and feared that Red forces were assembling in his rear, withdrew to Gatchina where informal negotiations soon began between representatives of the opposing sides. Many rank-and-file cossacks were easily convinced that they had no reason to fight on behalf of a government that no longer existed. They welcomed a suggestion that they hand over the unpopular Kerensky for trial by the Bolshevik authorities in return for a pardon and rapid dispatch to their homelands in the Don and Amur regions. In these circumstances Kerensky, who learned of these discussions on the afternoon of 1 November, decided to escape from Gatchina and to go underground. He abandoned his civil and military functions in favour of Avksentyev and General N. N. Dukhonin respectively.

In the account given here Krasnov feigns surprise and indignation at Kerensky's flight. Allowance must be made for the fact that his deposition was made shortly after he had fallen into Bolshevik hands. In his memoirs, written some years later, he states that he helped Kerensky to escape, but this claim is contested by the latter. Kerensky suspected treachery by Krasnov and other conservatives in the officer corps, but his

suspicions were greatly exaggerated. There is no evidence that
Krasnov acted improperly towards the fallen premier, or that
in advising him to go to Petrograd he hoped to encompass his
demise.

The failure of the 'Gatchina campaign' may be attributed to
the following causes: (a) the general war-weariness among the
soldiers, who instinctively opposed any active military operations against either external or internal enemies of the
Provisional Government; (b) similar sentiments among the
railwaymen, who in obedience to instructions from Vikzhel
(see above, p. 45) refused to assist in effecting troop movements
—a Vikzhel delegation saw Kerensky on 31 October in search
of a negotiated settlement, which he rejected; (c) the slowness
with which GHQ and other military authorities responded to
repeated appeals to assist the task force, especially to dispatch
infantry reinforcements, without which the cossacks were under-
standably reluctant to continue fighting—not until 30 October
were any sizeable relief forces concentrated, by which time the
outcome had been decided; (d) poor communications, ag-
gravated by the relatively rapid movement of the task force and
the control exercised by radicalized soldiers over transmission
of radio messages; (e) mutual distrust between senior military
officers, whose main concern was to 'save the army' from internal decay, and the democratic socialist intellectuals whom
Kerensky in some ways typified.

Kerensky's flight was by no means an act of cowardice, as
Krasnov here implies: it could be justified both on moral and
on political grounds. Nevertheless it had an unfortunate effect
upon his personal reputation. It also deprived democratic anti-
Bolsheviks of a possible figurehead around whom to rally, and
cast doubt on the legality of their claims to succeed the defunct
Provisional Government. These weaknesses were quickly seized
on by the Bolsheviks, as is evident from the tone of the appeal
adopted on this occasion by the CEC.

9   This was a roll-call vote, at which those present voted on
party lines. The reason for this is evident from the report in
Novaya zhizn': when first presented, a majority (33:30) voted
for the Left SR draft. This led the Bolsheviks to impose party
discipline on their followers and sympathizers. The Left SRs

did not join the USDI in their demonstrative departure from the CEC, although at 2 a.m. on 2 November their delegates discussed this possible course of action; the voting took place at 7 a.m. on 2 November (*Rabochaya gazeta*, 4 November). The USDI returned to the chamber on 17 November.

FOURTH SESSION

1   *Muravyev's 'Order no. 1' on the Defence of Petrograd.* This edict was issued by the eccentric lieutenant-colonel whom the MRC had appointed Commander-in-Chief of the Petrograd military district, with special responsibility for defence of the capital (see below, p. 302). It entrusted maintenance of order to 'soldiers, sailors, Red guardsmen, and the entire revolutionary proletariat', who were instructed to act 'mercilessly and without delay' against criminals. It also forbade searches of premises or expropriations except in the presence of an MRC representative or 'one or more soldiers, sailors, or Red guardsmen'—a provision which made the intended safeguard worthless. Muravyev did evidently want to restrain unruly elements from committing robberies and assaults, but placed a naïve confidence in his mutinous troops' capacity for self-discipline. This attitude reflected the revolutionary idealism of the Left SRs, to whose cause Muravyev was a recent convert: until September 1917 he had been a stalwart 'defensist'.

What was at issue here was not Muravyev's personal fitness for his post, as a casual reading of the minutes might suggest, but the licence to perpetrate arbitrary acts enjoyed by the MRC and other agencies of 'proletarian dictatorship'. The Bolsheviks were quick to countermand Muravyev's order, which they excused on grounds of political inexperience, but they themselves were soon to engage in terroristic measures on a far greater scale. On 7 November Muravyev was prevailed upon to resign (in favour of Antonov-Ovseyenko), only to cause his superiors further embarrassment a few days later: see above, p. 117. More seriously, early in 1918, when he was serving as chief of an expeditionary force sent into the Ukraine, he permitted his troops to commit numerous outrages which aroused popular opinion against the Bolsheviks. In the following June he rose to become commander of the Eastern front but turned against the

central authorities, of whose intransigent policy he now disapproved; he was shot in a scuffle, allegedly 'while resisting
arrest' (11 July).

2 The debate on this issue was so sharp because it raised the
touchy subject of the CEC's rights *vis-à-vis* the commissars and
the CPC as the executive authority, to which question the
delegates turned later in the session (item 4). As a result of the
rules now adopted, the CPC was to be informed of CEC
business by its chairman, but in practice the agenda was devised by the latter after discussion in the party CC or informal
consultation with leading colleagues.

3 *Inter-party Conference.* During the night of 1–2 November,
while the CEC was debating V. Volodarsky's resolution in-
corporating Lenin's stiff terms for an agreement with the moderate socialists (see above, p. 52), the conference itself maintained a shadowy existence. The next day the various parties
and organizations involved met separately to take stock of the
situation. Vikzhel issued a statement attributing the failure to
reach agreement to Bolshevik intransigence. The CC of the
PSR declared that there was no point in resuming the talks, and
a similar (but slightly more equivocal) stand was taken by the
Executive Committee of the All-Russian Soviet of Peasant
Deputies. The CEC of first convocation also resolved (by 29
votes to 13 with 7 abstentions) that no coalition with the
Bolsheviks was possible. The Menshevik CC issued a lengthy
statement to the effect that, despite the Bolsheviks' sole responsibility for the impasse, it would still continue the talks
'provided that, as an essential preliminary, the Bolsheviks fulfil
the following conditions: (a) free all those arrested on political
grounds or captured in armed combat . . . ; (b) cease the system
of political terror and restore freedom of the press, spoken word,
assembly, association, strike action, and personal and domi-
ciliar inviolability; (c) declare an armistice wherever civil war
is in progress; (d) hand over to the municipality enough armed
strength to maintain order . . .' Since these demands had already been rejected, this reassertion of fundamental principles
amounted to an acknowledgment that the talks were doomed.
An element of tactical calculation was also involved here. The
Mensheviks knew that the Bolshevik CC was divided on this

matter and hoped to strengthen the resolve of those who
advocated conciliation.

The Bolshevik CC session that same day (2 November) was
evidently stormy. (Unfortunately no minutes of meetings between 1 and 8 November have been preserved.) It prompted
Lunacharsky's resignation (see below, p. 297) and another
appeal, this time in writing, from Lenin for support by stalwarts
in the Petrograd committee; the latter body responded by
declaring the proposed agreement 'absolutely unacceptable'
(*Pervy legal'ny*, p. 342). The principal matter under discussion
in the CC was once again the conduct of the Bolshevik negotiators at the conference, which Lenin described as criminal
sabotage: 'without betraying the slogan of soviet power', he
averred, 'one cannot renounce a purely Bolshevik government
if this government has been entrusted with power by the majority [of delegates] at the Second Congress of Soviets.' His
more forceful criticisms of his comrades' attitude were excised
from the published text of the resolution which the CC finally
adopted (five members voting against it). This reiterated the
Bolsheviks' willingness to broaden the basis of the government
by admitting more soviet representatives (but not Duma
deputies) into the CEC and bringing some moderate socialists
into the CPC, provided they subscribed to the Bolshevik
programme.

The Left SRs evidently now decided to force the issue. When
the matter came up before the CEC that evening, they presented their demand for a homogeneous socialist ministry in
ultimatum form. Zinoviev, whose position had now apparently
softened, read out the CC's statement but added that it had
not yet been discussed by the Bolshevik fraction in the CEC—a
way of saying that he did not agree with it. During the ensuing
recess he and Kamenev decided to adopt a more co-operative
attitude. This is evident above all from clause 3(d) and the
penultimate sentence of the resolution which Kamenev then
presented. The figure of 50 Duma representatives was only half
that suggested by the moderate socialists, but the presence of
these men in the CEC might conceivably have turned the scales
in favour of the non-Bolsheviks. 'Systematic armament of the
workers' could be regarded as an attempt to dilute the programme endorsed by the Second Congress of Soviets. Nor had

the Bolshevik CC authorized a settlement giving the Bolsheviks half the portfolios in the reformed ministry.

These concessions, and perhaps above all the spirit that animated them, aroused the wrath of Lenin and some of his associates (see below, p. 297); how far the proposals actually endangered Bolshevik hegemony must remain a matter of opinion. For the moment they satisfied the Left SRs, but they were far from adequate to salvage the inter-party conference.

4 *Left SRs and Soviet Government.* In the afternoon of 26 October Lenin, and possibly some other Bolshevik leaders, held talks with three Left SR representatives (B. D. Kamkov, V. A. Karelin, and V. B. Spiro) with the object of persuading them to join the government they were about to set up. Their refusal meant that an all-Bolshevik ministry was presented to the Second Congress of Soviets for its endorsement a few hours later. No record has survived of these conversations. The Left SRs' refusal was evidently due to their objection to the intransigent line taken by the Bolsheviks towards the moderate socialists, whose presence in the government they deemed essential. They were also somewhat awed by the Bolsheviks' superior political expertise, which would enable them to impose their views upon the Left SRs if the coalition were restricted to these two parties. There may also be something to Lenin's argument (see above, p. 80) that the Left SRs wanted to keep their options open at a time when it seemed that the insurrection might still fail, and that they were influenced by their less radical comrades in the PSR (in which the breach had yet to become final).

5 *Representation of CEC Abroad.* This debate shows that the CEC delegates regarded their soviet institution as the real centre of power and the PCs as its instruments. It took time for them to realize that the Bolshevik leaders' view was very different. Trotsky's commissariat was intent on keeping full control over the foreign relations of the infant state.

Stockholm was the main transit point for communication with western Europe. In April 1917 the Bolsheviks had established there the so-called Foreign Bureau of their party CC. This consisted of J. S. Fürstenberg (Hanecki), K. Radek, and V. V. Vorovsky. They published a propaganda organ in German (*Russische Korrespondenz 'Prawda'*, followed by *Bote der russischen Revolution*) and endeavoured to win over left-wing socialists who supported the International Socialist Committee (generally known as the 'Zimmerwald committee'), which had moved to Stockholm. After the Bolshevik revolution Radek and Hanecki left for Petrograd (5 November). Lenin was keen to appoint Hanecki as the Bolsheviks' official representative in Stockholm, but many senior party comrades had scruples over Hanecki's part in transmitting to the Bolsheviks funds of dubious origin which were then generally believed, and are now definitely known, to have originated in part from the German government. In November Vorovsky was appointed ambassador to the Scandinavian countries (see below, p. 326).

6   *Statute of the CEC.* The Organization Commission set up on 27 October (see above, p. 41) had evidently been given, or had itself acquired, the task of devising a statute for the CEC. This showed a determination to institutionalize the machinery of government which had been lacking among the moderate socialists who ran the CEC of first convocation. The drafters of the statute assumed that the new CEC would play a key role in ruling the country.

In the short time at their disposal for preparing this document, they could not broach such vital matters as the scope of the CEC's powers *vis-à-vis* the CPC or the mode of election of deputies. Yet many points here are of great interest.

Section I. The term 'restricted session' applies to the number of members attending, not the publicity accorded to the debate. Such sessions were required because it was expected that most deputies would be busy with executive tasks that might well take them outside the city. Possibly one can also detect here a desire to concentrate power in the hands of a limited number of reliable or experienced deputies. The attempt to fix the periodicity of meetings suggests that the organizers were already eager to drop the practice of meeting almost daily, as a kind of 'revolutionary Convention'. On candidate members, see below, p. 306.

Section II. The Presidium, which was to meet much more frequently than the CEC plenum, was already allotted extensive powers. No machinery was provided whereby its decisions could be contested. The wording of the statute suggests that its framers wanted the CEC to meet daily and to hear a report from its Presidium; this, however, was not what happened in practice.

Section III. In reality a division already existed between the CEC's deliberative and executive functions, which according to Bolshevik constitutional theory were to be combined. A hierarchical order was set up, consisting of Presidium, commissions, and departments. No measures were taken to ensure rotation of members in order to prevent undue professional specialization. Departments were to have some operatives who were not deputies, i.e. full-time civil servants. The third sentence in clause 7 is not clear. Presumably it meant that not more than one-third of the departmental staff should be co-opted personnel.

A number of departments other than those listed came into being as and when required: see below, p. 305. Of the five commissions established on 27 October, none was explicitly mentioned here (although the Editorial Commission presumably managed the department of that name); some of them will have been of an *ad hoc* character.

The statute was not debated at length, ostensibly owing to the lateness of the hour. Characteristically, the only point which aroused discussion related to the practical but non-essential matter of members' earnings. The deputies were evidently little concerned about the statute's political implications, which would soon become all too apparent— requiring revision of the statute as early as 17 November (see below, p. 338).

7 The *All-Russian Central Council of Trade Unions* (ARCCTU) was set up at the Third conference of Russian trade unions, held from 21 to 28 June 1917. It had 35 members, elected in such a way as to give the Mensheviks a slight advantage. The leading Bolsheviks on ARCCTU were the secretary, S. A. Lozovsky, and the deputy chairman, D. B. Ryazanov. Both men advocated compromise with the moderate socialists, an attitude which reflected their sense of responsibility towards their trade-union followers. This 'softness' led them into trouble with Lenin, and Lozovsky's stand on freedom of conscience (see below, p. 299) brought him expulsion from the Bolshevik

party; Ryazanov was soon given a quasi-academic appointment.

The structure of the trade-union movement, at this time still very diverse, was clarified at the First all-Russian congress called by ARCCTU from 7 to 14 January 1918. This provided for a number of federations (*ob'yedineniya*), each of which united all workers employed in a particular branch of production. These are the bodies to which the CEC decided to give a (relatively modest) voice in its affairs.

8 *All-Russian Council of Factory Committees* (ARCFC). This body was set up to co-ordinate the factory-committee movement at a conference held from 17 to 22–3 October 1917. It was designed to supersede the Central Council of Factory Committees of Petrograd, which although formally an organ of regional scope had in fact played a national role. ARCFC had a brief life: the Bolsheviks, anxious to thwart the Anarcho-syndicalist tendencies that were widespread in the factory-committee movement, saw the institution as a potential rival to the central bodies for state control and management of the economy which they deemed essential under socialism. The ARCFC leaders had ideas of their own about workers' control in industry, and the decree of 14 November on this subject (see below, p. 317) was a compromise between them and Lenin. It gave ARCFC a mere five seats on an All-Russian Council of Workers' Control with some 40–50 members; the latter body was itself soon incorporated into the Supreme Economic Council (SEC: see below, p. 351), while ARCFC was integrated into the machinery set up to regulate economic life in the Petrograd region.

FIFTH SESSION

1 *The Social-Democratic Party of the Kingdom of Poland and of Lithuania* (SDKPiL), to give it its full name, was founded in December 1899. Its most prominent leaders were Rosa Luxemburg, L. Iogiches, and A. Warszawski (Warski). They differed from the Russian Bolsheviks over the question of national self-determination, but in 1906, after playing a major part in the Russian revolution of 1905, the SDKPiL joined the RSDRP as an autonomous organization. The outbreak of the First World

War, followed by the Central Powers' occupation of Russian Poland, strengthened the internationalist tendencies in the party. I. S. Unshlikht (Józef Unszlicht, pseud. Yurovsky) was one of several leaders—others included Radek and Dzerzhinsky—who became closely associated with the Bolsheviks. He represented the SDKPiL in the CEC of first convocation; later in 1917 he was a member of the Petrograd MRC and served on the directing board (*kollegium*) of the PC of Internal Affairs.

2 *The Inter-district Conference of District* (Rayon) *Workers' and Soldiers' Soviets of Petrograd* was set up on 12 April 1917 by the executive committee of the Petrograd soviet to co-ordinate the work of the district (borough) soviets in the city. From July onward it came under control of the Bolsheviks, who used it as a base from which to wrest from the moderate socialists the predominant influence in the Petrograd soviet. Once this body had come under their control early in September, the conference concerned itself in the main with the organization of Red guards units. After the October insurrection it faded from view, its functions passing to the regular executive apparatus of the Petrograd soviet.

3 Trotsky's resolution was worded more sharply than one drafted at this time by Lenin (*PSS*, xxxv. 51–2), which was not submitted to the CEC. This proposed the establishment of an investigating commission into management of the press as the first step towards a regime under which groups of citizens numbering 10,000 or more should have an equal right to stocks of newsprint and printing facilities. There was no difference of substance between the two leaders. The Bolsheviks apparently had no clear policy on this issue when they took power (see above, p. 252); they were presumably sincere in holding out the prospect of an eventual liberalization of press control measures once the political struggle had eased, but by the time the civil war ended their views had hardened considerably.

4 *Zemshchina:* a right-wing daily published in St. Petersburg/Petrograd from 1909 to 1917, edited by S. S. Glinka-Yanchevsky.

5 *Novoye vremya:* the leading conservative daily in the capital, founded in 1868 and published for many years by A. S.

Suvorin. It was closed down by the Petrograd MRC on 26 October 1917.

6 *Russkaya volya:* a Petrograd daily, founded in December 1916, which took a strong pro-war stand; suppressed by the insurgents on 25 October.

7 *Programme-Minimum and Programme-Maximum.* The RSDRP's official programme, adopted in 1903, distinguished schematically between demands thought to be appropriate to the 'bourgeois democratic' and 'proletarian socialist' phases of the revolutionary process. The former included a parliamentary republic, civil liberties, abolition of the standing army, compulsory education from public funds etc. The latter included socialization of all means of production and exchange and the establishment of a 'proletarian dictatorship'.

8 *Cirque Moderne:* a popular venue for mass meetings in revolutionary Petrograd, where Trotsky had made a name for himself as an effective orator.

9 *Kaledinites:* a term used loosely at this time to denote the counter-revolutionary forces mobilizing in the south-east of European Russia. On 31 October the 7th Cossack division was ordered to occupy Voronezh. The move was seen as the first step to the overthrow of Soviet rule; but it was an exaggeration at this juncture to speak of these forces posing a threat to Moscow. When General Dukhonin at GHQ asked Kaledin for aid (30 October), the latter replied that no men could be spared or transported to Mogilev because of the hostile attitude adopted by the railwaymen. Moreover, Kaledin's troops were unwilling to fight far away from their home territory. The Red forces were soon able to seize the initiative in this theatre. On 10 January 1918, spurred on by the approach of some 10,000 Soviet troops led by Antonov-Ovseyenko, disaffected cossacks decided to depose the regional government; thereafter the Taganrog workers in insurrection and Kaledin's forces were obliged to evacuate most of the Don territory. On 30 January Kaledin committed suicide. See also below, pp. 353, 368.

10 *Rech':* Petrograd daily, central organ of the Kadets (Constitutional Democrats, Party of People's Freedom). Published

from 1906, its chief editors were I. V. Gessen, V. D. Nabokov, and the party's principal leader and spokesman, P. N. Milyukov. The paper was suppressed after the issue of 26 October and its offices more than once raided by bands of Red guardsmen; nevertheless from 16 November it reappeared under different titles (*Nasha rech'*, *Svobodnaya rech'*, *Novaya rech'*, *Vek*, *Nash vek*), but with uneven frequency, until it was finally closed down early in August 1918. To equate the Kadets with Kaledinites is to commit a rhetorical exaggeration: although many liberals sympathized with Kaledin (and with the Volunteer Army being formed under his protection), they had little sympathy for the cossacks' autonomist tendencies.

11   The Kadet leader evidently realized that he was in serious danger if he remained in Petrograd. At the end of October he left the city for Moscow, whence he proceeded to Rostov-on-Don; for some months he served as a civilian adviser to leaders of the White Volunteer Army. The Bolsheviks thus had reason to rue their laxity in allowing him to escape their security net at a time when many less eminent democratic politicians were arrested and imprisoned on mere suspicion.

12   *Russkoye slovo*: Moscow daily, founded in 1895, and published from 1897 onwards by I. D. Sytin. Appreciated for the breadth of its news coverage, its circulation reached three-quarters of a million copies by 1916. After the February revolution it took a liberal stand. Closed down by order of the Moscow soviet authorities on 27 November, allegedly for 'slandering soviet power', it reappeared in January 1918 under the title of *Novoye slovo*, then *Nashe slovo*, but was finally suppressed in July 1918.

13   *Social-Democratic and Socialist-Revolutionary Agrarian Programmes*. In 1902 Lenin drew up an agrarian programme for the RSDRP in which he sought to reconcile the Marxist conviction that farming by peasant smallholders was reactionary with the tactical aim of exploiting disaffection among the land-hungry peasantry. One of the demands he put forward was for return to the peasants of the so-called *otrezki*, parcels of land 'cut off' from peasant allotments in favour of private proprietors by the 1861 reform. These proposals, less radical than those put forward at the time by the Socialist-Revolutionaries, the

Marxists' chief rivals, were soon overtaken by events, and in 1905 Lenin openly advocated nationalization of all the land. This represented a major shift away from standard doctrine among European Marxists.

By nationalization the Bolsheviks understood something different from the socialization favoured by the SRs. Whereas the latter were on the whole sympathetic to maintenance of the small family farm, and as democrats paid some heed to the peasants' actual preferences, the Bolsheviks, as whole-hearted partisans of state socialism and proletarian dictatorship, were anxious to refashion agrarian relations along collectivistic lines. The tensions between the Left SRs and the Bolsheviks over agrarian policy helped to bring about a breach between these two parties in the spring of 1918. However, at this moment they seemed to have reconciled their differences: Lenin's land decree, promulgated at the Second Congress of Soviets, and inspired chiefly by calculations of political strategy, appeared to embody the main demands put forward by the more radical Populists. Malkin and other Left SR spokesmen somewhat naïvely regarded the Bolsheviks as converts to their own ideas.

14 *Resignation of People's Commissars.* The CPC showed signs of cracking on 2 November, when Lunacharsky resigned, ostensibly in protest at the destruction wrought during the fighting in Moscow (see below, p. 310). Although he withdrew his resignation the following day, tension among the Bolshevik leaders persisted. A number of them had serious reservations about the general direction of internal policy, which seemed to be heading towards single-party, indeed personal, dictatorship. The immediate issues were press censorship, civil liberties, and the CPC's responsibility for its actions to the CEC; behind them lay the whole problem of the rights to be accorded to political opponents, in the party and in the country as a whole.

Disapproving of the Bolshevik representatives' conduct at the fourth session of the CEC (2–3 November: see above, p. 62), Lenin responded by presenting an ultimatum to 'the minority in the Central Committee', whom he charged with having infringed party discipline by defying a decision of the CC on composition of the (reformed) government. He demanded that they submit, threatening that otherwise he would take the matter before an extraordinary party congress, which would doubtless expel them from the party. Each member of the CC was summoned individually and requested to sign the ultimatum; ten of them did so.

The inter-party conference met again during the night of 3–4 November, but reached no agreement. The Bolsheviks and Left SRs reiterated their terms, holding out the prospect of concessions once they had been accepted and a new government formed. For the Mensheviks R. Abramovich insisted that the 'terroristic' measures must be repealed first; otherwise, he argued, the conference could not continue, still less produce a compromise, since the PSR could not be expected to attend so long as its leaders stood in danger of arrest. Asked whether the MRC had ordered the arrest of the Vikzhel leaders, Stalin gave an evasive reply. It was decided that the talks should be resumed the following afternoon, but this meeting had to be postponed since the CEC was then in session and the crisis had taken a new turn.

Lenin continued his campaign against the 'capitulationists' with a speech to the Petrograd soviet in which, without mentioning them by name, he condemned them for cowardice. At an emergency conference of Bolshevik organizations in the capital a resolution was passed affirming that 'our party does not need the aid of petty-bourgeois political groups' and 'calling to order those comrades who are vacillating, intimidated by the grandeur of the tasks lying before the party . . .'

The intransigent line which the Bolshevik leaders took at this session of the CEC on the issues of press censorship and responsible government came as the last straw to the right-wing Bolsheviks. By their resignation they evidently hoped to strengthen the moderate socialists' willingness to compromise with the Bolsheviks and to persuade their 'hard-line' comrades to yield under pressure. In this, however, they overestimated their own power and underestimated Lenin's personal authority in the party, which was all but absolute; if anything, it was further strengthened by this unequal test of political will.

The conflict may be seen as one which ranged revolutionary idealism against the exigencies of power politics, the individual conscience against *raison du parti*. The underlying moral issue was well put by Lozovsky, the Bolshevik trade-union leader, in a statement to the Bolshevik fraction in the CEC, which was published on the following day in the Menshevik *Rabochaya gazeta*. Revealing that at the fraction's private (caucus) meeting during the CEC session the issue had been presented as one of party discipline, he declared:

> I cannot remain silent in the name of party discipline when I feel with every fibre of my being that the CC's tactics are leading to the isolation of the proletariat, to civil war among working people, and to the defeat of the great revolution . . . I cannot suppress in the name of party discipline [my knowledge of] the sullen discontent of the working masses, who fought for soviet power [only to discover that] by some incomprehensible manœuvre that power is wholly Bolshevik
> . . .

Of the four people's commissars who resigned, only the first three were members of the party CC. They, together with Kamenev and Zinoviev, submitted their resignation from that body at a meeting held on 4 November (presumably just after the CEC session). The PC of Welfare, Alexandra Kollontay, was also said to have resigned her post, but *Izvestiya* of 10 November reported her as still in office. Another functionary who resigned was R. Arsky, who worked in the PC of Labour. K. K. Yurenev later issued a statement denying that he had resigned; his position was evidently similar to that of Shlyapnikov.

Very soon some of the dissidents were having second thoughts about their action. The first to recant was Zinoviev, who as early as 7 November wrote a 'Letter to my Comrades' in which he claimed that the Mensheviks were to blame for the collapse of the inter-party talks—implying that there was no longer any reason for the opposition to adhere to the demands it had put forward; he appealed to his comrades to join him in submitting to party discipline. According to the official CC record the opposition members submitted a statement which was considered by the committee on 29 November but found unsatisfactory by Lenin (no record of this exchange has been preserved); the same source adds that the date of their return to the CC is 'not known', but it is clear that Zinoviev attended the meeting of 11 December (and may well have been present earlier). He was re-elected to the CC in March 1918, whereas

Kamenev was not re-admitted until March 1919; A. I. Rykov and V. P. Nogin became respectively full and candidate members after the Ninth congress (March–April 1920). Nevertheless the Bolshevik dissidents continued to take an active part in political life. On 2 December 1917 Kamenev, V. P. Milyutin, Yu. Larin, and Ryazanov were appointed members of the bureau, or steering committee, of the Bolshevik fraction in the Constituent Assembly, but on 11 December the entire bureau was dismissed for taking too 'soft' an attitude toward the prospective national parliament (see below, p. 403).

The vacant ministerial posts took some time to fill. A. L. Kalegayev was reluctant to take his seat as PC of Agriculture until his party's conditions for joining the government had been met (see below, pp. 339, 373); he first attended a CPC session on 19 November and was appointed commissar five days later. The other three appointments were filled by Bolsheviks: G. I. Petrovsky became PC of Internal Affairs (17 November), V. V. Obolensky PC of Trade and Industry (15 December), and A. G. Shlikhter PC of Supply (December; succeeded in February 1918 by A. D. Tsurupa).

15 *Foreign Left-wing Socialists' Support for Soviet Government.* Receipt of news that the October insurrection was greeted favourably by internationalist (anti-war) socialists elsewhere in Europe strengthened the Bolsheviks' hand in the debate on the character of the new regime. The Left SRs were even more convinced than the Bolsheviks that the success of the revolution in Russia depended on its being emulated abroad.

Henri Guilbeaux had little standing among French socialists. A representative at the 1916 Kienthal conference, he resided in Geneva where, as a member of the *Swiss* socialist party, he edited the review *Demain* (and also performed public relations services for the Bolsheviks, with whose Foreign Bureau in Stockholm he was in regular contact).

Georg Ledebour was better known. He was one of three members of the executive (*Vorstand*) of the Sozialdemokratische Arbeitsgemeinschaft, an association of left-wing Social-Democratic deputies in the German Reichstag formed in March 1916, when the majority of the party once again approved a grant of credit to the Imperial government for waging the war. In the following month Ledebour became a member of the executive (*Aktionskomitee*) of the Independent Social-Democratic party (USDP) and later played a prominent part in the 1918 German revolution. The message quoted here suggests that he was ill informed as to the real situation in Petrograd. The Bolsheviks had of course sanctioned partition of landed properties as a temporary expedient to secure peasant support, and Lenin certainly had no intention of broadening the Soviet government along the lines which Ledebour evidently desired. However, these subtleties escaped the attention of the CEC deputies who heard Sokolnikov read the message.

The Austrian party's proper title, incorrectly given here, was 'the German Social-Democratic Labour Party in Austria'. Its congress of October 1917 resulted in a shift to the left, but the dominant group, the supporters of Otto Bauer, was 'centrist' rather than pro-Bolshevik. Its position was that the war should continue until a democratic peace had been negotiated. Nevertheless it was easier for this party than for the German Social-Democrats to ventilate its views in public. The news of the October insurrection in Russia was a contributory cause of mass demonstrations in Vienna: on 29 October/11 November the Vienna police reported that 20,000 persons took to the streets (higher figures are given in other sources); the marchers, who behaved in an orderly manner, called for an immediate democratic peace and recognition of the Soviet government. This popular discontent, together with the worsening food supply situation, led the Austro-Hungarian government to press for armistice negotiations and peace on the Eastern front (see below, p. 344).

Another telegram of support, not read out on this occasion, was received from the Dutch socialist leader Anton Pannekoek. The messages were brought from Stockholm to Petrograd by a Bolshevik courier named Kogan.

16   *Products Exchange.* The practice of bartering industrial commodities for foodstuffs grew up of its own accord during the latter half of 1917 as regular commercial channels dried up and Russia gradually reverted to a natural economy. Efforts were made both by the Provisional Government and by its successor to regulate this unofficial trade, but without much practical effect.

Lenin may here be said to make a virtue out of necessity. The practice could be presented as socialistic since it did not involve money, which was expected to die out as a medium of exchange once capitalism had been abolished. Lenin's argument that socialism was primarily a simple matter of workers learning to keep accounts and control production (developed at greater length in his *State and Revolution*) allowed him to claim that Russia was already mature for socialism—a point contested by many Russian Marxists, Bolsheviks included, as well as by European Social-Democrats. At the same time he was careful to say (see above, pp. 74, 88) that this made it possible only to *begin* (not to complete) the construction of a socialist society.

His emphasis on the merits of spontaneous revolutionary action, in reply to Left SR charges of excessive *dirigisme*, contrasts sharply with his writings of 1918 and later.

17 *Decree on Land Committees.* The rural district (*volost'*) land committees were often under maximalist influence and took the initiative in dividing up the proprietors' land and stock. They had been entrusted by Lenin's land decree of 26 October with the implementation of the agrarian reform. On 31 October an ordinance was issued by Milyutin, during his brief tenure as PC of Agriculture, specifying the duties of these committees. This instruction had been approved by the First Congress of Soviets on 23 June but had not been put into effect by the Provisional Government. Many of its provisions were no longer realistic, as the Left SRs were quick to note.

Kalegayev is also hinting at the ambiguity in the Bolsheviks' attitude toward individual peasant ownership of land and their readiness to maintain in being at least the more efficient private estates in the guise of state or collective farms—to the detriment, as the Populists saw it, of the peasants who wished to divide up all the land as smallholdings and to farm it without interference from the central government.

18 *Commander-in-Chief; Revolutionary Staff.* Proshyan is here referring to the Commander-in-Chief of the Petrograd military district, Lieutenant-colonel Muravyev (see above, p. 287).

By 'revolutionary staff' is meant the so-called 'field staff' (*voyenno-polevoy shtab*) set up on 25 October to effect the seizure

of power. This consisted of N. I. Podvoysky, A. S. Bubnov,
V. A. Antonov-Ovseyenko, G. I. Chudnovsky and K. S.
Yeremeyev. Modern Soviet writers attribute its formation to
the Bolshevik CC, but in fact it was more closely associated with
the MRC, in which Trotsky was one of the leading figures (see
above, p. 270). According to Antonov-Ovseyenko the field staff
also included several young officers, notably captain Lukin of
the Sveaborg fortress and captain Kazantsev of the 176th
infantry regiment.

After the insurrection it took over control of military instal-
lations and bodies of troops in the capital, and within a few
days found itself (its composition now slightly altered) directing
operations against the forces of Krasnov and Kerensky (see
above, p. 285). In practice the field staff acted much as it pleased,
but in principle it was responsible both to the MRC and the
the three commissars charged with responsibility for military
and naval affairs. This administrative overlap did not make for
smooth operations. Jurisdictional conflicts were frequent in the
chaotic early days of 'soviet power', when many revolutionaries
were eager to avoid legal 'formalism' yet issued a flood of
decrees, instructions, and orders. Proshyan would have been on
stronger ground had he emphasized the need for legality rather
than efficiency in the new administrative structure, but the
Left SRs shared Russian revolutionary intellectuals' general
prejudice against 'bourgeois legalism'.

19 *Bolshevik Leadership in Moscow.* Two of the four people's
commissars who resigned, Nogin and Rykov, were from the
Bolshevik committee in Moscow, which was split on factional
lines; N. I. Bukharin, G. I. Lomov (Oppokov) and G. Ya.
Sokolnikov emerged during 1917 as leaders of a vociferous
radical group. In August, when the CC nominated four of its
members from Moscow to direct work in the entire Central
Industrial region, either by chance or by design it balanced
two left-wingers against two right-wingers. In the following
month Nogin became chairman of the Moscow soviet of
workers' deputies. He and Rykov, who were senior in age and
party seniority to the radicals, took account of the mood of
Moscow workers, which was in general a little less 'advanced'
than in Petrograd. They were more favourable than the Bol-

shevik leaders in Petrograd (and Lenin) to the prospect of a compromise with the other socialist parties and slower to embark upon an insurrectionary path. This helps to explain why the struggle for control of Russia's second capital was relatively fierce and prolonged (see below, p. 310).

20   *The CEC and the CPC.* Clauses 2 and 3 of Uritsky's resolution (which was evidently written by Trotsky) contained a definition of the CEC's powers which significantly narrowed its right to control the executive. The Second Congress of Soviets had laid down the general rule that the CPC was responsible to the CEC, implying that the latter was the sovereign body between sessions of the Congress. Now: (i) the CPC was expressly given the right to issue 'urgent' decrees provided that they fell 'within the general programme adopted by the Congress'—and was free to determine for itself whether this condition applied; (ii) its control was characterized as 'general', implying that if it raised specific issues it would lay itself open to the charge of obstructing the government. To be sure, its right to dismiss the commissars, singly or *en bloc*, was now spelled out—but this was a serious step which the deputies could be expected to take only in the event of grave dereliction of duty. The final paragraph sought to turn the tables on the authors of the interpellation by presenting them as cowardly or deficient in civic sense.

The passage (by a narrow margin) of this resolution may be considered a major step towards the transformation of the Soviet regime into an oligarchic dictatorship. See below, p. 338.

21   *Revolutionary Movement in Germany.* Anti-war agitation by revolutionary sailors at Kiel in the spring of 1917 was put down firmly by the Imperial government: two men were shot for mutiny (5 September) and many others sentenced to long prison terms. The disaffection in the fleet anticipated the movement which erupted with such force in November 1918.

The so-called Spartakus group (its proper title was *Gruppe Internationale*; it published a series of 'Political Letters' signed 'Spartakus') was formed on 1 January 1916 by Karl Liebknecht, Rosa Luxemburg, Franz Mehring, Clara Zetkin and others. It stood on the extreme left of German socialist opinion; in 1917 it joined the USDP but preserved its autonomy, acting as a pressure group within the larger and more influential body.

Its leaders placed more emphasis on extra-parliamentary action and had a certain following among metallurgical workers in Leipzig and Berlin. Impressed by the course of events in Russia, they sought to assist the Bolsheviks by launching mass strikes and demonstrations—with some success, as the events of January 1918 were to show. Nevertheless their mass basis was too weak for them to think of taking power, and when revolution broke out in November 1918 the efforts of the Spartakus League (as it now called itself) to emulate the Bolsheviks' achievement soon led to its violent extinction.

22 *Lenin on Inevitability of Revolution in the West.* Lenin was non-committal on the question of the degree to which success of the 'proletarian revolution' in Russia depended on its emulation abroad—a matter that was to loom large in the ideological dispute between Stalin and Trotsky in the 1920s. While some other passages in his writings of this period (e.g. *PSS*, xxxvi. 11) give a more pessimistic view, this statement probably expresses accurately his frame of mind just after the October insurrection. It might be summarized as follows: (i) everything should be done to foment international revolution; (ii) unless this revolution took place soon the Bolsheviks were likely to be overthrown, but this fate was not inevitable; (iii) ultimately the western workers were bound to rise, and when they did so they would win; (iv) they would then have before them the heroic Bolshevik example, whether the Russian revolution had succeeded or not. Some other Bolsheviks took a more 'internationalist' stand, notably Trotsky and Lunacharsky (see below, p. 314).

SIXTH SESSION

1 *Departments of the CEC.* Although the statute provided for nomination by the Presidium (not the Organization Commission), and specified that departments should be headed by commissions rather than individuals, neither rule seems to have been observed. An effort was clearly made to preserve a balance between members of the two fractions when making these appointments. The list was evidently endorsed without debate.

The departments named here (fourteen excluding the Secretariat) include five that were not mentioned in the statute adopted on 2 November (see above, p. 66): Economic, Juridical, Military, Nationality Affairs, and Domestic (*Khozyaystvenny*). The department concerned with managing the printing press, not listed here, was presumably absorbed by the Editorial department. The department for struggle with counter-revolution, likewise absent from this list, may have preferred not to publicize its existence. At least four other departments are known to have existed: Credentials, Cossacks, Peasants, and Supply, of which the latter three came into being during December. Those with governmental functions lost influence to the corresponding PCs and were sooner or later abolished. V. M. Kleandrov (*Organizatsiya*, p. 77) states that this point was debated by the CEC in December, but as no record of this appears in the minutes the discussion was presumably at Presidium level. In July 1918 Sverdlov stated that the Juridical department ceased to exist shortly after it was established. The Economic department was absorbed into the SEC (see below, p. 351), and the Inter-city and Municipal departments into the PC of Internal Affairs. Those which survived longest were the Peasant and Cossack departments, to autumn 1918 and to 1921 respectively. Probably the most significant was the Agitation and Propaganda department, which dispatched many hundreds of emissaries to the provinces.

2 *Candidate Members of the CEC.* The practice of appointing candidate members was inherited from the pre-revolutionary underground, when clandestine organizations faced the constant risk of exposure and arrest. An additional motive for preserving it may have been a desire to maintain the interfractional balance when deputies were temporarily absent from Petrograd. Candidate (probationary) membership was retained in the Communist party but not in soviet organizations.

3 *Presidium.* This was conceived as a 'core organization' within the CEC, designed to direct and control its work. Such bodies were common in soviets and other popular deliberative organs during the Russian revolution.

After Kamenev's resignation from the CC on 4 November Lenin and other senior Bolsheviks took the view that he could no longer be relied upon to manage the CEC's affairs. His

inclusion on this list of nominees indicates that his party colleagues in the CEC thought otherwise. That same day the
Bolshevik CC charged Trotsky, Stalin, and A. A. Ioffe with
securing his removal. His replacement was Sverdlov (see below,
p. 311).

The Left SRs' attitude was one of characteristic vacillation.
Two days earlier they had announced that they would withdraw
from 'all responsible posts' (see above, p. 77). In the event they
seem to have adhered to this line until they joined the government (see below, p. 339).

4 *Elections to the Constituent Assembly.* The convocation of a
Constituent Assembly elected by universal, direct, equal and
secret suffrage was a major plank in the platform of all Russian
political parties in 1917. The arrangements (compilation of
electoral registers, receipt of candidates' nominations etc.) were
supervised by a 16-man All-Russian Electoral Commission,
which had subordinate commissions in each constituency.
Lists of candidates could be submitted by groups of one hundred
electors. In practice voters were presented with a choice between nominees of political parties rather than individual
representatives.

The election date, first fixed (14 June) for 17 September, was
on 9 August postponed until 12 November. Before their seizure
of power the Bolsheviks had denounced the Provisional Government for the delay. They now faced an embarrassing situation:
they would appear inconsistent if they now postponed the
elections again, still more so if they cancelled them completely.
The CPC had proclaimed itself a *provisional* 'workers' and
peasants' government' pending convocation of the Assembly;
and on 28 October it had formally committed itself to holding
the elections on the appointed day. It was common knowledge
that the Bolsheviks were fundamentally opposed to conventional
ideas of popular sovereignty: in a 'proletarian dictatorship',
according to their theory, power should lie wholly with the
soviets. Since the Bolsheviks and their allies could expect to
win only a minority of the votes, the election of the Constituent
Assembly could not fail to lead to a confrontation between
partisans and opponents of the new order.

The Bolsheviks' tactics were as yet undecided. V. A. Avanesov's remark suggests that he was not averse to delaying the elections provided the responsibility for this was seen to lie with the Left SRs. Lenin is also reliably reported (by Trotsky) to have uttered similar sentiments. However, it seemed more expedient to act with greater circumspection, and to begin by discrediting the Electoral Commission as 'counter-revolutionary'. This body at first ignored the Bolshevik regime as unconstitutional and protested at the measures it took, such as imposing martial law in Petrograd, which prevented it from exercising its normal functions. For later developments in Bolshevik policy, see below, pp. 340, 401.

The Left SRs' views were likewise flexible. According to *Znamya truda* for 7 November they declared against a postponement of the elections, or changes in the lists, before 12 November—but largely on pragmatic grounds. They did not share the moderate socialists' commitment to parliamentary institutions; nor did they agree with the Bolsheviks in condemning them as 'bourgeois'. During the next few weeks their position veered towards that of their allies: see above, p. 246.

5   *Inter-party Conference.* The refusal of the hard-line Bolsheviks to give way to the advocates of conciliation deprived the inter-party talks of their *raison d'être.* At a meeting during the night of 5–6 November the Mensheviks presented a resolution adopted by their CC stating that they would take no further part in the conference unless the Bolsheviks ceased all 'terroristic' measures. Zinoviev and Ryazanov defended their party's stand and blamed the moderate socialists for the breakdown. A Left SR motion to postpone the talks was accepted, whereupon the chairman, Krushinsky, announced that he and Malitsky would return to Moscow to consult other members of the railwaymen's union executive. Vikzhel's Petrograd bureau continued to liaise with the political organizations concerned, but no positive results were achieved.

Meanwhile equally fruitless negotiations were under way at Mogilev, under the auspices of the All-Army Committee, between moderate socialist leaders (7–10 November). The candidacy of Chernov for the post of prime minister in a reconstituted Provisional Government was unacceptable to his party colleagues who stood further to the right. In practice the

moderates now concentrated their attention on the Constituent
Assembly elections, which they expected to give them overwhelming popular endorsement: this, they believed, would
embarrass and discredit the Bolsheviks, forcing them to yield
peacefully to their rivals.

6 *Romanian Front.* The Romanian front, the most remote from
Petrograd in the European theatre of war, was the least affected
by indiscipline. The army committees backed the moderate
socialists, and the local Bolsheviks were seldom clearly differentiated from other partisans of 'revolutionary democracy'.
On 31 October an extraordinary congress of unit representatives on this front met at Roman (Romanů), Moldavia. The
Bolsheviks had only 25 mandates to 108 for the SRs and 40
for the Mensheviks. The congress expressed support for the
CSCR and called for a socialist coalition government. In the
Constituent Assembly elections the PSR won a clear majority
of the votes cast by soldiers on this front. It was not until late
November and early December that the Bolsheviks secured
strong support, initially in the VIIIth Army; even so their task
was complicated by the presence of Ukrainian and other
soldiers with their own national loyalties.

Although some unit committees adopted a pro-Bolshevik
stand from the start, this resolution cannot be regarded as
representative. The speaker's regimental affiliation and credentials are not given in the source. The 48th division, whose
spokesman also attended, was stationed on the same front; its
morale was officially described as excellent (Gen. I. P. Sytin to
GHQ, 8 November).

7 *'Petrograd Soviet of Peasant Deputies.'* This body, notwith-
standing its title, was actually a soldiers' organization. It had
been set up in April 1917 in the Petrograd garrison by left-wing
PSR activists. They and the Bolsheviks, who won a footing in it
from September, turned it into a focal point of opposition to the
moderate-controlled Executive Committee which claimed to
speak for peasants throughout the country. Its principal activity
was to propagandize soldiers returning to their villages: some
400–500 such individuals are thought to have been dispatched
up to October, and twice as many thereafter. The organization
was dissolved early in 1918.

8   *Tsentrobalt*. As the resolute tone of this message suggests, the Central Committee of the Baltic Fleet was a reservoir of extremist sentiment. It came under Bolshevik control on 19 September, when a plenary meeting acclaimed a resolution presented by P. E. Dybenko, its popular former chairman now released from a brief period under arrest, that it would no longer obey the Provisional Government. The Second Congress of Tsentrobalt, held in Helsingfors (Helsinki) from 25 September to 5 October, produced an executive of which some 70 per cent of the members were Bolsheviks or sympathizers. Its presidium, chosen on 16 October, was headed by Dybenko (chairman), V. P. Yevdokimov and A. V. Baranov (deputy chairmen). Tsentrobalt played an important part in aiding the Petrograd insurgents and then in bolstering Bolshevik power; it also supplied cadres for the restructured naval organization (of which Dybenko became the head) and sent detachments to fight Kaledin's forces in south-eastern Russia. The latter move was, however, resisted by an opposition group which on 14 November ousted Dybenko's successor as chairman, N. F. Izmaylov, and replaced him by I. I. Balakin (who was to be shot as a 'counter-revolutionary' in May 1918). The disaffection was contained only with some difficulty, and on 3 March 1918 Tsentrobalt was dissolved. The new Workers' and Peasants' Fleet had a centralized command structure.

9   *Battle for Moscow*. This vivid but impressionistic eyewitness account reflects the animus which the 29-year-old N. I. Bukharin, leader of the left wing in the Bolsheviks' Moscow party committee, felt against his more cautious comrades, Nogin and Rykov (see above, p. 303). Vacillation by the insurgent leaders was only one reason why the struggle for control of the city was so prolonged and costly; more important were the less feverish political atmosphere in Moscow by comparison with Petrograd and the different composition of its labour force and garrison.

While the non-Bolshevik press exaggerated the extent of the material damage wrought by the battle, it was certainly more serious than Bukharin here suggests. His figure of 5,000 casualties (suppressed in *Prot.*) is probably inflated, although no alternative estimate exists. Some 500 persons are thought to have been imprisoned by the victors after the engagement.

The Red guardsmen, as Bukharin correctly notes (in contrast to many later accounts), were less significant than rebellious soldiers: their numbers have been put at 3,000 and 15,000 respectively (Ovsyannikov, *Moskva*, p. 56), while their opponents are credited with 10,000 men. Most of the garrison remained neutral. The Red guards' organization was a good deal slacker than in Petrograd.

Although Bukharin speaks of the soviet as a united organization, there were actually two independent bodies representing the workers and soldiers; they merged shortly afterwards. The MRC, formed as late as 24 October, had no time to plan the operation on which it launched so hastily. Of its seven members three were non-Bolsheviks who hoped by their presence to minimize the rising's harmful effects; these men left the committee during the battle, so that their ambiguous stand was less of a handicap than one might suppose. It was partly under their influence that two armistice agreements were reached (26, 29 October) which were, however, soon broken, each side blaming the other for the breach. Efforts at mediation were undertaken by Vikzhel and then, more successfully, by the United Social-Democratic Internationalists. Bukharin fails to mention their role, but instead points to a peace-making effort by the Metropolitan, which most of his listeners, as atheists, could be expected to condemn out of hand.

10   See above, p. 275.

SEVENTH SESSION

1   *Sverdlov's Appointment as CEC Chairman.* Before the session opened the Bolshevik CC decided that Kamenev should be removed as chairman (see above, p. 307), but failed to nominate his successor. V. D. Bonch-Bruyevich relates (*Na boyevykh postakh*, pp. 161–74) that this matter was settled personally by Lenin. Sverdlov had previously demonstrated his talents as an organizer in the Bolshevik party secretariat. He combined an unusual capacity for hard work with affability and unquestioning loyalty to his leader. These qualities made him the ideal choice from Lenin's point of view, and Sverdlov remained CEC

chairman until his death in 1919. He was also *ex officio* chairman of the Bolshevik caucus in that body.

The query as to the existence of a quorum on this occasion suggests that some Bolsheviks who were opposed to the change may have absented themselves deliberately. The statute (see above, p. 64) prescribed that in a restricted session one-quarter of the members should be present for decisions to be valid; since the CEC at this moment had between 101 and 108 members, some 25 to 27 would have had to attend. *Prot.* (p. 40) lists 49 members 'and others'; but some of these may have arrived later in the proceedings.

The phrasing of the last sentence in this item of business shows that some CEC members were already viewing themselves as party representatives rather than as delegates of a particular enterprise, soviet etc.

2 *Civil Servants' Strike*. The CPC's efforts to assert its authority over the administration met with a campaign of passive resistance from civil servants who regarded its assumption of power as illegal. Many officials simply went home; those with strong political convictions passed formal resolutions of protest and voted on strike action. Such central direction as there was came from the CSCR, the democratic political parties, and the trade unions. The federated Union of Public Employees (*Soyuz soyuzov sluzhashchikh gosudarstvennykh uchrezhdeniy*) operated through branches in various ministries. One of the most active of these, in the Labour ministry, decided as early as 26 October to take strike action (by a vote of 130 to 14 with 5 abstentions). The campaign spread from the central government departments to the State Bank and other credit institutions, which declared a three-day strike on 14 November, the railways and postal services, municipal institutions, law courts, and some private businesses. The protesters were, however, hamstrung by their sense of responsibility to the public. Finance ministry employees voted to maintain essential services during their strike, which began on 1 November; officials concerned with national defence did not join the movement.

The Bolsheviks branded the strikes as 'sabotage', and despite its inaccuracy the term has found its way into the history-books. The officials were ordered to return to work; when this proved

fruitless, they were threatened with drastic penalties. On 7
November the MRC warned that 'if the wealthy classes do not
cease their sabotage and if this prevents transport of food . . .
they and their partisans will be deprived of the right to receive
food and any supplies they possess will be taken from them.'
Absentee officials were dismissed with loss of pension rights and
other privileges, and on 28–29 November twenty-seven union
activists were arrested. *Izvestiya* (27 November) characterized
the strikers as 'enemies of the people' and cried: 'To the scaffold
with these infamous saboteurs!' This pressure, coupled with
material hardship, caused many civil servants to return to their
jobs. The eventual dissolution of the Constituent Assembly, the
embodiment of hopes for a democratic legal order, made resistance seem less worthwhile.

3 *All-Russian Teachers' Union.* Founded in 1905, this was one
of the most important professional organizations in the country.
In so far as it engaged in politics, its sympathies were with the
parties of the centre and democratic left. Its summons to its
members to cease work in protest against the Bolshevik take-
over was widely followed: in Moscow, for example, a mere 34
out of 4,000 teachers remained at their posts and the strike did
not end until 11 March 1918; in Petrograd, where the response
was almost equally vigorous, the teachers returned to work on
6 January 1918, after the dissolution of the Constituent
Assembly. Despite its political role the union was not suppressed
at once. Instead the ministry fostered an alternative organization of 'internationalist teachers', led by V. M. Pozner, which
however won little support. Some union members were arrested
in August 1918 and their organization was finally dissolved in
December of that year.

4 *Foreign Reactions to the Bolshevik Revolution.* Trotsky's analysis
of the international situation was not unrealistic—if one allows
for the rhetoric to be expected in such circumstances. Germany's
attitude was indeed more ambiguous than Austria-Hungary's,
but the reasons must be sought in her leaders' greater confidence
in the military prospects. They were not as yet afraid of Bolshevism's appeal to German opinion, as Trotsky here suggests.
He was also incorrect in thinking that of the Entente powers
Great Britain was the most hostile: if anything the reverse was

the case. At the inter-Allied conference which opened in Paris on 17/30 November Balfour presented a suggestion that had originated with Sir George Buchanan, British ambassador in Petrograd, that Russia should be formally released from her treaty obligations to the Allies; but this encountered violent objections from the Italians and the French.

The informal contacts which Trotsky mentions had begun as early as 26 October, when Major-General Knox had interceded on behalf of the women soldiers captured after the surrender of the Winter Palace. Balfour later gave instructions that consular channels should be used in any dealings with the Soviet authorities necessary to safeguard the interests of Allied citizens. This did not of course imply recognition, which no Allied policy-maker was at this time willing to consider.

Trotsky's remarks on conditions in the United States seem to be based largely on his personal observation when in New York earlier in the year. The 'food riots' were of purely local significance and were touched off by the high prices charged by certain tradesmen; they were certainly less extensive and violent than the disturbances which took place during 1917 in many parts of Russia, where the food shortages were of course much more severe.

5 *Trotsky on the Superior 'Consciousness' of German Workers.* Trotsky shared with Mensheviks and many others on the left the view that the Russian proletariat was less developed politically, economically, and culturally than workers in western Europe, particularly in Germany; but from this proposition he deduced a revolutionary strategy that was closer to that of Lenin: namely, that the Bolshevik party, acting in the name of the workers and poorer peasants, should seize power in order to spark off a general European 'proletarian revolution', the results of which would amply compensate for the disadvantages of Russian backwardness.

Lenin's views (see above, p. 305) had a slightly different emphasis, a fact which many years later was to assume enormous significance. Stalin and his partisans branded 'Trotskyism' as a non-Leninist heresy, freely interpreting it to indicate lack of confidence in the Soviet people's ability to build socialism by its own efforts and a commitment to an 'adventuristic' foreign policy. Trotsky claimed that his views were in accord with Lenin's; and certainly towards the end of his life Lenin modified his earlier optimistic assessment of the Russian workers' cultural maturity, so approximating Trotsky's position in 1917. However, this circumstance was all but irrelevant in the power struggle of the later 1920s.

6   *Secret Treaties.* The various confidential agreements concluded by the belligerent powers concerning the settlement of territorial claims after the war were considered by left-wing socialists as examples of 'imperialistic' rapacity. The undertaking to publish them once 'soviet power' had been established was a powerful weapon in the maximalists' propaganda arsenal during 1917. 'The existence of these treaties, and even something of their nature, were matters of general knowledge, but they still represented a set of mysterious documents, capable of arousing strong passions' (Wade, *Russian Search*, p. 83). Publication began in *Pravda* and *Izvestiya* on 10 November. In a prefatory note Trotsky declared roundly that 'abolition of secret diplomacy is the first essential of an honourable, popular and really democratic foreign policy', such as the Soviet government was committed to pursue. The treaties were declared to be no longer binding upon the Russian people. Shortly afterwards the texts, more than one hundred in number, were published in book form.

The Bolsheviks of course gained access only to documents exchanged between Entente governments. Of these the most far-reaching concerned the Ottoman empire, which was to be forced to yield a large amount of territory to the Allies; Russia was promised the Straits and an adjoining region, as well as parts of Armenia and Kurdistan (agreements of 12 March 1915, 16 September 1916). Of more immediate significance was the accord of 1/14 February 1917 whereby France and Russia gave each other a free hand in determining their eastern and western borders respectively. Other documents related to the aspirations of Italy, Serbia, and Romania.

The immediate impact of publication was probably less sensational than Trotsky and other Bolshevik leaders hoped; but it was certainly a major embarrassment to the Entente governments. It contributed to the pressure in several countries for a policy of 'open covenants openly arrived at', a principle taken most seriously by the United States.

When the German Social Democrats came to power in November 1918 they failed to act in this matter as the Bolsheviks wished. Karl Kautsky was entrusted by the new government with the far more limited task of collecting and editing official German papers relating to the immediate antecedents of the war. This four-volume work appeared in 1919; its stated aim was to provide 'a scholarly collection of sources for impartial judgments on events by politicians and historians' —i.e. any revolutionizing intent was expressly disavowed.

7 *The Soviet Government and GHQ; Peace Note of 8 November.* With the defeat of the task force headed by Kerensky and Krasnov (see above, p. 285) the main potential threat to Bolshevik rule came from General Headquarters (*Stavka*) at Mogilev. This was now headed by Lieutenant-General N. N. Dukhonin, a 41-year-old officer who assumed the post of temporary acting Supreme Commander-in-Chief on 1 November, after learning of Kerensky's flight. Previously (from September 1917) Dukhonin had served as chief of staff at GHQ. He at once forbade all troop movements in the direction of Petrograd and called for a cessation of bloodshed pending formation of a democratic government enjoying broad public support. At first it seemed as if such a government might be formed at Mogilev, under the auspices of the army's most senior representative organ (see above, p. 308), but this idea found little favour among the troops, whose opinions were veering rapidly to the left under the impact of the 'peace decree' adopted at the Second Congress of Soviets.

By 8 November the Bolsheviks, having consolidated their hold over the principal cities and many army units (notably on the Northern and Western fronts), felt strong enough to challenge GHQ. At 4 a.m. Lenin, Trotsky, and Krylenko despatched by radio-telegraph an order to 'the citizen Supreme Commander-in-Chief' instructing him 'to approach immediately the authorities of the hostile armies with a proposal for immediate cessation of military action so that peace negotiations may begin'. He was to keep the CPC continuously informed of the progress of the negotiations and to sign an armistice only with the CPC's prior consent.

Trotsky's note, dispatched later that day, to Allied ambassadors in Petrograd informed them of the establishment of the Soviet government and drew their attention to the peace resolution adopted at the Congress, 'which I request you to regard as a formal proposal for an armistice on all fronts and for the immediate opening of peace negotiations'. He can have had few illusions that the Allies would respond favourably to this proposal for a *general* peace, particularly since the Bolsheviks had embarked on a course of action that seemed bound to lead to a *separate* peace on the Eastern fronts. Their strategy was based on the assumption that the very news of these negotiations would arouse the western European peoples and force their governments to join the talks.

Nor did the CPC seriously expect Dukhonin, who had not recognized its authority, to obey these instructions; but it was tactically expedient that the onus for the breach should fall upon GHQ and that it should occur over an issue which would mobilize the war-weary soldiers against their 'counter-revolutionary' officers. The terms of the order were such that, had Dukhonin complied with it, the CPC would still have been able to claim the credit for the armistice. For later moves, see below, pp. 323, 331.

8   *Decree on Workers' Control.* At the Second Congress of Soviets no decree comparable to those on peace and land was adopted in regard to workers' control, the third major plank in the Bolshevik programme. One reason for this was the latent tension between the Anarcho-syndicalists in the factory-committee movement, who understood socialism to mean thoroughgoing industrial democracy, and the Marxists, who were partisans of centralized state control and planning. Among the Marxists there were differences between Bolsheviks and Mensheviks, the latter favouring a mixed economy under state regulation but with some rights reserved to private employers. Similar views were held by right-wing Bolsheviks such as Ryazanov and Lozovsky (see above, p. 292), who had experience in the trade-union movement.

Lenin's approach was pre-eminently tactical: he was anxious

to disrupt the economic power of the employers, even at the risk of temporarily encouraging anarchistic excesses, by facilitating measures of control from below—evidently calculating that this experience would convince workers of the need for centralized direction. To reconcile the conflicting viewpoints a conference was held on 5 November under the chairmanship of Shlyapnikov. It was decided to take Lenin's draft as the basis of the decree, but to amend it in the spirit of the proposals put forward by ARCFC (see above, p. 293). The latter wanted an effective system of workers' control supervised by a national council (the All-Russian Council of Workers' Control, in which ARCFC would be prominently represented) and by subordinate control commissions; on the council one-third of the seats were to be reserved for representatives of employers, engineers, technicians, and foremen. Lenin's draft provided for more initiative from below and for a more broadly-based council in which ARCFC would have a mere five out of some 40 to 50 representatives. He was clearly anxious to prevent ARCFC from undermining the authority he sought to invest in the Supreme Economic Council (SEC: see below, p. 351).

Shlyapnikov was over-optimistic in telling the CEC that the decree would be published that same day (8 November). The commission set up here discussed the matter further, and it came before the CEC again on 14 November. As finally adopted, the decree appears to have made no concession to the views of Kamkov and G. Zaks, the Left SR members of the commission.

9 *The CPC and the State Bank.* Among the civil servants who resisted as illegal orders from the new government (see above, n. 2) those employed in the Finance ministry and State Bank held a key position. Their two unions were in contact with the CSCR, and defied an order (30 October) to resume normal working. V. R. Menzhinsky, whom Lenin charged with the task of securing control of the banks, requested an advance of ten million roubles for the CPC, but the manager of the State Bank, I. P. Shipov, refused to comply unless a special order were presented from the Treasury. The Bolsheviks then turned to the junior employees, whom they sought to agitate against their superiors; but this manœuvre was jeopardized by a rash

step on Menzhinsky's part. On 6 November he tried to obtain the money by force, relying on a detachment of armed men led by Lieutenant-Colonel Muravyev (see above, p. 287). The clerks, fearing that the premises would be looted, remonstrated, and the troops were withdrawn.

This CEC resolution sought to overcome the State Bank employees' resistance by appealing to their sympathies for the Constituent Assembly, for which elections were about to be held; in view of the Bolsheviks' own ambiguous attitude on this matter the argument was none too plausible. The charge that the bank employees were secretly subsidizing anti-Bolsheviks may have had some substance, but concrete evidence of this has yet to be produced. The frequently repeated claim that forty (or forty-two) million roubles were handed over (e.g. in *Hist. Civil War*, ii. 310) is exaggerated; although the clandestine Provisional Government did make appropriations totalling this amount, it does not seem to have actually disposed of such sums.

Menzhinsky's next move was to approach certain sympathetic officials, who were prepared to compromise so long as a minimum of formalities were observed in expenditure of the funds. On 13 November V. V. Obolensky was appointed commissar of the State Bank. The employees voted overwhelmingly to withdraw their labour in protest, but three days later the keys to the Treasury vaults were handed over. On 17 November the CPC received its first advance of five million roubles, and soon a skeleton banking service was in operation. For later developments, see below, p. 376.

10   *Abolition of Class Privileges.* The Left SRs yielded nothing to the Bolsheviks in egalitarian zeal, and it was they who took the initiative in raising this symbolic issue. Their draft decree was vaguely worded and was amended in the CPC; the revised text was presented to the CEC the next day by the Bolshevik jurist P. I. Stuchka and became law at once (the decree, dated 11 November, was published on the twelfth). This Bolshevik version characteristically shifted the emphasis from social *mores* to political struggle and extended the scope of the measure to include suppression of class *organizations*. The term 'citizen of the Russian republic', suggested by the Left SRs and incorporated

in the decree, was modelled on the French revolutionary precedent; it never struck root in Soviet Russia, where the appellation 'comrade', more expressive of proletarian class solidarity, found greater favour.

Perhaps the most important aspect of this matter was procedural. The Left SRs, anxious to affirm the sovereignty of the CEC against the CPC's pretensions, sought to dictate to the latter body the terms of the decree; this was no doubt one reason why the CPC modified the text.

11 *CEC of First Convocation.* This body, elected at the First Congress of Soviets on 17 June, was deemed by the Bolsheviks and their allies to have forfeited its authority by virtue of the decisions of the Second Congress in October. The moderate socialists claimed that the latter gathering was irregular and that the old CEC retained its legal title, as well as the right to dispose of the funds it had accumulated. It continued to meet clandestinely from 5 November to 11 January 1918. The minutes of ten of these meetings have been preserved and published (in 1925). It issued several appeals for public support, put out two small-circulation newspapers (*Za svobodu, Revolyutsionny nabat*), and tried to call a conference of provincial soviets that were out of sympathy with the Bolsheviks. It was also actively associated with the CSCR and its successor, the Union for the Defence of the Constituent Assembly. The results of its labours were slight, mainly because opinion in the soviets was flowing towards support for the Bolshevik regime and the moderates were unwilling to resort to more forceful methods of resistance lest thereby they play into the hands of 'reaction'.

EIGHTH SESSION

1 *Food Supply Committees.* During 1917 these elected organs acquired a key role in decisions on procurements and distribution of foodstuffs. Formally they came under the authority of local institutions of self-government as well as the central ministry; in practice many of their members took their cue from the soviets or other *ad hoc* bodies that had elected them. The resulting administrative chaos multiplied the adverse effects of the breakdown of market relationships and the com-

munications system under the strain of war. Efforts to mono-
polize trade in grain and to fix prices for staple items led to
hoarding and black marketeering. Official delivery targets were
often not met, so that the ration could not be honoured. The
situation was particularly acute in the 'consuming' provinces of
northern and central Russia, and the problems of Kostroma
(north-east of Moscow) were typical. Danilov, like many provincial activists, took a fairly pragmatic approach. The last
point in his address suggests that he was ill informed as to the
political situation in Petrograd.

2 *Bread Ration in Petrograd.* On 21 October the bread ration in
the capital had been lowered from $\frac{3}{4}$ to $\frac{1}{2}$ funt (0·22 lb.) per
person; manual labourers received a supplementary $\frac{1}{4}$ funt.
Yakubov was presumably envisaging that the ration might have
to be halved; this level was indeed reached early in the New
Year.

3 *Bolshevik Supply Policy.* This was a middle-of-the-road policy.
Opinions were divided among leading Bolsheviks on this matter.
On the right wing stood I. A. Teodorovich, who five days
earlier had resigned his post as PC of Supply. He favoured
conciliation of his former colleagues in the Moscow supply
organization, who were mostly socialists nominated by soviets
or other 'democratic' organizations. The radicals, among them
A. G. Shlikhter, who in December succeeded to the post of
commissar, (and notably Lenin, once he took up the problem),
favoured wholesale requisitioning and draconian punishments
for offenders. Neither method was a panacea. The extremist
course eventually adopted antagonized the peasants but at least
enabled the regime to survive. The allegations of 'sabotage' by
supply officials made in this discussion were greatly exaggerated.

4 *State Educational Commission.* This was a consultative body
designed to give general guidance on educational policy; it
succeeded the State Educational *Committee*, which was dissolved
on 20 November—despite the favourable view taken of it by
Lunacharsky (see above, p. 100). The commission's make-up
was weighted to ensure political conformity: in addition to a
chairman, secretary, and 16 elected representatives (six from
the central soviet organs and ten from various other public
bodies) there were to be 15 departmental chiefs nominated by

the CPC. Lunacharsky initially envisaged a highly decentralized form of administration, but by May 1919 his ministry's staff was ten times as great as it had been in October 1917; local educational councils, intended to be elective, were from April 1918 onwards composed of persons appointed by the local soviet authorities.

5 *Second (Extraordinary) Congress of Peasant Deputies.* The decision to hold this gathering in Petrograd, rather than in Mogilev where the moderate socialists were discussing formation of a rival government under Chernov, was a victory for the maximalists. According to one source the 330 delegates included 195 Left SRs, 37 Bolsheviks, and 15 other ultra-radicals. Many of them were soldiers fresh from the trenches. Constructive debate was rendered all but impossible. Much time was wasted over procedural issues, and on no less than three occasions the moderates walked out in protest. Nevertheless the congress, held from 10 to 25 November, voted to merge the central soviet organs representing the peasants with those that spoke for the workers and soldiers—an event of considerable significance (see below, p. 328).

6 *Zemsky Sobor.* This archaic title (= 'Assembly of All the Land') was popularly given to a gathering of municipal Duma and zemstvo representatives held on 9–10 November. The invitation was issued by the mayor of Petrograd, Shreyder (PSR), who was active on the CSCR and hoped that the conference might create a legal basis for a reconstituted Provisional Government. The response to his appeal was, however, disappointing, partly because of communications difficulties and partly because local politicians were preoccupied with the Constituent Assembly elections; moreover the centre and moderate left elements were confused and intimidated by the Bolsheviks' victory. A mere 30 delegates arrived from Moscow and the provinces, who were joined by 15 representatives from Petrograd. They agreed to call the gathering a conference (*soveshchanie*); I. G. Tsereteli spoke strongly on behalf of the Constituent Assembly, but the delegates dispersed with no real achievements to their credit.

7 *Reform of the Law Courts.* Despite Stuchka's emphasis on the urgency of the measure, no decision was taken at this session of

the CEC. The matter was raised again the following day and referred to a commision (see above, pp. 122, 148); but apparently this commission did not meet. This allowed the CPC to handle the matter alone. As the text of the draft as printed in *Prot.*, pp. 74–6, is identical with the published version, it may be assumed that Stuchka had everything his own way. Shortly afterwards he admitted that his ideas, which reflected Lenin's, 'aroused many protests even among our closest colleagues' ('Prol. revol.', 3).

The decree was strong medicine indeed. It not only abolished all existing legal institutions, including the bar of advocates, but introduced a new concept of legality based on political criteria which gave ample scope for infringements of basic human rights by the new authorities. Article 5 laid down that local courts were to be guided in their judgments by existing laws 'only to the extent that these have not been repealed by the revolution and do not contradict [their] revolutionary consciousness and sense of revolutionary legality'. All laws were declared automatically repealed if they conflicted with the new government's decrees or the 'minimum programme' of the RSDRP or PSR. Revolutionary tribunals were set up to deal with security cases as well as certain economic offences.

NINTH SESSION

1   *The CPC and General Headquarters.* Dukhonin was placed in a dilemma by the CPC's instructions of 8 November (see above, p. 316) to commence negotiations for an immediate armistice. If he obeyed them he would, as he saw it, pave the way for a separate peace, so fatally compromising his authority in the eyes of all who wanted to keep Russia in the war, not least the Allied governments. If he disobeyed them, he would incur the enmity of the soldiers and of the new régime. He therefore delayed his response in the hope that the Entente powers might come to his rescue, for he realized that they would not respond to Trotsky's invitation to join in the peace talks.

The CPC's message had been sent *en clair*—evidently so that it should become known to the troops—and bore neither an official number nor a date. This gave Dukhonin a pretext for delay. At 7.50 p.m. on 8 November he sent a message by radio and direct-wire apparatus to General A. A. Manikovsky, former

deputy War minister under the Provisional Government, who
had stayed on after the insurrection as the ministry's senior
administrative officer, asking him to retransmit the instructions
in code. Manikovsky replied (no doubt truthfully) that he had
no knowledge of the order, whereupon Dukhonin, after waiting
until 1 a.m. for some further communication from Petrograd,
retired to bed. One hour later Smolny communicated directly
with GHQ by direct-wire apparatus, Stalin now taking
Trotsky's place. The chief of staff, General M. K. Diterikhs,
explained what had been done in response to the CPC's
instructions. Krylenko asked why GHQ had not verified the
message with him rather than Manikovsky. Diterikhs, unwilling
to state categorically that GHQ did not recognize the Soviet
government's authority, made no reply. Dukhonin was then
awakened. He said he was now satisfied as to the veracity of the
instructions but could not comply with them until the following
points were clarified: (a) had the CPC heard from the Allied
governments? (b) what did the CPC propose to do about the
Romanian army, which was an integral part of the forces on the
Russian front? (c) did the CPC intend to enter into separate
peace talks with Germany alone or with the Central Powers?

By forcing the Bolsheviks to define their peace policy more
precisely, Dukhonin evidently hoped to show that it was out of
step with the aspirations of most soldiers, who were by no
means reconciled to a separate 'annexationist' peace. But his
interlocutors refused to be drawn: their instructions, they held,
were clear enough and any 'technical details' would be settled
as they arose. Once again the Supreme Commander-in-Chief
was ordered, this time in the form of an ultimatum, to comply
with the order. Dukhonin replied:

> I can only gather that you cannot enter into direct talks with
> [all] the powers. This is even less possible for me on your
> behalf. Only a central government backed by the army and
> the country can have enough weight and significance [in the
> eyes of our] enemies for these talks to have enough authority
> [and] attain results. I also consider that a speedy general
> peace is in Russia's interests.

He thus refused to contemplate negotiations for a separate (as
distinct from a general) peace and to acknowledge the CPC's

authority to conduct such talks. A skilled politician would have kept these two issues separate; as it was, Dukhonin had been manœuvred into defying the Soviet government, and his deposition followed at once:

In the name of the government of the Russian Republic, at the behest of the CPC, we dismiss you from your post for disobedience to the government's instructions and for conduct leading to untold misery for the toiling masses and especially the armies of all countries.

Dukhonin was ordered to remain at his post until the arrival of his successor. This was to be Krylenko, a Bolshevik activist of long standing (and joint PC of War), whose military rank was no higher than ensign (*praporshchik*). This revolutionary gesture was designed to impress ordinary soldiers and to arouse their passions. Lenin and Krylenko drove the point home in a message sent later that day (9 November) to all army committees, soldiers, and sailors, which ended:

Soldiers! The cause of peace is in your hands. Do not allow counter-revolutionary generals to sabotage the great cause of peace. Keep them under guard to prevent lynching unworthy of a revolutionary army and evasion of the justice that awaits them. Maintain strict revolutionary and military order. Regiments in the front line should immediately elect plenipotentiaries to enter formal negotiations on an armistice with the enemy. The CPC gives you the right to do so. Keep us informed by every means of each step in the negotiations. Only the CPC has the right to sign a final armistice agreement. Soldiers! The cause of peace is in your hands. Vigilance, self-restraint, energy—and the cause of peace will conquer!

The appeal, together with the record of the conversation with GHQ, was published in Petrograd newspapers on 10 November and widely circulated. Many soldiers and others who were generally sympathetic to the new regime doubted the wisdom of fraternization at unit level, as was evident in this debate. Lenin had to assume a defensive stance. He admitted that the 'struggle for peace' would be long and arduous, but still refrained from making clear the principal difference between himself and most of his listeners: his willingness to make far-reaching sacrifices of the national interest, as conventionally seen, for the sake of preserving the revolutionary dictatorship. Fraternization resulted in local armistice agreements from 15 November. Dukhonin had wired all front commanders (9 November) that he would neither yield nor resign; however, his resistance lasted only a week: see below, p. 331.

2 *Criticism and Self-criticism.* The limits of permissible criticism of the CPC's actions soon came to be defined more narrowly than Lenin here suggests. In practice decisions by major policymakers had to be accepted without question; only the mode of their implementation might be a legitimate matter for discussion. Criticism of those who executed their policy helped the leaders to maintain their control, as did the 'self-criticism' required of those alleged to have deviated from the correct 'line'. All criticism was supposed to strengthen the state and society. This became a key component of Communist political culture.

3 *Lenin on Capital Punishment Without Trial.* This appears to be the first instance after the Bolshevik seizure of power when Lenin publicly advocated that opponents of the regime should be put to death without judicial process. The category of such potential victims was soon to be extended to members of 'bourgeois' parties (see below, p. 356), speculators, and other so-called 'class enemies', and a political security organ was established to co-ordinate these measures.

4 *CEC's Representation Abroad.* 'Orlovsky' was a pseudonym of V. V. Vorovsky, who had stayed on in Stockholm after his colleagues in the Foreign Bureau had left for Petrograd (see above, p. 291). Some weeks elapsed before he could commence his work as official representative of the Soviet government to the Scandinavian countries (whose governments did not, however, recognize Soviet Russia).

The soldiers' newspaper to which Zinoviev refers was *Die Fackel*, edited in Petrograd by Karl Radek's 'section for international propaganda'. On 19 December responsibility for this activity was transferred from the PC of Foreign Affairs to the

CEC, presumably to avoid diplomatic embarrassment; the paper was then renamed *Der Völkerfriede*. It was distributed freely among German and Austro-Hungarian prisoners of war; some copies also reached troops across the front line.

P. B. Axelrod, the veteran Menshevik leader, and five other moderate socialist politicians had been delegated by the CEC of first convocation to prepare a conference of anti-war socialists. This was never held, since the other Entente governments refused to issue passports to their citizens who wished to attend, but at a preliminary meeting organized by the International Socialist Committee, known as the Third Zimmerwald Conference (5–12 September), Axelrod participated in a stormy exchange with Radek and Vorovsky, who set forth Lenin's views on ending the war by revolutionary violence.

TENTH SESSION

1   *Workers' Control.* Milyutin did not reveal to the CEC many details of the discussions held in the commission set up by the CEC on 8 November (see above, p. 106). The objections to which he first referred were evidently raised by Lozovsky, Ryazanov or some other partisan of state planning of the economy. His defence, essentially that the Bolsheviks had been overtaken by events, suggests that he did not understand the approach taken by Lenin, who was primarily concerned with political tactics. Milyutin failed to deal with the objection that concessions to the Anarcho-syndicalists in the factory-committee movement were bound to add to the economic chaos, at least temporarily. Nor was he quite accurate in saying that there was no disagreement over the functions of workers' control, for the question was whether these bodies were to play a destructive or constructive role in economic affairs—as Lozovsky made clear later in the debate.

The provision in the decree (clause 9) giving employers three days in which to complain about decisions by workers' control organs was a far from adequate safeguard against anarchistic abuses. The scheme could have worked only if a proper legal framework had been devised, with an impartial tribunal as final instance: but this was excluded by the Bolsheviks' class-oriented approach to law. Even on administrative grounds the decree is to be faulted for setting up an unnecessarily complicated and expensive four-tier structure of agencies at the enterprise, city-district, municipal, and national levels, which could not be implemented in practice.

The 'all-Russian centre' to which Milyutin refers is the All-Russian Council of Workers' Control. This consisted of five representatives of the CEC, the central peasant executive, ARCCTU, the bureau of ARCFC, and the union of engineers and technicians; two from the workers' co-operatives, the union of agronomists, and the Petrograd trade-union council; and one or two from each major trade union (clause 4). It was too large to have any real decision-making power and held only two sessions before it was absorbed into the Supreme Economic Council (SEC).

Clause 10 specified the offences as: concealing materials, goods or orders; incorrect maintenance of accounts; and 'similar abuses'. These were directed against managerial personnel, and no provision was made to cover offences by the controllers themselves.

Instructions along the lines specified in clause 12 were issued on 13 December.

Lozovsky's statement that workers' control did not represent 'the beginning of socialism' would have been disputed by most of his party colleagues.

ELEVENTH SESSION

1 *Merger of Central Soviet Executives.* The Second Congress of Soviets, from which the Bolshevik 'workers' and peasants' government' derived its legitimacy, could plausibly claim to represent the radicalized workers and soldiers, but not peasants: only 19 (4·7 per cent) of its deputies had been from peasant soviets (although some joint soviets had peasant sections). Rural soviets were far fewer in number and in so far as their leaders concerned themselves with national politics they favoured a compromise between extremists and moderates. Bolshevik influence was slight compared with that wielded by Socialist-Revolutionaries of the centre and left.

The Bolsheviks were naturally eager to secure the assent to their programme of the central peasant organization. In this

they were aided by the Left SRs, who dominated the Second
Extraordinary Congress of Peasant Deputies (see above, p. 322).
On 12 November, in a somewhat disorderly debate on 'the
question of power', strong pressure made itself felt, especially
among the soldiers present, for unity among all revolutionary
groups and broadening of the Soviet government. The assembly
endorsed a Left SR resolution that the two central soviet
executives should merge on a parity basis; the government
should comprise representatives of all the socialist parties 'from
the Popular Socialists to the Bolsheviks', but be bound by the
programme endorsed at the Second Congress of Soviets. This
decision in effect paved the way for a coalition between Left
SRs and Bolsheviks. Talks were thereupon held in private
between leaders of these parties (and the Menshevik Internationalists). No record has survived of these conversations,
which on 14 November eventuated in a compromise along the
lines foreshadowed in the inter-party conference held earlier
under the auspices of Vikzhel. The government was to be 'organized' (i.e. reconstituted) and to be accountable to a greatly
expanded CEC. In the latter body the existing 108 worker and
soldier members were to be joined by the same number of
'peasant' representatives (most of whom would in practice be
soldiers), nearly as many members of certain armed forces'
organizations, and about half as many trade-unionists. This
scheme ensured that the peasant (and trade-union) delegates
would be swamped by men in uniform of proven militancy.
Thus the parity so loudly proclaimed at this ceremonial session
was more apparent than real: it conferred a somewhat spurious
'democratic' legitimacy upon a régime whose strength was still
confined to the major urban centres and to the front. At best it
symbolized the new rulers' aspirations to govern in the interests
of the workers and peasants.

Both parties sought to extract the maximum propaganda
advantage from the merger. It was hailed with great enthusiasm
by the delegates, whose morale was raised by news of the imminent armistice. They were in no mood to reflect that the
projected expansion of the CEC would diminish its significance
as a policy-making body. In the event no measures were taken
to ensure that the new entrants were truly representative of
their 'constituencies': the military and naval organizations

subsequently presented a list of 58 of their delegates, as did Vikzhel for its ten (*Prot.*, pp. 105–7, 25 November; cf. *ZT*, 19 November, for a breakdown by units), but whether the full complement was ever attained remains uncertain. Another point lost sight of in the euphoria was that the agreement of 14 November was linked to concessions on policy matters by the Bolsheviks that were never honoured—notably in the matter of press freedom. In sum, the occasion was indeed a triumph—but for the actual masters of the new Russia rather than for its plain citizens.

For the subsequent negotiations on formation of a coalition CPC, see below, p. 339.

2 *Left SR 'Revolutionary Messianism'*. In this emotional address Mariya Spiridonova, the eloquent tribune of the emergent Left SR party, expresses clearly the messianic fervour that distinguished its partisans from most of the Bolsheviks. They held that revolutionary Russia had an overwhelming moral obligation to extend its influence abroad by forceful means. Many Bolsheviks, of course, shared such sentiments, but Lenin was concerned above all with preserving and consolidating the regime's power within the country (see above, p. 305) and regarded the extension of that power to other countries as something to be undertaken only as expediency dictated, after cool calculation of all pertinent factors. The Left SRs' impetuosity sprang from their less doctrinaire (and more moralistic) approach to politics; this was in turn a legacy of the Russian Populist tradition. The religious imagery employed by Spiridonova at the end of her speech should be noted. This ideological difference also helps to explain Left SR objections to Bolshevik agrarian policy and readiness to resort to terroristic methods of rule.

3 *Trotsky's Premature Announcement of Armistice*. Trotsky here allowed himself to be carried away by rhetoric (*Pravda*, 16 Nov., reported that his speech 'breathed fire and poison'). The Germans had so far agreed only to hold negotiations for an armistice, and had no intention of making it general. The relationship between the Bolsheviks and the Central Powers was far less favourable to the former than Trotsky here suggests, as the Brest-Litovsk conference would soon reveal. His ex-

pectation of an immediate popular outburst in the Entente
countries was exaggerated, to say the least. The last paragraph
of his speech may have been excised from *Prot.* because of its
admission of the possibility of 'honourable defeat', which seemed
less likely, or less creditable, some months later.

4   *Trotsky's Second Note to Allies on Armistice.* Although the
Bolshevik leaders realized that the German government and
high command were interested only in a separate peace, they
hoped that the Allied governments could be prevailed upon to
join in the negotiations as the first step towards a *general* cessation of hostilities. Following up his initial message (see above,
p. 317), and the establishment of contact with the German high
command (see n. 5), he and Lenin on 14–15 November
addressed a radio-telegraph message and notes to these governments inviting them to take part. In this message they gave the
impression that the Germans had already agreed to enter *peace*,
as distinct from armistice, talks, which was not yet the case. This
was evidently done to increase pressure upon the addressees,
who, however, ignored the approach. Since only five days were
to elapse before talks began, participation would in any case
have been impossible, even if the political will had existed. The
Allied position, as defined by the inter-Allied conference which
opened in Paris on 17–30 November, was that war aims could
be revised only once 'a stable government acceptable to the
Russian people' had been installed—i.e. once the Bolsheviks
had been removed from office. On 16 November Trotsky
repeated the invitation, but again received no reply.

5   *The CPC and General Headquarters.* The last round in the
struggle for control of GHQ was a test of wills between General
Dukhonin and N. V. Krylenko, whom the CPC had nominated
as his successor (see above, pp. 316, 323), with the belligerent
powers endeavouring to influence the outcome.

    On 10 November the chiefs of the six Entente military
missions sent Dukhonin a joint letter protesting 'in the most
energetic manner against violation of the treaty signed . . . on 5
September 1914' which prohibited a separate termination of
hostilities by any of the Allies. The signatories knew that the
initiative in seeking an armistice lay not with Dukhonin but
with the CPC; but they hoped that their move would strengthen

the former's hand. Dukhonin circulated the text, but its impact on the war-weary troops was minimal, and possibly even counter-productive. Trotsky, in a message for general distribution (11 November), characterized it as 'a flagrant interference in the domestic affairs of our country with the object of bringing about civil war'. The Allied chiefs of mission followed up their demarche with another letter urging Dukhonin to appeal for civil peace and stricter discipline.

On the same day Krylenko left Petrograd with a small escort, bound for Mogilev. He had a dual task: to establish contact with the Germans and to bring GHQ under Bolshevik control. He proceeded first to Pskov and then to Dvinsk (12 November), where he arrested the commander of the Vth Army, General V. G. Boldyrev, for failing to comply with his instructions regarding the armistice; it was from here that emissaries were sent across the front line (13 November) bearing the Soviet request for an armistice: the request was accepted within 24 hours, and it was agreed that talks should begin at Brest-Litovsk on 19 November. Addressing a meeting of Vth Army soldiers, Krylenko declared that all 'counter-revolutionary' officers must be removed and threatened that 'the masses will obtain peace over their dead bodies'. The Germans' assent to armistice talks greatly strengthened his position and emboldened soldiers' committees all along the front to depose their commanders or at least to bring their activities under close control, notably by censoring military communications. Among those dismissed were Generals A. V. Cheremisov and P. S. Baluyev, Commanders-in-Chief of the Northern and Western fronts respectively; Baluyev's self-appointed successor, General B. S. Malyavin, was in turn arrested. Some senior field officers, such as General N. A. Danilov, commander of the IInd Army, chose to collaborate with the insurgents.

Dukhonin ordered troops of the Finland division to halt Krylenko's movement toward Mogilev and summoned cossack reinforcements from the South-western front, but even these troops were no longer wholly reliable. On 14 November Krylenko, now at Polotsk (HQ of IIIrd Army), formed a detachment of men from 35th corps to move on GHQ; other units were readied at Minsk and Petrograd. In Mogilev itself the soldiers' leaders and the All-Army committee hoped to avoid bloodshed, and at first did not hinder preparations by Dukhonin's staff for evacuation to Kiev, where they hoped for protection from units loyal to the Ukrainian Rada. On 18 November Dukhonin learned of a report that the Allies would after all permit Russia to conclude a separate peace, which led him to delay his departure, since in his view this would remove the main obstacle to agreement between the army and the Bolsheviks. However, the report was false, and by the next day opinion in the garrison had hardened. An MRC was formed which subordinated itself to Krylenko, dissolved the All-Army committee, and placed Dukhonin under house arrest. On 20 November Krylenko and his men entered Mogilev and took over GHQ, meeting no resistance. Dukhonin lost his life that same afternoon under particularly odious circumstances.

Accounts of his death at the hands of a mob of enraged soldiers differ in some particulars; but it is well attested that Krylenko tried to save the general's life. His intention was evidently to remove him to Petrograd to stand trial, and he is even said to have told the crowd that he would give his own life to spare that of his captive. However, he then left the scene, allowing the soldiers to drag Dukhonin from his railway-coach and to kill him (according to Krylenko's account, he was present but was roughly pushed aside). In either case the new Supreme Commander-in-Chief bears a heavy moral responsibility for the death of his predecessor. His inflammatory statements—among them his speech at this session of the CEC—had led many soldiers to see Dukhonin and other generals as 'enemies of the people' who richly deserved death at that same people's hands. In defence of Krylenko it may be noted that (a) he at once issued a statement deploring this excess as 'a stain on the banner of the revolution' and (b) the soldiers were angered by news of the escape, from their nearby place of confinement, of several generals arrested in connection with the 'Kornilov affair', whose release had evidently been sanctioned by Dukhonin. However, these men had not been found guilty of any crime, and had they not escaped might well have shared Dukhonin's fate.

Dukhonin was the first notable casualty in the incipient Russian civil war. His murder did much to harden attitudes on the White side.

6 *Soviet Aid to Finnish 'Reds'.* Leading Bolsheviks were at this
time outspoken about their readiness to intervene on behalf of
the Finnish 'Reds', a factor of crucial significance in the outbreak of civil war in that country.

Some 30,000 to 40,000 soldiers and sailors were stationed in
Finland at the end of 1917. These troops had become increasingly radical, and the Bolsheviks hoped to use them to help the
Finnish Social Democrats to seize power. This party had likewise moved far to the left, but only a few extremists thought
that the Finnish revolution should follow the Bolshevik model:
most activists expected to achieve power by parliamentary
means. National independence was one of their foremost goals
and their pro-Bolshevik sympathies may be attributed in part
to their belief that a Soviet regime would favour this aspiration.
Their policy was sufficiently radical to frighten many Finns
that a 'Red dictatorship' was imminent, but it lacked the
determination shown by the Russian Bolsheviks.

On 26 October Finnish Social Democrats and trade-
unionists set up a 27-man Central Revolutionary Council, which
on 30 October decided (by 18 votes to 8) not to seize power but
instead to call a general strike in order to force the 'bourgeois'
Senate to carry through a programme of reforms. The Social
Democrats in the Diet agreed that the legislature should
assume supreme authority, and on 2 November the reforms
were promulgated. This took the wind out of the sails of the
Central Revolutionary Council. At an extraordinary party
congress (12–14 November) Stalin offered 'fraternal aid' and
urged greater boldness, but the extremists found themselves in
a minority. Power passed to a broad coalition headed by the
constitutionalist P. E. Svinhufvud; one of the first moves of
this government was to seek recognition of Finland's independence from the Soviet regime (see below, pp. 350, 400).

7 *Vikzhel and the CEC.* After the failure of the inter-party
conference and the departure from Petrograd of the railwaymen's union leaders, a conference of line organizations was held
in Moscow (13–15 November). The attitudes of the participants,
and their reports on the chaos afflicting the transport system,
convinced Krushinsky and his colleagues that they should no
longer hold out against collaboration with the Bolsheviks,

especially now that the latter seemed prepared to grant Vikzhel's demand for a broadening of their government. Vikzhel's entry into the CEC was hedged with conditions for which its representatives continued to press so far as their numerical weakness permitted; they rejected an invitation to fill the post of PC of Transport. Their ten delegates included one Popular Socialist (D. A. Planson), one centre SR (M. Kondratyev), four Left SRs and four United SDs.

8 *Constituent Assembly Election Results in Petrograd.* Of the 942,333 voters who went to the polls in metropolitan Petrograd, 424,027 (45·2 per cent) chose the Bolshevik list. The next strongest parties were the Kadets with 246,506 (26·3 per cent) and the PSR with 152,230 votes (16·2 per cent). In Moscow the Bolsheviks won 47·9 per cent and the Kadets 34·5 per cent of the total votes cast.

9 Lunacharsky's statement is incorrect: no state had as yet extended *de facto*, let alone *de jure*, recognition to the Soviet government; some neutrals, however, had permitted their representatives to contact the Soviet authorities informally—as indeed had the Entente powers.

10 *Fifth All-City Conference of Factory Committees.* The conference was held on 15–16 November. The sharpness of this resolution, which implicitly criticized the compromise with the Left SRs, reflected the strength of the Anarcho-syndicalist element. These extremists, led by I. S. Bleykhman and V. ('Bill') Shatov, advocated thorough-going workers' control through the factory committees and resented the Bolshevik (and Menshevik) aspiration to control the economy by means of a powerful central bureaucracy. A resolution endorsing the workers' control decree of 14 November was passed by all the 250–300 delegates present but for one lone dissentient and 20 who abstained; but the vote understated the extent of ultra-left-wing sentiment.

11 The *Novaya zhizn'* reporter notes that the speaker was 'a grey-haired old man'—a rarity at this assembly of youthful revolutionaries. Stashkov was the symbolic peasant representative on the armistice delegation sent to Brest-Litovsk: the fact that he was on the presidium of the Congress of Peasant

Deputies casts doubt on the story (Fokke, 'Na stsene', p. 16) that he was a totally unknown individual casually picked up in the street and persuaded to accompany the delegation to Brest instead of returning to his village.

12 *American Socialist Labor Party.* This party was less influential than its rival, the Socialist Party of America, and its following was almost wholly restricted to unassimilated foreign immigrants to the United States. Boris Reinstein, who was of Russian Jewish origin, had been sent to represent his party at the Stockholm socialist conference, where he came into contact with Bolshevik representatives (see above, p. 290) who persuaded him to return to Russia. He was the first foreigner to address the CEC, whose members were eager for evidence of external support. He held no mandate to speak for his party, but he probably represented its mood at the time: American socialists opposed to the war in both parties were generally sympathetic to Bolshevism, of which they knew almost nothing. In March 1919 Reinstein represented the United States at the First Congress of the Communist International.

TWELFTH SESSION

1 *Dissolution of Petrograd Municipal Duma.* The moderate socialist-led Duma had provided a harbour for the CSCR (see above, p. 283), the focal-point of resistance to the Bolshevik take-over by left-wing democrats. It was only a question of time before the Petrograd MRC emulated its Moscow counterpart by dissolving this elected authority. The decree was issued by the CPC on 16 November without prior consultation with other groups represented in the CEC. A blow against the spirit, if not the letter, of the 14 November compromise, it provoked angry scenes in the chief revolutionary forum. On the first occasion when the matter was raised, the Bolsheviks were obliged to beat a tactical retreat and to devise a document (see n. 3 below) designed to meet their critics' objections to the arbitrary way in which important political decisions were taken.

The decree was to come into effect on 17 November. New elections were to be held on 26 November on the basis of certain rules published simultaneously (*Izvestiya*, 17 Nov.). These rules provided for universal adult suffrage and secret balloting; seats were to be allocated in proportion to the votes cast for each list of candidates—as in the Constituent Assembly elections; no restrictions were placed on submission of lists; and the elections were to be supervised by a commission consisting of nine individuals chosen by the Petrograd soviet executive and one representative of each party or group taking part in the election. Despite these formal safeguards the election was a travesty of democratic principles, since it was held under duress. A mere nine days separated publication of the decree from election day, which was insufficient for the compilation of candidates' lists or an adequate campaign. The decree was silent as regards freedom of electoral propaganda, and in practice this was inhibited by the activities of the MRC. For this reason the centre and moderate left parties boycotted the election, which they regarded as illegal in any case.

2 *Appeal by Provisional Government Ministers.* After their release from the Peter and Paul fortress several ministers of the deposed Provisional Government and their aides met regularly at the home of Countess S. V. Panina, a leading Kadet politician and philanthropist. Ten such gatherings were held between 28 (or 29) October and 16 November, when the ministers dispersed after issuing a public statement. This urged the population to rally round the forthcoming Constituent Assembly, to oppose the illegal actions of the Bolshevik authorities, and to reject the proposed armistice, which the signatories contended could lead only to a 'shameful' separate peace with the Central Powers. The appeal—signed *inter alia* by S. N. Prokopovich (Supply), P. N. Malyantovich (Justice), A. M. Nikitin (Posts & Telegraph) and S. L. Maslov (Agriculture)—was published in a number of Petrograd newspapers the next day.

The MRC responded to this challenge by ordering nine daily papers to be closed down (*Novaya zhizn'* and *Delo naroda* were spared). Some of those banned managed to survive under different titles: for example, the Menshevik organ *Rabochaya gazeta* became successively *Luch* (19 November), *Klich* (23 November), *Plamya* (24 November), *Fakel'* (25 November), *Molniya* (26 November), *Shchit* (30 November) and finally *Novy luch* (1 December), a title under which it was permitted to survive for some months. The MRC also ordered the signatories of the appeal to be re-arrested, ostensibly 'in order to prevent violence against them by the justly indignant revolutionary workers and soldiers'.

3 *'Constitutional Instruction' on CEC–CPC Relations.* This document is now known (Gorodetsky, *Rozhdenie*, p. 202) to have been agreed by the Bolshevik and Left SR leaders on 17 November. The Left SRs hoped that it would place relations between the CPC and the CEC (which they regarded as a 'people's parliament') on a regular legal basis. Sverdlov was careful to avoid the term 'constitution', which smacked of 'bourgeois' notions of representative government, preferring the less precise term *konstitutsiya—nakaz*. Its provisions were open to various interpretations. Although it went further than the resolution of 4 November (see above, p. 86), it did not seriously limit the powers of the CPC. Indeed, it seems that Lenin, true to the organizational precepts of Bolshevism, sought to checkmate the dilution of the CEC that resulted from the 14 November compromise by reinforcing the authority of the CPC. Later, when the CPC itself was thrown open to Left SR commissars, the actual decision-making centre passed naturally to the Bolshevik party's Central Committee. In this way he could ensure that control of the government rested in the hands of individuals on whom he could rely.

Paragraph 1 of the document, which re-asserted the principle adopted at the Second Congress of Soviets, was counterbalanced by paragraph 2, which in effect limited the assembly's ostensibly sovereign rights: for who was to determine which ordinances were of a 'general political character'? In the absense of any impartial arbiter this could only be decided by the CPC itself, or by those who directed its affairs. Likewise these men could decide what constituted the 'measures of struggle against counter-revolution' they were empowered to take under paragraph 3. Nor was any time limit specified within which either routine or emergency measures had to be justified before the CEC. Finally, the CPC was left free to publish decrees *before* submission to the CEC, which were to go into effect as soon as they were published in the official journal (now called

Gazeta Vremennogo Rabochego i Krest'yanskogo Pravitel'stva): a decree to this effect was signed the same day (*Izvestiya*, 18 November).

In sum the 'constitutional instruction' may be regarded as a *ruse de guerre*. Its provisions were honoured more in the breach than in the observance. Despite objections by critics of the CPC, many measures were passed without any reference (even *ex post facto*) to the assembly; weekly reports were not rendered; and interpellations were left unanswered.

4 *Bolshevik–Left SR Coalition.* As the inter-party conference had shown, Lenin had no objection to a coalition with non-Bolshevik socialist parties provided that (a) they were committed to the 'soviet' (i.e. Bolshevik) platform and (b) a majority of portfolios, including certain key posts, were reserved to Bolsheviks. On the contrary, he was eager to broaden the government on this basis in order to confer upon it a more 'democratic' appearance; action to this effect had been agreed with the Left SRs on 14 November. That party's success at the Second (Extraordinary) Congress of Peasant Deputies made them seem more acceptable as governmental partners. The chief value of their presence in the CPC in Bolshevik eyes was that the government could then plausibly claim to represent the will of many millions of peasants and not just the workers and soldiers.

Already on 4 November Lenin had proposed that the Left SR leader A. L. Kalegayev be appointed PC of Agriculture, which was of key importance to Populists. Reconstruction of the CPC was discussed in that body on 15 and 16 November (Gorodetsky, *Rozhdenie*, pp. 201 f.); simultaneously talks continued with the Left SR leaders, which eventuated in an understanding of which the substance is embodied in these three points. Power was to be shared in *each* of the people's commissariats, which were supposed to be managed collectively by boards (*kollegii*) under overall direction by the commissar concerned. The Left SRs were not, however, content to play second fiddle in all commissariats other than Agriculture and insisted on more generous terms. Negotiations continued until 8 December: see below, p. 373. Thus the coalition proved more difficult to achieve in the executive branch of government than

it did in the legislature (if one may use constitutional terminology).

THIRTEENTH SESSION

1   *Right of Recall*. The revocation of mandates by electors was
an integral part of 'soviet power' as envisaged by Lenin and
other Bolshevik theorists in 1917. Before October Lenin did not,
however, spell out in detail how he expected such a procedure
to be implemented; and in the practice of the soviet movement
recall of deputies seems to have been applied in rare instances
as when, for example, one was discovered to have served as an
agent of the Okhrana. After October, on the other hand, it was
used more extensively, under the direction of Bolshevik activists,
to eliminate from the soviets Mensheviks and other advocates
of moderation, so paving the way for maximalist supporters
to replace them. (Later still, the same treatment was applied to
anarchists and other ultra-leftists.) Where tension was most
acute, such quasi-constitutional methods were dispensed with
and recalcitrant soviets simply dissolved by force in favour of
rival bodies with more 'reliable' political affiliations.

It was precisely this kind of situation that Lenin had in
mind when at the end of his speech he advocated use of this
procedure to enable power to 'pass from one party to another
bloodlessly'—it being understood, of course, that this was to
be strictly a one-way process: replacement of maximalist candidates by moderates or other critics was in his eyes evidence of
'counter-revolutionary' tendencies. The application of the right
of recall to a body such as the Constituent Assembly, which had
been elected by universal suffrage (and so represented the entire
population, and not simply one social class) was anomalous—as
indeed Lenin recognized. The problem was that the Bolsheviks,
although they had won about one-quarter of the total votes
cast, had no hope of a majority in the assembly, even with the
support of their Left SR allies. They therefore had to devise
tactics to deal with an assembly whose prestige would stand
high with the population in general, and which would inevitably serve as a rallying-point for opponents of the dictatorship.
Forceful measures were likely to provoke considerable discontent; and therefore a cautious cat-and-mouse strategy was

expedient. Having reluctantly agreed that the elections should go ahead (see above, p. 308), they could scarcely prevent the deputies gathering, or outlaw the assembly by decree.

This measure represented a less violent alternative: the Constituent Assembly would be allowed to meet, but those deputies whose presence was found undesirable would be excluded on the grounds that they had lost the confidence of the electorate. The disadvantage of this course, from the Bolsheviks' viewpoint, was that it would give the moderates ample time in which to take counter-measures and to appeal for support to the electorate. With tension mounting, the CPC realized that its power was likely to be endangered. A few days later the Bolshevik authorities resorted to strong-arm methods: the arrest of certain deputies and also of officials charged with supervising the elections (see below, pp. 347, 354).

The Left SR attitude on this question, as exemplified by Karelin, was still relatively moderate; but it was the United SD representative, Kramarov, who seems to have best appreciated what was at stake in this debate.

2 *Reform of Law Courts.* For the decree, see above, p. 323. The CPC was in no mood to wait for the next session of the CEC, held three days later. On 22 November it discussed the matter and adopted the decree as an emergency measure; it was published in *Pravda* on the following day and in the official gazette on 24 November. The Ruling Senate prohibited application of the decree, but this body and other judicial organs were promptly closed down.

FOURTEENTH SESSION

1 *Brest-Litovsk Armistice Negotiations.* The first round of the armistice talks between Russia and the Central Powers took place on 20–2 November. The Russian negotiating team consisted of three Bolsheviks (A. A. Ioffe, chairman; L. B. Kamenev; G. Ya. Sokolnikov) and two Left SRs (A. A. Bitsenko; S. D. Mstislavsky). In this report Kamenev was naturally at pains to present its performance in the most favourable light and to show the Central Powers as yielding before the threat of international revolution fostered by the Bolsheviks. In fact the

balance of forces was very different: how far Kamenev and his colleagues deceived themselves as to the power-political realities remains uncertain. An element of bluff was involved on either side, for each saw the armistice talks as the preliminary to a peace settlement that would vastly enhance its strength. The Central Powers were intent on a separate peace which would bring them territorial gains and free their troops to fight on the Western front; for diplomatic reasons they pretended to be willing to conclude a democratic peace between all belligerents. The Bolshevik leaders (particularly Lenin) were prepared in the last resort to settle for a separate peace on the Eastern front on whatever terms they could get; but they had to profess the conviction that the Allied governments could soon be forced by popular pressure to join in the talks. The Russians were more aware than the Central Powers of the propaganda implications of Brest-Litovsk.

Kamenev's report is detailed, and is by and large borne out by the agreed official protocol of the talks. (This was published in full in *Izvestiya* on 26–8 November; the text as given in *Prot.*, pp. 95–104, is incomplete; for a contemporary English translation, see *Proceedings*, pp. 12–29.) There are, however, some important omissions and distortions; nor is there any reference to the subtle power play that was actually involved.

During the preliminary sparring the real Soviet objective was to force the Central Powers to clarify their attitude in the forthcoming peace talks, so that their imperialistic ambitions should be evident to all. Major-General Hoffmann skilfully avoided this trap by refusing to discuss political questions; the sole 'concession' he would make was to include the text of the Soviet peace offer in the minutes. In the second session the Russians were bluntly informed that it was up to them to obtain their allies' assent to the armistice, whereupon Ioffe 'took note' of the point (i.e. dropped the matter) and went on to set out the Russian delegation's terms for a *separate* armistice. Kamenev states here that this step was taken while the German government was considering a request to send a message of invitation to the Allies; however, this was just a face-saving device, since it must have been clear to the Soviets that such a message, if sent, would make even less impact on the Allied governments than their own appeals in the same sense.

The Russian armistice terms included a bold demand for unilateral territorial withdrawal: German forces were to evacuate the Moon Sound islands, which they had occupied in late September and early October. This was clearly unacceptable, as Hoffmann at once indicated ('such terms could only be presented to a defeated country'). This being so, the Russian delegation scored a tactical success in having its terms discussed at all. Here their opponents' eagerness for a quick decision was to the Soviet advantage.

Kamenev's account omits the next stage in the talks. On the duration of the armistice the Russians proposed six months, the Germans fourteen days. Ioffe proposed a compromise of twenty-eight days (with automatic renewal), which Hoffmann accepted in principle. After raising some other objections the Germans then presented their own terms, of which Ioffe took note.

On the third day the Soviet delegation unexpectedly announced that these terms needed examination by 'our high command' (i.e. the CPC) and suggested a one-week recess. This was another skilful move, since in the interim the strains between the Central Powers could be expected to intensify. The recess would also allow a further appeal to the Allies, which if ignored would strengthen the Soviet case for independent action. It seems doubtful whether Kamenev was really so naïve as to expect, as he states here, that a revolutionary upsurge would force the Allied governments' hands within a week. It was abundantly clear that there was no alternative to acceptance of the German terms for a separate armistice. Nor can this have seemed a shocking prospect, as he implies, for these terms contained nothing prejudicial to Russian (or 'world-revolutionary') interests—as the Soviet negotiators could establish from the semi-official talks held later that day.

The point that aroused most difficulty was how, if at all, Germany could be prevented from moving troops from the Eastern front to Italy or France: a verbal assurance was clearly insufficient, and some face-saving formula had to be found (see below, p. 352). Secondly, the German terms did not provide adequate opportunity for the fraternization between the troops to which the Russians attached such significance. These two points needed top-level discussion in Petrograd before the armistice could be finally concluded after a second round of talks.

The principle of an interim armistice had already been accepted by the Central Powers. A ten-day cessation of hostilities from 2 p.m. on 24 November was agreed without difficulty. An armistice took effect on the Romanian front two days later.

2   *German and Austrian Statements on Armistice.* These statements, transmitted to Russia by radio on 18 November, were formal replies by the German and Austro-Hungarian ministers of Foreign Affairs to Trotsky's messages and notes. Kühlmann also relayed part of Chancellor Hertling's speech in the Reichstag on 16/29 November (excluding those passages in which the chancellor held out the prospect of close economic relations with Russia after the war and promised Poland, Lithuania, and Kurland 'a form of state corresponding to the tendency of their culture'). The Austrian reply was more forthcoming: it stated clearly that the Dual Monarchy was willing to enter talks on an immediate armistice and a *general* peace, and that the Soviet 'guidelines' (i.e. the peace decree) were an acceptable basis for these negotiations.

The differences of emphasis were probably noted by the Soviet leaders. Steglich (*Friedenspolitik*, p. 246) suggests that Kamenev may have deliberately attempted to exploit them when he expressed regret that these statements fell short of Soviet desiderata. The published text of the minutes does not contain the challenging remarks which Kamenev quotes himself as having uttered at this point.

3   A reference to Rear-Admiral V. M. Altfater, the senior member of the group of nine officers who accompanied the Soviet negotiators to Brest-Litovsk for this round of the talks. Their task was to advise the delegation on technical military problems and to preserve, so far as possible, the country's defence capacity. The Bolshevik press (and *Prot.*) made no mention of Altfater's speech to this session of the CEC, presumably on security grounds. Later the admiral was active in building up the infant Red Army, but in 1919 he was shot by the Bolsheviks as a hostage.

4   *Ukrainian Trophies.* The CPC was anxious to demonstrate

its commitment to the principle of national self-determination, enshrined in the 'Declaration on the Rights of the Peoples of Russia' (2 November). In fact the Bolsheviks interpreted this principle in a flexible ('dialectical') manner, holding that aspirations for national independence merited support only in so far as they were compatible with the interests of the 'proletarian revolution' as they themselves interpreted them.

Although the immediate significance of this particular episode was slight, it indicates that the Bolsheviks underestimated the strength of Ukrainian national feeling, which was not to be assuaged by such gestures. The trophies concerned included historical documents as well as the items mentioned. (The *bulava* was the symbol of authority used by cossack hetmans.) They had been taken by the Imperial government in the eighteenth century and were housed in the Hermitage Museum and in the church of the Preobrazhensky guards regiment. A ceremony such as Lunacharsky proposed was indeed held (23 November) but the trophies were apparently not returned to the Ukraine for some years owing to the conflict that broke out shortly afterwards between the Soviet government in Petrograd and the Central Rada in Kiev (see below, p. 364).

5 *Dissolution of Petrograd Municipal Duma.* The Left SR resolution on this issue was ambiguous and indicated a shift to the left in that party's stand, since on 17 November Spiridonova had condemned the measure as 'crude and mistaken' (see above, p. 140). Now the emphasis was placed on a procedural point, the manner in which the decree had been promulgated.

The dissolution of the Duma clearly foreshadowed similar action against the Constituent Assembly and may be regarded as a probing operation designed to weaken the moderates' will to resist. It was undertaken less on account of the Duma members' 'counter-revolutionary' activities than from an unwillingness to tolerate an institution in which maximalist elements continued to sit side by side with moderate socialists and other advocates of democracy, the very existence of which cast doubt on the need for dictatorial measures.

As a result of the boycott by all major non-Bolshevik groups (even the Left SRs were unable in the time allowed to put up their own list of candidates), the new Duma was dominated by

FIFTEENTH SESSION

the Bolsheviks: of 199 deputies elected they had 185 and the Left SRs 10. It coexisted uneasily for some months with city-ward Dumas, several of which remained under moderate control.

The narrowness of the vote indicates the strength of constitutionalist sentiment in the newly expanded CEC, which, however, the opposition was unable to turn to its advantage.

6 Steklov's argument is disingenuous. While it is true that the 'constitutional instruction' had only been adopted on 17 November, in response to opposition protests over the CPC's decree dissolving the Duma, this latter act was also in breach of the provisions adopted on 4 November (see above, p. 86), whereby the CPC was empowered to act on its own only in an emergency situation and on matters that fell within the programme adopted by the Congress of Soviets. Forcible dissolution of an elected local government body was not covered by this programme and was scarcely a matter of urgency; but the Bolsheviks could fall back on the argument that they themselves were the best judges of their government's actions.

FIFTEENTH SESSION

1 *Constituent Assembly Electoral Commission.* The commission, set up by the Provisional Government to oversee conduct of the elections, denounced the October insurrection as an illegal usurpation of power and thereupon suspended its sessions. Its members considered that with the government's collapse the commission had lost its *raison d'être*; that the Bolsheviks would ban or disrupt the elections; and that their own non-cooperation would help discredit the new regime and bring about its early overthrow. When these expectations were proved false, the commission resumed its meetings, first in the Mariyinsky and then in the Tauride Palace (the latter being the designated venue of the Constituent Assembly), whence it issued instructions and advice to its provincial subordinates.

The MRC first reacted by asking local soviets to gather and submit evidence of alleged malpractices by the local electoral commissions, which evidence would then be used to justify the holding of fresh elections (*Pravda*, 22 November). Soon afterwards, however, the Bolshevik leaders decided to employ more forceful tactics. The apparent reason for the change was the resurfacing, on 22 November, of the CSCR in new guise as a 'Union for the Defence of the Constituent Assembly', which expressed publicly its determination to open the assembly's proceedings on 28 November, the due date fixed in August by the Provisional Government. On 23 November a squad of armed men headed by ensign M. V. Prigorovsky, chief (security) commissar at Smolny, entered the building and ordered the commission to disband. When the members refused he left, to return shortly afterwards with an order signed by Lenin for the arrest of the 'Kadet' commission. The officials, twelve to fifteen in number, were taken to Smolny and detained in conditions of considerable discomfort. No charges were preferred against them, the measure being largely a gesture of intimidation. On 27 November they were released. In the meantime M. S. Uritsky, later head of the Petrograd Cheka (security police), was appointed by the CPC to handle all matters relating to the commission, with the right to reconstitute it and to supervise all arrangements for convocation of the assembly.

2 *Prisoners of War.* According to Russian general staff data, based on reports from the International Red Cross, by December 1917 3,638,271 Russians were held prisoner by enemy powers. These figures evidently excluded those who had died in captivity. Several years later the military historian General N. N. Golovin, on the basis of archival research, arrived at a much lower estimate of 2,410,000 prisoners (in November 1917). M. Klante, a German historian who used the papers of E. Brändström, estimated the total at 2·8 million in mid-1918.

In any event the figure will have been greater than that for prisoners of war held by the Russians. This was put by the general staff at 1,813,458 (1 September 1917) and by Klante at 2,272,000. The disparity was one of the factors impeding speedy agreement on an exchange. The matter was supposed to be settled by the Brest-Litovsk peace treaty of March 1918 (arts. VIII, XII; supplementary treaty, arts. 18–20). Repatriation missions were exchanged, but their task had not been completed by the time Germany collapsed, when some 700,000 former Russian soldiers are thought to have still been in Ger-

many alone; after many further vicissitudes those who wished
to return to Soviet Russia were repatriated under an agreement
signed on 19 April 1920.

Kamenev is remarkably outspoken here in discussing the
political motives that underlay the Bolsheviks' reluctance to
initiate such an exchange at once, which the PPS spokesman
urged on humane grounds.

3 *Opposition Arguments on Armistice Talks.* Since the Left SRs
were represented on the armistice delegation, it was left to
spokesmen for two of the small minority groups, the PPS and
the United SDs, to voice the reservations felt by many even in
the maximalist camp at the Soviet government's apparent
readiness to bow before German dictates. However, although
they had a more realistic appreciation of the actual ratio of
forces than the Bolshevik leaders (if, indeed, the latter's enthusiasm was not somewhat feigned), they could not put forward any
more effective alternative policy. In particular:

(a) on the non-transfer of troops (see below, p. 352), it was
clear to everyone that the Russians were in no position to enforce such a demand, and that the German authorities were
bound to evade their formal obligations in this regard so long as
the war in the West continued; insistence on this point was of
moral rather than practical significance, in so far as it could be
invoked to counter allegations of 'treachery' to the Entente by
pro-war elements in the Allied countries. Kamenev in his speech
mentions the need for controls, but apparently said nothing
about this during the negotiations.

(b) on the term of the armistice, even a three-month period
offered no guarantee that German workers would revolt and
end the war from below. Kamenev can scarcely have believed
that twenty-eight days would suffice for convocation of an international peace congress. Both the Bolsheviks and their critics in
the CEC were in effect reduced to an *attentiste* policy. As Lenin
realized more clearly than anyone, although he had yet to make
his pessimistic assessment of the situation public, the Soviet
regime had to accept an onerous 'imperialistic' peace at German hands.

Although the critics' rhetoric had little substance behind it,
Łapiński seems to have anticipated the Bolsheviks in his realiza-

tion of the need for a strong revolutionary army. It was not until mid-December that the CPC was converted to this idea, and two months or so elapsed before this armed force came into being. At the present time the Bolsheviks gave top priority to demobilizing the army they had inherited.

4 *Evacuation of Persia (Iran)*. A Russian expeditionary force had entered northern Persia in 1916 to create a secondary front against Turkey; some other troops had been stationed in that country under the provisions of the 1907 Anglo-Russian convention. The CPC's 'appeal to Muslims of Russia and the East', published on 24 November, voided the treaty of partition and declared that troops would be withdrawn 'as soon as military operations are brought to an end'. The armistice of 2 December (art. 10) provided that the signatories would respect 'the freedom, independence and territorial inviolability of neutral Persia'. However, it proved difficult to implement this agreement in practice. In correspondence with the Persian chargé d'affaires, Assad Khan, Trotsky urged a co-ordinated evacuation plan, and on 14 January 1918 the Soviet government formally repudiated the 1907 convention. The Persian government, with some support from the western Allies, refused to recognize the Soviet diplomatic emissary, and senior Russian officers in Persia delayed the evacuation of the troops until March 1918: even after that date some anti-Bolshevik Russians stayed behind, and in 1919–20 Persia became tangentially embroiled in the Russian civil war. Contentious issues between Russia and Persia were cleared away by the treaty of 26 February 1921, which *inter alia* modified the original pledge: renunciation of pre-war privileges was now made conditional on Persia maintaining its integrity against threats from a third party (such as Great Britain).

5 *The Right of National Self-Determination, the Ukraine, and Finland*. The right of national self-determination 'up to secession and formation of an autonomous state' was proclaimed in a formal document, 'the Declaration of Rights of the Peoples of Russia', adopted by the CPC on 2 November 1917. In practice the Bolshevik attitude to national claims was governed by their assessment of the advantage which their satisfaction would bring to their cause. 'The principle of self-determination must

be a means in the struggle for socialism and must be subordinated to the principles of socialism' (Stalin, *Soch.*, iv. 32; 15 January 1918). During the Russian civil war many national minority leaders in the former empire faced a Hobson's choice between the old-fashioned imperialism of the Whites and the revolutionary centralism of the Reds. Independence was won only by those peoples that enjoyed a favourable geographic situation, an advanced political and social structure, and above all effective foreign aid. Whereas the CPC was in no mood to treat with the Ukrainian Rada (see below, p. 364), which it dismissed as 'bourgeois' and 'counter-revolutionary' despite its socialist colouring, in the case of Finland it was obliged to enter into a compromise which it no doubt hoped would be temporary. One week after taking office the Svinhufvud government (see above, p. 334) submitted to the Finnish House of Representatives a declaration in favour of immediate independence, which that body approved on 23 November. Svinhufvud was reluctant to approach the CPC at once, lest this damage his standing in Allied eyes, but the Finnish Social Democrats were anxious that the break with Russia should come about by mutual agreement. On 25 November a delegation of three FSDP deputies, led by K. Manner, was received by Lenin, who questioned them at length as to their party's intentions. Manner's replies, although somewhat equivocal, apparently convinced Lenin that the risk was worth taking. Another factor in the situation was the knowledge on both sides that the Germans wanted to maintain Finnish independence. See also below, p. 400.

6 *Interference in Internal Affairs of Other Countries.* Carried away by his rhetoric, Kamenev here committed an indiscretion which no Bolshevik would have permitted himself once the Soviet regime had consolidated its hold and begun to struggle for recognition as a member of the international community. In these early weeks Russian maximalists (Left SRs included) did not conceal their fundamental hostility to the existing order in all countries, or their readiness to assist international revolution by propaganda, financial aid, and in the last resort by military action (as in the Ukraine and Finland). In the case of Germany efforts to spread revolution were at this time confined to propa-

ganda, which however played a relatively slight role in bringing about revolution in November 1918.

7 *Supreme Economic Council.* The establishment of a body for central planning and direction of economic life was implicit in the Bolsheviks' understanding of socialism—as it was also in that of the Mensheviks, who did not, however, believe the present revolution was socialist. For the Left SRs, as for many rank-and-file Bolsheviks, this seemed to signify a move away from the libertarian goal of 'workers' democracy'. Their spokesmen objected not only to the content of the proposal but also to the covert manner in which it had in their view been brought forward. The draft was prepared by a commission set up on 11 November by the CPC, which approved it one week later. Though this information is suppressed in recent Soviet sources, a leading role in this commission was played by N. I. Bukharin, the left-wing Bolshevik leader in Moscow. The Left SRs claimed half the places on the new council on the grounds that they spoke for the peasants, the bulk of the 'toiling' population. In response to their protests they were admitted to the final stage of the discussions (see above, pp. 169, 172), but evidently exercised no influence on the framing of the measure, since the decree's final text is identical with the draft.

The draft provided for far-reaching nationalization of industry and the establishment of state-controlled 'trusts' (combines). The management was to be in the hands of functionaries drawn from the appropriate people's commissariats and trade unions; on these boards (*glavki, tsentry*) the former managerial or technical personnel were to have only a consultative voice. Many moderate socialists who worked in these bodies considered that the organizational structure was top-heavy and likely to lead to unnecessary tension with middle-class elements who, if handled reasonably, would collaborate with the new authorities in reconstruction of the economy.

SIXTEENTH SESSION

1 By this is meant the opening, on the initiative of moderate (mainly PSR) deputies, of the Constituent Assembly on the appointed date.

2 *Non-Transfer of Troops to Western Fronts.* This was the key point in the armistice talks, since such troop transfers jeopardized the prospect of a *general* armistice and peace, to which the Bolsheviks were ostensibly committed. The formula that was adopted left the Central Powers free to act as they pleased, for as Steglich (*Friedenspolitik*, p. 248) comments: 'Since the German army command had taken the precaution during the armistice negotiations of ordering the transfer of more than one-third of the divisions stationed in the east, the provision merely enabled the Russians to save face *vis-à-vis* their allies; in practical terms it was without significance.'

According to a British military historian 42 divisions were moved westward between autumn 1917 and 1 March 1918, enabling 192 divisions to be concentrated on the Western fronts as against 59 on the Eastern (including Romania). These figures are roughly corroborated by German sources. See also below, p. 359.

3 *Arrest of Supply Chiefs.* In their efforts to take over the Supply ministry and the elected organizations nominally subordinate to it, the Bolsheviks encountered a good deal of passive resistance. Many of these officials sympathized with the moderate socialists, and their opposition combined political with professional motives. So far as the latter were concerned, they feared that further disruption of the intricate supply apparatus would lead to starvation conditions in the northern cities and at the front.

Their first move was to call a conference of supply officials in Moscow (18 November), which decided not to co-operate with the Bolshevik people's commissariat and set up a ten-man provisional executive board (here referred to as a commission or council) to co-ordinate action by supply committees until a legitimate government had been restored. The deputy PC of Supply, A. G. Shlikhter (who had in effect succeeded I. A. Teodorovich when he resigned earlier in the month) responded by ordering the board dissolved and its members arrested. A decree of 26 November dismissed all the alleged 'saboteurs' in the supply organization. Among those arrested the next day was V. G. Groman, chief of the supply department in the Petrograd soviet and one of the leading economic experts in the

RSDRP; (in the 1920s he was to become a leading Soviet planner). The action aroused a storm of protest which seems to have forced Shlikhter to retreat. Possibly he had only intended the arrests as a political ploy; in any case the men were speedily released. Talks with them followed, but these broke down on 3 December.

It is worth noting that on this occasion the pragmatically inclined Bolshevik trade-union leader Lozovsky acted jointly with the Left SRs.

4 *Cossacks and the CEC.* The defeat of General Krasnov's forces (see above, p. 286) and the armistice negotiations helped the Bolsheviks to win a foothold among the cossack troops, notably in Petrograd military district and on the Northern and Western fronts. This was of considerable importance in view of the fighting now in progress in south-eastern Russia between 'Red' forces and those of Kaledin (see above, p. 295), the outcome of which depended very largely on the political allegiance of the rank-and-file cossacks in the region. On 25 and 26 November the CPC issued two appeals for support to 'toiling cossacks' and on 10 December it followed up this move by releasing the cossacks from their traditional obligation to perform military service. This request for representation was granted on 15 December (Fedorov, *VTsIK*, p. 39). *Znamya truda* reports a 'Cossack committee attached to the CEC' as carrying through on 29 November the dissolution of the Council of Cossack Forces and arresting seven of its leaders.

SEVENTEENTH SESSION

1 *Railwaymen's Wages.* The relatively well-organized railwaymen were among the first groups of workers—another group was the metallurgical workers—to put forward proposals for new wage scales after the Bolshevik insurrection. Their demands were reasonable, given the rapid rise in the cost of living, and were in large measure granted by the CPC on 11 December (see below, p. 372). The point that aroused debate here, characteristically, was that of differentials: the Left SRs wanted them narrowed; the Bolsheviks, not to be outdone, suggested an even more egalitarian structure. The object of these manœuvres was to curry favour with the lower-paid railwaymen and to embar-

rass the railwaymen's union, which was under non-Bolshevik
leadership.

2 *Outlawing of Kadets.* The CPC's decree of 28 November outlawing the liberal Constitutional-Democratic (Kadet) party as
'a party of enemies of the people' and ordering the arrest of its
leaders marked a significant step along the road to dictatorial
rule—and was at once seen as such by the socialist opposition,
who filed an interpellation on the matter.

The event which provoked this decree was the attempt, by a
group of Constituent Assembly deputies, mainly from the PSR,
to open its proceedings on the date fixed by the Provisional
Government (see above, p. 307). Several dozen deputies succeeded in making their way past the guards into the chamber;
here they decided, since no quorum was present, to hold a
private meeting—and to repeat the procedure until such time
as a quorum had assembled. This was of course an open defiance of the CPC's decree, published on 27 November, prescrib-
ing that the assembly would open only when 400 deputies had
arrived and registered their presence with Uritsky's commission. The Bolsheviks regarded the deputies' action as a 'counter-
revolutionary demonstration' and made it a pretext for repressive action against those political leaders whom they regarded
as most dangerous. Although the Kadets had not initiated the
plan to enter the Tauride Palace, their pro-Allied sympathies
made them a logical target. Four of their leaders were arrested
early in the morning of 28 November: A. I. Shingarev, F. F.
Kokoshkin, P. D. Dolgorukov and S. V. Panina; F. I. Rodichev
and N. N. Kutler were seized shortly afterwards.

In the Bolshevik press much was made of the Kadets' alleged
contacts with Kaledin's supporters. The evidence suggests, however, that the Kadet leaders were slow to proffer assistance
either to Kaledin or to other White leaders, and that contacts
were at best intermittent; in the Don region Kaledin's relations
with the local Kadets were strained. It was thus a potential
rather than an actual threat which the Bolsheviks sought to
counteract.

At the end of his speech Shteynberg set forth what was to become the Left SRs' official attitude towards the Constituent
Assembly.

Lenin's reply developed a principle which was central to his political thought but which contemporaries did not readily recognize: namely, that political disagreements were inseparable from the 'class struggle'; that every social class had its party or parties which expressed its interests; and that under a 'proletarian dictatorship' there was room for only one party, that of the Bolsheviks who represented its immanent interests, and who were justified in suppressing all rivals. The theory was to be taken to its logical conclusion in 1918, when the Left SRs, Anarchists, and other maximalist groups were in turn suppressed as allegedly 'counter-revolutionary'. Lenin also propounds here the notion of collective guilt, an integral element of the totalitarian *Weltanschauung*.

3   The reference is to the CPC's declaration on 26 October that it was assuming power provisionally, pending a decision by the Constituent Assembly on Russia's form of government, and to its ordinance that elections to the assembly be held on the duly appointed date.

4   *Kadets and Kornilov*. In August 1917 many people on the right and centre, alarmed by the Provisional Government's drift to the left, looked to the Supreme Commander-in-Chief at that time, General L. G. Kornilov, as an individual capable of restoring order and discipline. Leaders of the Kadet party were involved in talks about a possible reconstitution of the government to make it less dependent upon the soviets, but (contrary to Lenin's insinuations here) there is no evidence to support the contention that they were associated in any way with an attempt to impose a government more to their taste by military force—or indeed that General Kornilov himself made such an attempt. (He did not disobey the Provisional Government until he was dismissed for alleged conspiracy by prime minister Kerensky on 27 August; prior to that the military moves which he authorized were made with Kerensky's explicit or tacit consent.) Milyukov did endeavour to reconcile Kerensky and Kornilov after the breach, but was unsuccessful.

The allusion to Chernov relates to his leading articles in *Delo naroda* early in September 1917, when the PSR leader (and former minister of Agriculture) sought to discredit Kerensky and other former colleagues in the government who had opposed his policies.

5   *Trotsky on Revolutionary Terror.* Trotsky's sense of history and fondness for dramatic effect seem to have got the better of him here: other Bolshevik leaders were more circumspect about openly advocating such terroristic measures. Lenin had expressly denied any intent to use the guillotine against 'enemies of the people', explaining that the Bolsheviks should emulate the French Jacobins' 'good example' without copying it exactly; however, he remained convinced that violence was necessary and legitimate to suppress resistance to Bolshevik rule. Trotsky's speech was not reported in the maximalist press, although a similar one before the Petrograd soviet on 2 December was published in *Izvestiya* four days later. In this he stated: 'we have not executed anyone and do not intend to, but there are moments when the people's fury is aroused . . . None of us can say that the people, driven to an extreme, will renounce even this ultimate measure.' This formulation made no explicit reference to the *mode* of execution. Trotsky was thought to have said that the guillotine 'could serve to shorten people by a head', to which Martov retorted (4 December) that it could also 'lengthen the ears . . . of those who purported to solve social problems with its assistance'. Trotsky's threats caused a commotion at the second (regular) Congress of Peasant Deputies on 3 December: when he appeared he was howled down, whereupon the Bolsheviks demonstratively left the hall.

The CPC lost no time in acting upon these suggestions. On 7 December it resolved to establish a national security organ, the All-Russian Extraordinary Commission for Combating Counter-Revolution, Sabotage and Speculation (Cheka), under F. E. Dzerzhinsky. This took over and expanded the work of two Petrograd soviet organs, the MRC and its 'Military Investigating Committee', some of whose personnel it inherited. At first it limited itself to arresting and investigating suspects, but it soon assumed a punitive role as well. The first known execution by the Cheka (*not* by the guillotine!) took place on 24 February 1918. Trotsky remained consistent in his views on this matter, which in 1920 he reiterated in a pamphlet entitled *Terrorism or Communism*, a reply to K. Kautsky's *Terrorism and Communism*.

I. S. Bleykhman, mentioned here, was secretary of the Petrograd Federation of Anarchist-Communists and a member of the MRC.

6 *Unemployment Insurance.* The wholesale closure of factories for lack of supplies and fuel was causing serious distress in Petrograd and other cities at this time. It seemed likely to turn working-class opinion against the Soviet regime. The Bolsheviks sought above all to establish the basic principle of nation-wide unemployment insurance, which was bound to be attractive to industrial labour, and regarded the present measure as a temporary stopgap. It provided for local labour exchanges and relief funds, initially financed by levies on employers. Benefits were supposed to be paid at a rate equivalent to the average local wage for a day labourer. In practice the resources available were quite disproportionate to actual needs: Petrograd alone had 120,000 registered unemployed.

The matter was passed to the CEC after consideration by the CPC on 30 November; the commission it set up consisted mainly of officials in the PC of Labour, among them Dr. A. N. Vinokurov, who is believed to have composed the final draft. The text was approved by the CPC and published on 13 December; the decree bears the date of 11 December.

EIGHTEENTH SESSION

1 *Brest-Litovsk Armistice Agreement.* On 2 December representatives of the belligerent powers at the Brest-Litovsk conference agreed that an armistice between their forces should take effect at midday on 4 December. The armistice was to last for twenty-eight days and to be subject to denunciation on seven days' notice. The agreement was a landmark in the history of the First World War. It was also a considerable success for the German high command, which had for long been anxious to free its hands in the east in preparation for an offensive planned on the Western front in the spring of 1918. The Bolsheviks, who tended to exaggerate the international impact of their diplomacy, interpreted the armistice as a signal victory for their revolutionary cause. They lost no time in exploiting its propaganda value both at home and abroad. Such was clearly the intent of the

eighteenth session of the CEC. The second session to have a ceremonial rather than a business-like character (for the first see above, p. 130), it was in effect little more than a mass meeting which served to whip up support for the regime, not least among the war-weary troops.

The armistice talks had been initiated on 20 November but were broken off two days later, ostensibly to give the Allies another chance to define their attitude, and in the absence of any response were resumed on 29 November. An interim agreement on suspension of hostilities for ten days entered into force on 24 November, the provisions of which in certain respects anticipated those incorporated in the final document. The main provisions were as follows:

(i) The agreement applied only to the forces of the signatory states on the Eastern front. (An armistice between the Central Powers and Romania was signed on 26 November: see p. 344.) The Central Powers' representatives refused to be drawn into a discussion of a *general* armistice, maintaining that this was a 'political' question beyond their competence. Since the Soviet negotiating team obviously could not speak for the Entente as a whole, it had no option but to concede this point, which appears to have been raised chiefly 'for the record'.

(ii) The demarcation line followed the existing front line, no intermediate neutral zone being established. Several months earlier the German high command had decided not to seek unilateral military advantages from the prospective armistice agreement, lest they thereby reduce the chances of obtaining a favourable early separate peace. The Soviet negotiators, unaware of this decision, seem to have misinterpreted their adversaries' apparent restraint as a sign of weakness. They suggested that the Germans should withdraw their forces from the Moon Sound islands, which had been occupied a few weeks earlier, and where their presence constituted a security threat to Petrograd. This proposal was naturally rejected out of hand, Hoffmann observing tartly that it could be made only by a victorious power to a vanquished enemy (see above, p. 343).

(iii) The agreement incorporated a provision permitting 'fraternization' between soldiers along the demarcation line. The Bolsheviks set great store by this as a means of carrying on revolutionary agitation among the Central Powers' troops.

However, the German command took steps to maintain close control over these contacts in order to limit their potentially subversive effect.

(iv) The most vital clause stated that until 1/14 January 1918 'operational troop movements may be carried out only if they have been initiated prior to signature of the agreement'. This phrasing gave the Central Powers a legal loophole to act as they pleased on such transfers (see above, p. 352). In fairness it should, however, be added that: (a) no precise information is available as to the subsequent deployment or commitment to action of the troops so transferred; (b) their movement was governed by several other factors independent of the armistice talks (e.g. the availability of transport and of replacements); (c) it was probably inaugurated before these talks had begun; (d) the Soviet government had no means of enforcing observance of the agreement by the other side. Therefore Allied charges that the armistice amounted to collusion between Soviet Russia and the Central Powers should not be accepted without qualification.

2   Hermann Molkenbuhr (1851–1927) was elected secretary of the German Social Democratic party each year from 1905 to 1913, and again in October 1917; in 1916, together with F. Ebert and P. Scheidemann, he became joint chairman of the party's fraction in the Reichstag.

3   *Trotsky on Revolutionary War.* Trotsky's 'revolutionary defensism', evidently acceptable to his listeners, was soon to get him into trouble and to be officially repudiated. In January 1918, when the Soviet leaders had to define their attitude to the Central Powers' demand that their government sign a peace treaty imposing major territorial and other sacrifices upon the infant republic, opinions were sharply divided. Lenin, supported by Sverdlov and Stalin, insisted on acceptance of the German terms. The 'Left Communists', as they came to be known, held to the traditional policy of waging revolutionary war against the 'imperialist' aggressor. Trotsky adopted an intermediate position summed up in the celebrated phrase 'neither war nor peace'. The Soviet delegation was to 'break off the negotiations but state that we are not going to fight'; this was designed to expose the aggressive nature of German policy

and to encourage the revolutionary forces in that country to
rise up against the government. This line was endorsed in the
Central Committee by 9 votes to 7 on 11 January. However,
when it was put into practice on 28 January/10 February the
Central Powers responded by moving their forces further into
Russia, in defiance of the armistice agreement, and stepping up
their demands. The Soviet government had no alternative but
to accept Lenin's arguments, with which Trotsky now concurred. The peace of Brest-Litovsk, signed on 3 March (see
below, p. 395), represented a victory for pragmatism over the
internationalist idealism well exemplified in this speech.

4   *The Kalpashnikov Affair* has its place in the history of Soviet–
American relations as the first diplomatic confrontation between the two future super-powers. In 1916 Colonel Andrey
Kalpashnikov, of the 1st Siberian corps, was sent by the Russian Red Cross to the United States (where he had previously
served in the Russian embassy) to raise money for the purchase
of ambulances and other relief supplies. By chance he returned
to Russia on the same ship as Trotsky and other internationalist
émigrés; at Halifax, where Trotsky was detained at the request
of the British, Kalpashnikov served as interpreter during his
interrogation—'a fact which Trotsky . . . found it difficult to
forget or forgive' (Kennan, *Russia Leaves the War*, p. 195).
Subsequently Kalpashnikov was attached to the U.S. Red
Cross Commission in Romania. Owing to the military situation
this mission, based at Jassy and headed by Colonel H. W.
Anderson, could only communicate with Washington, or
obtain supplies, through Russia.

   Immediately after the October insurrection Kalpashnikov
returned to Petrograd to supervise assembly of his vehicles,
which had in the meantime arrived there, with the intention of
taking them back to Romania. However, in the last days before
the armistice of 26 November on the Romanian front political
and military leaders in Jassy conceived a desperate plan for
certain units whose morale remained high to force their way
across southern Russia to the Don, where they were to help
Kaledin reconstitute an eastern front. Among supporters of this
scheme was Anderson, who hoped to evacuate his mission to
British-occupied Mesopotamia. He took the view that if Kal-

pashnikov's vehicles were diverted from Jassy, where they might fall into enemy hands, to the Don, they could be useful to these forces; there is, however, no evidence of any intention on his part to place them at Kaledin's disposal.

On 22 November Anderson sent two telegrams to the American embassy in Petrograd. One of these is quoted here by Trotsky; the other requested the ambassador, Francis, to give Kalpashnikov every assistance and to supply him on demand with up to 100,000 roubles from American Red Cross funds. The message, although received on 24 November, was not passed on to Kalpashnikov for eight days, apparently owing to opposition within the embassy to action deemed likely to embroil the United States in the incipient civil war. The military attaché, Brigadier-General W. V. Judson, advocated a flexible policy towards the Soviet regime; so did Colonel R. Robins, who headed the U.S. Red Cross Commission in Petrograd. Since its inception in August this organization, which was independent of the embassy (and of its counterpart in Jassy), had intervened actively in Russia's internal affairs, first backing the moderate socialists but then veering towards support for the Bolsheviks. On 24 November Robins, who frequently paid unofficial visits to Smolny, discussed with Trotsky the proposed despatch to Jassy of a trainload of Red Cross supplies. The evidence suggests that Trotsky nourished Robins's suspicions of Kalpashnikov, and that he already knew of Anderson's scheme as the latter's telegrams had been intercepted.

On 28 November Anderson countermanded his earlier instructions, since the Romanian armistice had shown evacuation through southern Russia to be impracticable. He now wished the mission to return to Petrograd, but this plan was obstructed by Robins, who feared that the vehicles might fall into the hands of the Ukrainian autonomists. Robins also had foreknowledge of Kalpashnikov's arrest by the Soviet authorities, which ensued on the night of 7–8 December.

The American embassy's reaction was to empower Robins to approach Trotsky unofficially and to show him copies of Anderson's three telegrams. Such frankness, it was hoped, would convince the Soviet government that the Americans were innocent of any collusion with Kaledin. No formal demand was made for Kalpashnikov's release. This 'soft' approach did not prevent Trotsky from making the charges public at this expanded session of the CEC, where they had a considerable impact. In presenting the evidence Trotsky showed political acumen. He made no mention of Anderson's third telegram (countermanding the vehicles' proposed dispatch to Rostov), since this did not suit his purpose. Nor did he cite a letter dated 4 December from Perkins to Anderson corroborating this decision—although the letter was reproduced along with the other documents in *Izvestiya* on the following day. The third document he cited was quite innocuous; the object was evidently to implicate Francis personally in the alleged plot.

The ambassador—stung, no doubt, by Trotsky's irony in according him a knighthood—responded with a public disavowal of complicity; this was printed in *Izvestiya* three days later. The official Soviet view then and since has been that Anderson's third telegram was insufficient evidence that the Rostov evacuation plan had been abandoned.

The Kalpashnikov affair was certainly, as Kennan writes, 'murky and confused'; but four conclusions suggest themselves.

(i) There is no evidence to link Kalpashnikov with Kaledin's enterprise. Although strongly anti-Soviet, he had no opportunity to assist Kaledin at this time since he was not even informed of the proposed evacuation through Rostov (which might or might not have aided Kaledin) until after it had been abandoned.

(ii) Kalpashnikov's role was that of a scapegoat. As a Russian subject working for a semi-official organization he had no diplomatic privileges and was exposed to the risk of arbitrary arrest. His officer's rank and his part in the Halifax interrogation made him doubly suspect in Trotsky's eyes. He later protested that he had been the innocent victim of a 'provocation' engineered by the Soviet authorities with the connivance of sympathizers in the American community in Petrograd. There is something to this claim, although it is impossible to corroborate his statement that a senior Cheka official told him that the affair had been devised to create a scandal which would force Francis to take a position more in line with Soviet wishes.

(iii) The American response to Trotsky's challenge was weak and confused. The Red Cross mission chiefs' lobbying complicated the ambassador's efforts to pursue a consistent line. How-

ever, the aid they thus rendered Trotsky was given from mis-
guided fellow-feeling rather than at his behest.

(iv) Trotsky's main motive was probably to teach the Allies
a humiliating lesson for their refusal to take part in the Brest-
Litovsk negotiations. The armistice terms pointed to the likelihood of a separate peace, which was bound to be unpopular; a
successful blow against the Entente would deflect criticism by
demonstrating the Soviet government's continued adherence to
a revolutionary line. The Americans, less hostile to Bolshevism
than the British or French, were 'the weakest link in the chain'
and thus a natural target.

If this was the purpose, it may be said to have succeeded,
since by sending Robins to Smolny a move was made towards
de facto recognition.

5 *Soviet Attitude to Diplomatic Privileges.* This threat was taken
seriously by Francis, who was also receiving menacing letters
from anarchists in Petrograd. The fate of General Dukhonin
was fresh in his mind. Moreover, the early Bolsheviks, confident
that the revolution would soon sweep away the 'bourgeois'
order, scorned accepted norms of diplomatic protocol, to which
their successors would later attach such importance. The right
of embassy personnel to immunity from arrest or maltreatment
was not regarded as sacrosanct, as was shown a few weeks later
by the Diamandi incident (see below, p. 412).

6 *Chicherin and Petrov.* The future PC of Foreign Affairs (1918–
30) was the instrument of one of Trotsky's earliest successes in
his campaign to have the Soviet government treated as an equal
by the 'imperialist' powers of the Entente. During the First
World War G. V. Chicherin was prominent in the affairs of the
Russian émigré community in Great Britain. A forthright internationalist, who had abandoned his former Menshevik convictions for a viewpoint close to Lenin's, he agitated successfully
against a scheme for forced repatriation of Russian political
émigrés (1916) and then, after the February revolution, cam-
paigned on behalf of their return to Russia. This activity led to
his arrest in the autumn of 1917 and to his imprisonment in
Brixton Gaol, London, for 'anti-Ally and pro-German activities'. One of his comrades, P. Petrov, had been arrested on a
similar charge early in 1916.

Among Trotsky's first acts on assuming control of the Foreign Affairs ministry was to send the British ambassador, Sir George Buchanan, a peremptory demand for the release of the two men (13 November). Their detention, he argued, was unjustified since 'counter-revolutionary British citizens are in no way oppressed in the territory of the Russian republic'. The note contained a clear hint of retaliatory action; and four days later, without waiting for a reply from London, Trotsky issued an order that no British subject would be allowed to leave Russia until the two men were freed. The move alarmed the British community in Petrograd and Buchanan advised his government to concede the point. Balfour, who was anxious to avoid a complete break in Anglo-Russian relations lest the Soviet government fall wholly into the German embrace, agreed. Although the War Cabinet had decided on 16/29 November to ignore Trotsky's request, on 27 November/10 December it reversed its stand and gave the Foreign Secretary discretion to handle the affair as he chose. Smolny was informed that the two men's cases would be reconsidered with a view to their repatriation, and on 1 December the ban on British subjects leaving Russia was rescinded. Chicherin was released from Brixton on 21 December 1917/3 January 1918 and on reaching Petrograd became Trotsky's deputy in the PC of Foreign Affairs. In Soviet eyes the affair was regarded as a precedent establishing the principle of reciprocity in relations with non-Communist states.

7   *The CPC and the Central Rada.* Moiseyev's intervention spoiled the outward harmony of this ceremonial session and obliged Zinoviev to make an unscheduled statement to explain why, without any previous discussion in this supposedly sovereign soviet body, the CPC had announced that a state of war existed between it and the Central Rada in Kiev—a development of portentous significance which the Bolshevik leaders clearly found embarrassing.

After the local Bolsheviks' failure to seize power in Kiev (25 October–1 November) *de facto* authority in that city lay with the Ukrainian autonomists. Their central executive body, which assumed governmental powers, was known as the General Secretariat; headed by V. Vinnichenko (Vynnychenko), it consisted in the main of Ukrainian Socialist-Revolutionaries and Social Democrats but included some Russians. Through a committee of representatives, the Small (Mala) Rada, it was responsible to a larger deliberative body, the Central Rada, whose members were nominated or elected by a wide range of public and private organizations. (In common parlance the government was often referred to simply but incorrectly as 'the Rada'.)

The Rada leaders stood for a speedy democratic non-annexationist peace, to be negotiated by all the belligerent powers, and at home for an orderly transfer of large landed properties to peasant ownership, state control of industry, and far-reaching 'democratization'. They reluctantly recognized the CPC's claim to be the legitimate government of (Great) Russia but resisted its pretensions to speak for Ukrainian or other non-Russian workers or peasants; invoking the principle of national self-determination, to which the CPC had formally pledged allegiance (2 November), they looked forward to a federal union of the various regions making up the former Russian empire, in which each republic would enjoy extensive autonomy and in which the Ukraine, by reason of its economic and strategic importance, would naturally play a leading role.

By the so-called 'Third Universal', promulgated on 7 November, the General Secretariat claimed full executive power throughout the Ukraine, whose territorial limits it had previously defined, pending convocation (in January 1918) of a Ukrainian Constituent Assembly. The establishment of a Ukrainian People's Republic did not arouse as much enthusiasm as its initiators hoped among ordinary Ukrainians, whose national self-awareness was as yet little developed; such popular support as the regime could muster came largely from its espousal of social revolutionary objectives, in which it seemed to have much in common with the Bolsheviks (the strong authoritarian streak in Leninist doctrine was not generally apparent). In a trial of strength between the Rada and the CPC the advantage could be expected to lie with the latter.

The CPC was at first too busy establishing its power in Great Russia and at the front to concern itself closely with Ukrainian affairs, and the Kievan Bolsheviks confined themselves for the moment to verbal criticism of the Rada. Some of the Kievans were sympathetic to Ukrainian national aspirations, but such 'compromising' tendencies were abhorrent to Lenin and other leading Bolsheviks (notably Stalin and Sverdlov; Trotsky's attitude was slightly more equivocal). It appears that they were never prepared to tolerate the existence of an autonomous Ukraine, even if its government were socialist: apart from the obvious strategic and econom'c disadvantages, a policy of co-existence would endanger the Bolshevik dictatorship ideologic-ally by holding out a pluralistic alternative. These underlying reasons for the growing tension between Kiev and Petrograd were obscured in contemporary polemical exchanges, which revolved around concrete issues of secondary importance.

These latter issues were, in order of significance, military, foreign political, and economic:

(i) S. Petlyura (Petlura), secretary for Military Affairs and the strongest personality in the Rada government, actively promoted the 'ukrainization' of former Imperial Army troops, i.e. their re-formation into units constituted on national lines and stationed as far as possible on Ukrainian territory—where they could bolster the Rada's shaky authority and also stiffen the front against the Central Powers until a general peace had been signed.

(ii) The Rada leaders opposed the Bolsheviks' unilateral action in liquidating GHQ and instituting negotiations that would clearly result in a *separate* armistice and peace treaty. Although they were later obliged to modify their stand (see below, n. 10), their natural sympathies lay with the Allies, whose representatives in Kiev endeavoured to stiffen their opposition to both the Germans and the Bolsheviks (see below, p. 390).

(iii) The population in northern and central Russia, which normally depended on supplies of grain and other foodstuffs from the south, were on the verge of starvation. The chief obstacle to maintenance of supplies was the breakdown of the railway network, but the Rada's efforts to protect the Ukraine's own economic interests were naturally taken by the hard-pressed and suspicious Bolsheviks as corroborative evidence of alleged 'counter-revolutionary' propensities (see below, p. 392).

These three issues brought to a head the latent antagonism between the two rival centres of authority. On 17 November Stalin, PC for Nationality Affairs, communicated by direct wire with N. V. Porsh, secretary for Labour in the Rada government, and with a local Bolshevik activist. (The text of this conversation was later suppressed from Stalin's published works.) His tone was relatively mild: he confirmed that the Soviet government recognized the Ukraine's right to self-determination and specified that this right might be exercised either through a referendum or by a decision of the two Constituent Assemblies; but simultaneously he insisted that an all-Ukrainian congress of soviets be convoked and that 'soviet power' be implemented throughout the region. He was evidently willing to grant pro-Rada organizations a modest share in power temporarily, until they could be 'squeezed out' by pro-Bolshevik bodies. This was a standard Bolshevik tactic wherever the struggle was prolonged. Although often successful elsewhere, in Kiev the plans went awry. M. Kovalivs'kyi, secretary for Supply in the Rada government and a leading Ukrainian SR politician, devised a scheme whereby the delegates of workers' and soldiers' soviets who attended this gathering, which opened on 4 December, were 'swamped' by hundreds of rural delegates loyal to his own party. The radicals were obliged to leave, whereupon the congress endorsed the Rada's policies.

This manœuvre had been preceded by military action to disarm and to expel from the Ukraine certain units sympathetic to the Bolsheviks, notably from Kiev on 29–30 November. Although this operation was carried out bloodlessly it was bound to antagonize Petrograd. In an ultimatum dispatched by radio on 4 December, Lenin and Trotsky charged the Rada with 'carrying on an ambiguous bourgeois policy under cover of national phrases' and posed four questions:

Would the Rada undertake to cease disorganizing the common front? Would the Rada undertake not to allow any military units to the Don, the Urals or elsewhere, except with the consent of the [Bolshevik] Commander-in-Chief? Would the Rada aid the revolutionary armies in their struggle against the counter-revolutionary Kadet–Kaledin uprising? Would the Rada cease all its efforts to disarm Soviet regiments and workers' Red guards in the Ukraine and at once return their arms to those who had been disarmed? [The message concluded:] If no satisfactory reply to these questions is received within 48 hours, the CPC will consider the

Rada in a state of open war against soviet power in Russia and the Ukraine.

The CPC evidently did not expect its ultimatum to be accepted: the questions were rhetorical and their main purpose 'agitational'. The Rada's spirited reply (5 December) accused the CPC of pursuing a contradictory policy, simultaneously promising the Ukraine the right of national self-determination in theory while denying that right in practice. It demanded an end to all interference in the Ukraine's domestic affairs, dismissed the Bolshevik charges in detail, and concluded by declaring that force would be met with force. It was to this message that the CPC responded by affirming that a state of war now existed (6 December).

Meanwhile small bodies of troops were being concentrated for an offensive on Kiev. It was, however, difficult to persuade men to fight in such an unpopular cause and the first units sent against pro-Rada troops disintegrated. The campaign was to be fought as much by political propaganda as by arms. As yet not all efforts at a mediated settlement had been exhausted: see below, p. 387.

8 *Central Rada and Kaledin.* The charge of collusion between the Rada government in Kiev and General Kaledin's cossack forces on the Don was prominent in Bolshevik rhetoric at the time and has become standard in Soviet historiography since. Such allegations served to discredit the Rada by associating it with a force whose aims were clearly anti-Soviet.

There is no evidence of military collaboration between Kiev and Novocherkassk; indeed, their forces appear to have clashed at some places in the Donets region. Although they cannot be documented, there were undoubtedly instances when local Ukrainian authorities permitted cossack troops making their way home from the front to pass through their territory. They considered that they had neither the strength nor the right to prevent them; and they took the same attitude towards the still more numerous parties of men returning in the same way to Great Russia. It was another matter to tolerate the transit of organized bodies of men who were sent for an offensive purpose, since this would compromise the Ukraine's neutrality in the incipient Russian civil war. For this reason on 24 November

Petlyura declined a request by Krylenko, the Bolshevik Commander-in-Chief, that such facilities be extended to Red troops
being sent against Kaledin. This demand may have been motivated by political rather than military considerations, namely
to force the Rada to define its attitude to the conflict. There is
no evidence that the denial of transit rights impeded Bolshevik
operations and it can scarcely be regarded as proof of indirect
collaboration between the Rada and Kaledin.

In the political sphere the relationship between the two
regimes was intermittent and tentative. On 10 November
Vinnichenko secured endorsement by the Small Rada for the
principle of talks with other regional authorities, including
those of the Don and the Kuban, on formation of an all-Russian
federal government. Later in the month a delegation from the
so-called South-eastern Cossack Union (the only such authority
to respond) came to Kiev. No record of these conversations has
survived, but they evidently did not lead to any agreement. The
two regimes were far apart ideologically. As the later history of
the civil war was repeatedly to demonstrate, the deep divisions
between right and left prevented effective collaboration against
the Bolsheviks. The latter, however, were prone to exaggerate
their adversaries' cohesion.

9 *Central Rada and the Provisional Government.* Disagreements
over the granting of autonomous rights to the Ukraine provoked the collapse of the first coalition cabinet early in July
1917. Its two successors were no better able to resolve this
thorny problem. On 4 August temporary instructions were
drawn up to define the powers of the General Secretariat; these
failed to satisfy the partisans of Ukrainian autonomy, yet went
too far for the Senate, which on 2 October refused to endorse
them. On 19 October the third coalition cabinet invited two
Ukrainian politicians, A. N. Zarubin and I. M. Steshenko, to
Petrograd for talks. These were still in progress when the Provisional Government was overthrown by the Bolsheviks. N. V.
Nekrasov, a left-wing Kadet, was appointed governor-general
of Finland in September 1917.

10 *Central Rada and Brest-Litovsk.* Zinoviev's statement is ironic
in view of later Soviet complaints of Ukrainian 'treachery' at
the Brest-Litovsk peace conference.

The initial position of the General Secretariat, as set forth on 10 November, on the question of concluding peace was similar to that of most Russian moderate socialists: it was to be general and to renounce annexations or indemnities. It further maintained that Russia could only be properly represented at international negotiations by a federal government responsible to the all-Russian Constituent Assembly; the Bolsheviks, as usurpers, had no such right. In practice this rigorous stand soon had to be modified—less in response to pressure by radical elements within the Ukraine, as Zinoviev here suggests, than from the need to react to the Soviet government's unexpected success in winning control of GHQ and initiating armistice talks with the Central Powers. These developments, together with the general breakdown of order at the front, threatened the security of the infant Ukrainian People's Republic. On 21 November the General Secretariat decided to participate in the talks which five days later eventuated in an armistice on the Romanian front. The corresponding decision to attend the Brest-Litovsk talks was evidently taken immediately afterwards, although the Rada delegation, led by M. Lyubynsky, did not arrive at the conference location until 3 December, by which time the armistice had already been concluded.

The delegates had been instructed to enter the Russian negotiating team 'for purposes of information and control'. During the first round of the peace talks (9–15 December O.S.) the Ukrainians did not intervene in the discussions and their presence caused the Soviet representatives no embarrassment. Trotsky had initially recommended that a conciliatory line be taken towards them (*vide* his message to Krylenko of 24 November, reproduced in Antonov-Ovseyenko, *Zapiski*, p. 47), evidently in the hope that their 'separatist' inclinations could be held in check—a policy for which he was later to be excoriated by the Stalinists. However, the growing antagonism between Petrograd and Kiev, reflected in the exchange of verbal broadsides and intermittent fighting, led the Ukrainian delegates to insist more strongly on their autonomous status. This change of attitude was made explicit by the Rada government in a statement broadcast on 11 December, to which the Central Powers promptly sent an encouraging reply. For their part they were eager to offset the influence in Kiev of the Entente representatives and hoped to exploit the Russo-Ukrainian conflict in their own interests.

When the Brest-Litovsk talks were resumed on 27 December/ 9 January the Ukrainian delegates, who were privately rebuffed by Trotsky, entered into separate negotiations with representatives of the Central Powers (31 December–6 January O.S.) and drew up a draft agreement whereby, in return for certain concessions by the Dual Monarchy, the Ukraine would secure peace under the Central Powers' *de facto* 'protection'. The Ukrainian treaty was signed on 27 January/9 February 1918. It gave the Central Powers a trump card in their ensuing dealings with the Bolsheviks. The natural indignation of Petrograd was enhanced by the fact that the Rada government had meanwhile been driven out of Kiev by the advancing 'Red' forces and had thus, in the Soviet view, forfeited all claim to speak for the Ukraine.

NINETEENTH SESSION

1 In lieu of 'for two weeks' *Novaya zhizn*' and *Znamya truda* read: 'for a long time'. Presumably the speaker had in mind the sixteenth session on 27 November. Of the two intervening sessions the first (1 December) had evidently been restricted and the second (8 December) of a ceremonial character; at neither had any real debate on policy been possible. The Bolsheviks' readiness to ignore the rights of this supposedly sovereign legislative body testified to their growing self-assurance. The CEC, wrote the Menshevik Internationalist N. N. Sukhanov, was 'a sorry parody of a revolutionary parliament' (*Novaya zhizn*', 8 Dec.)

2 *First Congress of All-Russian Union of Railwaymen.* Vikzhel had summoned an extraordinary congress of the union for 15 December in Petrograd. A fierce political struggle for control of this gathering developed between supporters of the present executive and maximalist elements; a favourable outcome of this was presumably what the CPC meant here by 'new circumstances'. The left-wingers, based in the Petrograd and Moscow regional networks, seized the initiative by calling a rival congress, which opened on 12 December. The next day it was ad-

dressed by Lenin, Zinoviev, and M. T. Yelizarov (Lenin's brother-in-law, who had taken over from Vikzhel control of the ministry of Transport). It endorsed the CPC's suggestions on a pay rise. The terms of this settlement (published on 14 December and evidently agreed the previous day, although the decree was backdated to the eleventh) were relatively generous, especially to the lower-income groups, who received an immediate advance of 200 roubles. A very narrow differential (1·79:1 in the Petrograd region) was fixed between the highest and lowest of the fourteen service grades. Political calculations were clearly not absent from the deal, and on 15 December the delegates responded by condemning Vikzhel, which they held to blame *inter alia* for the delay in meeting the men's wage demands. On 19 December, four days behind schedule, the union's extraordinary congress began its deliberations. The delegates, over 600 strong, were faced with constant obstruction by the radicals, whose assembly continued in session and acted as a kind of caucus. Although they eventually (29 December) succeeded in imposing their own nominee as chairman, these tactics aroused exasperation among many rank-and-file delegates, and on two occasions (27 December, 4 January) maximalist resolutions were defeated. On 6 January the radicals countered by declaring that Vikzhel had no further right to exist, which deprived the congress of its *raison d'être*. They finally approved a new union executive, called Vikzhedor, in which the Bolsheviks held a comfortable majority.

3 *Nation-wide Pay Scales.* M. F. Krushinsky was here assuring his egalitarian-minded listeners that the railwaymen did not seek to restore the relatively favoured status, in respect to pay and benefits, which they had previously enjoyed. Nation-wide wage scales (*tarify*), agreed between the employers and employees concerned with the sanction of the PC of Labour, were introduced in certain branches of industry from January 1918 onward. The first such agreement (19 January), applying to metallurgical workers, set a differential between the highest and lowest grade of 1·50:1, which was slightly narrower than that fixed for the railwaymen. The practical effect of these agreements was, however, limited.

4 *Emergency Security Measures.* In December 1917 Petrograd

and Moscow were placed in a state of enhanced security in order to quell riotous disorders among troops and others carried away by the licentious spirit of the times. On the night of 23–4 November a mob of soldiers forced its way into the Winter Palace (which had already suffered at the insurgents' hands) for a carousal in its well-stocked cellars; quarrels broke out which were settled by exchanges of gunfire. A rash of similar incidents followed. Gangs of rowdies entered shops and private homes in search of spirits, and the streets became dangerous after dark. On the night of 3–4 December no less than 69 instances of rioting and looting (and 611 other crimes) were reported (Bonch-Bruyevich, *Na boyevykh postakh*, p. 184). The leisurely approach hitherto taken by the MRC, which itself had been responsible for many arbitrary acts, was clearly inadequate. An army ensign, G. I. Blagonravov, was appointed 'extraordinary military commissar' for Petrograd and a 'committee for struggle against pogroms' set up; the latter body issued an order placing the city under martial law (6 December). All public meetings were banned, a curfew imposed, and rioters warned that they were liable to summary shooting. Within hours machine-guns had been brought into play against one group of looters which refused to disperse. The number of such incidents was thereafter much reduced.

In Moscow, where the problem was rather less acute, emergency measures were imposed for a twelve-day period on 8 December. They included preliminary press censorship, which led the non-Bolshevik newspapers to suspend publication as a protest gesture.

At the time and later the riots were often blamed on 'counter-revolutionary provocateurs', but there is no evidence that any organized political group was involved.

5 *Bolshevik–Left SR Coalition.* The understanding reached on 17 November (see above, p. 339) was at first jeopardized by continuing disagreement over the dissolution of the Petrograd municipal Duma. Although the Left SRs' opposition to this move soon softened, their leaders decided (19 November) to hold out for the commissariats of Interior, Justice, and Military Affairs. Kalegayev, who had participated in the CPC's deliberations since 19 November, had his membership of that body formally

confirmed five days later, but this was not made public. The two parties co-operated fairly smoothly at the second (regular) Congress of Peasant Deputies, although hard-line Bolsheviks were disturbed that the Left SRs joined their moderate comrades in protesting at the decree outlawing the Kadets. Lenin, concerned as ever with the realities of power, was still anxious to bring the coalition into being. He praised the Bolsheviks' prospective partners as 'loyal guardians of the SR doctrine, programme and demands' who had 'remained faithful to the interests of the toiling peasantry', and on 7 December (according to a well-informed recent Soviet source) the CPC decided to concede their request for more portfolios in the cabinet. However, at least three private meetings (8, 9–10, 11 December) had to be held with the Left SR chiefs before the agreement could be finalized.

The bargain gave the Left SRs nominal control of two important commissariats (Agriculture, Justice); the PC of Posts and Telegraphs came under P. P. Proshyan (whom the agreement evidently named as a commissar 'without portfolio'; his appointment followed shortly afterwards: see above, p. 251). V. E. Trutovsky's responsibilities were carved out of the domain of the PC of Internal Affairs; this was now headed by the Bolshevik G. I. Petrovsky, so that V. A. Algasov's title, as given here, was ambiguous. V. A. Karelin's relatively unimportant civilian post was likewise created at the expense of the PC of Education (managed by Lunarcharsky); so too was the curiously named 'State Commissariat for Palaces of the Republic', which was entrusted to another Left SR, Alexandra Izmaylovich; their functions appeared to overlap. Izmaylovich became, after Kollontay, the second woman member of the government. 'Mikhaylov' was evidently a pseudonym for Karelin, who thus held two posts; he was formally the equal of the three Bolshevik joint commissars for military and naval affairs (V. A. Antonov-Ovseyenko, N. V. Krylenko, P. E. Dybenko). In addition to these appointments the PLSR obtained representation in all other PCs as members of their boards (*kollegii*); one of the most significant such posts was that held by P. Alexandrovich as vice-chairman of the Cheka.

Since the CPC was not a conventional cabinet, it means little to state that the Left SRs had seven seats to the Bolsheviks' thirteen (if military representatives are included). Many of their posts were nominal; the status of a PC was ill defined; and no limitation was set on the number of board members. One western historian comments: 'Obviously, Lenin had let none of the real power out of his hands . . . The chief means at [the Left SRs'] disposal for influencing policy was the threat of resignation. They were guests in the house; Lenin held the title' (Radkey, *Sickle*, p. 149). Commenting on the agreement at the time (14 December), S. D. Mstislavsky claimed that the PLSR commissars would preserve their independence and follow party directives; but he added that the coalition might well collapse. Evidently he and his colleagues realized the precariousness of their situation.

6 *Civil Marriage and Divorce.* Although this issue appeared on the CPC's agenda on three occasions (18–20 November), it does not seem to have been discussed there, and the draft decrees were prepared in Stuchka's PC of Justice. They received only cursory attention in the CEC on this occasion, and no record has survived of the two speakers' arguments. The large number of amendments that were submitted suggests that a full-scale debate would have been welcomed, but the Presidium evidently wished to avoid any delay. The two decrees were confirmed by the CPC on 16 December and published respectively three and four days later. The sole amendment to be accepted, that of Kharitonov, was presumably no. 5 and was of purely verbal import; however, at some stage in the private discussions another amendment was passed in the sense of that listed here as no. 8. Clause 1 of the civil marriage decree contained a footnote: 'A church marriage along with the obligatory civil marriage is the private affair of the parties concerned.' This concession to religious belief was withdrawn in September 1918, when the two decrees were incorporated into the RSFSR Code on the Registration of Civil Acts.

In the Imperial era registration of civil acts had been the duty of the ecclesiastical authorities. This reform was therefore, in Marxist eyes, 'bourgeois-democratic' rather than socialist: it brought Russian practice into line with that of most western European states. The principal innovations were the attempt to eliminate legal discrimination against illegitimate children and the provision that marriage partners might choose either the husband's or wife's surname. The divorce decree, however, went further than any measure known elsewhere by introducing what was in effect 'divorce on demand'. Article 1 stated baldly: 'A marriage is dissolved at the request of both partners or even of one of them.' Such a request had merely to be made to the local court or registration office, which had only to satisfy itself that it was genuine; no inquiry was made into the grounds for the request. If the spouse's whereabouts were unknown, the divorce took effect automatically two months after publication of a notice in the press; amendment no. 7, which sought to extend the term to 12 months, relates to this point.

The divorce decree was designed to weaken the family as an institution, which many Marxists viewed as inherently exploitative. Its effects went far beyond formalization of the breakdown of numerous marriages. It encouraged Soviet citizens, especially men, to behave promiscuously and callously, so contributing to the social anarchy that characterized the post-revolutionary epoch. A number of unwanted wives and children were simply abandoned and became a charge upon public authorities unable to care for them; court orders for alimony payments were not rigorously enforced. The regime's policy on these matters was not popular with country-dwellers or women in general, and in the 1920s voices were raised in favour of moderation; however, a substantial change in official attitudes towards the family did not occur until the mid-1930s.

TWENTIETH SESSION

1 *Nationalization of Banks.* Having won control over the State Bank (see above, p. 318), the Bolsheviks were in a position to launch an attack upon private credit institutions. When the matter was discussed in the CPC on 27 November Lenin evidently had some difficulty in getting his way, for it was decided merely to set up a commission under G. L. Pyatakov and N. I. Bukharin to examine questions of basic economic policy. These men shared Larin's and Obolensky's preference for a more moderate approach. At two conferences with the Committee of Commercial Banks (1, 2 December) a compromise was drafted whereby the State Bank was to supply a certain amount of cash

daily to this committee, which would allocate it among its member organizations; the latter were to supply information about the state of their balances and accept certain limitations upon their disbursements. Such an arrangement was in line with earlier Bolshevik thinking, but Lenin now wanted to reduce the private banks to complete subordination by an act of force. He turned to G. Ya. Sokolnikov to draft, with the assistance of pro-maximalist bank employees, a decree nationalizing all credit institutions outright. Meanwhile V. D. Bonch-Bruyevich, the CPC's office manager, had been collecting information on the location of certain bank directors' homes; also privy to the plan were N. I. Podvoysky and (probably) I. V. Stalin.

At dawn on 14 December a number of bank executives were arrested in their homes, whence most of them were taken to Smolny. A few hours later, when the banks had opened for business, two commissars, each with an escort of Lettish riflemen or sailors from the Baltic fleet, entered the premises of twenty-eight Petrograd banks (and their local branches). The staff was assembled and the cashiers forced to hand over the keys to their desks and to the vaults. That evening the CEC was invited to endorse the *fait accompli*. The decree declared banking a state monopoly and merged all existing private banks with the State Bank. Article 6 promised that 'the interests of small depositors will be fully safeguarded'. On 26 January 1918 the private banks' share capital was declared the property of the People's Bank (as the State Bank was now called).

On 15 December the bank employees responded by calling a general strike. The Committee of Commercial Banks demanded the release of their arrested colleagues, which was speedily granted on payment of a 5 million rouble 'deposit' (*zalog*). This concession did not prevent further arrests from taking place. With the aid of the maximalist elements on their staff some banks resumed operations on a much reduced scale. Each transaction had to be verified by a commissar; private account-holders were permitted to withdraw only modest amounts; and cheques drawn by business concerns had to be counter-stamped by the appropriate enterprise committee. The object of these restrictions was not just to prevent 'speculation', as was publicly stated, but to oblige depositors to keep their money in the bank, where its value would rapidly decline as inflation gathered pace. (The new government was printing currency at a rate three times higher than its predecessor.)

Those whose savings were in the form of precious metals were expropriated outright. The law of 14 December provided for the compulsory opening of safe deposits and confiscation of all gold, silver, and foreign currency. This measure was carried out from 23 December onwards with great strictness; but the authorities did not render due account of the valuables they thus acquired.

The bank employees' union was officially closed down (20 December), although in practice it survived in other forms until January 1919, when it was replaced by a new organization under Communist control. Some of its members found employment with the People's Bank.

2 '*Instant Socialism*'. This phrase, if it may be taken literally, suggests that Sokolnikov, like many other Bolshevik leaders at this time, saw nationalization of the banks not just as a short-term expedient designed to weaken private capital and con-solidate 'soviet power', but as a step towards achievement of an ultimate Marxist goal, a moneyless economy. In 1917–18 Sokolnikov stood on the left wing of party opinion, but there-after he moved to the right, and as PC of Finance from 1921 to 1926 he became identified with cautious orthodox policies.

3 *Left SRs' Economic Programme*. V. E. Trutovsky was the leading Left SR spokesman on economic affairs. His use here of the term 'socialization' rather than 'nationalization' reflects the long-standing ideological difference between Populists and Marxists as to the proper role of the state in a socialist society. Traditionally most SRs had expected the revolution to result in a mixed economy, in which the agricultural sector alone would be publicly owned; however, during 1917 the views of the SR Maximalists, who since 1906 had insisted on wholesale socializa-tion, gained support within the party. At the present juncture the Left SRs were too preoccupied with immediate problems to reconsider their fundamental beliefs. The resolution passed at the party's first congress (20–8 November) stressed municipal and co-operative ownership and a monopoly on foreign trade, but said nothing about the fate of large-scale industry. In 1918, when a revision of the party programme was under discussion,

Trutovsky came out in favour of the compulsory syndication and nationalization of industry, whereas Izmaylovich was more critical of bureaucratic management. The debate was never resolved, since the party was driven underground. Those party members who remained politically active during the 'war communism' period generally advocated a decentralization of the economic control mechanism, as indeed did many Marxists.

4   *Financial Aid to Whites.* Selivanov's strictures had some point, since Russian bankers did provide White military leaders with some of the financial assistance they received during these early months—funds which they thought far from adequate to meet their needs. Information on these matters is naturally sparse, particularly in regard to ataman Dutov's forces in distant Orenburg, which presumably had to make do with local resources. In the Don Kaledin obtained access to tax revenues collected in the local branch of the State Bank and agreed to hand over one-quarter of this money to the Volunteer Army. General Alexeyev's account book notes the receipt of 10·5 million roubles from this source between December 1917 and February 1918. This was about two-thirds of his army's total recorded income (November–February) of 15,365,065 roubles. Businessmen in Rostov-on-Don provided 575,000 and sympathizers in Moscow over 260,000 roubles; other sums were received from local sympathizers and 975,000 roubles on loan from 'a special source' ('Denezhnye dokumenty', p. 352). Other White sources put the total amount received from Moscow (to the spring of 1918?) at 500,000 to 800,000 roubles.

In regard to foreign donors, Alexeyev's account book documents three payments by 'the French mission' between 2 and 10 January 1918, amounting to 305,000 roubles. This evidence cannot, however, be corroborated from French sources. Although a French representative, Colonel Hucher, was in Novocherkassk from 9 November, his mission was purely one of reconnaissance. He urged his government to extend financial aid, and Paris decided to appropriate 100 million francs; but the agent bearing the first instalment of 7 million francs, captain Bordes, did not arrive until February 1918, by which time Kaledin's government had fallen. The British government on 1/14 December 1917 assigned £20 million to support pro-Allied

forces in southern Russia, of which half was to go to the south-
east; but owing to communications difficulties 'it can be assumed that no British money ever reached Kaledin or the
Volunteer Army' (Bradley, 'Allies', p. 176)—that is, in the
period under consideration. The United States government
decided to subsidize Kaledin indirectly by loaning money to the
British and French, but nothing came of this plan.

5 *Brest-Litovsk Peace Negotiations, First Phase.* Although Trotsky
here gives an optimistic assessment of the first round in the
peace talks, he must have heard from A. A. Ioffe, head of the
Soviet delegation, that the Central Powers' intentions towards
Russia were a good deal less benevolent than it was politic to
proclaim in public.

When the talks formally commenced on 9 December, Ioffe
set forth a six-point declaration of the principles upon which, in
the Soviet view, a general democratic peace should be based.
Amplifying the 'peace decree' adopted by the Second Congress
of Soviets on 26 October, it called for speedy evacuation of
occupied territories and restoration of independence to nations
which had lost it during the war; those which had not been
independent before 1914 should be free to determine their
future by a referendum, organized in such a way as 'to give full
voting rights to the entire population of the country, including
émigrés and refugees'; minorities should be assured rights of
cultural and 'where possible' administrative autonomy; no
country should be required to pay compensation for war
expenditure; colonial questions should be decided in accordance with the principles outlined in the first five points.

Such a programme, had it been applied, would clearly have
crippled the German and particularly the Austrian empires.
Although phrased in democratic terminology, it could easily be
interpreted in such a way as to serve the ends of Soviet policy
(e.g. by insisting that only a 'revolutionary' expression of the
popular will could be considered 'democratic'), and was thus
quite compatible with the view, enunciated most clearly by
Stalin (see above, p. 350), that the right of national self-determination should be granted only where it served to promote the
cause of international socialism. These dialectical subtleties
were disregarded by the Central Powers' representatives who,

indifferent to the revolutionary implications of Bolshevism, sought to exploit their military advantage to gain strategically valuable territory in Poland and the Baltic region. Nevertheless Baron Richard von Kühlmann, 'political leader' of the German delegation and a skilled diplomatist, endeavoured to conceal these purposes and to give an impression of reasonableness.

The Central Powers' joint reply was delivered by Count Czernin at the second session of the conference on 12 December. It stated that the basic principles contained in the Russian declaration could serve as the basis of a just peace 'without forcible annexations or contributions' between all belligerents. It went on to express certain reservations about the six points, notably in regard to minority rights (an internal matter for each state to decide according to its own constitution) and self-determination for German colonies (impracticable at present). The nuances of this statement were evidently overlooked by the inexperienced Ioffe, who welcomed it as 'an enormous step forward to a general peace'. He apparently did not recognize that the Central Powers' acceptance of the Soviet negotiating position was conditional upon acceptance within the next ten days by the Western Allies of the same principle of renunciation of annexations and indemnities—an eventuality remote in the extreme. The peace offer may best be seen, in the phrase of Chancellor G. von Hertling, as 'a skilful chess move' designed above all to deepen the rift between Russia and her allies and so to complete the Bolsheviks' isolation.

German eastern policy had been clarified on 5 December at a high-level conference at Bad Kreuznach. Overruling Kühlmann's mild objections, the Kaiser had endorsed the military leaders' scheme to establish Kurland and Lithuania as nominally independent states closely bound to Germany and with German troops in indefinite occupation. To appease democratic scruples resolutions expressing assent to such arrangements had been secured from the territories' representative institutions, although their claim to speak for the population was tenuous. The military also hoped by similar means to extend German control to the *unoccupied* Russian Baltic provinces (i.e. to part of Livonia and to Estonia). As for Poland, whose disposition had yet to be agreed between Vienna and Berlin, it was considered that the Bolsheviks would have no choice but to accept the legality of the existing puppet government headed by J. Kucharzewski. Kühlmann also seems to have thought that German designs in the Baltic would encounter no great objection from a government committed to self-determination for all peoples of the former Russian empire. He differed from his colleagues mainly in his concern to ensure that these annexations should be carried through with least damage to Germany's future relations with a (non-Bolshevik) Russia.

The Central Powers' representatives feared that if the Soviet delegation persisted in its over-optimistic misreading of their intentions this might provoke a nationalistic reaction in Russia that would imperil the chances of peace. Accordingly Major-General Max Hoffmann, chief representative of the high command, was commissioned to explain privately that the Central Powers would not regard as 'annexationist' a peace which provided for continued presence of their troops in occupied areas where the population had already expressed its consent. This revelation had a bombshell effect upon Ioffe—or so at least Hoffmann states in his memoirs, which pro-Entente historians have cited with relish; however, since Ioffe had had confidential discussions with both Czernin and Kühlmann on 7 December, before the conference began, he probably had some foreknowledge of his adversaries' intentions. In any case, when the conference resumed a few hours later (17.05 hours, 14 December), the Soviet delegation put forward a formula specifying that all foreign troops should be evacuated from regions where the referendum was to take place. It was added that indigenous forces and 'local militia' should remain and that the interim administration should be 'in the hands of democratically elected representatives of the local population', by which was presumably meant soviet-type bodies: for the text, see above, p. 228. Kühlmann responded with an alternative formula whereby the Russians would explicitly bind themselves to recognize decisions of the existing German-backed representative institutions.

At this point the territorial issue was left suspended while the conference was recessed for ten days, at the Soviet side's request, to enable their government to address a final invitation to the Allies to attend the talks, coupled with a warning that if they failed to do so the responsibility for a separate Russo-German peace would be theirs alone (see above, p. 237). Ioffe and his colleagues left for Petrograd on 15 December. They could take with them the preliminary text of several articles of the future separate peace, which had in the meantime been concerted in the conference's 'political commission'. But agreement on these secondary points depended on a settlement of the all-important territorial problem. This dispute was a confrontation between two abusive interpretations of the democratic principle of national self-determination as applied to the territories which each side hoped to bring under its control—a struggle destined to continue for several more weeks, until the Germans imposed their will by military force.

In this exposition of the Soviet standpoint, designed to allay fears among the CEC delegates of a surrender to German 'imperialism', Trotsky presented the Soviet bargaining position as a good deal stronger than it was. A few days later the government was obliged to strike a different note and to envisage armed resistance to German pressure: see below, p. 393.

6 *Strategic Consistency and Tactical Flexibility.* Trotsky was here enunciating a cardinal principle of Communist operational doctrine. In directing the class struggle the party should undertake a 'scientific' analysis of the correlation of forces, strike a 'correct' balance between short-term and long-term objectives, select carefully the direction of its principal blow, utilize to the full the support of allies and auxiliaries, and adjust the means employed to the ends sought. Whereas its strategic aims were to be determined by basic principles, in the tactical sphere expediency should prevail. To cite an authoritative modern text: 'If political strategy remains fundamentally unchanged during a given historical epoch, tactics change with alterations in the milieu, in concrete historical conditions . . . Tactical flexibility, the capacity to resolve new tasks in the class struggle rapidly and correctly, to direct this struggle skilfully, is an indicator of a political party's maturity' (*Osnovy*, pp. 121–2).

7 This statement suggests that Trotsky, generally seen as the most 'internationalist' of Bolshevik leaders, was by no means indifferent to the 'national-liberation' aspect of the October revolution. He was particularly sensitive to Russia's backwardness *vis-à-vis* western Europe (cf. above, p. 314), for which it

was tempting to hold foreign 'imperialism' responsible, especially when addressing a popular assembly such as this. The 'robber treaty' alluded to is presumably the London declaration of 23 August/5 September 1914.

8   Read: 'and if Wilson grants it to Panama'. Presumably a stenographic error—although Trotsky later recalled having written propaganda material to be broadcast to France in which 'I reminded them of certain forgotten facts in their past history, beginning with the Panama business' (*My Life*, p. 359), meaning the Panama scandal of 1892–3. He may have confused the two issues at the time.

9   *French Trade-Union Conference*. The third national conference of French trade-union federations and labour exchanges—wartime substitutes for regular congresses of the CGT—was held at Clermont-Ferrand on 23–5 December 1917 (N.S.). It was attended by 141 delegates representing 36 trade-union federations, 57 unions and 70 labour exchanges. On the issue of the war the radical elements were divided, which enabled the leadership (L. Jouhaux and others) to secure overwhelming support for a resolution which acclaimed both the Russian revolution and the stand taken by President Wilson. Although the tide was running strongly to the left in the French trade-union movement, the radical leaders made less of an impression than they had at the two preceding conferences (August 1915, December 1916). They were above all concerned to preserve the movement's unity and, although sympathetic to the Bolsheviks, did not share their sectarian zeal.

10   Trotsky's confused reply suggests that B. V. Avilov had hit a raw nerve by drawing attention to Soviet Russia's diplomatic isolation. He appears to mean that, in the event of a separate Russo-German peace, German policy would be more favourable towards Russia than towards the Western powers, and that the resulting tension could be exploited for revolutionary ends. This indeed became a major goal of Soviet policy in the 1920s.

11   *Trotsky and Allied War Aims*. Trotsky's strictures, which echoed a major current Soviet propaganda theme, helped to promote a modification in the Entente powers' attitude on the war aims question which removed much of the grounds for this

charge. The Soviet 'peace decree', publication of the secret treaties, and the armistice on the Eastern front all contributed, along with the military stalemate in the west, to intensify domestic pressures for a change of policy—although these fell far short of Soviet expectations. In Britain Arthur Henderson, who had been forced out of Lloyd George's cabinet on this issue, emerged as leader of a loose grouping of radical politicians, trade unionists and others who favoured an explicit statement of the democratic ideals for which the war was being fought. A draft declaration embodying these principles was endorsed at a rally held on 28 November (N.S.). On the following day there appeared in the *Daily Telegraph* Lord Lansdowne's historic letter advocating a negotiated settlement, the first overt expression of a conciliatory tendency in the highest political circles. Its publication was timed to coincide with the delayed opening of the inter-Allied conference in Paris (at which the Russians were no longer officially represented).

At this meeting Colonel E. M. House for the United States and Lloyd George in turn submitted draft resolutions setting out the Allies' 'non-annexationist' intentions, but these encountered strong opposition from the Italians and the French. The conference did nothing to co-ordinate the diplomatic, as distinct from the military, strategy of the Entente. So far as relations with Russia were concerned, it led to a hardened attitude, since soon afterwards the Supreme War Council which it established resolved to give indirect support to pro-Allied forces in southern Russia, while maintaining informal contacts with the Bolsheviks.

Nevertheless both Lloyd George and President Woodrow Wilson realized that the Central Powers were making a favourable impression on Russian and world opinion by their apparently conciliatory attitude at Brest-Litovsk. They were anxious to prevent the Russians from coming to look upon the Germans as their deliverers and believed that a solemn public statement of purpose would constitute an effective reply to the Bolsheviks' peace propaganda, while simultaneously encouraging moderate opposition forces within Germany. In an address to the Trades Union Congress on 5 January 1918 (N.S.) Lloyd George hinted at the catastrophe that would befall Russia if she signed a separate peace and spoke of 'fighting to the end' alongside Russian democracy—presumably after overthrow of the Bolsheviks, whom he did not mention. He made no specific suggestions about eastern European territorial problems, apart from a commitment to Polish independence. There was little in the speech to hearten either the war-weary peoples of the former Russian empire or the regimes that claimed to represent them, and the Bolsheviks could plausibly construe it as a threat to work towards a peace at their expense; nevertheless it did mark a considerable step forward in British official thinking.

Far more influential was President Wilson's address to Congress delivered three days later (the 'Fourteen Points' speech). In the preamble he praised both the Russian people *and their leaders* for resisting the Central Powers' 'unjust demands' at Brest-Litovsk and promised American friendship and aid. The implication was that the United States might co-operate even with the Bolshevik government provided that it resisted German pressure energetically. The Fourteen Points included some basic principles which were later to underlie the post-war international order, and statements on policy objectives in regard to specific territorial problems. Point VI, dealing with Russia, provided for evacuation of enemy forces and independent determination of the country's future; but it was couched in vague and confused terms. Wilson may be faulted for failing to come to grips with Bolshevism, but his speech also contained an element of political calculation and to some extent attained its purpose. It made a favourable impression not only upon ordinary Russians (among whom three and a half million copies were distributed by American agencies with the Soviet authorities' consent) but also upon Lenin. He appreciated that the prospect of American support could strengthen the Russian bargaining position at Brest-Litovsk, and at once had the text wired to Trotsky. Nevertheless he did not revise in the slightest his hostility towards Wilson's 'bourgeois pacifism'. The president's proposals for a League of Nations, peaceful arbitration of disputes and world disarmament must have appeared to him at best Utopian and at worst nefarious. Soviet commentators have made much of President Wilson's alleged 'hypocrisy' in proffering friendship to the Russian people while simultaneously extending covert support to the anti-Bolsheviks, but in his mind there was no necessary contradiction.

The historical significance of Trotsky's challenge is thus two-fold. In the short term it helped to bring about a leftward shift in Allied policy, which in turn was reflected (albeit imperfectly) in the 1918–19 peace settlement. In the long term it foreshadowed the ideological rivalry between the USSR and the USA, each 'super-power' having its own concept of a global order.

12   *The CPC and the Central Rada.* The CPC was now better prepared than it had been six days earlier (see above, p. 364) to face a debate in the CEC on Ukrainian affairs, since in the interim its position *vis-à-vis* the Rada had significantly improved. The Bolshevik leaders dealt firmly with an effort at mediation by a Ukrainian soldiers' organization in Petrograd, the 'Ukrainian staff of the Petrograd regional military Rada'. After consulting with the Central Rada in Kiev this body put forward five conditions for an agreement: the CPC was to pledge itself to recognize the Ukrainian People's Republic and to abstain from interference in its affairs, to proceed with re-patriation of Ukrainian troops, to admit Rada representatives to the Brest-Litovsk peace talks, and to regulate outstanding economic problems. Reasonable as these terms might seem, the CPC was in no mood to consider them seriously. Not only did it reject the offer, stating that agreement was possible only if the Rada formally renounced its (alleged) aid to Kaledin's forces: it also sent a posse of Red guards to arrest the mediators (7–8 December). Ukrainian spokesmen in Petrograd protested against these reprisals to the All-Russian Congress of Peasant Deputies, which thereupon attempted a mediation mission itself. A delegation led by P. P. Proshyan, one of the putative Left SR people's commissars, was sent to Kiev. But these men were no match for Stalin, who gave private assurances that the arrested men would be released as soon as their innocence was established but simultaneously drew up a statement reiterating the CPC's grievances against the Rada. Entitled 'Reply to Ukrainian Comrades in the Rear and at the Front' and published in *Pravda* on 13 December, its terms were similar to those he was to use the next day before the CEC.

Meanwhile in the Ukraine the Bolsheviks and other radical elements who had withdrawn from the All-Ukrainian Congress of Soviets after this had come under Ukrainian autonomist control left Kiev for the relative sanctuary of Kharkov (7–8 December). Here they expected the political climate to be more favourable to their cause: the city was more industrialized and had a large Russian element in the population. It was ruled by a loose coalition of left-wing groups in which the Bolsheviks had a strong but not dominant position. Their leaders, notably F. A. Sergeyev, held that premature action for partisan ends would jeopardize this alliance, essential to avert the threat posed by Kaledin's forces to the east. But on 8 December effective power in Kharkov passed into the hands of the Bolsheviks, who were fortified by the arrival from Petrograd of a detachment of troops and Red guards on its way to fight Kaledin.

A congress of soviets from the Donets and Krivoy Rog region (i.e. the eastern part of the Ukraine) was due to open at Kharkov on 9 December. The delegates to this gathering generally shared Sergeyev's apprehensions. They also manifested regionalist tendencies, preferring an autonomous status within a *Russian* Soviet republic to the prospect of incorporation into a largely agrarian Ukraine ruled from Kiev; national antipathies were involved here as well. The autonomy scheme had previously been endorsed by the Bolshevik Central Committee in Petrograd, which hoped thereby to undercut the Central Rada's authority; it was, however, fiercely opposed by the Bolsheviks who now arrived in the delegates' midst from Kiev. The 'Kievans', probably between 100 and 150 strong (lower figures are encountered), insisted that they should be allowed to merge forces with the Kharkov congress (i.e. should assume its direction); the joint organ was then to claim sovereign power in all the Ukraine and elect an executive which would provide an alternative focus of mass loyalties to the 'bourgeois' Rada in Kiev. To many of the delegates assembled in the Kharkov congress such a course seemed risky: they could not speak for the entire Ukraine since there were scarcely any peasant representatives among them, and a campaign against the Rada would divert attention from the far more urgent struggle against Kaledin. Nevertheless after feverish debates these hesitations were overcome (9 December). The final vote on this issue was 43:11; since 77 delegates to the Donets–Krivoy Rog congress had full voting rights, 23 men must have absented themselves or abstained.

This was the dubious origin of the First All-Ukrainian Congress of Soviets (11–12 December), which sanctioned the establishment of a 41-man Central Executive Committee of Soviets of the Ukraine (CECU), a counterpart to the CEC in Petrograd. On 17 December there was also established a 'People's Secretariat', or government, modelled on the CPC. This government, headed (according to one near-contemporary source) by E. G. Medvedev, a Left SR, was a compromise between the 'Kievans' and the Bolsheviks of Kharkov; most of its members regarded themselves as Russians rather than Ukrainians. CECU really existed only on paper: in practice the government simply submitted a few major decisions to its Presidium for endorsement. It lost no time in issuing a number of edicts similar to those promulgated by the CPC, which immediately recognized it as the sole legitimate authority in the Ukraine. Among these acts was one deposing the Rada government in Kiev. Although initially far weaker than its adversary, within a few weeks the People's Secretariat had managed to establish a tenuous hold over much of the Ukraine; crucial in this success was the presence of Russian troops. It moved first to Yekaterinoslav and then, on 30 January 1918, to Kiev, shortly after that city had been taken by the Reds after a bitter ten-day battle. Two weeks later it was again forced to flee, whereupon Kiev was occupied by troops of the Central Powers (3 March).

13 *Siberia, Turkestan, and Belorussia.* These centres of 'soviet power' existed for some time in virtual isolation from Petrograd; in consequence the local leaders often took a more inflexible line towards non-Russian elements than the Bolshevik leaders, especially Lenin, thought desirable.

In Siberia a soviet executive body known as Tsentrosibir was set up by the first All-Siberian congress of soviets (16–23 October). Its activities were confined to propaganda, for Irkutsk, the city where it was situated, did not come under Bolshevik control until the latter half of December; even then power was assumed, not by Tsentrosibir as an all-Siberian agency, but by the local soviet and a regional (*okrug*) bureau. This testified to the strength of localist sentiment, as did the decision by the Siberian CPC, formed in February 1918, not to recognize the peace of Brest-Litovsk.

In Belorussia there existed from November onward a regional soviet executive, in which soldiers predominated, and a 'CPC of the Western Region and the Front', a government whose shadowy claim to represent the Belorussian population was strongly contested by local civilian politicians. The Belorussian Central Rada, set up in July 1917, stood for self-determination, democracy and agrarian reform on the PSR model. Its leaders convoked a National Congress at Minsk for 15 December, which was attended by 1872 delegates, 716 of them from the army. The congress was willing to recognize the Soviet government in Petrograd but not its local equivalent, since the Belorussian leaders now sought independence. This caused the Bolsheviks, led by N. I. Krivoshein of the Minsk garrison, to disperse the congress by force (17–18 December), on the pretext that the organizers had not obtained prior approval from the local soviet authorities. The CPC of the Western Region and the Front lasted until 4 March 1918, when Belorussia came under German occupation. The nationalist leaders then re-emerged and declared their country independent (25 March), but were too weak to withstand opposition by the two major powers on their flanks.

In Central Asia the non-Russians were numerically far stronger but their national movement was still in an embryonic stage. The Bolsheviks' strength was concentrated in Tashkent, which they seized after a four-day battle on 1 November. The CPC of Turkestan (Turksovnarkom) was established by the third regional (*kray*) congress of soviets, held in Tashkent from 15 to 22 November. It had 15 members, of whom 7 were Bolsheviks and 8 Left SRs; a noteworthy feature was the absence of any native members. To this omission the Muslims responded by setting up a government of their own at Kokand in December. This consisted of a 'people's council' (*halk şurasi*) and an executive headed by M. Tinishbayoglu. It was forcibly deposed in February 1918 when Red forces stormed and largely destroyed the town of Kokand, but the CPC of Turkestan still faced a long struggle before its power became a reality in the region.

14 *The Central Rada and the French Mission.* The telegram, dated 28 November, was published the next day in *Pravda* as an ap-

pendix to an article by Stalin entitled 'What is the Rada?'. No particulars were given by whom or to whom it was sent. From internal evidence the originator was a member of the General Secretariat, who was relaying to some subordinate(s) a French appreciation of the local situation which may or may not have accorded with his own views; he had evidently just seen a French representative (probably General Tabouis: see below). The telegram stated that the French military mission in Romania had been instructed to maintain the closest relations with the Rada and to support it by every means in the hope of maintaining 'the appearance of an [Eastern] front' until the spring, when conditions would be more favourable to the Allies. The 'ukrainized' units on the South-western and Romanian fronts were thought capable of undertaking this task. Some French officers had been sent to the Don on a 'special mission' to ask the Cossack authorities to dispatch supplies of coal and wheat to the Romanian and South-western fronts. The French took the view that the Romanian armistice was due to intrigue by pro-German elements. Finally, the British were said to have received instructions to withdraw their medical detachments from the Ukraine.

The interception of this telegram was an embarrassment to the Rada, since it could be interpreted as evidence that it was in league with Kaledin and the Allies. The relationship between the parties was actually much more equivocal, and the situation had evolved since the telegram had been dispatched. Romania's withdrawal from the war (see above, p. 344) made plans for a pro-Allied *bloc* in southern Russia quite unrealistic; nor had there ever been any real prospect of effective collaboration between the Ukrainians and the Don cossacks. The final blow to the scheme was the Rada's decision to seek peace with the Central Powers. Proponents of Allied intervention could now look only to the Don cossacks and to the feeble White forces sheltering under their protection.

France was the Allied power most actively interested in this theatre, but her policy was inconsistent. The Quai d'Orsay and French diplomats in Petrograd wanted to maintain Russia's territorial integrity, whereas the military mission in Romania, under General Berthelot, was more sympathetic to Ukrainian strivings for autonomy. Shortly after the Rada assumed power a liaison officer was sent from Jassy to Kiev, and later all French officers in the Ukraine were placed under Berthelot's authority. The senior French officer in Kiev was General Tabouis, formerly attached to South-western front headquarters. Although under instructions not to interfere in local politics, he was actually allowed considerable discretion, especially once the Allied military missions had been forced out of GHQ; he could not be controlled from Petrograd.

On 18 November Tabouis saw Petlyura and A. Shulgin (O. Shulhyn), secretary for External Affairs in the Rada government, and offered French moral and material assistance, including a large loan. The Ukrainian socialist politicians were loath to become dependent on a foreign power and asked France first to grant the Ukraine formal recognition; but this no Allied government could do. After the CPC's ultimatum of 4 December Tabouis's hopes revived; the next day he saw the premier, Vinnichenko, and suggested that talks on an aid programme be initiated forthwith, yet still the Ukrainians dragged their feet. By an Anglo-French convention of 10/23 December the Ukraine was allocated to the French sphere of influence. Simultaneously the Supreme Allied War Council resolved to 'keep in touch' with local governments. At a suggestion from Jassy Tabouis was appointed 'Commissioner-General' in the Ukraine (16 December) and on the twenty-second he presented his credentials. This amounted to *de facto* recognition, although neither he nor the French government would refer to the Ukrainian People's Republic by its official title. Nothing much came of the Entente's aid offers, and although some money may have been transferred through private channels, it cannot be said that the Rada was dependent upon such support.

15 *Central Rada's Supply Policy.* The incident is not discussed in Kovalivs'kyi's memoirs; nor do other published sources throw light upon the movement of goods at this time between the territories controlled by the Rada and the CPC. This order, if indeed it was given in these terms, may have been intended to embarrass the CPC as well as to maintain reserves of scarce foodstuffs in the Ukraine, which was also experiencing a lack of currency (normally supplied by the State Bank in Petrograd). This led the General Secretariat to permit Treasury loan certifi-

cates to circulate in lieu of cash, and later to issue its own currency unit, the *karbovanets*.

TWENTY-FIRST SESSION

1 *Brest-Litovsk Peace Negotiations, First Phase.* This session of the CEC assumed the form of a mass meeting whose main purpose was to whip up popular support for the Soviet negotiators' stand against German territorial demands once the peace conference resumed on 27 December. The American journalist Edgar Sisson, who attended the meeting, noted that the Bolsheviks did not want the soldiers' natural indignation to develop into a mood of patriotic defiance, which would have cast doubt on the wisdom of the effort to conclude a separate peace (*One Hundred Red Days*, p. 191).

Five days earlier Trotsky had addressed the CEC on this subject in his capacity as PC of Foreign Affairs (see above, p. 212), but he had not as yet been to Brest-Litovsk; a report by the senior Bolshevik member of the delegation could be expected to make a greater impact. As an orator Kamenev was not in Trotsky's class, yet he was an effective speaker and adopted the appropriate tone of outraged innocence. The decision to convoke this session was probably taken by the CPC on 15 or 16 November, after it had heard the returning delegates' account of the first phase of the talks. G. F. Kennan (*Russia Leaves the War*, p. 224) notes that the Bolshevik-controlled press, which had at first hailed the Central Powers' reply as a Soviet victory, said nothing about the German menace until 17 December. On that day *Pravda* published side by side Trotsky's invitation to the Allied governments to join the talks (in which the Germans were over-optimistically said to be willing to withdraw from *all* occupied territory, in the west as in the east) and an editorial whose author was clearly cognizant of German territorial ambitions in Poland and the Baltic: the fate of these territories, it declared, would be decided by 'the popular masses'.

A massive demonstration was held in Petrograd on 17 December. This had originally been cast as a celebration of the success supposedly achieved at Brest-Litovsk, but was now given the character of a military parade. One of its objects was to show the German diplomats who had arrived in the capital (see be-

low, n. 10) that Russia was determined to resist any aggression;
another was to raise morale among soldiers in the Petrograd
garrison and to prepare them psychologically for a possible
resumption of hostilities. The same purpose was served by the
interventions at this CEC session by men from the front, although according to Sisson their remarks were often less belli-
cose in tone than would appear from the press reports (and
Prot.), which played down their evocative descriptions of the
soldiers' hardships.

2 Kamenev's statement is inaccurate. Ioffe's response to the
Central Powers' declaration was given immediately, not after
three hours; in it he noted certain shortcomings of that statement, but his general tone was favourable. He adopted a far
more critical stance two days later, after he had been appraised
informally of the Germans' intentions: see above, p. 382.

3 *Russo-German Commercial Relations.* The Russo-German commercial convention of 1904, concluded at a time when Russia
badly needed German goodwill, was generally condemned by
public opinion on the grounds that the tariff rates conferred
unfair advantages on Germany, which in 1914 supplied about
half Russia's imports. Some critics even spoke of a semi-colonial
relationship, although Russia's poor competitive position was
basically due to her state of under-development.

It was clearly in Germany's interest to try to restore this
relationship once the war ended. On 13 December the Brest-
Litovsk negotiators agreed that all pre-war treaties should re-
cover force in so far as they were not at variance with changed
conditions. Kühlmann went on to propose an interim commercial agreement based on application of the 'most-favoured
nation' principle; such an agreement could accommodate the
Soviet desire for state regulation of international trade.

These exchanges paved the way for more detailed discussion
in committee (6–15 January) of a German draft treaty. Some
progress was made, but these talks were soon overtaken by
events: the breakdown of the conference and the German military offensive. The ultimatum of 21 February incorporated
what was in effect a demand for a return to the 1904 convention. This had already been conceded by the Ukrainian Rada
in the treaty which it signed on 27 January/9 February 1918.

Similar provisions were now presented to the Russians as article 7 of the Brest-Litovsk treaty, signed on 3 March. The interim agreement was now to last until the end of 1919 at the earliest, and to be followed by a long-term treaty; 'most-favoured nation' provisions (with exemption clauses narrowly defined) were to continue at least until 1925; Russia was not to impose duties on timber or ores exported to Germany; finally, the pre-war tariff rates were to apply, although these had of course been outdated by inflation.

In practice these terms were less onerous than many Russians (or Allied observers) expected. There was no massive influx of competitive German goods which, had they been available, could only have benefited the hard-pressed Russian consumer. Russia did suffer economically from the treaty in other respects (notably by loss of control over the Ukraine), but its apparent threat to her vital interests could be evaded without much difficulty: see below, n. 4.

4   *Soviet Foreign Trade Policy.* In the light of later Soviet history it is ironic that Kamenev should have based his justification of the delegation's conduct upon its defence of socialist principles, not of Russia's economic interests; the latter argument would not have been ideologically acceptable at this time.

The Bolsheviks were only feeling their way towards a coherent doctrine in this field. Lenin considered state regulation of foreign trade to be essential, and this was endorsed by the CPC on 27 November when it decided to establish the Supreme Economic Council. But the new government lacked the necessary apparatus to enforce such a monopoly, and those responsible (especially M. G. Broński and G. I. Lomov-Oppokov) did little more than grant licences to individual applicants on an *ad hoc* basis. Foreign trade all but ceased in 1918 owing to the Allied blockade, and although the Brest-Litovsk treaty restored commercial ties with the Central Powers exchanges were on a very limited scale.

Soviet fear of German penetration of the Russian economy, though understandable, was greatly exaggerated. The treaty expressly allowed for relations between state monopolies in one country and private enterprises in the other, and reserved to *governments* the right to determine the conditions in which foreign-owned companies should be permitted to operate. These provisions gave the Soviet authorities the opportunity to pass measures to safeguard Russian enterprises from possible German encroachment, notably by a decree of 28 June 1918 nationalizing several hundred concerns in which German capital was involved. The supplementary agreements of 27 August brought important alleviations of the burdens imposed by the Brest-Litovsk treaty, which was unilaterally denounced on 13 November after Germany's collapse.

5 *'Mitteleuropa.'* This term was used very loosely by both proponents and opponents to denote a concept first popularized in 1915 by the German political writer (and Progressive deputy) Friedrich Naumann. Impressed by the Reich's military successes, he had suggested that the Central Powers' war aim should be the political and economic integration under their hegemony of various territories, some but not all located in central Europe (*Mitteleuropa*). Only such a 'super-state' (*Oberstaat*), he contended, could compete effectively with Russia, America, and the British Empire in the struggle for world power that was expected to continue after the war's end. It could provide capital and modern skills *inter alia* to develop Russia's rich natural resources, 'so giving the Russian masses form and content'. The boundaries of *Mitteleuropa* were not clearly defined, but some advocates of the scheme hoped to include Poland, the Baltic provinces, and other parts of the Russian empire. By 1917 proponents of this eastern orientation had prevailed over those who had initially looked rather to southeastern Europe, and strictly speaking the term *Mitteleuropa* was no longer applicable to them. Opponents of German expansion, in Russia as elsewhere, did not distinguish carefully between the several tendencies in this movement and also exaggerated its impact upon official German policy. However, the general drift of opinion was certainly towards a more egotistical and intransigent interpretation of the concept, which at first had had some liberal and beneficent features.

6 Kamenev here comes close to repeating an earlier indiscretion (see above, p. 350) by suggesting that the Bolsheviks should help the peoples of Poland, Lithuania, and Latvia to determine their future in such a way that they would be ab-

sorbed within the Soviet state, whose border would thus be coterminous with 'the limits within which the Russian revolution expands', as he put it. He omitted to consider that these peoples might choose independence from both Germany and Russia.

7 In the text of this proposal as submitted by Ioffe on 14 December this noun occurs in the singular, referring to the Russian army alone. If the plural rendering here is not just an oversight, it may indicate that the Soviet government hoped to include a provision for mutual demobilization in the terms of the peace treaty.

8 *Liebknecht's Release.* This forecast came to pass, but only in an indirect manner. In the autumn of 1918, as revolutionary pressures in Germany mounted, Chancellor Max von Baden responded favourably to a suggestion by Philip Scheidemann, the SPD leader, that Liebknecht be released before expiry of his 49-month jail term, as a gesture of appeasement to the left-wing socialists. On 23 October, after having served 25 months of his sentence by the Higher Military Court, Liebknecht was allowed to leave the prison at Luckau. He proceeded to Berlin, where he played a leading role in the Spartakus League and helped to found the German Communist party (KPD) at the end of December. Shortly afterwards—against his better judgement, as it seems—he became involved in an insurrectionary bid for power which led to his death, at the hands of troops of the Guards cavalry division, on 15 January 1919.

9 *First All-Russian Naval Congress.* Organized by the Naval Revolutionary Committee (see above, p. 272), this congress was held in Petrograd from 18 to 25 November. It was attended by 190 delegates, of whom 82 and 65 came from the Baltic and Black Sea fleets respectively; 116 men registered as Bolsheviks. Most had been present at the Second Congress of Soviets and their support for the new regime was not in doubt. A. V. Baranov, a welder on the training-ship *Argun*, had been deputy chairman of Tsentrobalt and his election as chairman of this gathering was unopposed. The congress was addressed by, *inter alia*, Trotsky and Lenin (18, 22 November) and adopted by an overwhelming majority (160 votes to 2, with 28 abstentions) a resolution endorsing the government's policy. It also approved

a scheme whereby the Naval ministry was to be run by a five-man 'collegium', responsible to the CEC; the Admiralty Council was to be replaced by a consultative organ familiarly known as 'the council of 20', consisting of 20 CEC members (13 Bolsheviks, 7 others) who constituted its 'Naval section'. The congress drew up an instruction for its deputies, whom it evidently intended to keep under its constant control, but this aim proved difficult to achieve.

10   *Talks on Repatriation of Prisoners and Internees.* On 4 December *Pravda* reported that an annex to the armistice agreement provided for the speedy establishment in Petrograd of a mixed commission of representatives from the eastern belligerent powers to settle certain technical questions such as repatriating prisoners of war and internees, restoring communications and trading ties, and enforcing the cessation of hostilities at sea. The news aroused intense interest in pro-Allied circles in the capital: some conservatives and liberals believed that the Bolsheviks were in collusion with the Germans, others that the Germans might come to their own rescue. Fly-sheets were distributed to the effect that two German army corps would intervene against the Bolsheviks. However, the moderate press (e.g. the socialist daily *Den'*) published accurate reports about the composition and functions of the mission. The first officials to arrive (14 December) were the naval experts under Freiherr Walter von Keyserlingk; they were soon followed by the civilians whose chief, Count Wilhelm von Mirbach, was later to serve as German ambassador to Soviet Russia. The talks proceeded discreetly and eventuated in an agreement on repatriation of prisoners and internees which was incorporated into the Brest-Litovsk treaty.

11   *Germany and the Russian Right.* The identity of this alleged would-be negotiator is not known; in any case his attitude was unrepresentative of Constituent Assembly supporters. It was only after the dissolution of this body that some conservative and liberal members of the so-called 'Right Centre', a loose grouping of anti-Bolshevik politicians in Moscow, began seriously to consider co-operation with the Germans as a lesser evil than continued Bolshevik rule. Later in 1918 a similar attitude was taken by the Kadet leader P. N. Milyukov, but his insis-

tence on preservation of Russia's territorial integrity prevented any agreement.

12 *Trotsky on the Need for Organization.* Trotsky is here expressing an attitude as yet uncommon among Bolshevik leaders, who were still swayed by the revolution's libertarian ideals. He himself was to take the supply problem in hand six weeks later when he was appointed chairman of an extraordinary inter-departmental commission on food supply (Chokprod). His organizational work in this sphere was soon overshadowed by much more important duties as PC of War; in establishing the Red Army, he took as his slogan: 'Work, discipline, and order will save the Soviet republic.'

13 *The Mensheviks and the CEC; Demobilization Congress.* V. N. Rozanov and Henryk Erlich (G. M. Erlikh), respectively a Menshevik and a (Jewish) Bundist, were both among the six delegates dispatched by the CEC of first convocation to attend the projected international socialist conference in Stockholm (see above, p. 327).

After the October insurrection neither the orthodox Mensheviks nor Martov's Menshevik Internationalists took part in the affairs of the CEC, whose legality they contested, although in 1918 the latter group modified its stand. Thus this unheralded intervention from the floor came as a shock to the maximalist delegates, not least to chairman Sverdlov. There was of course no 'constitutional' reason why the speaker should have been prevented from finishing his remarks. This A. Ioffe should not be confused with his better-known namesake, the Bolshevik representative at Brest-Litovsk (and later a prominent supporter of Trotsky). A Menshevik in uniform, he was active politically at Lepel (Vitebsk province); on 24 November he was arrested for anti-Bolshevik agitation and forced to march 50 miles under escort to Polotsk, where the MRC of the IIIrd Army set him at liberty. At their extraordinary congress in Petrograd the Mensheviks elected him a member of their party's central electoral committee (2 December).

The All-Army Demobilization Congress, members of which were invited to attend this session of the CEC, was held in Petrograd from 15 December to 3 January 1918. At its peak it had 272 delegates from various army organizations, about half of whom were Bolsheviks. It took practical steps to effect de-mobilization and approved various Bolshevik measures, including formation of the nucleus of a new Red Army (28 December). This latter step was decided upon in part because delegates to the congress, in response to a questionnaire submitted by Lenin, reported that the armed forces were in no state to resist a German offensive.

TWENTY-SECOND SESSION

1   *Recognition of Finnish Independence.* The Svinhufvud government was under considerable pressure from Finnish Social-Democratic leaders to enter into direct negotiations with the CPC over the country's national independence. The assurances received from Lenin on 25 November (see above, p. 350) were confirmed at another interview on 14 December. On this occasion the Finnish delegates (K. Manner, E. Gylling, and K. Wiik) handed over an official letter in which they asked the Bolshevik Central Committee to support their demand for independence. This contained an assurance that the Finnish Social Democrats considered that 'the Finnish proletariat must carry on the fight to complete victory by its own efforts, not permitting national disputes to obstruct the class struggle'; Soviet consent, they added, would give the lie to 'bourgeois' allegations that Soviet Russia was imperialistic and hostile to Finnish national aspirations.

Svinhufvud had as yet received no favourable response from the Western Powers to his approaches; he was also becoming increasingly concerned at the activities of the Red guards and their close ties with the revolutionary-minded Russian troops in the country. Accordingly he decided that he had no option but to turn directly to the Soviets. On 15 December two senior officials with experience of Russo-Finnish relations, C. Enckell and K. Idman, went to Petrograd and were received by Lenin, who stated that a direct request for recognition addressed to the CPC would undoubtedly be granted. On the following day Svinhufvud, armed with an official document in this sense from the Senate, joined the two men. The Soviet leaders insisted that this document be reworded to include explicit mention of the CPC, which could be interpreted as a recognition of its legitimacy. On the evening of 18–31 December they were summoned to Smolny, where the CPC was in session, and after a long New Year's Eve vigil in the unheated building were rewarded by the appearance of V. D. Bonch-Bruyevich bearing the document of which the text is reproduced here.

Confirmation by the CEC was of course a mere formality. It was not in the Bolsheviks' interest to permit any debate, lest dissenters ask embarrassing questions about their ultimate intentions, the apparent inconsistency in the treatment of Finland and the Ukraine, or the role played in the affair by German pressure. In the brief remarks he was permitted to make Moiseyev confined himself to the point that the CPC had no popular mandate to conclude an agreement of such import; although true, this was somewhat academic in the light of the repressive measures which the Bolsheviks were known to be preparing in regard to the Constituent Assembly.

That the grant of independence was intended to be merely nominal is evident from Stalin's last sentence. This was undoubtedly more than a mere ritual statement; it expressed his belief that 'proletarian revolution' in Finland was imminent and that Soviet aid would help to ensure its success. Both the Red and White forces in that country were now readying themselves for civil war. The hostilities that broke out in earnest on the night of 14–15 January 1918 resulted in a White victory. One reason for this was that, owing to the breakdown of the Brest-Litovsk talks and the ensuing German advance into Russia (and then to the terms of the peace treaty), Soviet Russia was obliged to withdraw the bulk of her troops from Finland, whereas in the final stages of the war the White Finns received substantial military aid from Germany. A more profound reason lay in the attitude of the Finnish Social-Democratic leaders. In accusing them here of cowardice Stalin was wide of the mark. The reasons for their conduct must be sought in the western European orientation of their party and of the Finnish labour movement, and beyond that in the differences between Russian and Finnish political culture.

2 *Preparations for the Constituent Assembly.* The outlawing of the Kadets on 28 November (see above, p. 354) made it abundantly clear that the Bolsheviks were determined to deal firmly with

the Constituent Assembly, so that both its supporters and its adversaries prepared for a showdown. As elections in the more distant provinces were completed, more and more deputies made their way to Petrograd. By 5 December the number had passed 200 and by 15 December had risen to 400, the figure set by the CPC as the quorum. However, by the latter date only 73 deputies had registered their presence with Uritsky's team, which had taken over from the dissolved Electoral Commission. Most of the remainder refused to have anything to do with a body they considered illegal, and they were fortified in this stand by leaders of the various democratic parties. Both the moderates and maximalists sought to keep 'their' deputies occupied, e.g. by addressing meetings, until the assembly opened.

The PSR deputies were soon obliged to abandon their efforts to hold regular gatherings in the Tauride Palace, access to which was now controlled more closely by Red guardsmen loyal to Uritsky. Much time was spent discussing legislative proposals to be placed before the assembly; these were to include resolutions on peace, land reform, and workers' control—the main planks in the programme of 'revolutionary democracy' which the Bolsheviks were now implementing in their own way. Early in December 109 PSR deputies issued a statement apprising the public of their intentions in the hope of consolidating popular support for the assembly, so that any act of force against it would unleash a wave of indignation which might even bring down the Bolshevik regime. Meanwhile some PSR leaders attempted, through the party's Military Commission, to build up a small body of troops and civilians capable of turning this mood to the moderates' advantage.

Meanwhile the Bolshevik leaders were divided as to their tactics; the Central Committee (CC) discussed the question on 29 November without coming to a clear decision. A bureau was set up to guide the actions of the Bolshevik caucus ('fraction') of assembly deputies. Evidently under pressure from below, this agency took a 'soft' line, even requesting the CC to call a special party conference or congress to thrash out policy in this matter. The bureau's proceedings have not been published. It included Kamenev, Rykov, Ryazanov, Larin, Milyutin, and Nogin—all right-wingers who had previously opposed the tendency towards dictatorship (see above, pp. 77, 85); Stalin was also a member, and it has been suggested that he, too, may have vacillated, but the evidence on this point is inconclusive (Gorodetsky, *Rozhdenie*, p. 442). In any case Lenin reacted decisively. When the CC met on 11 December, with this question the only item on its agenda, he proposed that the bureau be dissolved and that the party's attitude to the Constituent Assembly be set forth in the form of theses; the Bolshevik deputies were to be reminded that they were under the CC's authority and rules were to be drawn up for their future guidance. The CC did not endorse this proposal unreservedly (it stated that the bureau was to be 're-elected'), but it commissioned Sokolnikov and Bukharin 'to work in the caucus' and convened a meeting of the bureau at which the CC was to report. No more was heard of the bureau, and on 12 December the Bolshevik caucus duly endorsed Lenin's 'Theses on the Constituent Assembly', which were published on the fourteenth.

This lengthy (19 articles) document in essence made two points: (a) the elections had not properly expressed the voters' will, since the Left SRs had shared a common list with their former party comrades and 'the overwhelming majority of the people could not then appreciate the whole scope and significance of the October . . . revolution'; (b) the civil war had so 'sharpened the class struggle' that the country's problems could be solved only by 'merciless military suppression of counter-revolutionaries, not 'by formal democratic means'. 'Any attempt, direct or indirect, to consider the question of the Constituent Assembly from a formal legalistic viewpoint . . . is a betrayal of the proletarian cause' (Lenin, *PSS*, xxxv.166). This amounted to a warning that the assembly would be forcibly broken up unless it complied absolutely with the Bolsheviks' demands. Uritsky made this quite plain; addressing the Petrograd party committee on 12 December, he recommended flexible tactics so that the party should retain the initiative: 'Shall we dissolve [the assembly]? Yes, perhaps. Everything depends on the circumstances' (*Pervy legal'ny*, p. 373).

On the night of 16–17 December N. D. Avksentyev, a prominent PSR deputy and former Provisional Government minister, was arrested by the Cheka and taken to the Peter and Paul fortress. Also apprehended at this time were twenty-four members of the Union for the Defence of the Constituent Assembly, some of whom were deputies; orders had been issued (in secret, but the fact became known) for the arrest of several other moderate leaders, including Chernov and Tsereteli. Having thus prepared the ground, the CPC decided, on 20 December, that it was safe to fix a date for the assembly to open.

That day *Pravda* carried an article signed 'E.P.' (E. A. Preobrazhensky?) entitled 'Speculation on the Constituent Assembly' which complained that some 'genuine democrats' and participants in the October insurrection had not yet shaken off their 'constitutional illusions'. This was directed against those Left SRs (and indeed Bolsheviks) who still held that the assembly should at least be given a chance 'to pass a test before the people'; if it failed that test, the radical deputies should withdraw, form a 'revolutionary convention' which would attract greater popular support, and then merge with the Third Congress of Soviets. In this way that body would inherit the prestige and legitimacy of the Constituent Assembly. Lenin, however, preferred a tactic which would rule out temporary coexistence of the two representative institutions.

3 *Third Congress of Soviets.* Zinoviev was an advocate of the tactical line just described. It was clearly politic to convene another soviet congress ahead of schedule, whether or not it were to incorporate the 'rump' of the Constituent Assembly. Should more forceful methods be employed against the latter, the soviet body could simply step into its shoes.

In the event the Third Congress of Soviets opened two days later than the date projected here (and the congress of peasant deputies two days earlier). The merger of these two gatherings on 13 January created an assembly of no less than 1,866 deputies (including those with a consultative vote). It could clearly do no more than echo impulses transmitted to it by the organizers. No proper provision was made to ensure an orderly system of representation, and as at the Second Congress the military element loomed large. The congress formally approved the CPC's and CEC's conduct to date and endorsed a programmatic statement embodying the basic principles of the Soviet order. It also elected a new 306-man CEC, consisting of 160 Bolsheviks, 125 Left SRs, 10 'sympathizers' with these two parties and 11 moderate oppositionists (7 SRs, 2 Mensheviks, and 2 USDI members); this CEC of third convocation remained in being until March 1918.

4 *Zinoviev on the Constituent Assembly and the Soviets*. On 11 October Zinoviev had written, in a letter expressing reservations about the projected Bolshevik insurrection: 'The Constituent Assembly will be able to rely in its revolutionary work only on the soviets. The Constituent Assembly plus the soviets—this is the mixed type of state institution toward which we are moving' (*Bolsheviks*, p. 90). Now, over two months later, he was stating a directly contrary view. He was evidently anxious to rehabilitate himself in the eyes of Lenin and the 'hard-liners' on the Bolshevik Central Committee, to which he had just been re-admitted (see above, p. 299).

5 *Second (Regular) Congress of Peasant Deputies*. This gathering (26 November–11 December), like the extraordinary congress which preceded it (see above, p. 322), was dominated by the Left SRs, many of whose supporters were soldiers fresh from the front. Its claim to represent the 'organized' peasantry was thus in some doubt. It was the scene of violent polemics over political and ideological issues. On 4 December the moderate deputies withdrew, and two parallel assemblies, each claiming legitimacy, coexisted uneasily for a week until the minority group was forcibly dispersed. Thereupon the radicals assumed the right to choose which of their number should attend the Third Congress of Peasant Deputies, which opened on 13 January and promptly voted to merge with its urban–military counterpart, the Third Congress of Soviets of Workers' and Soldiers' Deputies.

6 This tactic presupposed a period of coexistence between the rival all-Russian representative institutions (see above, n. 2). The phrase 'the Constituent Assembly *as at present composed*', in the first paragraph of the resolution, left open the possibility that the assembly might be reconstituted by invoking the right of electors to recall their deputies.

7 i.e. conditional support. The phrase became notorious in the spring of 1917 when the Executive Committee of the Petrograd soviet resolved to support the Provisional Government 'in so far

as' (Russian: *postol'ku—poskol'ku*) its actions corresponded to the demands which it had put forward, notably for democratization of the army and retention of the Petrograd garrison in the capital. This attitude, which at the time was endorsed by all the left-wing parties, including the Bolsheviks, combined constant criticism and control of the government's actions with a refusal to accept a share of the responsibility for ruling the country. It helped to undermine the Provisional Government's authority and soon proved unworkable, as the moderate socialists implicitly recognized by entering the governmental coalition in May 1917; by this time the Bolsheviks had adopted Lenin's irreconcilable stand towards both the government and the moderate socialists. The formula first appeared in the 1905 revolution.

8 *Annulling of Public Debts.* In raising this important issue so casually the Left SRs gave further proof of their impetuosity where international affairs were concerned; the Bolsheviks, aware that such a measure would have a profound impact upon Soviet Russia's foreign relations, were more circumspect. Pressure from this quarter may have led the CPC to resume discussion of this measure, which it had first considered on 21 November when, however, it took no action. On 23 December it decided to suspend provisionally all dealings in government bonds; meanwhile the SEC was to devise laws on the liquidation of the state debt. This formulation still reflected the views of the CPC's more prudent members, but when the decree was published five days later (initially in the Left SR paper *Znamya truda*) its provisions were expanded to cover dealings in privately issued securities as well as governmental ones. The matter was raised again in the CEC on 3 January: see below, p. 415.

8 So far as is known, no such delegation was sent. Soviet interests in Stockholm continued to be handled by Vorovsky until he returned to Russia in January 1919, after the Swedish government withdrew permission for his mission to operate.

9 *Sickness Insurance Law.* Like the decree on unemployment insurance (see above, p. 357), this law was highly unrealistic in Russia's present desperate economic circumstances, and its promulgation had a 'declarative' or propagandist character— as indeed Lenin later acknowledged (*PSS*, xxxviii.198). The CEC implicitly recognized this by endorsing it without debate

in an apparently casual manner. It was not even published in *Izvestiya* or *Pravda*, but appeared in the official gazette on 31 December. The scheme was to be compulsory and to apply to hired agricultural workers and 'the poorest peasants' as well as to industrial employees (art. 1). Local sickness benefit funds (*kassy*) were to pay contributors the equivalent of their normal wage in the event of sickness, pregnancy, or injury (art. 26). Medicines were to be free (art. 39). Benefits were to be financed mainly from employees' contributions, fixed at 10 per cent of wages or salary. Each *kassa* was to enjoy considerable internal autonomy, the members of its board being elected by and responsible to the contributors. All this reflected the thinking of the (predominantly Menshevik) specialists in the ministry of Labour under the Provisional Government who were responsible for the initial draft of this measure. The provisions of this law were superseded by the statute of 31 October 1918 which introduced a more centralized form of administration of all current insurance programmes.

TWENTY-THIRD SESSION

1   *Food Supply.* The 'council of ten' was the provisional executive set up in November at the conference of supply officials in Moscow, whose members had been briefly detained on Shlikhter's orders (see above, p. 352). The Moscow Bolsheviks took a more lenient line than the PC of Supply in Petrograd, of which Shlikhter was on 18 December formally placed in charge. On 28 December they permitted the officials to hold another congress which gave the provisional executive a more permanent character under the title of All-Russian Supply Council. It was to have twenty-five members, most of them representatives of provincial areas (including those with grain surpluses); two seats were given to the pragmatically-inclined Moscow Bolshevik leaders Rykov and Milyutin. This body then suggested establishing a national body as an integral part of the SEC in Petrograd, a move clearly designed to weaken the PC of Supply.

Shlikhter responded by building up an alternative representative organization under his own control which rested mainly on the supply committees in the armed forces—a powerful consumers' lobby. He also won Lenin's backing for an uncompromising line. The result was that in January 1918 a rival body to the (Moscow-based) All-Russian Supply Council came into being, subordinate to the CPC. However, Shlikhter himself was obliged to yield his position to A. D. Tsurupa (and in part to Trotsky's Chokprod), and to leave for Siberia in search of supplies.

These squabbles impeded practical efforts to feed the hungry millions in the 'consuming provinces'. The commissar's claims here were over-optimistic, for famine was indeed already stalking the Russian north-west where, according to a recent Soviet historian, 'a significant part of the rural population . . . were living off substitutes: cereals were mixed with oil-cake and wood bark, and some people had to eat moss or straw' (Sautin, *Vel. Okt.*, pp. 130 f.)

2 '*Bagmen*' (*meshochniki*) were individuals—not only soldiers but also town-dwellers of various social categories—who sought to feed themselves and their families by travelling to country districts and buying or exchanging commodities for edibles, which they then brought back with them, often by train. Such measures of self-help contravened the state grain monopoly introduced by the Provisional Government, and were regarded by the Bolsheviks as 'speculation'. Trotsky's first step as chairman of Chokprod (see p. 399) was to set a limit for each traveller of half a pud (18 lb.) of foodstuffs; any surplus was to be confiscated, and those offering armed resistance were to be summarily shot. In practice it proved difficult to control this trade, which continued throughout the period of 'war communism' (1918–21), so long as supplies were to be had, with the authorities' tacit consent.

3 *State Publishing; Copyright Law.* The angry exchanges which this matter occasioned may have been due to the Presidium's action in tabling, at a time when the regime's very survival was at stake, what seemed to be a relatively trivial issue. Sukhanov's taunt evidently provoked Volodarsky, a 'hard-line' Bolshevik, to launch an indirect attack on the more easy-going Lunacharsky, who was responsible for the proposed measure. This had first been presented to the CPC on 18 December, but had not been discussed there; Lenin is said to have endorsed it, and it was then passed to the CEC. After cursory examination here it

was published on 4 January 1918 without any notable modification to the original draft.

The decree gave the PC of Education the right to impose a five-year monopoly on the works of any author and to publish cheap popular editions of literary and other classics on which copyright had expired. The matter of authors' royalties raised a basic ideological problem: what should be the scope of private rights to intellectual property in a socialist order? In the early years of the Soviet regime a restrictive policy was followed. Writers and artists were expected to toil for the common good, not for personal profit, and in return were to be cared for by state agencies. In June 1918 inheritance rights were abolished altogether, but a decree of 26 November 1918 permitted royalty payments according to a tariff in which the size of the edition was the main criterion, and allowed the heirs of deceased authors, if they were impoverished, to apply for a maintenance grant payable from accumulated royalties. It extended the state's monopoly rights to all scientific and artistic works, whether published or not. Several dozen deceased writers' and composers' works had meanwhile been declared public property. In the 1920s these restrictions were somewhat relaxed. The state was still empowered to purchase a writer's or artist's work without his permission, but copyright was reintroduced; fees were calculated from the year of first publication, and royalty payments could be inherited for a limited term (maximum fifteen years).

Publishing by various state authorities went ahead without much effort at co-ordination until 1919, when a decree of 29 May established a system of central control through Gosizdat (State Publishing House), which combined a censorship function with positive 'guidance'. Political direction of cultural life, which was to become one of the key characteristics of Soviet socialism, may be said to have originated with the modest measure which Polyansky here set before the CEC.

4 *Left SRs and the New Judicial System.* The Left SR Shteynberg's approach to his responsibilities as PC of Justice was considerably more restrained than that of his predecessor Stuchka, and from the start he found himself in conflict with his 'hardline' Bolshevik colleagues, notably Lenin, Trotsky, and Dzer-

zhinsky. On 16 December he issued an order listing the agencies in Petrograd empowered to make arrests, search premises, and confiscate property. The list was extensive—it included the 'investigating committees' of the city and district soviets as well as the Cheka—but it did at least allow complaints against arbitrary actions to be filed with the PC of Justice. In the CPC Shteynberg protested at individual Cheka abuses, asked for certain corrupt or arbitrary interrogators to be dismissed, and sought to make prior consent by his commissariat mandatory in effecting arrests. Lenin is said to have angrily dismissed such pleas as 'common tittle-tattle' (*obyvatel'skaya spletnya*) prejudicial to state security (Shlikhter, *Ilyich*, pp. 60–2). In his memoirs Shteynberg himself gives a lively, but inaccurate and self-serving, account of some of these disagreements.

In this speech he repeated the suggestion that the new 'people's judges' should decide cases according to their own discretion, which of course opened the way to the arbitrary acts he professed to deplore. Nevertheless it is plain from the provisions of this ordinance, which was discussed in the CPC on 27 and 29 December and published on 12 January, that he was endeavouring to limit the sweeping impact of Stuchka's 'decree no. 1' (see above, p. 323). It provided for transfer of unsettled cases from judicial institutions that had been liquidated, such as the Ruling Senate, to courts of cassation, circuit, and 'local' courts. These were therefore expected to exist alongside the new revolutionary tribunals (although in several cities, Petrograd and Moscow included, the circuit courts had actually already been closed down). They were to function under the control of commissars entitled to interfere at will in their proceedings (art. 7), but such individuals were required to report both to their electors in the local soviet and to the PC of Justice (art. 9). The minimal safeguards of legality which the decree sought to provide could not, however, be enforced in practice owing to the extremists' opposition, although 'decree no. 2' on the judicial system, adopted by the CPC on 15 February 1918, did make some concessions to the Left SR viewpoint.

5 *Welfare.* Alexandra Kollontay is best known today as an apostle of revolutionary feminism. As PC of Social Welfare her responsibilities covered a large field (pensions, veterans' affairs,

women's education etc.) but she gave priority to the care of infants and nursing mothers. The homes and hostels referred to here were designed to cater mainly to the needs of orphans, whose numbers had been tragically swollen by the war. Like many maximalists at the time, Kollontay believed that if such children were brought up institutionally, without the constraints of family ties, they could become leaders in the construction of a socialist society. Her somewhat naïve idealism is also reflected in her remarks here about the clergy: two weeks later she was to create trouble for the government, and to earn herself a reprimand, for ordering the confiscation of the property of the Alexander Nevsky monastery in Petrograd. No special decree was passed on monasterial possessions, as she intimated; this question was covered by the edict of 20 January 1918, article 12 of which expropriated *all* ecclesiastical and religious bodies. (Their land had already been declared confiscated by the decree of 26 October.)

In March 1918 Kollontay resigned from the CPC in protest against the Brest-Litovsk treaty, which the 'Left Communists' regarded as a betrayal of internationalist principles, and in 1921 she joined another dissident group, the 'Workers' Opposition'.

TWENTY-FOURTH SESSION

1   *Soviet–Romanian Relations.* The ultimatum in question (31 December) was the second of three such demands by the CPC, each of which marked an aggravation in Soviet–Romanian relations.

After the armistice of 26 November Romania's military leaders were predominantly concerned with bolstering their armies' security against revolutionary influences from the rear. This coincided with a political interest in Bessarabia, where Romanian-speaking 'Moldavians' formed a sizeable element of the population. At Kishinev, the provincial capital, on 21 November local Moldavian politicians had set up a representative 'regional council' (*sfatul tseriy*), initially with the limited aim of preserving order against depredations by undisciplined Russian troops. Friction soon broke out between Russian and Romanian forces along the front over food allocations and other material problems, which were complicated by national and political antagonisms. On 2 December the Bolshevik-led MRC of the Romanian front, which had been established at Jassy after the congress at Roman (see above, p. 309), made a bid for power, but the *coup* was frustrated by soldiers loyal to the Ukrainian Rada. Shortly afterwards four insurgent leaders were summoned for talks to the headquarters of General G. D. Shcherbachev, where despite a safe-conduct they were arrested; subsequently one of them, a Kronshtadt sailor and activist named S. G. Roshal who had been appointed commissar of the Romanian front, was killed. The incident helped to radicalize the mood of the armed forces' delegates who attended the second congress of Rumcherod (the chief deliberative body in the region), held at Odessa from 10 to 22 December. This congress declared itself the sole legitimate source of power in the area from which its members came and elected a new pro-Bolshevik executive.

Petrograd did not hear of Roshal's death until 15 December, when it was reported by Bolshevik leaders at Kishinev, who also stated that Romanian troops had occupied the frontier village of Leovo and several other places in Bessarabia. The news evoked a prompt protest from Trotsky to the Romanian ambassador, Count C. Diamandi, who was peremptorily requested to reply on the same day (16 December) explaining what steps his government had taken to punish the 'criminals' responsible for these misdeeds; 'the severest measures' were threatened against anyone, of whatever rank, who assisted Kaledin or other foes of the Soviet regime. Diamandi replied that he had not been informed of details of the incidents; that the Romanian forces had to protect their vital interests from infringement by disorderly Russian soldiers; that contacts with Kaledin and the Rada were concerned solely with supply matters; and that neighbouring states should maintain friendly relations. This reply was less than frank, but Trotsky evidently decided not to press the issue at a moment when a much greater menace was looming from the Central Powers.

Two weeks later, however, Smolny resolved on more forceful action. On the night of 30–1 December the CPC was informed by the commander of the 49th division that several more clashes had taken place, involving the 194th and 195th infantry regiments; some of the men had been disarmed and sent to the rear, while others who had fraternized with nearby Austro-Hungarian troops had been arrested. (The Romanian actions may have been prompted by the formation at Jassy on 28 December of the so-called 'front detachment' of Rumcherod, which was' clearly preparing to seize power, as well as by a further outbreak of looting.) Evidently at the suggestion of Trotsky, now absent from the capital attending the peace talks, the CPC decided to arrest as hostages the Romanian envoy and four members of his staff, who were taken to the Peter and Paul fortress. This breach of diplomatic immunity shocked the Allied representatives in Petrograd. The more conservative of them wanted to leave the city at once, but the moderates, led by the American ambassador Francis, who had just succeeded as *doyen* of the corps, advocated a collective diplomatic *démarche*. A meeting was arranged with Lenin (1 January) at which a letter of protest was solemnly read out in the presence of members of the diplomatic corps. Lenin is said to have replied that 'for a socialist the lives of a thousand soldiers are dearer than the tranquillity of a single diplomat' (*Pravda*, 3 January), but one may doubt whether he voiced such sentiments in public. A few hours later the CPC decided to release the men. *Pravda* stated that their arrest had served its purpose, and although it did not specify what that purpose had been the claim was not without validity. The arrest drove a breach in the Allies' policy of renouncing all official dealings with the Soviet government; furthermore the CPC secured from Francis (through Robins) an informal undertaking to press the Romanians to moderate their policy. Neither the Soviets nor the Americans seem to have taken this engagement very seriously. If anything the 'Diamandi incident', as it came to be known, hardened the Romanian attitude, for on 10 January the occupation of Bessarabia, which had hitherto been on a limited scale, began in earnest. The action was ostensibly taken at the behest of the local Moldavian authorities and the Russian military leaders. The Soviet government did not, as one might have expected, reply to this new provocation with a declaration of war, but was content to order Diamandi to leave the country at a few hours' notice and to seize the Romanian gold reserve, which had previously been evacuated to Russia (13 January).

2 *Final Preparations for the Constituent Assembly.* During the twelve days that had elapsed since the CEC had last considered this matter (see above, p. 242), tension in Petrograd had steadily mounted. It was heightened by further outbreaks of rioting, during which machine-guns were again brought into play (night of 23–4 December) and the city was placed under martial law. On 24 December *Delo naroda* appealed to the Russian people to defend their assembly if it were forcibly dissolved. Meanwhile the Bolshevik leaders set up an emergency military staff comprising prominent politicians (Trotsky, Sverdlov, and the Left SR Proshyan), activists with military and police responsibilities (Podvoysky, Yeremeyev, Blagonravov, and Uritsky), and military officers who had entered the Soviet government's service. Uritsky was (according to some sources) appointed commandant of the Tauride Palace, where the assembly was to meet, and Bonch-Bruyevich commandant of the Smolny, which it was feared might be attacked. Some 5,000 troops and perhaps as many Red guardsmen were held in readiness. The city was placarded with appeals by both sides, headed respectively 'All Power to the Constituent Assembly' and 'All Power to the Soviets', the former urging people to demonstrate on the assembly's behalf and the latter warning them to stay off the streets.

The PSR deputies' views as to the attitude they should take on the questions of land and peace had been moving to the left. This made it all the more urgent for their adversaries to prevent them broadcasting the fact from the tribune of the assembly. Lenin drafted a programmatic statement which, as Sverdlov states here, was to be presented for the deputies' endorsement, on the assumption that by refusing to comply they would provide a pretext for dissolution. The document was a cross between a draft constitution (many of its provisions were in fact embodied in the RSFSR constitution of July 1918) and a summary of the ruling parties' objectives. It declared Russia to be a Soviet republic and proclaimed the intention 'to crush the exploiters' resistance mercilessly, organize society on a socialist basis, and bring about the triumph of socialism in all countries'. It committed deputies who endorsed it to approval of the chief measures undertaken or decreed by the Soviet government and in effect to their own elimination: 'the Constituent Assembly considers that it has no other task than to work out the fundamental principles of the socialist reconstruction of society.'

The accompanying ordinance made it clear that the Bolshevik leaders had abandoned the scheme whereby the assembly would be permitted to continue in being temporarily as a rump parliament, which had still been urged in a message from the CEC published in *Znamya truda* on 29 December.

3 *Annulling of Public Debts.* Despite the CEC's endorsement of this draft measure, the text of which appeared in *Pravda* on 2 January, its promulgation was delayed until 28 January, evidently at the behest of those within the CPC—and the SEC—who were nervous about its probable international repercussions; the delay was not explained at the time. The CEC approved the final text on 21 January.

This was perhaps the most revolutionary of all the Bolsheviks' early edicts, in that it challenged the principle, generally accepted among modern states, that a national government is at least morally responsible for obligations entered into by its predecessors. The Allied and neutral powers promptly stated that they regarded it as 'non-existent' and reserved their right to demand retribution for loss or damage suffered by their subjects as a result of this measure as well as from confiscation of their property. The Soviet standpoint was that 'the expropriators had been expropriated': Russian revolutionaries had indicated as early as 1905 their intention to repudiate foreign loans to the tsarist regime, and the wartime loans from the Allies had been amply repaid in Russian soldiers' blood. To these arguments was later added the claim that Russian losses due to Allied intervention in the civil war outweighed those incurred by her foreign creditors.

The Soviet government subsequently modified its rigid stance in regard to the foreign loans which the decree annulled 'unconditionally and without exception' (art. 3). Under the Brest-Litovsk treaty it was obliged to pay compensation to Germany, and some 120 million gold roubles were transferred before this treaty was denounced in November 1918. In February 1919 the PC of Foreign Affairs suggested that certain pre-war debts might be honoured if trade with the Entente countries were resumed, but this offer was ignored. After the civil war ended this issue became central to Soviet Russia's efforts to rejoin the international community. The terms were now stiffened: the creditor nations were to cease all hostile acts against the Soviet republic and to afford it diplomatic recognition. The respective demands were discussed at international conferences held at Genoa and The Hague in 1922, but no general settlement was reached; however, by the treaty of Rapallo Soviet Russia and Germany agreed to drop all reciprocal financial claims. This breached the common front of Russia's creditors. In subsequent negotiations with Britain and France the USSR insisted on the grant of fresh long-term credits in exchange for any recognition of Russia's pre-war debt, but this demand proved unacceptable (although the British Labour government of 1924 was prepared to concede it); there matters rested. The failure to reach a settlement on the issue of debts and claims did not preclude *de jure* diplomatic recognition by the major European powers, the USSR's entry into the League of Nations, or conclusion of the 1935 Franco-Soviet pact.

In October 1917 Russia's total public debt was reckoned at some 60 milliard roubles, about a quarter of which was held abroad. The best estimate of the pre-war foreign state debt is 3,971 million roubles; to this must be added the foreign share of government-backed railway bonds (975 m.r.), state mortgage bonds (230 m.r.) and municipal loans (420 m.r.), making a total of 5,596 m.r. (Vaynshteyn, *Nar. bogatstvo*, pp. 444–5). The wartime debt has been put at 7,788 m.r. (Michelson, *Public Finance*, p. 322), from which approximately 1 milliard roubles should be deducted to allow for Russian assets deposited with or seized by the Allies. The amount of foreign capital investment, mostly in private enterprises and railway companies, is thought to have amounted to 2,849 m.r. The total foreign debt must therefore have been in the region of 15 milliard roubles. The Soviet delegation to the Genoa conference was presented with a demand for 18½ milliard roubles, including interest, which of course it considered inflated.

The total internal public debt in October 1917 has been put at 44 milliard roubles, of which 25 milliard are accounted for by long-term loans (Ryvkin, *Fin. pol.*, p. 105). Both the Imperial and Provisional governments had resorted to the money market on an extensive scale to meet war expenditure; the 1917 'Liberty loan' alone was subscribed to the tune of 4 milliard roubles. The decree of 28 January 1918 repeated earlier assurances that the interests of small-scale investors would be safeguarded. It defined these as persons holding up to 10,000 roubles' worth of government securities bought from earned income. (Slightly more generous terms had been suggested by the SEC.) They were to receive nominal certificates in a new Soviet government loan. However, owing to the rapid progress of inflation this loan could not be floated, and instead in October 1918 they were offered compensation in the form of credit with the People's Bank to the nominal value of these annulled securities. If this left them below the 'subsistence norm' they could apply for monthly cash payments in addition, but these soon dried up. Securities also circulated in lieu of currency. One Soviet author acknowledges that State security-holders incurred a loss equivalent to 99 per cent of the nominal value of their holdings (Shmelev, 'Public Finance', p. 119). The decree also declared savings bank deposits 'inviolate' but this promise could not be honoured either.

TWENTY-FIFTH SESSION

1 *Shooting of Constituent Assembly Demonstrators.* At 11 p.m. on 3 January the emergency military staff reimposed martial law in Petrograd on the grounds that a 'counter-revolutionary demonstration' in defence of the Constituent Assembly was planned for 5 January by PSR leaders who were allegedly in touch with Kaledin. Workers and soldiers were told to remain in their factories or barracks, where on 4 January they were addressed by agitators sent out by the Petrograd soviet. The PSR's Military Commission, under G. I. Semenov, had established a network of contacts with a few hundred sympathizers in three military units stationed in the city. They planned to stage an armed demonstration with the vague idea that, if it were actively supported by the populace at large, it might lead to the collapse of the Bolshevik government. Their deliberations did not remain a secret, although how far foreknowledge of their plans influenced maximalist counter-moves cannot be determined. (Semenov later went over to the Bolsheviks and gave evidence for the prosecution in the 1922 trial of PSR leaders, where much

was made of these conspiratorial goings-on; this evidence must, however, be handled with caution.) On 4 January at the latest (according to PSR sources, already on 26 and 29 December) the party's Central Committee decided that the plan should be abandoned, and that evening A. R. Gots so informed the military commission. This decision was probably due to realization that the plan was known and that the Bolsheviks' countermeasures would prevent mobilization of popular support. The PSR leaders did not want bloodshed, and were in any case not accustomed to taking determined or forceful action. Instead they decided to call for an *unarmed* demonstration, an idea which some of them had favoured from the start. This call was followed by several hundred men and women (higher figures are encountered), from every walk of life, including a few workers and even some soldiers. Considering the demoralization occasioned by the last-minute change of plan and the risk involved in facing well-armed patrols of sailors and Red guardsmen, this must be accounted something of an achievement.

Shortly before midday a column of marchers approached the Tauride Palace but found their way barred. When they refused to turn back shots were fired, first in the air and then at the demonstrators. There were several casualties, including a member of the former central peasant executive, G. I. Loginov (Logvinov?), and a woman PSR activist named Gorbachevskaya. Another column, which included some men from the Obukhov munitions factory, was fired on near the same spot. In all ten demonstrators are thought to have been killed and many more injured.

The Petrograd soviet executive later claimed that the demonstrators had fired 'provocative shots' at the guardians of order. This assertion may be discounted. Although a few marchers may have brought weapons, or obtained them by disarming their assailants, there is no independent evidence that such arms were used. The soviet executive, in announcing that an investigation would be held, made no pretence of objectivity, stating that anyone found to have 'spilled the blood of revolutionary workers' would be brought to trial but saying nothing about any action against over-zealous Red guardsmen. Such shooting was, indeed, denied both in *Izvestiya* and *Znamya truda* as a false rumour (7 January). Four days later the PLSR organ named some of the members of the investigating team, but no report of its findings has been traced.

2   *Dissolution of the Constituent Assembly.* The assembly convened at 4 p.m. on 5 January in an atmosphere heated by news of the shootings. Uritsky had ensured that the galleries of the Tauride Palace were filled with a crowd of government supporters. These soldiers, sailors, and workers, some of whom were armed, made no secret of their feelings and occasionally hurled insults at the deputies gathered below. When the *doyen d'âge* attempted to open the proceedings he was jostled aside by Sverdlov, who said that he had been authorized by the CEC to perform that role. He read out the 'declaration of the rights of the toiling and exploited masses' and the *Internationale* was sung. Thereupon Chernov was chosen as chairman in preference to the PLSR leader Mariya Spiridonova, whose candidacy was advanced by the left. He delivered a long rambling speech evidently designed to bridge the gulf between the moderate socialists and the maximalists. After Bukharin and Shteynberg had rejected these advances and restated the views of the government parties, Tsereteli spoke for the Mensheviks. He delivered a powerful indictment of the new regime's record to date, pointing to its abuses of power—a matter calculated to elicit some PLSR sympathy—and called upon all authorities in the land to submit to the people's sovereign will. After some further debate the Bolsheviks and Left SRs tabled a resolution that the assembly should take their programmatic declaration as the basis of its agenda. Predictably, this was rejected by a vote of 237 to 146.

A recess followed (11.10 p.m.) while the government leaders met privately to decide how they might best proceed with dissolution of the assembly. The Left SRs wanted to delay the move until the deputies had voted on the peace issue. Thus when the session was resumed the Bolsheviks delivered a separate statement indicting the assembly's 'counter-revolutionary majority' and withdrew. A tumult broke out, during which weapons were brandished. Eventually the chairman managed to restore order and the debate continued in a rather confused fashion until the Left SRs in turn decided that their patience was exhausted. The PSR leaders, in no doubt as to what lay in store, decided to push through in rapid succession a number of

fundamental measures which, they hoped, would show the
general public that the deputies shared their revolutionary
aspirations. The first of these acts abolished private landed
property without compensation; the second expressed regret at
the negotiations for a separate peace and urged speedy conclusion of a general one; the third proclaimed the Russian state a
democratic federative republic. Although there was of course
less chance than ever of such a programme being implemented
under the moderate socialists' auspices, these declarative decrees did at least make it difficult for the maximalists to discredit the assembly as 'bourgeois'; on the contrary, it could
serve as a symbol around which some Russian democrats could
rally during the civil war. This struggle was bound to receive a
further impetus from the suppression of the only nation-wide
political forum in which opposition to the dictatorship could
have been ventilated.

The assembly was permitted only a single session, which
ended at 4.40 a.m. on 6 January. When some deputies returned
to the Tauride Palace that afternoon, they were denied entrance
by the guards. It remained for the CEC to adopt a decree dissolving the assembly, and this was published the following day.
It recapitulated the familiar arguments which Lenin developed
in this two-hour speech. The incorporation of the maximalist
Constituent Assembly deputies into the CEC was a substitute
for the rump parliament scheme advocated by some Left SRs
and Bolsheviks. It could not serve to confer additional legitimacy on the CEC, since this body did not meet again before the
Third Congress of Soviets, to which it formally surrendered its
powers.

3   A reference to the propositions, commonly known as the
'April Theses', which Lenin had first put forward on 4 April
1917, on the morrow of his arrival in Petrograd, to Bolshevik
delegates attending the All-Russian Conference of Soviets. The
fifth thesis reads, in part: 'Not a parliamentary republic—[this]
would be a retrograde step—but a republic of soviets of workers', farm labourers' and peasants' deputies throughout the
country, from top to bottom'. At that time Lenin did not
counterpose the soviets to the Constituent Assembly so absolutely as he was to do once the Bolsheviks had seized power, but

rather implied that the two forms of representation were complementary: 'without the soviets of workers' and soldiers' deputies', he wrote, 'convocation of the Constituent Assembly is not guaranteed and its success is impossible.'

4   The demonstrations of 20–1 April 1917 in Petrograd ('April Days') led to the resignation of Milyukov as minister of Foreign Affairs and to the formation of the first coalition cabinet with strong socialist participation.

References to Notes

This list is restricted to the principal works consulted and excludes newspaper sources. Wherever possible anonymous works are identified by the names of their editors or compilers. For full titles see Bibliography.

Session	Note	
I	1	Russia. *II Vseross. s'yezd*; Butenko and Chugayev, *II Vseross. s'yezd*; Startsev, 'Bol'sheviki', 35–45; B & F, 109–38; Lenin, xxxv. 444; Melgunov, *Kak bol'sheviki*, 82.
	2	Vompe, *Dni*, 10, 15–17; *II Vseross. s'yezd*, 87 ff.
	3	*PVRK*; Lenin, xxxv. 442; Gorodetsky, *Rozhdenie*, 189; Orekhova, 'O sostave'.
	4	Melgunov, *Kak bol'sheviki*, 306–82; Mints, *Ist. Vel. Okt.*, iii. 294; *IGV*, iii. 24–5 (map); Sobolev, *Istoriya*, 300–1.
	5	*VMRK*, 17–21, 31–2, 39, 269; Chugayev, *Prot. i post. TsKBf*, 23–6, 274–5; Drezen, *Balt. flot*, 12–14, 332; Kudelli, *Okt. shkval*, 65.
	6	*DSV*, i. 24–5; Volin, *Deyatel'nost'*, 23–5; Popov, *Okt. perevorot*, 262–3, 362–5; Garvi, *Prof. soyuzy*, 29–30.
II	1	*DSV*, i. 9–10; *II Vseross. s'yezd*, 57; B & F, 124; B & K, i. 199 f., ii. 982–4; Trotsky, *Lenin*, 133–4.
	3	*Prot. TsK*, 144–7 (*Bolsheviks*, 126–8).
	5	Nikolayevsky, *Men'sheviki*, 27–41; *Prot. TsK*, 144–7 (*Bolsheviks*, 126–8); Gorodetsky, *Rozhdenie*, 162; Mints, *Ist. Vel. Okt.*, iii. 166–80 (citing TsGAOR, f. 5498, op. 1).
	6	Radkey, *Sickle*, 18–39.
	8	Radkey, *Agr. Foes*, 440–2; *idem*, *Sickle*, 95–162, esp. 102, 110–12.
	9	Sobolev, *Istoriya*, 257–60; Gaponenko, *Okt. revol. i armiya*, 51; Radkey, *Sickle*, 40–2.
III	1	Nikolayevsky, *Men'sheviki*, 42–43; RSDRP, *Pervy*

legal'ny, 337–42; *Prot. TsK*, 148–61 (*Bolsheviks*, 128–35); Gorodetsky, *Rozhdenie*, 163–6; Mints, *Ist. Vel. Okt.*, iii. 166–80.

2 Lenin, xxxiv. 108–16; B & K, iii. 1721–42; Rabinovitch, *Bolsheviks*, 185–6, 201–2, 255–62; *Bolsheviks*, 67, 278.

3 Rosenberg, 'Municipal Duma Elections', 131–63, esp. 159–63; *idem, Liberals*, 220.

5 Tych, *PPS–Lewica*; Dziewanowski, 'World War I'.

6 Rosenberg, 'Municipal Duma Elections', 137–40; Voznesensky, *Moskva*, 98–105; Radkey, *Agr. Foes*, 240–2, 244, 430, 432–4.

7 *PVRK*, ii. 276–7; Gorodetsky, *Rozhdenie*, 202; Popov, *Okt. perevorot*, 337–44; B & F, 118–19, 150–3; Demyanov, 'Zapiski', 45–6.

8 Kerensky, 'Gatchina', 147–80 (also in *Izdaleka*, 194–225); Kerensky, *Russia*, 438–49; Krasnov, 'Na vnutr. fronte', 97–190, esp. 148–72; Shlyapnikov, 'Okt. perevorot i Stavka'; Avdeyev, 'Vokrug Gatchiny'; 'Okt. na fronte'; Kozmin, 'Podgotovka'; Nesterenko, 'Gatchina'; Lutovinov, *Likvidatsiya*; Kenez, *Civil War*, 140 n.; B & F, 139–44, 160–5; Milyukov, *Istoriya*, pt. 3, 240–80; Radkey, *Sickle*, 39–47.

IV 1 *VMRK*, 271; Trotsky, *Soch.*, iii(ii). 86–8, 396.

3 Nikolayevsky, *Men'sheviki*, 44–52; Vompe, *Dni*, 38; RSDRP, *Pervy legal'ny*, 337–44; Lenin, xxxv. 44–5; Gorodetsky, *Rozhdenie*, 165–6; *Prot. TsK*, 161–2 (*Bolsheviks*, 136–8).

4 *II Vseross. s'yezd*, 83; Lenin xxxv. 72; Ilyukhina, 'K voprosu', 11; Schapiro, *Origin*, 69–70; Keep, *Russ. Revol.*, 315.

5 *Leninskiy sb.*, xxxvi. 18–20; RSDRP, *Pervy legal'ny*, 290; *Bolsheviks*, 161, 316–17; Piyashev, *Vorovsky*, 205–8; Zeman, *Merchant of Revol.*, 219–20, 239; Zeman, *Germany and the Revol.*, 87; Carr, *Bolsh. Revol.*, iii. 30; Lerner, *Radek*, 54–75; Futrell, *Northern Underground*, 156, 158, 175–6.

6 *DSV*, i. 36–8.

7 *Leninskiy sb.*, xxxvi. 24–5; VTsSPS, *III Vseross. konferentsiya*; VTsSPS, *Otchet*; VTsSPS, *I Vseross. s'yezd*; Keep, *Russ. Revol.*, 111–12, 299–304.

Session *Note*
8 *DSV*, i. 77–85; Keep, *Russ. Revol.*, 272–4; Amosov, *Okt. revol.*, ii. 138–214, esp. 193; Avrich, 'Bolsh. Revol.', 57.

V 1 Dziewanowski, *Comm. Party*, 27–34, 64–5.
   2 Sidorov, *VOSR*, vi. 9, 193, 359.
4–6, 12 Cherepakhov & Fingerit, *Russkaya period. pechat'*.
   9 Shlyapnikov, 'Okt. perevorot i Stavka', 170; Kenez, *Civil War*, 59, 73–5.
  10 BDIC MS. catalogue; Rosenberg, *Liberals*, 300.
  11 Gessen, *V dvukh vekakh*, 381.
  13 Keep, *Rise*, 75, 81–4; Radkey, *Agr. Foes*, 24–41.
  14 Lenin, xxxv. 47–9, 128–9; *Prot. TsK*, 162–4, 167–9, 193 (*Bolsheviks*, 138–42, 160–7); Gavrilov, *Bor'ba*, 140–1; Schapiro, *Origin*, 79, 84; Gorodetsky, *Rozhdenie*, 157, 206.
  15 Neck, *Arbeiterschaft*, 111; Hannak, *Im Sturm*, 225–30; May, *Passing*, ii. 642–52; Braunthal, *Geschichte*, 117; Osterroth and Schuster, *Chronik*, 187–8, 197; *Dict. biog.* xiii(iii). 11–12.
  18 Anikeyev, *Deyatel'nost' TsK* (1969), 442; Antonov–Ovseyenko, *Zapiski*, i.10; Sobolev, *Istoriya*, 177, 219.
  20 Trotsky, *Soch.*, iii(ii). 108–9.
  21 Stern, *Einfluss*, 94, 125, 129.

VI 1 Gorodetsky, *Rozhdenie*, 181–2; Iroshnikov, *Sozdanie*, 243; Kleandrov, *Organizatsiya*, 77–9.
  2 *DSV*, i. 38–9.
  3 *Prot. TsK*, 178–9 (*Bolsheviks*, 151–2).
  4 B & K, i. 445, 456–62; Malchevsky, *Vseross. Uchred. Sobr.*, 139–44; Kropat, 'Lenin u. die Konst. Vers.', 96; Kochan, 'Kadet Policy'.
  5 Radkey, *Sickle*, 73–91 (Mogilev talks).
  6 Frenkin, *Revol. dvizh.*, 209–25; Bereznyakov, *Bor'ba*, 165; Gaponenko, *Okt. revol. i armiya*, 71–9; Golub, *Partiya, armiya*, 270–3; Keep, 'October', 261–2.
  7 Smirnov, 'Petrogr. Sovet krest. dep.', 90–110.
  8 Chugayev, *Prot. i post. TsKBF*, 5–30, esp. 18, 25; 221–4, 274–5; Drezen, 'Tsentral'nye'.
  9 Melgunov, *Kak bol'sheviki*, 277–382; B & F, 174–80; Milyukov, *Istoriya*, pt. 3, 295–306; Bradley, 'Allies', 170; Tsypkin, *Kr. gvardiya*, 110–38; Podvoysky, *Kr. gvardiya*, 57–103; *Hist. Civil War*, ii. 393–478; Mints,

Session Note

Ist. Vel. Okt., iii. 189–306; neither of the latter two sources offer alternative casualty figures.

VII   1   *Prot. TsK*, 178 (*Bolsheviks*, 151); Bonch–Bruyevich, *Na boyevykh postakh*, 161–74 (reproduced with minor excisions in *Vosp. o Lenine*, 124–31). On Sverdlov's role earlier in 1917: Odom, 'Sverdlov'; Duval, 'Bolsh. Secretariat'.

2   Popov, *Okt. perevorot*, 365–78; B & F, 224–31; Golinkov, *Krakh*, 34–46.

3   Fitzpatrick, *Enlightenment*, 34–42; Korolev, *Ocherki*, 124–45.

4   Ullman, *Intervention*, 16–30; Bradley, 'Allies', 170–2.

6   Wade, *Russ. Search*, 83–5, 102–4; Taylor, *Struggle for Mastery*, 543, 557, 581–2; B & F, 243–4; Epstein, 'Accessibility', 172; *DDK*, i. viii.

7   B & F, 233–5; *DVP*, i. 5–6, 16–17; *DSV*, i. 53; *SDFP*, i. 3–4.

8   Keep, *Russ. Revol.*, 270–5; Lazarev, 'Iz istorii', 136–7.

9   *Hist. Civil War*, ii. 370; B & F, 318–27; Gindin, *Kak bol'sheviki* (1961); Rivkin, *Fin. pol.*, 73–83; Arnold, *Banks*, 58–9; Fleer, 'Vrem. Prav.', 203–4.

10   *DSV*, i. 71–2; B & F, 279–80 (wrongly dated).

11   Yakovlev, 'Protokoly', 95–137.

VIII   1   B & K, ii. 618–22, 629–30; Pethybridge, *Spread*, 83–105; Keep, *Russ. Revol.*, 34–8, 177–9.

2   Davydov, *Bor'ba*, 21, 27, 29; Fraiman, *Okt. vooruzh. vosstanie*, ii. 517; Keep, *Russ. Revol.*, 420.

3   Orlov, *Prod. rabota*, 18–39; Keep, *Russ. Revol.*, 422–35.

4   *DSV*, i. 59–62, 111–12; Fitzpatrick, *Enlightenment*, 18–27.

5   Radkey, *Sickle*, 207–23; Keep, *Russ. Revol.*, 439–41.

6   Gorodetsky, *Rozhdenie*, 202; Nikolayevsky, *Men'sheviki*, 71–83.

7   *DSV*, i. 126; Stuchka, 'Prol. revol.', 1–8.

IX   1   'Nakanune peremiriya', 195–249; Gaponenko, *Okt. revol. i armiya*, 83–9, 416 n. 40 (citing archival source on local fraternization agreements).

2   Ponomarev, *Polit. slovar'*, 297–8; Fainsod, *How Russia*, 210–12.

4   Piyashev, *Vorovsky*, 208–10; Tsereteli, *Vosp.*, i. 271–339, esp. 301–3; Fainsod, *Internat. Socialism*, 180–1,

Session *Note*

203, 206–9; Ascher, *Axelrod*, 327–31; Carr, *Bolsh. Revol.*, iii. 30; Wade, *Russ. Search*, 105–17.

XI   1   Gorodetsky, *Rozhdenie*, 198–9; Gimpelson, *Iz istorii*, 24; Keep, *Russ. Revol.*, 321, 441.

     4   Text in *FRUS*, i. 250; Kennan, *Russia Leaves the War*, 111 (and facsimile between 114 and 115); B & F, 258–9 (excerpted); *SDFP*, i. 11; *DVP*, i. 28–30. Cf. also Ullman, *Intervention*, 23, 25–7; Steglich, *Friedenspolitik*, 243.

     5   Gessen, 'Dukhonin v Stavke', 304–7; B & F, 232–68; Gaponenko, *Okt. revol. i armiya*, 110–20; 'Nakanune peremiriya', 195–249; Kennan, *Russia Leaves the War*, 101–10; *Hist. Civil War*, ii. 531–42; Golub, *Partiya, armiya*, 266–7; Bradley, 'Allies', 173.

     6   Kuusinen, 'Fin. revol.', 6–11; Kirby, *Finland & Russia*, 188–201; Smith, *Finland*, 25–8; Hodgson, *Comm. in Finland*, 33–49; Syukiyaynen, *Revol. sobytiya*, 101–40; Puntila, *Hist. politique*, 143–4.

     7   Vompe, *Dni*, 77.

     8   Radkey, *Election*, 34–5 (left-hand column total emended), 80.

   10   Gavrilov, *Bor'ba*, 233; Venediktov, *Natsionalizatsiya*, i. 92. For relevant statements by Anarchist leaders: Avrich, *Anarchists*, 100–6.

   11   Fokke, 'Na stsene', 16 (repeated by Trotsky, *My Life*, 378).

   12   Draper, *Roots*, 148–9, 153, 364, citing Reinstein's memoirs in *The Communist International*, 9–10 (1929), 428–35.

XII   1   *DSV*, i. 91–9; *PVRK*, iii. 109.

     2   B & F, 263; *PVRK*, iii. 112, 114, 145 (newspaper confiscations); 143–4, 165, 167 (arrest of journalists); Medlin & Parsons, *Nabokov*, 167–9; Demyanov, 'Zapiski'; Fleer, 'Vrem. Prav.'; Rosenberg, 'Russ. Liberals', 330 and *Liberals*, 264–6.

     4   *DSV*, i. 102; Gorodetsky, *Rozhdenie*, 201–4; Ilyukhina, 'K voprosu', 23; Schapiro, *Origin*, 69–70, 79.

XIII   2   *DSV*, i. 124, 126; Kucherov, *Organs*, 22–3, citing an article by T. Malkovich (1940) in which the dates are in error.

Session   Note
XIV   1   *Mirnye peregovory*; B & F, 268–71; Ludendorff,
           Kriegserinnerungen, 408–9; Nowak, *Aufzeichnungen* . . .
           Hoffmann, ii. 189–94; Wheeler–Bennett, *Brest-Litovsk*,
           83–95, 379; Steglich, *Friedenspolitik*, 236–48.
       2   Steglich, *Friedenspolitik*, 243–6.
       3   *Proceedings*, 12; Fokke, 'Na stsene', 18; Wheeler-
           Bennett, *Brest-Litovsk*, 87; Erickson, *Soviet High Com-
           mand*, 26–7, 674, 776. In B & F, 268, the names are
           garbled and incomplete.
       4   *DSV*, i. 169; Pidhainy, *Formation*, 405 and personal
           communication to editor.

XV   1   Radkey, *Election*, 49 (citing the Commission's *Izves-
           tiya*); Medlin & Parsons, *Nabokov*, 166–75.
       2   TsSU. *Rossiya v mir. voyne*, 15, 30 (Tab. 22); Golovin,
           Voyenniya usiliya, 148 (*Russ. Army*, 92); Williams,
           'Russ. War Prisoners', 27; Kohn & Meyendorff, *Cost
           of the War*, 38–9, 135–6; Klante, *Wolga . . . Amur*, 109;
           DVP, i. 123–4, 176–7, 639–43.
       4   B & F, 467–9; *DVP*, i. 51, 72–4, 91–3, 104–5, 712,
           714; Lenczowski, *Russia & the West*, 48–56; Wheeler-
           Bennett, *Brest-Litovsk*, 127, 383; Carr, *Bolsh. Revol.*,
           iii. 246, 293–4.
       5   B & F, 282–3; Stalin, *Soch.*, iv. 32; Kirby, *Finland &
           Russia*, 201–3; Smith, *Finland*, 29.
       7   *DSV*, i. 73, 172–4; B & F, 310–15; Voronetskaya,
           'Organizatsiya', 7–8; Gershberg, 'Lenin'; Oppen-
           heim, 'Sup. Econ. Council', 4; Drobizhev, *Glavny
           shtab*, 31–101, esp. 61.

XVI   2   Edmonds, *History*, 264; Ludendorff, *Kriegserinnerungen*,
           408; Stegemann, *Gesch. des Krieges*, iv. 522 (who
           points out that the divisions were at three-quarter
           strength); more recently Strokov, *Vooruzh. sily*, 523.
       3   Jasny, *Soviet Economists*, 94–9; Keep, *Russ. Revol.*, 422–
           4.
       4   *IGV*, iii. 78; B & F, 407–9; Mints, *Ist. Vel. Okt.*, iii.
           501–2.

XVII   2   B & F, 357–60; *DSV*, i. 159; *PVRK*, iii. 431 (arrests);
           Rosenberg, *Liberals*, 278, 308–13.
       4   Milyukov, *Istoriya*, pt. 2, 251–2; Rosenberg, *Liberals*,
           226–33.
       5   Trotsky, *Soch.*, iii(ii). 132, 138; xii. 50–68; Scott,

Session Note

'Cheka', 7; Latsis, 'Dzerzhinsky', 81–97, esp. 81–5; Latsis, *Chrez. komissii*, 7; Kanev, *Krakh anarkhizma*, 34, 54, 84 (Bleykhman).

6 *DSV*, i. 200–4; B & F, 204–8; Shvarts (Schwarz), *Sots. strakh.*, 99–132, esp. 123 f.

XVIII 1 See XIV, n. 1.

3 Wheeler-Bennett, *Brest-Litovsk*, 184–7, 191–5; *Bolsheviks*, 177.

4 Kennan, *Russia Leaves the War*, 194–217; Kalpashnikov, *Prisoner*, 12–78; Sisson, *One Hundred Red Days*, 449–51.

6 Ullman, *Intervention*, 33–35; Buchanan, *Mission*, ii. 228; Debo, 'Chicherin', 660–2; Lloyd George, *War Memoirs*, v. 2566, 2575, 2580.

7 Lenin, xxxv. 143–5; Reshetar, *Ukr. Revol.*, 94–5; Doroshenko, *Istoriia*, i. 214–24; Khristiuk, *Zamitki*, ii. 72–4; Yurchenko, *Ukr.-ros. stosunki*, 126–8; Mints, *Ist. Vel. Okt.*, iii. 561–2; Pidhainy, *Formation*, 401–19; Kovalivs'kyi, *Pry dzherelakh*, 437–9.

8 Doroshenko, *Istoriia*, i. 205–7; Reshetar, *Ukr. Revol.*, 93; Khristiuk, ii. 88–9; Yurkevich, *Ukr.-ros. stosunki*, 129–30; Shkilnyk, *Ukraina u borot'bi*, 155.

9 Pidhainy, *Formation*, 146–7; B & K, i. 383–402.

10 Reshetar, 103–5; Pidhainy, *Formation*, 457–87; *Mirnye peregovory*, 247–52; Trotsky, *My Life*, 392–3; Fischer, *Griff*, 642–4 (*Germany's Aims*, 486–7; slightly abridged).

XIX 2 Gavrilov, *Bor'ba*, 452–3; Keep, *Russ. Revol.*, 291–3.

3 Carr, *Bolsh. Revol.*, ii. 116–19, 205–6.

4 Bonch-Bruyevich, *Na boyevykh postakh*, 180–5 (not reprinted in *Vosp. o Lenine*).

5 Lenin, xxxv. 100–2, 152; Ilyukhina, 'K voprosu', 23–4; Radkey, *Sickle*, 149; Gorodetsky, *Rozhdenie*, 204–12 (citing unpublished materials); Gusev and Yeritsyan, *Ot soglashatel'stva*, 188–91.

6 *DSV*, i. 237–40, 247–9; iii. 320 (§52); Orlova, *Prav. regul.*, 8–10, 94–6; Carr, *Socialism*, i. 37–48 (where the extent of reformist trends under NEP are exaggerated); Halle, *Women*, 106–19; Geiger, *Family*, 43–75.

XX 1 B & F, 323–5; Gindin, *Kak bol'sheviki* (1962); Bonch-Bruyevich, *Na boyevykh postakh*, 197–207 (not reprinted in *Vosp. o Lenine*); Arnold, *Banks*, 59–61; Carr,

Session Note

Bolsh. Revol., ii. 138–41; Garvy, 'Origins'; Rivkin, *Fin. pol.*, 64–6, 83–97.

2 Carr, *Bolsh. Revol.*, ii. 149, 261–8.

3 PLSR. *Rezol. i post.*, 20–3; PLSR. *Sb. statey*, 5–18, 21– 6, 38–42; Izmaylovich, *Posleokt. oshibki*, 23; Radkey, *Agr. Foes*, 32–7, 66; Radkey, *Sickle*, 327.

4 'Denezhnye dokumenty', 345–57; Bradley, 'Allies', 166–85, esp. 176–7, 179; Kenez, *Civil War*, 72–3 (who does not cite 'Denezhnye dokumenty'); Ullman, *Intervention*, 46–7, 49; *FRUS*, ii. 591–2, 595–6; Kennan, *Russia Leaves the War*, 177–8; Rosenberg, *Liberals*, 289; Lukomsky, *Vosp.*, i. 288–9; Kazanovich, 'Poyezdka', 185; Solovyev, *Vel. Okt.*, 145–6; Fischer, *Soviets*, i. 836 (abr. ed., 617)—where the 14 December convention was first published; see now *DBFP* (I), iii. 369.

5 *Mirnye peregovory*; *SDFP*, i. 20–2; B & F, 476–84; Wheeler-Bennett, *Brest-Litovsk*, 111–29; Nowak, *Aufzeichnungen . . . Hoffmann*, ii. 197–202; Kühlmann, *Erinnerungen*, 520–4; Kennan, *Russia Leaves the War*, 219–24; Steglich, *Friedenspolitik*, 297–310.

6 *Osnovy*, 120–9; Varlamov, 'O nauchnykh', 172; Stalin, *Foundations*, 88–106; Keep, 'Lenin', 142–3.

8 Trotsky, *My Life*, 359.

9 Brécy, *Mouvement syndical*, 96–100.

11 Graubard, *Brit. Labour*, 46–8; Mayer, *Polit. Origins*, 181–3, 255, 267–90, 313–67; Lloyd George, *War Memoirs*, iv. 1898–1924, v. 2483–8, 2515–27.

12 Lapchinskyi, 'Pershii period'; Sh[reyberg], 'Iz istorii', 166–85, esp. 172–6; Doroshenko, *Istoriia*, i. 222; Bosh, *God bor'by*, 85–108; Kovalivs'kyi, *Pry dzherelakh*, 440; Reshetar, *Ukr. Revol.*, 94; Sobolev, *Istoriya*, 322–6; Mints, *Ist. Vel. Okt.*, iii. 561–3, 574–6; Pipes, *Formation*, 123–6; Pidhainy, *Formation*, 436–49; Heinzig, 'Kampf'.

13 Gavrilov, *Bor'ba*, 105, 117–18, 260, 270, 315, 420, 428, 526 (Siberia); 106, 240 (Central Asia); 321, 477 (Belorussia); Leykina, 'Oktyabr'', 228–9; Sobolev, *Istoriya*, 340–2, 398–401; Kudryavtsev & Vendrikh, *Irkutsk*, 267–89; Pipes, *Formation*, 74–5, 91–3, 174–6; Lubachko, *Belorussia*, 7–24; Abetsedarsky, *Ist. Belor. SSR*, ii. 74–7.

430 REFERENCES TO NOTES

Session Note

14 Bradley, 'Allies', 175, 180–3; Doroshenko, *Istoriia*, i. 233–5; Kovalivs'kyi, *Pry dzherelakh*, 426–34; Tabouis, 'Commissaire', 142–64; Pidhainy, *Formation*, 294–303, 315–17, 322–5, 329, 336–7, 345–7, 354–9.

15 Korolivsky *et al.*, *Pobeda*, 328; Reshetar, *Ukr. Revol.*, 110.

XXI 1 Kennan, *Russia Leaves the War*, 224–7; Sisson, *One Hundred Red Days*, 191–6; see also XX, n. 5.

2 *Mirnye peregovory*, 11–13, 28–9.

3 *Russia. Post. o pravakh*, 17–25; *Mirny dogovor*, 11–22, 35 ff.; Goldshteyn, *Voyna*; Pokrovsky, *Vneshnyaya torgovlya*, 345–95, esp. 361–4; Shteyn, *Torg. pol.*, 7–49; Shteyn, *Brest*, 3–34, esp. 19–20; Wheeler-Bennett, *Brest-Litovsk*, 256, 266–8, 270–4, 392–408.

4 *Leninskiy sb.*, xxi. 106–7; *DVP*, i. 125–35, 141–6; Sonkin, *Okno*, 32–41, 60–5.

5 Naumann, *Mitteleuropa*, 72, 101, 168, 193; Meyer, *Mitteleuropa*, 194–217, 260–80; Epstein, *Germany & the East*, 61, 65.

8 Kerff, *Liebknecht*, 327–36; Scheidemann, *Zusammenbruch*, 177; Hannover-Drück and Hannover, *Mord*, 20–4.

9 Selivanov, 'Pervy s'yezd'.

11 Baumgart, 'Militärpolit. Berichte', 92; Gurko, 'Iz Petrograda', 14; Rosenberg, *Liberals*, 290, 295, 313–20.

12 B & F, 661–2; Trotsky, *Kak vooruzhalas'*, i. 31; Deutscher, *Prophet Armed*, 407, 426.

13 Lenin, xxxv. 179–80, 472–3; Nikolayevsky, *Men'sheviki*, 114; Tsereteli, *Vosp.*, i. 301; Haimson, 'Les Mencheviks', 26–8.

XXII 1 Smith, *Finland*, 32–3; Syukiyaynen, *Revol. sobytiya*, 147–56; Kirby, 'Finnish S.D. Party', 193–6; *idem*, 'Stockholm', 81–4; Hodgson, *Comm. in Finland*, 59–78 (civil war).

2 *Prot. TsK*, 180–3, 194–5 (*Bolsheviks*, 153–6, 162, 167–8, 306–7); RSDRP, *Pervy legal'ny*, 371–4; Lenin, xxxv. 160–6; PLSR. *Rezol. i post.*, 23–4; *DSV*, i. 266, 549; B & F, 360–7; Schapiro, *Origin*, 80–5; Gorodetsky, *Rozhdenie*, 429–94, esp. 442; Kropat, 'Lenin u. die Konst. Vers.', 497; Radkey, *Sickle*, 336–49;

Session *Note*

Semenov, *Voyennaya*, 10–12; Keep, *Russ. Revol.*, 324–8.

3 Gimpelson, 'Nek. novye dannye', 214–17; B & F, 389–99; Keep, *Russ. Revol.*, 335–8; the congress minutes were published as *Tretiy Vseross. s'yezd Sovetov* . . . , Pg., 1918.

4 B & F, 59–62; *Prot. TsK*, 87–92 (*Bolsheviks*, 89–95); Schapiro, *Origin*, 60–1, 82; Anweiler, *Soviets*, 186–7.

5 Keep, *Russ. Revol.*, 441–4.

7 B & K, i. 126, iii. 1203; Sukhanov, *Zapiski*, i. 260–1, ii. 89–90; Sidorov, *VOSR*, i. 24.

8 *DSV*, i. 285; Rivkin, *Fin. pol.*, 104.

9 Piyashev, *Vorovsky*, 208; Carr, *Bolsh. Revol.*, iii. 121 n., 129; Kan, *Nov. ist. Shvetsii*, 73–5.

10 Shvarts (Schwarz), *Sots. strakh.*, 68, 70–9, 166.

XXIII 1 *DSV*, i. 460, ii. 4; Davydov, *Bor'ba*, 36–8; Keep, *Russ. Revol.*, 420–5.

2 B & F, 661–2; Chamberlin, *Russ. Revol.*, ii. 101, 338; Carr, *Bolsh. Revol.*, ii. 128, 242–3; Kritzman, *Heroische Periode*, 219–20.

3 Gordon, *Sov. avt. pravo*, 20–24; Levitsky, *Introduction*, 31–2; Gsovski, *Soviet Civil Law*, i. 606–17, esp. 611–12; Hazard *et al.*, *Soviet Legal System*, 342–50.

4 *DSV*, i. 294–6, 463–74; *Leninskiy sb.*, xxi. 111–15; Shlikhter, *Ilyich*, 60–2; Shteynberg, *Volkskommissar*, 15–40, 88–99, 123–38; Kucherov, *Organs*, 35.

5 *DSV*, i. 374, 565; B & F, 587; Kollontai, *Autobiography* 35–9; Schapiro, *Origin*, 109, 291.

XXIV 1 Frenkin, *Revol. dvizh.*, 258–74, 305–11, 319, 321–3, 339; Bereznyakov, *Bor'ba*, 198–208, 234–8, 251–3, 266–9; Aftenyuk *et al.*, *Za vlast'*, 199–211; Gaponenko, *Okt. revol. i armiya*, 230–1; Nartsov, 'Vel. Okt.', 134–8; Kennan, *Russia Leaves the War*, 330–42.

2 Oganovsky, 'Dnevnik', 143–9; Bonch-Bruyevich, *Na boyevykh postakh*, 227–53 (reference to pogroms omitted in *Vosp. o Lenine*, 140–54); Lenin, xxxv. 221–3; B & F, 372–4; Radkey, *Sickle*, 320, 365–6, 375, 428; Keep, *Russ. Revol.*, 328–9.

3 *DSV*, i. 386–7, iii. 455–6; B & F, 632–4; *SDFP*, i. 43, 138, 192, 270–2, 309–15, 322, 453–7; Vaynshteyn, *Nar. bog.*, 444–5 (Tab. 13); Michelson *et al.*, *Public Finance*, 322; (for other figures: Pasvolsky and Moul-

Session   Note
          ton, *Russian Debts*, 16–22, 175–81); Shmelev, 'Public
          Finance', 74–137, esp. 119; Davies, *Development*, 3–10.

XXV 1–2   Malchevsky, *Vseross. Uchred. Sobr.*; Semenov, *Voyen-
          naya*, 14–15; Bonch-Bruyevich, *Na boyevykh postakh*,
          241; Shteynberg, *Volkskommissar*, 71–3; Sokolov,
          'Zashchita', 62–68; Mstislavsky, *Pyat' dney*, 135–61.
      3   Lenin, xxxi. 99, 103–18, 351, 532; Sukhanov, *Zapiski*,
          iii. 28–42.
      4   B & K, iii. 1242–4; Milyukov, *Istoriya*, pt. 1, 93–117;
          Milyukov, *Polit. Memoirs*, 445–9; Sidorov, *VOSR*, ii.
          727, 729, 741–50, 840; Kazovskaya, 'Nota'; Rakhme-
          tov, 'Aprel'skiye dni' (report of government investiga-
          tion).

Bibliography

A. BOOKS AND ARTICLES

ABETSEDARSKY, L. S. *et al.* (eds.), *Istoriya Belorusskoy SSR*. 2 vols. Minsk, 1961.

AFTENYUK, S. YA. *et al.* (eds.), *Za vlast' Sovetov. Khronika revolyutsion-nykh sobytiy v Moldavii, mart 1917—yanvar' 1918*. Kishinev, 1969.

AMOSOV, P. N. *et al.* (eds.), *Oktyabr'skaya revolyutsiya i fabzavkomy. Materialy po istorii fabrichno-zavodskikh komitetov*. 2 pts. Moscow, 1927.

ANDREYEV, A. M., *Sovety rabochikh i soldatskikh deputatov nakanune Oktyabrya. Mart—oktyabr' 1917 g.* (Sovety v period Oktyabr'skoy revolyutsii i grazhdanskoy voyny, 1.) Moscow, 1967. Eng. trans.: *The Soviets of Workers' and Soldiers' Deputies on the Eve of the October Revolution, March—October 1917*. Tr. J. Langstone. Moscow, 1971.

ANIKEYEV, V. V., *Deyatel'nost' TsK RKP(b) v 1917 g.* Moscow, 1969.

——, *Deyatel'nost' TsK RKP(b) v 1917–1918 gg.* Moscow, 1974.

ANTONOV-OVSEYENKO, V. [A.], *Zapiski o grazhdanskoy voyne*. 2 fascs. Moscow, 1924–8.

ANWEILER, O., *Die Rätebewegung in Russland, 1905–1921*. Leyden, 1958. Eng. trans.: *The Soviets. The Russian Workers', Peasants' and Soldiers' Councils, 1905–1921*. Tr. R. Hein. New York, 1974.

ARNOLD, A. Z., *Banks, Credit and Money in Soviet Russia*. New York, 1937.

ASCHER, A., *Pavel Axelrod and the Development of Menshevism*. (Russian Research Center Studies, 70.) Cambridge, Mass., 1972.

AVDEYEV, N., 'Vokrug "Gatchiny" ', in: *KA* 9 (1925), pp. 171–94.

AVRICH, P. H. (ed.), *The Anarchists in the Russian Revolution*. Ithaca, N. Y.–London, 1973.

AVRICH, P. H., 'The Bolshevik Revolution and Workers' Control in Russian Industry', in: *SR* 22 (1963), pp. 47–63.

BAUMGART, W., 'Die militärpolitischen Berichte des Freiherrn von Keyserlingk aus Petersburg, Januar–Februar 1918', in: *VfZ* 15 (1967), 1, pp. 87–104.

BEREZNYAKOV, N. V. *et al.* (comps.), *Bor'ba za vlast' Sovetov v Moldavii, mart 1917–mart 1918 gg. Sbornik dokumentov i materialov.* Kishinev, 1957.

BONCH-BRUYEVICH, V. D., *Na boyevykh postakh fevral'skoy i Oktyabr'skoy revolyutsii.* 2nd ed. Moscow, 1931.

——, *Vospominaniya o Lenine.* Moscow, 1965.

BOSH, E. B., *God bor'by. Bor'ba za vlast' na Ukraine s aprelya 1917 g. do nemetskoy okkupatsii.* Moscow–Leningrad, 1925.

BRADLEY, J. F. N., 'The Allies and Russia in the Light of French Archives, 7 November 1917—15 March 1918', in: *SS* 16 (1964–5), pp. 166–85.

BRAUNTHAL, J., *Geschichte der Internationale*, Bd. 2. Hanover, 1963.

BRÉCY, R., *Le Mouvement syndical en France, 1871–1921. Essai bibliographique.* Paris–The Hague, 1963.

BROWDER, R. P. and KERENSKY, A. F. (eds.), *The Russian Provisional Government, 1917. Documents.* 3 vols. Stanford, 1961. [B & K].

BUCHANAN, SIR G., *My Mission to Russia and Other Diplomatic Memories.* 2 vols. London–New York, 1923.

BUNYAN, J. and FISHER, H. H., *The Bolshevik Revolution, 1917–1918. Documents and Materials.* Stanford, 1934; reprinted 1965. [B & F].

BUTENKO, A. F. and CHUGAYEV, D. A. (eds.), *Vtoroy Vserossiyskiy s'yezd Sovetov rabochikh i soldatskikh deputatov. Sbornik dokumentov.* Moscow, 1957.

CARR, E. H., *The Bolshevik Revolution, 1917–1923.* (A History of Soviet Russia.) 3 vols. London–New York, 1950–3; reprinted 1966.

——, *Socialism in One Country.* (A History of Soviet Russia.) 3 vols. London–New York, 1958–64; reprinted 1970.

CHAMBERLIN, W. H., *The Russian Revolution, 1917–1921.* 2 vols. New York, 1935; reprinted 1965.

CHEREPAKHOV, M. S. and FINGERIT, E. M. (comps.), *Russkaya periodicheskaya pechat', 1895–oktyabr' 1917. Spravochnik.* Moscow, 1957.

CHERNOV, V. M., ' "Sovety" v nashey revolyutsii', in: Bakh, A. N. *et al.* (eds.), *God russkoy revolyutsii, 1917–1918 gg. Sbornik statey,* Moscow, 1918, pp. 47–66.

CHUGAYEV, D. A. (ed.), *Protokoly i postanovleniya TsK Baltiyskogo flota, 1917–1918.* Moscow–Leningrad, 1963.

CHUGAYEV, D. A. *et al.* (eds.), *Petrogradskiy voyenno-revolyutsionny komitet. Dokumenty i materialy.* 3 vols. Moscow, 1966–7. [*PVRK*].

DANIELS, R. V., *The Conscience of the Revolution. Communist Opposition in Soviet Russia.* Cambridge, Mass.–London, 1960.

BIBLIOGRAPHY

435

DANIELS, R. V., *Red October. The Bolshevik Revolution of 1917.* New York, 1967–London, 1968.

DAVIES, R. W., *The Development of the Soviet Budgetary System.* Cambridge, 1958.

DAVYDOV, M. I., *Bor'ba za khleb. Prodovol'stvennaya politika Kommunisticheskoy partii i Sovetskogo gosudarstva v gody grazhdanskoy voyny, 1917–1920.* Moscow, 1971.

DEBO, R. K., 'The Making of a Bolshevik. Georgi Chicherin in England, 1914–1918', in: *SR* 35 (1966), pp. 651–62.

DEGRAS, J. (ed.), *Soviet Documents on Foreign Policy,* vol. 1. 1917–24. London–New York, 1951. [*SDFP*].

DEMYANOV, A. S., 'Zapiski o podpol'nom Vremennom Pravitel'stve', in: *ARR* 7 (1922), pp. 34–52.

'Denezhnye dokumenty gen. Alekseyeva', in: *ARR* 5 (1922), pp. 345–57.

DEUTSCHER, I., *The Prophet Armed. Trotsky, 1879–1921.* London–New York, 1954.

Dictionnaire biographique du mouvement ouvrier français, vol. 13(iii). 1871–1914. Ed. H. Dubief *et al.* Paris, 1975.

DOROSHENKO, D., *Istoriia Ukraini, 1917–1923 rr.* 2 vols. Uzhgorod, 1930–2.

DRAPER, T., *The Roots of American Communism.* New York, 1957.

DREZEN, A. K. (ed.), *Baltiyskiy flot v Oktyabr'skoy revolyutsii i grazhdanskoy voyne.* Leningrad, 1932.

——, 'Tsentral'nye matrosskiye i ofitserskiye organizatsii Baltiyskogo flota v 1917 g.', in: *KL* (1929), 3, pp. 43–104.

DROBIZHEV, V. Z., *Glavny shtab sotsialisticheskoy promyshlennosti. Ocherki istorii VSNKh, 1917–1932 gg.* Moscow, 1966.

DSV: see Russia (Laws).

DUVAL, C., 'The Bolshevik Secretariat and Yakov Sverdlov. February to October 1917', in: *SEER* 51 (1973), pp. 47–57.

DVP: see Russia (Ministry of Foreign Affairs).

DZIEWANOWSKI, M. K., *The Communist Party of Poland. An Outline History.* Cambridge, Mass.–London, 1959.

——, 'World War I and the Marxist Movement of Poland', in: *ASEER* 12 (1953), pp. 72–92.

EDMONDS, SIR J. E., *A Short History of World War I.* London–New York, 1951.

EPSTEIN, F. T., 'The Accessibility of Source Materials Illuminating the History of German Foreign Policy . . .', in: Epstein, F. T. and Byrnes, R. F. (eds.), *Germany and the East. Selected Essays,* Bloomington, Ind.–London, 1973, pp. 169–90.

436 BIBLIOGRAPHY

EPSTEIN, F. T. and BYRNES, R. F. (eds.), *Germany and the East. Selected Essays*. Bloomington, Ind.–London, 1973.

ERICKSON, J., *The Soviet High Command. A Military–Political History*. London, 1962.

FAINSOD, M., *How Russia is Ruled*. (Russian Research Center Studies, 11.) Rev. ed. Cambridge, Mass.–London, 1963.

——, *International Socialism and the World War*. Cambridge, Mass., 1935; reprinted Garden City, N.Y., 1969.

FEDOROV, K. G., *VTsIK v pervye gody Sovetskoy vlasti, 1917–1920 gg*. Moscow, 1957.

FISCHER, F., *Griff nach der Weltmacht*. 3rd ed. Wiesbaden, 1964. Engl. trans.: *Germany's Aims in the First World War*. Introd. J. Joll. London, 1967.

FISCHER, L., *The Soviets in World Affairs. A History of Relations between the Soviet Union and the Rest of the World, 1917–1929*. London–New York, 1930; reprinted Princeton, 1960.

FITZPATRICK, S., *The Commissariat of Enlightenment. Soviet Organization of Education and the Arts under Lunacharsky*. Cambridge, 1970.

FLEER, M. G., 'Vremennoye Pravitel'stvo posle Oktyabrya', in: *KA* 6 (1924), pp. 195–221.

FOKKE, D. G., 'Na stsene i za kulisami brestskoy tragikomedii', in: *ARR* 20 (1930), pp. 5–207.

FRAIMAN, A. L. *et al.* (eds.), *Oktyabr'skoye vooruzhennoye vosstanie 1917 g. v Petrograde*. 2 vols. Leningrad, 1967.

FRENKIN, M. S., *Revolyutsionnoye dvizhenie na rumynskom fronte, 1917 g.–mart 1918 g. Soldaty 8-go armii rumynskogo fronta v bor'be za mir i vlast' Sovetov*. Moscow, 1965.

FUTRELL, M., *Northern Underground. Episodes of Russian Revolutionary Transport and Communications through Scandinavia and Finland, 1863–1917*. London, 1963.

GAPONENKO, L. S. (ed.), *Oktyabr'skaya revolyutsiya i armiya, 25 oktyabrya 1917–mart 1918 g. Sbornik dokumentov*. Moscow, 1973.

GARVI, P. A., *Professional'nye soyuzy v Rossii v pervye gody revolyutsii, 1917–1921*. Ed. G. Ya. Aronson. New York, 1958.

GARVY, G., 'The Origin of Lenin's Views on the Role of Banks in the Socialist Transformation of Society', in: *HPE* 4 (1972), pp. 252–63.

GAVRILOV, L. M. *et al.* (comps.), *Bor'ba za ustanovlenie i uprochenie Sovetskoy vlasti. Khronika sobytiy, 26 oktyabrya 1917 g.–10 yanvarya 1918 g*. Ed. I. G. Dykov *et al*. Moscow, 1962.

GEIGER, H. K., *The Family in Soviet Russia*. Cambridge, Mass.–London, 1968; reprinted 1970.

Germany. Aussenamt. *Die deutschen Dokumente zum Kriegsausbruch. Vollständige Sammlung* . . . Ed. Graf M. Montgelas and W. Schücking. 4 vols. Vol. 1. Charlottenburg, 1919. [*DDK*].

GERSHBERG, S. R., 'V. I. Lenin i sozdanie VSNKh', in: *VI* (1958), 7, pp. 3–24.

GERSON, L. D., *The Secret Police in Lenin's Russia.* London–Philadelphia, 1976.

[GESSEN], I. V., 'General Dukhonin v Stavke', in: *GM* (1918), 1–3, pp. 289–308.

GESSEN, I. V., *V dvukh vekakh. Zhiznenny otchet. ARR* 22 (1937).

GETZLER, I., *Martov. A Political Biography of a Russian Social Democrat.* Melbourne–London–New York, 1967.

GIMPELSON, E. G., *Iz istorii stroitel'stva Sovetov, noyabr' 1917 g.–iyul' 1918 g.* Moscow, 1958.

——, 'Nekotorye novye dannye o sostave III-go Vserossiyskogo s'yezda Sovetov rabochikh i soldatskikh deputatov', in: *VI* (1960), 9, pp. 214–17.

GINDIN, I. F., *Kak bol'sheviki natsionalizirovali chastnye banki. Fakty i dokumenty posleoktyabr'skikh dney v Petrograde.* Moscow, 1962.

——, *Kak bol'sheviki zakhvatili Gosudarstvenny Bank.* Moscow, 1961.

GOLDSHTEYN, I. M., *Voyna, russko-germanskiy torgovy dogovor, i: Sleduyet li Rossii byt' 'koloniyey' Germanii?* 2nd ed. Moscow, 1915.

GOLINKOV, D. L., *Krakh vrazheskogo podpol'ya. Iz istorii bor'by s kontrrevolyutsiyey v Sovetskoy Rossii v 1917–1924 gg.* Moscow, 1971.

GOLOVIN, N. N., *Voyennye usiliya Rossii v mirovoy voyne.* 2 vols. Paris, 1939, Engl. ed.: Golovine, N. N., *The Russian Army in the World War.* New Haven, 1931.

GOLUB, P. A., *Partiya, armiya i revolyutsiya. Otvoyevanie partiyey bol'shevikov armii na storonu revolyutsii, mart 1917–fevral' 1918.* Moscow, 1967.

GORDON, M. V., *Sovetskoye avtorskoye pravo.* Moscow, 1955.

GORIN, P. O. (ed.), *Organizatsiya i stroitel'stvo Sovetov rabochickh i soldatskikh deputatov v 1917 g. Sbornik dokumentov.* (Materialy po istorii Sovetskogo stroitel'stva, 1.) Moscow, 1928.

GORODETSKY, E. N., *Rozhdenie Sovetskogo gosudarstva, 1917–1918 gg.* Moscow, 1965.

GORODETSKY, E. N. and SHARAPOV, YU. P., *Sverdlov. Zhizn' i deyatel'nost'.* Moscow, 1961.

GRAUBARD, S. R., *British Labour and the Russian Revolution, 1917–1924.* Cambridge, Mass., 1956.

Great Britain. Foreign Office. *Documents on British Foreign Policy, 1919–1939.* Series I, vol. 3. London, 1949. [*DBFP*].

GSOVSKI, V., *Soviet Civil Law. Private Rights and their Background under the Soviet Regime.* 2 vols. Ann Arbor, Mich., 1948–9.

GURKO, V. I., 'Iz Petrograda cherez Moskvu, Parizh i London v Odessu, 1917–1918 gg.', in: *ARR* 15 (1924), pp. 5–84.

GURVICH, G. S., 'Vsya vlast' Sovetam', in: *Proletarskaya revolyutsiya i pravo*, fasc. 1, n.p., 1918, pp. 1–21.

GUSEV, K. V. and YERITSYAN, KH. A., *Ot soglashatel'stva k kontrrevolyutsii. Ocherki istorii politicheskogo bankrotstva i gibeli Partii Sotsialistov-Revolyutsionerov*. Moscow, 1968.

HAIMSON, L., 'Les Mencheviks face à la révolution d'octobre. Le Congrès extraordinaire du RSDRP, novembre–décembre 1917', in: *CMRS* 14 (1973), pp. 5–32.

HALLE, F. W., *Women in Soviet Russia*. London, 1934.

HANNAK, J., *Im Sturm eines Jahrhunderts. Eine volkstümliche Geschichte der Sozialistischen Partei Österreichs*. Vienna, 1952.

HANNOVER-DRÜCK, E. and HANNOVER, H., *Der Mord an Rosa Luxemburg und Karl Liebknecht. Dokumentation eines politischen Verbrechens*. Frankfurt, 1968.

HANNULA, J. O., *La Guerre d'indépendance de Finlande*. Tr. J.-L. Perret. Paris, 1938.

HAZARD, J. N. *et al.*, *The Soviet Legal System. Contemporary Documentation and Historical Commentary*. Rev. ed. Dobbs Ferry, N.Y., 1969.

HEINZIG, D., 'Der Kampf der Bolschewisten um die Bildung der ersten ukrainischen Sowjetregierung im November–Dezember 1917', in: Frenzke, D. and Uschakow, A. (eds.), *Macht und Recht im kommunistischen Herrschaftssystem*, Cologne, 1965, pp. 95–112.

The History of the Civil War in the USSR, vol. 2. *The Great Proletarian Revolution, October–November 1917*. London, 1947; reprinted Gulf Breeze, Fla., 1975.

HODGSON, J. H., *Communism in Finland. A History and an Interpretation*. Princeton, 1967.

ILYUKHINA, R. M., 'K voprosu o soglashenii bol'shevikov s levymi S-Rami, oktyabr' 1917–fevral' 1918 g.', in: *IZ* 73 (1963), pp. 3–34.

IROSHNIKOV, M. P., *Sozdanie Sovetskogo tsentral'nogo gosudarstvennogo apparata. Sovet Narodnykh Komissarov i narodnye komissary, oktyabr' 1917 g.–yanvar' 1918 g.* Moscow–Leningrad, 1966. 2nd ed. Leningrad, 1967.

Istoriya grazhdanskoy voyny v SSSR, vol. 3. *Uprochenie Sovetskoy vlasti, nachalo inostrannoy interventsii i grazhdanskaya voyna, noyabr' 1917 g.–mart 1919 g.* Moscow, 1958. [*IGV*].

IZMAYLOVICH, A., *Posleoktyabr'skiye oshibki*. [Moscow, 1918].

JASNY, N., *Soviet Economists of the Twenties. Names to be Remembered*. Cambridge, 1972.

KALPASHNIKOV (KALPASCHNIKOFF), A., *A Prisoner of Trotsky's*. Foreword by D. R. Francis. Garden City, N.Y., 1920.

KAN, A. S., *Noveyshaya istoriya Shvetsii*. Moscow, 1964.

KANEV, S. N., *Oktyabr'skaya revolyutsiya i krakh anarkhizma. Bor'ba partii bol'shevikov protiv anarkhizma, 1917–1922*. Moscow, 1974.

KAZANOVICH, V., 'Poyezdka iz Dobrovol'cheskoy Armii v "Krasnuyu Moskvu", may–iyul' 1918 g.', in: *ARR* 7 (1922), pp. 184–202.

KAZOVSKAYA, A., 'Nota Milyukova i aprel'skiye dni', in: *PR* 63 (1927), pp. 83–100.

KEEP, J. L. H., 'Lenin as Tactician', in: Schapiro, L. B. and Reddaway, P. (eds.), *Lenin. The Man, the Theorist, the Leader. A Reappraisal.* London–New York, 1967, pp. 135–58.

——, 'October in the Provinces', in: Pipes, R. (ed.), *Revolutionary Russia*, Cambridge, Mass., 1968, pp. 229–75.

——, *The Rise of Social Democracy in Russia*. Oxford, 1963.

——, *The Russian Revolution. A Study in Mass Mobilization.* London, 1976–New York, 1977.

KENEZ, P., *Civil War in South Russia, 1918. The First Year of the Volunteer Army*. Berkeley–Los Angeles–London, 1971.

KENNAN, G. F., *Russia and the West under Lenin and Stalin.* Boston, 1960–London, 1961.

——, *Russia Leaves the War.* (Soviet–American Relations, vol. 1.) Princeton–London, 1956; reprinted New York, 1967.

KERENSKY, A. F., 'Gatchina', in: *SZ* 10 (1922), pp. 147–80.

——, *Izdaleka. Sbornik statey, 1920–1921 gg.* Paris, 1922.

——, *Russia and History's Turning-Point.* New York, 1965–London, 1966.

KERFF, W., *Karl Liebknecht, 1914–1916. Fragment einer Biographie.* East Berlin, 1967.

KHESIN, S. S. *et al.* (eds.), *Voyenno-morskoy revolyutsionny komitet. Sbornik dokumentov.* Leningrad, 1975. [*VMRK*].

KHRISTIUK, P., *Zamitki i materiyali do istorii Ukrains'koi revoliutsii, 1917–1920 rr.* 2 vols. Vienna, 1921; reprinted New York, 1969.

KIRBY, D. G., *Finland and Russia, 1808–1920. From Autocracy to Independence. A Selection of Documents.* London, 1975.

——, 'The Finnish Social-Democratic Party and the Bolsheviks', in: *JCH* 7 (1972), 1–2, pp. 181–98.

——, 'Stockholm–Petrograd–Berlin. International Social-Democracy and Finnish Independence, 1917', in: *SEER* 52 (1974), pp. 63–84.

KLANTE, M., *Von der Wolga zum Amur. Die tschechische Legion und der russische Bürgerkrieg.* Berlin, 1931.

KLEANDROVA, V. M., *Organizatsiya i forma deyatel'nosti VTsIK, 1917–1924 gg.* Moscow, 1968.

KOCHAN, L., 'Kadet Policy and the Constituent Assembly', in: *SEER* 45 (1967), pp. 183–93.

KOHN, S. and MEYENDORFF, A. P., *The Cost of the War to Russia. The Vital Statistics of European Russia during the World War, 1914–1917.* New Haven, 1932.

KOLLONTAI (KOLLONTAY), A., *The Autobiography of a Sexually Emancipated Woman* [1926]. Ed. I. Fetscher. New York, 1971.

KORENEVSKAYA, E. I., 'Organizatsionno-pravovye formy deyatel'nosti Soveta narodnykh komissarov RSFSR, 1917–1922', in: *SGP* (1968), 7, pp. 93–7.

KOROLEV, F. F., *Ocherki po istorii Sovetskoy shkoly i pedagogiki.* 2 vols. Vol. 1. *1917–1920.* Moscow, 1958–61.

KOROLIVSKY, S. M., RUBACH, M. A., and SUPRUNENKO, N. I., *Pobeda Sovetskoy vlasti na Ukraine.* Moscow, 1967.

KOVALENKO, D. A. *et al.* (eds.), *Sovety v pervy god proletarskoy diktatury, oktyabr' 1917–noyabr' 1918 g.* (Sovety v period Oktyabr'skoy revolyutsii i grazhdanskoy voyny, 2.) Moscow, 1967.

KOVALIVS'KYI, M. M., *Pry dzherelakh borot'bi. Spomini, vrazhennia, refleksii.* Innsbruck, 1960.

[KOZMIN, A. I.], 'Podgotovka k nastupleniyu na Petrograd', in: *KA* 24 (1927), pp. 201–8.

KRASNOV, P. N., 'Na vnutrennem fronte', in: *ARR* 1 (1921), pp. 97–190.

KRITZMAN (KRITSMAN), L. N., *Die heroische Periode der grossen russischen Revolution. Ein Versuch der Analyse des sogenannten 'Kriegskommunismus'.* Vienna–Berlin, 1929; reprinted Frankfurt, 1971.

KROPAT, W.–A., 'Lenin und die Konstituierende Versammlung in Russland', in: *JGOE* 5 (1957), pp. 488–98.

KUCHEROV, S., *The Organs of the Soviet Administration of Justice. Their History and Operation.* Leyden, 1970.

KUDELLI, P. F. (ed.), *Oktyabr'skiy shkval. Moryaki Baltiyskogo flota v 1917 g. Sbornik.* Leningrad, 1927.

KUDRYAVTSEV, E. A. and VENDRIKH, G. A., *Irkutsk. Ocherki po istorii goroda.* Irkutsk, 1958.

KÜHLMANN, R. VON, *Erinnerungen.* Heidelberg, 1948.

KUUSINEN, O., 'Finlyandskaya revolyutsiya' [1918], in: *Finlyandskaya revolyutsiya. Sbornik statey,* Moscow, 1920, pp. 3–24.

LANDE, L., 'The Mensheviks in 1917', in: Haimson, L. (ed.), *The Mensheviks from the Revolution of 1917 to the Second World War,* Chicago–London, 1974, pp. 3–91.

LAPCHINSKYI, G. [F.], 'Pershii period radians'koi vladi na Ukraini. TsKVU ta Narodnyi Sekretariat', in: *LR* 28 (1928), pp. 159–75.

LATSIS, M. YA., *Chrezvychaynye komissii po bor'be s kontr-revolyutsiyey*. Moscow, 1921.

——, *Dva goda bor'by na vnutrennem fronte*. Moscow, 1920.

——, 'T. Dzerzhinsky i VChK', in: *PR* 56 (1926), pp. 81–97.

LAZAREV, A. B., 'Iz istorii razrabotki leninskogo dekreta o rabochem kontrole', in: *VI KPSS* (1960), 3, pp. 131–40.

LENCZOWSKI, G., *Russia and the West in Iran. A Study in Big Power Rivalry*. Ithaca, N.Y., 1949.

LENIN, V. I., *Polnoye sobranie sochineniy*. 5th ed. 55 vols. Moscow, 1959–65. [Lenin, *PSS*].

Leninskiy sbornik. 38 vols. Moscow, 1924–75.

LERNER, W., *Karl Radek. The Last Internationalist*. Stanford–London, 1970.

LESNOY, V. M., *Sotsialisticheskaya revolyutsiya i gosudarstvenny apparat*. Moscow, 1968.

LEVITSKY, S. L., *Introduction to Soviet Copyright Law*. Leyden, 1964.

LEYKINA, V., 'Oktyabr' po Rossii', in: *PR* 49 (1926), pp. 185–233; 58 (1926), pp. 234–55; 59 (1926), pp. 238–54.

LLOYD GEORGE, D., *The War Memoirs*. 6 vols. London, 1933–6.

LUBACHKO, I. S., *Belorussia under Soviet Rule, 1917–1957*. Lexington, Ky., 1972.

LUDENDORFF, E., *Meine Kriegserinnerungen, 1914–1918*. 3rd ed. Berlin, 1919.

LUKOMSKY, A. S., *Vospominaniya*. 2 vols. Berlin, 1922.

LUNACHARSKY, A. V., *Revolutionary Silhouettes*. Tr. M. Glenny. Introd. I. Deutscher. London–New York, 1968.

LUTOVINOV, I. S., *Likvidatsiya myatezha Kerenskogo–Krasnova*. Moscow, 1965.

LYUBIMOV, I. N. (comp.), *Revolyutsiya 1917 g. Khronika sobytiy*, 6. *Oktyabr'–dekabr'*. Moscow, 1930.

McNEAL, R. H. (ed.), *Resolutions and Decisions of the Communist Party of the Soviet Union*, vol. II: The Early Soviet Period, 1917–1929, ed. R. Gregor. Toronto, 1974.

MALCHEVSKY, I. S. (comp.), *Vserossiyskoye Uchreditel'noye Sobranie*. Moscow–Leningrad, 1930.

MAY, A. J., *The Passing of the Hapsburg Monarchy, 1914–1918*. 2 vols. Philadelphia, 1966.

MAYER, A. J., *Political Origins of the New Diplomacy, 1917–1918*. New Haven, 1959.

MEDLIN, V. D. and PARSONS, S. L., *V. D. Nabokov and the Russian Provisional Government, 1917.* New Haven–London, 1976.

MELGUNOV, S. P., *Kak bol'sheviki zakhvatili vlast'. Oktyabr'skiy perevorot 1917 g.* Paris, 1953. Engl. trans.: *The Bolshevik Seizure of Power.* Ed. and abridged by S. G. and B. S. Pushkarev. Tr. J. S. Beaver. Santa Barbara, Calif.–Oxford, 1972.

MEYER, H. C., *Mitteleuropa in German Thought and Action, 1815–1945.* The Hague, 1955.

MICHELSON, A. M., APOSTOL, P. N., and BERNATZKY, M. W., *Russian Public Finance during the War.* New Haven, 1928.

MILYUKOV, P. N., *Istoriya vtoroy russkoy revolyutsii.* 3 pts. Sofia, 1921–3.

——, *Political Memoirs, 1905–1917.* Ed. A. P. Mendel. Ann Arbor, 1967.

MINTS, I. I., *Istoriya Velikogo Oktyabrya.* 3 vols. Moscow, 1967–73.

Mirnye peregovory v Brest-Litovske s 22/9 dekabrya 1917 g. po 3 marta/18 fevralya 1918 g. Vol. 1. *Plenarnye zasedaniya. Zasedaniya politicheskoy komissii. Polny tekst stenogramm.* Ed. A. A. Ioffe (V. Krimsky). Foreword by L. Trotsky. Moscow, 1920.

Mirny dogovor mezhdu Rossiyey s odnoy storony i Germaniyey, Avstro–Vengriyey, Bolgariyey i Turtsiyey s drugoy. Moscow, 1918.

MOROZOV, B. M., *Partiya i Sovety v Oktyabr'skoy revolyutsii.* Moscow, 1966.

MOULTON, H. G. and PASVOLSKY, L., *World War Debt Settlements.* New York, 1926.

MSTISLAVSKY, S., *Pyat' dney. Nachalo i konets fevral'skoy revolyutsii.* 2nd ed. Berlin–Petrograd–Moscow, 1922.

'Nakanune peremiriya', in: *KA* 23 (1927), pp. 195–249.

NARTSOV, V. N., 'Velikaya Oktabr'skaya sotsialisticheskaya revolyutsiya i Rumyniya, 1917–1918 gg.', in: *Voprosy novoy i noveyshey istorii. Uchenye zapiski Barnaul'skogo Gosudarstvennogo Pedagogicheskogo Instituta,* vol. 19, Barnaul, 1972, pp. 125–59.

NAUMANN, F., *Mitteleuropa.* Berlin, 1916.

NECK, R., *Arbeiterschaft und Staat im ersten Weltkrieg, 1914–1918.* A. *Quellen.* Vol. 1. *Der Staat.* Vienna, 1968.

NESTERENKO, P., 'Gatchina v dni bor'by so bol'shevizmom', in: *BA* 1 (1926), pp. 72–80.

NIKOLAYEVSKY, B. I., *Men'sheviki v dni Oktyabr'skogo perevorota.* (Inter-University Project on the History of Menshevism, Paper 8.) New York, 1962.

NOWAK, K. F. (ed.), *Die Aufzeichnungen des Generalmajors Max Hoffmann.* Vol. 2. Berlin, 1930.

ODOM, W. E., 'Sverdlov, Bolshevik Party Organizer', in: *SEER* 44 (1966), pp. 421-44.

OGANOVSKY, N. [P.], 'Dnevnik chlena Uchreditel'nogo Sobraniya', in: *GM* (1918), 4-6, pp. 143-72.

'Oktyabr' na fronte', in: *KA* 20 (1927), pp. 149-94; 24 (1927), pp. 71-107.

OPPENHEIM, S. A., 'The Supreme Economic Council, 1917-1921', in: *SS* 25 (1973), pp. 3-27.

OREKHOVA, E. D., 'O sostave Petrogradskogo voyenno-revolyutsion-nogo komiteta', in: *IS* (1971), 2, pp. 118-30.

ORLOV, N. [A.], *Prodovol'stvennaya rabota Sovetskoy vlasti. K godov-shchine Oktyabr'skoy revolyutsii.* Moscow, 1919.

ORLOVA, N. V., *Pravovoye regulirovanie braka v SSSR.* Moscow, 1971.

Osnovy nauchnogo kommunizma. Ed. Maj.-Gen. Sulimov *et al.* Moscow, 1968.

OSTERROTH, F. and SCHUSTER, D., *Chronik der deutschen Sozialdemokratie*, vol. 1. Bonn, 1973.

OVSYANNIKOV, N. (ed.), *Oktyabr'skoye vosstanie 1917 g. v Moskve. Sbornik dokumentov.* Moscow, 1922.

PASVOLSKY, L. and MOULTON, H. G., *Russian Debts and Russian Reconstruction. A Study of the Relation of Russia's Foreign Debts to her Economic Recovery.* New York-London, 1924.

PETHYBRIDGE, R. W., *The Spread of the Russian Revolution. Essays on 1917.* London-New York, 1972.

PIDHAINY, O. S., *The Formation of the Ukrainian Republic.* Toronto-New York, 1966.

PIETSCH, W., *Revolution und Staat. Institutionen als Träger der Macht in Sowjetrussland, 1917-1922.* Cologne, 1969.

PIONTKOVSKY, S. A., *Oktyabr' 1917 g.* Moscow-Leningrad, 1927.

—— (ed.), *Sovety v Oktyabre. Sbornik dokumentov.* Moscow, 1928.

PIPES, R., *The Formation of the Soviet Union. Communism and Nationalism, 1917-1923.* Cambridge, Mass., 1954; revised ed., 1964; reprinted New York, 1968.

—— (ed.), *Revolutionary Russia.* Cambridge, Mass.-London, 1968; reprinted as *Revolutionary Russia. A Symposium*, Garden City, N.Y., 1969.

PIYASHEV, N., *Vorovsky.* (Zhizn' zamechatel'nykh lyudey, 275.) Moscow, 1959.

PODVOYSKY, N., *Krasnaya gvardiya v oktyabr'skiye dni. Leningrad i Moskva.* Moscow-Leningrad, 1927.

POKROVSKY, S. A., *Vneshnyaya torgovlya i vneshnyaya torgovaya politika Rossii.* Moscow, 1947.

POLOVTSOV, P. A., *Dni zatmeniya. Zapiski glavnokomanduyushchego voyskami Petrogradskogo voyennogo okruga . . . v 1917 g.* Paris, 1927.
PONOMAREV, B. N. (ed.), *Politicheskiy slovar'*. Moscow, 1958.
POPOV, A. (comp.), ROZHKOV, N. A. (ed.), *Oktyabr'skiy perevorot. Fakty i dokumenty*. Petrograd, 1918.
Proceedings of the Brest-Litovsk Peace Conference. The Peace Negotiations between Russia and the Central Powers, 21 November 1917–3 March 1918. Washington, 1918.
Prot. TsK: see Russia. Russian Social-Democratic Labour Party.
PUNTILA, L. A., *Histoire politique de la Finlande de 1809 à 1955*. Tr. J.-L. Perret. Neuchâtel, 1966.
PVRK: see Chugayev, D. A.

RABINOWITCH, A., *The Bolsheviks Come to Power. The Revolution of 1917 in Petrograd*. New York, 1976.
——, *Prelude to Revolution. The Petrograd Bolsheviks and the July 1917 Uprising*. Bloomington, Ind.–London, 1968.
RADKEY, O. H., *The Agrarian Foes of Bolshevism. Promise and Default of the Russian Socialist Revolutionaries, February to October 1917*. New York–London, 1958.
——, *The Election to the Russian Constituent Assembly of 1917*. Cambridge, Mass., 1950.
——, *The Sickle under the Hammer. The Russian Socialist Revolutionaries in the Early Months of Soviet Rule*. New York–London, 1963.
RAKHMETOV, V., 'Aprel'skiye dni v Petrograde', in: *KA* 33 (1929), pp. 34–81.
REED, J., *Ten Days that Shook the World*. London, 1926; reprinted Harmondsworth, 1966.
RESHETAR, J. S., *The Ukrainian Revolution, 1917–1920. A Study in Nationalism*. Princeton, 1952; reprinted New York, 1972.
REYSNER, M., 'Oktyabr'skaya revolyutsiya i gosudarstvennaya vlast'', in: *Oktyabr'skiy perevorot i diktatura proletariata. Sbornik statey*, Moscow, 1919, pp. 31–51.
RIVKIN, B. B., *Finansovaya politika v period Velikoy Oktyabr'skoy sotsialisticheskoy revolyutsii*. Moscow, 1957.
ROSENBERG, W. G., *Liberals in the Russian Revolution. The Constitutional-Democratic Party, 1917–1921*. Princeton–London, 1974.
——, 'Russian Liberals and the Bolshevik Coup', in: *JMH* 40 (1968), pp. 328–47.
——, 'The Russian Municipal Duma Elections of 1917. A Preliminary Computation of Returns', in: *SS* 21 (1969–70), pp. 131–63.
RSDRP. See Russia. Russian Social-Democratic Labour Party.

BIBLIOGRAPHY 445

RUSSIA. Laws and Statutes. *Dekrety Sovetskoy vlasti*. 7 vols. Moscow, 1957–75. [*DSV*].

RUSSIA. Russian Empire. Ministry of Trade and Industry. *Postanov-leniya o pravakh naibol'shego blagopriyatstvovaniya v torgovykh dogovorakh zaklyuchennykh Rossiyey s inostrannymi gosudarstvami v 1901 g. i pozd-neye*. Petrograd, 1915.

RUSSIA. RSFSR/USSR. All-Union (All-Russian) Central Council of Trade Unions (VTsSPS). *Otchet VTsSPS za iyul'–dekabr' 1917 g.* (By S. Lozovsky.) Petrograd, 1918.

——, *Pervy Vserossiyskiy s'yezd professional'nykh soyuzov, 7–14 yanvarya 1918 g. Polny stenograficheskiy otchet*. Foreword by M. Tomsky. Moscow, 1918.

——, *Tret'ya Vserossiyskaya konferentsiya professional'nykh soyuzov, 3–11 iyulya (20–28 iyunya st. st.). Stenograficheskiy otchet*. Moscow, 1927.

RUSSIA. RSFSR/USSR. Central Executive Committee of Soviets of Workers', Soldiers' and Peasants' Deputies (VTsIK). *Protokoly zasedaniy Vserossiyskogo Tsentral'nogo Ispolnitel'nogo Komiteta Sovetov Rabochikh, Soldatskikh, Krest'yanskikh i Kazach'ikh Deputatov, II sozyv, 27 oktyabrya–29 dekabrya 1917*. Moscow, 1918. [*Prot.*].

RUSSIA. RSFSR/USSR. Central Statistical Administration (TsSU). *Rossiya v mirovoy voyne v tsifrakh*. Moscow, 1925.

RUSSIA. RSFSR/USSR. Congress of Soviets. *Vtoroy Vserossiyskiy s'yezd Sovetov rabochikh i soldatskikh deputatov. Protokoly*. Compiled by K. G. Kotelnikov. Foreword by Ya. A. Yakovlev. Moscow–Leningrad, 1928.

RUSSIA. RSFSR/USSR. Ministry of Foreign Affairs (MID). *Doku-menty vneshney politiki SSSR*. 20 vols. Moscow, 1957–76. [*DVP*].

RUSSIA. Party of Left Socialist-Revolutionaries (PLSR). *Rezolyutsii i postanovleniya I-go i II-go s'yezdov Partii Levykh Sotsialistov-Revolyu-tsionerov (Internatsionalistov)*. Moscow, 1918.

——, *Sbornik statey po peresmotru programmy*. Moscow, 1918.

RUSSIA. Russian Social-Democratic Labour Party (Bolsheviks). (RSDRP(b)). Central Committee. *Protokoly Tsentral'nogo Komi-teta RSDRP(b), avgust 1917–fevral' 1918*. Ed. M. A. Savelev, comp. V. Rakhmetov. Moscow–Leningrad, 1929. (New edition of text: Moscow, 1958.) Engl. trans. (of 1958 ed.): *The Bolsheviks and the October Revolution. Minutes of the Central Committee of the RSDLP(B), August 1917–February 1918*. Tr. A. Bone. London, 1974. [*Prot. TsK*].

——, Petrograd Committee. *Pervy legal'ny Peterburgskiy komitet bol'-shevikov v 1917 g. Sbornik materialov i protokolov zasedaniy Peterburgs-kogo komiteta RSDRP(b) i yego ispolnitel'noy komissii za 1917 g. . . .* Ed. P. F. Kudelli, comp. by G. L. Shidlovsky. Moscow–Lenin-grad, 1927. [RSDRP, *Pervy legal'ny*].

RYABINSKY, K. (comp.), *Revolyutsiya 1917 g. Khronika sobytiy*, 5. *Oktyabr'*. Moscow–Leningrad, 1926.

SAUTIN, N., *Velikiy Oktyabr' v derevne na severo-zapade Rossii (oktyabr' 1917–1918 gg.).* Leningrad, 1959.

SCHAPIRO, L. B., *The Communist Party of the Soviet Union.* 2nd ed., revised and enlarged. London–New York, 1970; reprinted 1971.

——, *The Origin of the Communist Autocracy. Political Opposition in the Soviet State, First Phase, 1917–1922.* London–Cambridge, Mass., 1955; reprinted New York–Washington, 1965.

SCHEIDEMANN, P., *Der Zusammenbruch.* Berlin, 1921.

SCOTT, E. J., 'The Cheka', in: *SAP* 6, *Soviet Affairs* 1 (1956), pp. 1–23.

SDFP: see Degras, J.

SELIVANOV, V., 'Pervy Vserossiyskiy s'yezd voyennogo flota, 1–8 dekabrya 1917 g. n. st.', in: *KL* (1929), 1, pp. 89–114.

SEMENOV, G., *Voyennaya i boyevaya rabota Partii Sotsialistov-Revolyutsionerov za 1917–1918 gg.* Berlin, 1922.

SHKILNYK, M., *Ukraina u borot'bi za derzhavnist' v 1917–1921 rr. Spomini i rozdumi.* Toronto, 1971.

SHLIKHTER, A. [G.], *Ilyich kakim ya yego znal. Koye-chto iz vstrech i vospominaniy.* Kharkov, 1924.

SHLYAPNIKOV, A. G. (ed.), 'Oktyabr'skiy perevorot i Stavka', in: *KA* 8 (1925), pp. 153–75; 9 (1925), pp. 156–70.

SHMELEV, K., 'Public Finance during the Civil War, 1917–1921', in: G. Ya. Sokolnikov *et al.*, *Soviet Policy in Public Finance, 1917–1928*, ed. L. Hutchinson and C. C. Plehn, tr. E. Varneck, Stanford, 1931, pp. 74–137.

SH[REYBERG], S., 'Iz istorii Sovvlasti na Ukraine. O pervom Vseukrainskom s'yezde Sovetov i pervom Sovetskom pravitel'stve Ukrainy', in: *LR* 9 (1924), pp. 166–85.

SHTEYN, B. E. (ed.), *Brest-Litovskaya konferentsiya. Zasedaniya ekonomicheskoy i pravovoy komissii.* Moscow, 1923.

——, *Torgovaya politika i torgovye dogovory Sovetskoy Rossii, 1917–1922.* Moscow–Petrograd, 1923.

SHTEYNBERG: see Steinberg.

SHVARTS (SCHWARZ), S. M., *Sotsial'noye strakhovanie v Rossii v 1917–1919 gg.* New York, 1968.

SIDOROV, A. L. *et al.* (eds.), *Velikaya Oktyabr'skaya sotsialisticheskaya revolyutsiya. Dokumenty i materialy.* 9 vols. Moscow, 1957–63. Vol. I. *Revolyutsionnoye dvizhenie v Rossii posle sverzheniya samoderzhaviya.* 1957. Vol. 2. *Revolyutsionnoye dvizhenie v Rossii v aprele 1917 g. Aprel'skiy krizis.* 1958. Vol. 6. *Revolyutsionnoye dvizhenie v Rossii v sentyabre 1917 g. Obshchenatsional'ny krizis.* 1961. *Triumfal'noye shestvie Sovetskoy vlasti.* (2 parts.) 1963. [Sidorov, *VOSR*].

SISSON, E., *One Hundred Red Days. A Personal Chronicle of the Russian Revolution*. New Haven, 1931.

SMIRNOV, A. S., 'Petrogradskiy Sovet krest'yanskikh deputatov v 1917 g.', in: *IZ* 83 (1963), pp. 90–110.

SMITH, C. Jay, Jr., *Finland and the Russian Revolution, 1917–1922*. Athens, Ga., 1958.

SOBOLEV, P. N. *et al.* (eds.), *Istoriya Velikoy Oktyabr'skoy sotsialisticheskoy revolyutsii*. Moscow, 1967.

SOBOLEVA, P. I., *Bor'ba bol'shevikov protiv men'shevikov i S-Rov za leninskuyu politiku mira, noyabr' 1917–1918 gg*. Moscow, 1965.

SOKOLOV, B., 'Zashchita Vserossiyskogo Uchreditel'nogo Sobraniya', in: *ARR* 13 (1924), pp. 5–70.

SOLOVYEV, O. F., *Velikiy Oktyabr' i yego protivniki. O roli soyuza Antanty s vnutrenney kontr-revolyutsiyey v razvyazyvanii interventsii i grazhdanskoy voyny, oktyabr' 1917–iyul' 1918*. Moscow, 1968.

SONKIN, M. E., *Okno vo vneshniy mir. Ekonomicheskiye svyazi Sovetskogo gosudarstva v 1917–1921 gg*. Moscow, 1964.

STALIN, J. V., *Foundations of Leninism* [1924]. New York, 1939; reprinted 1970.

——, *Sochineniya*. 13 vols. Moscow, 1946–52.

STARTSEV, V. I., 'Bol'sheviki, Vtoroy Vserossiyskiy s'yezd Sovetov i sozdanie Sovetskoy sistemy', in: Tokarev, Yu. S. *et al.* (eds.), *Problemy gosudarstvennogo stroitel'stva v pervye gody Sovetskoy vlasti. Sbornik statey*. (Trudy Leningradskogo otdeleniya Instituta Istorii Akademii Nauk SSSR, fasc. 14.) Leningrad, 1973, pp. 7–45.

STEGEMANN, H., *Geschichte des Krieges*, vol. 4. Stuttgart–Berlin, 1921.

STEGLICH, W., *Die Friedenspolitik der Mittelmächte, 1917–1918*, vol. 1. Wiesbaden, 1964.

STEINBERG (SHTEYNBERG), J., *Als ich Volkskommissar war. Episoden aus der russischen Oktoberrevolution*. Munich, 1929.

STERN, L., *Der Einfluss der Grossen Sozialistischen Oktoberrevolution auf Deutschland und die deutsche Arbeiterbewegung*. East Berlin, 1958.

STRIEVSKAYA, S., 'V novom VTsIK', in: *NM* (1957), 10, 178–82.

STROKOV, A. A., *Vooruzhennye sily i voyennoye iskusstvo v pervoy mirovoy voyne*. Moscow, 1974.

STUCHKA, P. I., 'Proletarskaya revolyutsiya i sud', in: *Proletarskaya revolyutsiya i pravo*, Moscow, 1918, 1, pp. 1–8.

SUKHANOV, N. N., *Zapiski o revolyutsii*. 7 vols. Berlin–Petrograd–Moscow, 1922–3. Engl. trans.: *The Russian Revolution, 1917. Eyewitness Account*. Edited, abridged and translated by J. Carmichael. 2 vols. London, 1955. New ed., New York, 1962.

SYUKIYAYNEN, I. I., *Revolyutsionnye sobytiya 1917–1918 gg. vo Finlyandii*. Petrozavodsk, 1962.

Tabouis, General, 'Comment je devins Commissaire de la République Française en Ukraine', in: *Spohady* (Ukrainian Scientific Institute in Warsaw, *Pratsi*, vol. 8, 1932), pp. 142–64.

Taylor, A. J. P., *The Struggle for Mastery in Europe, 1848–1918*, Oxford, 1954; reprinted 1965.

Trotsky, L. D., *Kak vooruzhalas' revolyutsiya*. 3 pts. Moscow, 1923–5.

——, *My Life. An Attempt at an Autobiography* [1931]. Introd. J. Hansen. Harmondsworth, 1975.

——, *Lenin*. New York, 1925.

——, *Sochineniya*. 12 vols. Moscow/Moscow–Leningrad, 1924–7. Vol. 3. *1917*. pt. 2. *Ot Oktyabrya do Bresta*. Vol. 12. *Osnovnye problemy proletarskoy revolyutsii*. Vol. 17. *Sovetskaya Respublika i kapitalisticheskiy mir*. Pt. 1. *Pervonachal'ny period organizatsii sil*.

Tsereteli, I. G., *Vospominaniya o fevral'skoy revolyutsii*. 2 vols. Paris–The Hague, 1963.

Tsypkin, G. A., *Krasnaya gvardiya v bor'be za vlast' Sovetov*. Moscow, 1967.

Tych, F., *PPS–Lewica w latach wojny, 1914–1918*. Warsaw, 1960.

Ullman, R. H., *Intervention and the War*. (Anglo-Soviet Relations, 1917–1921, vol. 1.) Princeton, 1961.

United States. *Papers Relating to the Foreign Relations of the United States. 1918. Russia*. 3 vols. Washington, 1931–2. [*FRUS*].

Varlamov, K. I., 'O nauchnykh osnovakh marksistsko-leninskoy politicheskoy strategii i taktiki', in: *PNK* 3 (1969), pp. 134–84.

Varlamov, K. I. and Slamikhin, N. A., *Razoblachenie V. I. Leninym teorii i taktiki 'levykh kommunistov', noyabr' 1917–1918 gg.* Moscow, 1964.

Vaynshteyn, A. L., *Narodnoye bogatstvo i narodno-khozyaystvennoye nakoplenie predrevolyutsionnoy Rossii*. Moscow, 1960.

Venediktov, A. V., *Natsionalizatsiya promyshlennosti i organizatsiya sotsialisticheskogo proizvodstva v Petrograde, 1917–1920. Dokumenty i materialy*. 2 vols. Leningrad, 1957–60.

Vishnyak, M., *Vserossiyskoye Uchreditel'noye Sobranie*. Paris, 1932.

Vladimirova, V. (comp.), *Revolyutsiya 1917 g. Khronika sobytiy*. Vol. 3. *iyun'–iyul'*. Moscow–Petrograd, [1923]. Vol. 4. *avgust–sentyabr'*. Leningrad, 1924.

VMRK: see Khesin, S. S.

Volin, S., *Deyatel'nost' men'shevikov v profsoyuzakh pri Sovetskoy vlasti*. (Inter-University Project on the History of Menshevism, 13.) New York, 1962.

Vompe, P., *Dni Oktyabr'skoy revolyutsii i zheleznodorozhniki. Materialy po izucheniyu revolyutsionnogo dvizheniya na zheleznykh dorogakh.* Moscow, 1924.

VORONETSKAYA, A. A., 'Organizatsiya VSNKh i yego rol' v natsionalizatsii promyshlennosti', in: *IZ* 43 (1953), pp. 3–38.

VOZNESENSKY, A. N., *Moskva v 1917 g.* Moscow–Leningrad, 1928.

VTsSPS. See Russia. RSFSR/USSR. All-Union (All-Russian) Central Council of Trade Unions.

WADE, R. A., *The Russian Search for Peace, February–October 1917.* Stanford, 1969.

WHEELER-BENNETT, J. W., *Brest-Litovsk. The Forgotten Peace, March 1918.* London, 1938; reprinted London–New York, 1963.

WILLIAMS, R. C., 'Russian War Prisoners and Soviet-German Relations, 1918–1921', in: *CSP* 9 (1967), pp. 270–95.

YAKOVLEV, N. (ed.), 'Protokoly zasedaniy TsIK i byuro TsIK Sovetov rabochikh i soldatskikh deputatov pervogo sozyva posle Oktyabrya', in: *KA* 10 (1925), pp. 95–137.

YURCHENKO, O., *Ukrains'ko—rosiys'ki stosunki pislia 1917 r. v pravnomu aspekti.* (Ukrainian Free University Monographs, 19.) Munich, 1971.

ZEMAN, Z. A. B. (ed.), *Germany and the Revolution in Russia, 1915–1918. Documents from the Archives of the German Foreign Ministry.* London–New York, 1958.

ZEMAN, Z. A. B. and SCHARLAU, W., *The Merchant of Revolution. The Life of Alexander Israel Helphand (Parvus), 1867–1924.* London, 1965.

B. UNPUBLISHED MATERIAL

Protokoly Tsentral'nogo Komiteta Partii Sotsialistov-Revolyutsionerov, 2 sentyabrya 1917–30 yanvarya 1918 g. Zenzinov Papers (0.9.11), Russian Archive, Columbia University, New York.

C. JOURNALS, NEWSPAPERS AND SERIALS

Arkhiv russkoy revolyutsii. Ed. I. V. Gessen. 22 vols. Berlin, 1921–37. [*ARR*].

Bely arkhiv. Ed. Ya. M. Lisovoy. 10 parts. Paris, 1926–8. [*BA*].

Bulletin de la Presse. Ambassade de la République Française, Petrograd, 1917–18.

Cahiers du monde russe et soviétique. Paris, 1959– [*CMRS*].

Canadian Slavonic Papers. Ottawa, 1956– [*CSP*].

Delo naroda. Petrograd, 1917–18.

Den' : *organ sotsialisticheskoy mysli.* Petrograd, 1917.

Golos minuvshego. Zhurnal istorii i istorii literatury. Moscow, etc., 1913–23. [*GM*].

History of Political Economy. Durham, N.C., 1969– [*HPE*].

Iskra. Organ men'shevikov-internatsionalistov. Petrograd, 1917–18.

Istoricheskiye zapiski. Moscow, 1937– [*IZ*].

Istoriya SSSR. Moscow, 1957– [*IS*].

Izvestiya VTsIK i Petrogradskogo Soveta rabochikh i soldatskikh deputatov. Petrograd, later Moscow, 1917– [*Iz.*].

Jahrbücher für Geschichte Osteuropas, N.F. Munich–Wiesbaden. [*JGOE*].

Journal of Contemporary History. London. [*JCH*].

Journal of Modern History. Chicago. [*JMH*].

Krasnaya letopis'. Petrograd/Leningrad. [*KL*].

Krasny arkhiv. 106 vols. Moscow, 1922–41. [*KA*].

Letopis' revolyutsii. Khar'kov. [*LR*].

Luch. Petrograd, 1917. Followed by *Klich, Plamya, Fakel', Molniya, Shchit, Novy luch.*

Narod. Vechernaya gazeta. Organ Petrogradskoy gruppy Sotsialistov-Revolyutsionerov–oborontsev. Petrograd, 1917.

Nash vek. Petrograd, 1917–18. (Successor to *Rech'.*)

Novaya zhizn'. Obshchestvenno-literaturnaya sotsial-demokraticheskaya gazeta. Petrograd, later Moscow, 1917–18.

Novy luch. Petrograd, 1917–18.

Novy mir. Moscow. [*NM*].

Pravda. Petrograd, later Moscow, 1917– [*Pr.*].

Problemy nauchnogo kommunizma. Moscow, 1966– [*PNK*].

Proletarskaya revolyutsiya. Moscow, 1921–40. [*PR*].

St. Antony's Papers. Oxford. [*SAP*].

Slavic Review, formerly: *American Slavic and East European Review.* Seattle, later Columbus, Ohio. [*SR; ASEER*].

Slavonic and East European Review. London, 1922– [*SEER*].

Sovetskoye gosudarstvo i pravo. Moscow. [*SGP*].

Soviet Studies. Glasgow, 1949– [*SS*].

Sovremennye zapiski. Paris. [*SZ*].

Vecher. Petrograd, 1917.

Vecherneye slovo. Petrograd, 1918.

Vierteljahreshefte für Zeitgeschichte. Munich. [*VfZ*].

Voprosy istorii. Moscow. [*VI*].

Voprosy istorii KPSS. Moscow. [*VI KPSS*].

Znamya truda. Yezhednevnaya rabochaya gazeta, izd. Petrogradskim komitetom Partii Sotsialistov–Revolyutsionerov. Petrograd, 1917–18. [*ZT*].

A NOTE ON THE COMPOSITION OF THE CEC

In the index of personal names which follows an asterisk denotes those members of the CEC (second convocation) who are referred to either in the text or in the notes. These numbered about one-third of the total complement. Where there is some doubt as to the identity of an individual or the spelling of his name, this is indicated. Forenames and dates of birth and death have been given where available.

Party affiliation is indicated by the following symbols: B = Bolshevik (i.e., RSDRP(B)); LSR = Left Socialist-Revolutionary (PLSR); USDI = United Social-Democratic Internationalist; other affiliations are given in full, as is non-party status; a question mark means that the affiliation is unknown. Where such a symbol or affiliation follows directly after the member's name, this shows that he or she belonged to the core group in the assembly, which consisted of party nominees. Most of these persons were chosen by their respective party or group leaderships at the close of the Second All-Russian Congress of Soviets or shortly thereafter, but a number were added (co-opted) later. Candidate membership has been disregarded since this distinction was of no practical account.

The CEC broadened its composition to include individuals who represented certain working-class organizations (ARCCTU, ARCFC, Vikzhel) and—far more numerous—organizations which spoke for peasants, soldiers, and sailors. The peasant members, who were in fact designated by the executive committee of the second (regular) congress of peasant deputies and for the most part belonged to that body, are indicated here by the symbol 'p'. The armed forces' members represented, and were actually or supposedly elected by, organizations at a variety of levels: fronts, armies, regiments, etc. Their provenance is likewise noted, although in the case of sailors, most of whom were chosen by the first naval congress, information on their specific units has been omitted. In regard to all these delegates, who joined the CEC during the latter half of this convocation, their party affiliation is given *after* their organizational one.

Also indicated are major missions undertaken by members outside Petrograd and offices held in the CEC apparatus during this convocation, as well as those held at this time in the CPC or in the Central Committees of either of the two main maximalist parties.

Some individuals for whom there is no definite evidence in *Prot.* or elsewhere that they were either elected or co-opted to the CEC nevertheless participated actively in its debates and/or occupied office in its Presidium, commissions or departments. Of these persons some subsequently appear to have had their status regularized by co-option, without any mention of the fact in the published materials, whereas others did not. A dagger symbol (†) has been prefixed to the names of all such persons, meaning 'membership or status uncertain'.

Index of Personal Names

General Index

162, 190, 230f., 348; and inter-party conference, 53f., 276; and soviet power, 141, 143, 282; and Ukraine, 190, 199, 221f.

United States, 4, 64, 104, 144, 195, 215, 314; and CPC 360–3, 413; Red Cross, 189f., 360–3; socialists in, 138, 336; war aims, 316, 385f.; and Whites, 216, 380

Vikzhel: *see* All-Russian Union of Railwaymen
Vitebsk, 399
Vladimir, 94, 110
Völkerfriede, Der, 327
Vologda, 254
Volunteer Army, 296, 379f.
Voronezh, 295
Vyazma, 123

wages, 173, 199f., 353, 372
War, ministry and PC of, 324f., 373, 399
war, revolutionary, 187f., 359f.
workers, industrial: armament of, 62f.; culture of, 315; economic conditions of, 13, 15, 353, 372; and foreign affairs, 7, 150; and inter-party conference, 280
'workers' control', 14f., 41, 88, 94, 135, 206, 293, 402; decree on, 106, 124–8, 246, 317f., 327f., 335
'Workers' Opposition', 411

Zemshchina, 71, 294
Zemsky Sobor, 114, 320, 322
Zimmerwald: *see* International
Znamya truda, vii, 270f., 308, 353, 406, 415, 418f.